# The Quest for God and the Good

Diana Lobel

# The Quest for God and the Good

## • WORLD PHILOSOPHY AS A LIVING EXPERIENCE •

Columbia University Press

*New York*

COLUMBIA UNIVERSITY PRESS
*Publishers Since 1893*
New York Chichester, West Sussex


Library of Congress Cataloging-in-Publication Data
Lobel, Diana.
The quest for God and the good : world philosophy as a living experience /
Diana Lobel.
p. cm.
Includes bibliographical references (p. ) and index.
ISBN 978-0-231-15314-0 (cloth : alk. paper) — ISBN 978-0-231-15315-7 (pbk.) —
ISBN 978-0-231-52701-9 (electronic)
1. Philosophy and religion. 2. God—Comparative studies. 3. Good and evil—Religious aspects—Comparative studies. 4. Religious life—Comparative studies. I. Title.
BL51.L5755 2011
202'.11—dc22 2010033894

Columbia University Press books are printed on permanent
and durable acid-free paper.
This book is printed on paper with recycled content.
Printed in the United States of America
c 10 9 8 7 6 5 4 3 2 1
p 10 9 8 7 6 5 4 3 2 1

For Albert, Francine, and Janet Lobel

In countless ways, you have each shown me

the beauty of genuine kindness.

And indeed it was very good.

GENESIS 1:31

# Contents

# Acknowledgments

I REMEMBER VIVIDLY a moment in my first philosophy course at Oberlin College. The course was "Ancient Philosophy," and given the intensive liberal arts institution that Oberlin is, six students sat in a discussion section for the course once a week with the instructor, a full professor. I remember raising a point I didn't understand in Aristotle, and the thorough joy of traveling from not understanding to understanding. At that moment I knew that this was what I wanted to do with my life.

I remember another moment, when I taught my first section on Aristotle's *Nicomachean Ethics* for Professor Twersky's course, "Moderation and Extremism," as a graduate student at Harvard. The class met on the afternoon before Rosh Hashanah. I remember the utter joy of exploring the first few pages of the *Ethics*, and dancing off to services with a sense that I was fulfilling my life's purpose. This book is simply another moment of fruition in a long process of delightful engagement with philosophy and religious thought.

The book grew out of a course I have been teaching for many years, first as "The Search for God and the Good" in the Honors Program at the University of Maryland, College Park, then as "The Quest for God and the Good" at Rice University and Boston University. The course itself evolved gradually from courses for which I had served as a teaching fellow in the Core Curriculum at Harvard University: Isadore Twersky's "Moderation and Extremism,"

Michael Sandel's "Justice," and Jay Harris's "If There is No God, All is Permitted: Theism and Moral Reasoning." In its inception, the class read Plato, Aristotle, Augustine, Maimonides, and al-Ghazālī. I found that I repeatedly drew upon Asian parallels to make concepts in the Western texts clear; as a textualist, I decided it would be worthwhile to have students read the original Asian sources as well. In my year at Maryland, I remember the interest of student Marc Fox spurring my decision to include these Asian classics, and I thank him for his enthusiasm and engagement.

At some point I became fascinated by Plato's *Timaeus*, and brought in the Bible's book of Genesis as a natural parallel. I found students love reading the Bible with unprejudiced eyes; whenever I want to increase the engagement of the class, I bring in a Biblical text. However, I have found that students today do not necessarily know how to read primary texts themselves, and genuinely appreciate the guidance of study questions. I have included a full list of readings and study questions on the book's Web site. This should make the volume user-friendly for students, instructors, and lay readers who want to delve into the works explored in these pages. I see reading as a living experience; my goal in this book is to guide readers through these classics, not to substitute for reading of the primary sources.

There are numerous people I could cite from this long journey; I will mention those who come to mind specifically regarding the present book. My research assistant Scott Girdner read through the entire manuscript and made suggestions on content, writing, organization, and structure. The book was greatly enriched by his clarity and critical judgment. Warren Zev Harvey has been a stimulating and challenging conversation partner, particularly on matters related to chapter 4. While I regret taking issue with Professor Harvey's view, I hope I have done justice to his formulation, and take comfort that I share the view of the late Shlomo Pines. I am grateful to David Roochnik for his generosity in discussing Platonic and Aristotelian philosophy, looking together at texts, and sharing an unpublished manuscript on Aristotle. Stephen Scully was also wonderfully generous in poring over difficult texts of Plato, Aristotle, and Plotinus. With tremendous appreciation, I thank those with whom I have had the joy of learning Greek and reading Greek philosophy: Martin Black, Claire Olwen Cairo, Tom Marre, Mark Sentesy, Tyler Travillian, and Mindy Wolfrom. To actually read philosophy in Greek has been the realization of a lifelong dream. I am also grateful for the pleasure of reading philosophical texts with Stan Dorn, Colby Phillips, and Tony Rivera. I appreciate the suggestions of David Eckel on matters related to the philosophies of India, and those of Eric Dorman, who read and critiqued that entire chapter. I am grateful to my colleagues Gina Cogan and Tom Michael for assistance with the Buddhism chapter and many matters Buddhist and Taoist. John Berthrong graciously read the chapter on Chinese religion; Brook Ziporyn shared not only his Zhuangzi book, but also material from his unpublished tome on *li*, *The Pattern and the Pendulum*. I also thank the two anonymous readers for Columbia University Press for their stimulating critique and suggestions, and my editor, Wendy Lochner, and copy editor, Kerri Cox Sullivan, for their enthusiasm for the project and their expert guidance. My thanks go to Hee Kyung Kim, who prepared the bibliography, and Brian Jenkin, who added its finishing touches. I am especially grateful to the Boston University Humanities foundation for their generous Publication Production Award for the indexing of the book.

I appreciate the friendship and support of colleagues in the Department of Religion and the Division of Religious and Theological Studies at Boston University. In particular, I would like to thank the chairs of the Department of Religion, Deeana Klepper and Stephen Prothero, for their support for my work and teaching in unimaginably kind ways. There is nothing more powerful than being seen for who we are, in our weakness as well as our strength. I am also grateful to Wendy Czik, Administrator of the Department of Religion; Melissa Merolla, Program Coordinator the Division of Religious and Theological Studies; and Karen Nardella, Administrator of the DRTS, each of whom has been a rare and delightful gem. I appreciate the support of Jonathan Klawans, currently Director of the Division of Religious and Theological Studies, who has created and modeled a culture of warmth and collegiality. I also extend thanks to Steven Katz, Director of the Center for Judaic Studies, and Pagiel Czoka, the center's administrative assistant, for their patience and kindness amidst unforeseen changes. I cannot imagine a better environment in which to teach and work.

Tom Alden has seen this book come to light from its inception and nurtured its vision of the aesthetic beauty of philosophy. Tina Mulhern and Carol Hevia are fountains of joy. Reb Moshe Holcer *z"l* and Rabbi Yonah will always be a source of inspiration. Robin Rosenberg has given me more than I can express in words. My prayer is that I can express my gratitude through my life.

In addition to my family, this book is dedicated to the wonderful students with whom I have had the joy of sharing this quest each year. Some of their names appear in the notes; all of their responses are present throughout these pages. My hope is that this book will allow others to join us on this journey of understanding.

# The Quest for God and the Good

# Introduction

Among the enduring works of twentieth-century literature is Victor Frankl's *Man's Search for Meaning*. A psychoanalyst and concentration camp survivor, Frankl testifies that human beings can survive tremendous suffering if they understand it to have some purpose. Any of us can triumph over incomprehensible pain if we can reframe our challenges to discover their hidden meaning and value.

Drawing upon this insight, Frankl developed the psychological discipline of logotherapy (from the Greek *logos*, "meaning," and *therapeia*, "healing, care, or attention"). He posits that the fundamental human drive is not the search for pleasure or power, but the search for meaning; each individual must find a personal understanding of his or her own life purpose.[1] The search for the meaning and purpose of life is indeed universal. Human beings want to know why we are here, whether there is a transcendent being or dimension in the universe, and whether reality is fundamentally good. Above all, we want to know whether the search for God and the good will bring us happiness and fulfillment.

The discipline of philosophy has traditionally addressed these fundamental questions. Contemporary historian of philosophy Pierre Hadot has shown that for ancient thinkers, philosophy was not simply a theoretical discipline, but a way of life. Philosophical arguments were in essence spiritual exercises whose goal was to transform the self. "Philosophy," he writes, "then appears in its original aspect not as a theoretical construct, but as a method for training people to live and to look at the world in a new way. It is an attempt to transform mankind."[2] The truths revealed by ancient texts may appear simple at first glance, even banal. "Yet for their meaning to be understood, these truths must be *lived*, and constantly re-experienced. Each generation must take up, from scratch, the task of learning to read and to re-read these old truths" (108). The task of reading for self-transformation is itself a spiritual discipline, for "we have forgotten *how* to read, how to pause, liberate ourselves from our worries, return into ourselves, and leave aside our search for subtlety and originality, in order to meditate calmly, ruminate, and let the texts speak to us" (109).

Dale Wright, a scholar of Buddhist philosophy, likewise advocates a meditative reading practice that entails philosophical, reflective activity, one that "is never content with the obvious; it will refuse to hold onto customary forms of understanding in order to push beyond what is already within grasp. The initial act of reading serves to lure the mind out of complacency and inertia by challenging it to consider something new, or to experience more deeply what has already been thought."[3]

In that spirit, the goal of this study is to explore the insights of central thinkers and texts from throughout the world that address fundamental existential questions. Specifically, we will explore the connections between concepts of divinity or an absolute and the good life. While we as moderns often associate religion with the search for eternal liberation or immortality, central texts of many of the world's religious and philosophical traditions are equally concerned with uncovering the meaning and purpose of life in this world. These key texts and thinkers maintain that human beings find true fulfillment by making contact with fundamental values at the heart of their lived reality.[4]

Our first question as we undertake this search: Why is spiritual life so often described using metaphors of quest and journey? A "journey" implies movement in space, a physical going out toward a destination. A "quest" too requires setting forth in search of something. The quest and the journey suggest that history, events, and narrative are meaningful—perhaps that they even hold intrinsic, sacred importance. In contrast, many traditions speak of God, ultimate reality, or *nirvāṇa* as a spiritual absolute that does not move or change; they suggest that the ultimate human goal is to arrive at a static eternal perfection. For example, Aristotle's philosophical God does not change—it is pure Being, the Unmoved Mover, thought thinking itself. It does not seek or lack; it eternally contemplates its own nature. Similarly,

Plato's realm of the Forms is a beautiful mosaic of eternal, unchanging essences. The metaphor of the quest, in contrast, suggests that narrative, search, and change are meaningful; that the journey itself is its own reward. The latter perspective is at the heart of this study. It is not my goal to arrive at a universal definition of God and the good. Rather, I will endeavor to present the aesthetic beauty of multiple visions presented by thinkers across history and across cultures. I will suggest that investigation and discovery are themselves processes of value.

The book begins by examining the relationship between God and the good in the creation accounts of the Bible and Plato. Why does the Bible begin with creation? And do we have a real creation here? In fact, if we examine the text of Genesis closely, we discover that God does not create from nothing; "in the beginning" we find darkness, water, a formless void, and the deep. Creation is really the shaping of chaos into an orderly, intelligible cosmos. God does not appear to be all-powerful; rather, God does the best God can with the materials he has to work with. Nor does God appear to be omniscient; God does not necessarily know beforehand how his work will turn out. God is rather like an artist who is pleased with his or her creation. In the second creation story, which we find in Genesis 2, humans choose the tree of knowledge of good and evil—adult life, with painful consequences and moral maturity—over the innocent childhood of Eden. It is not that God punishes the first human beings; they discover the realities of adulthood. All of life, with its hardships and difficulties, is part of the good world God created.

Why is there an orderly cosmos? In chapter 2 we explore Plato's answer: God is good, and wanted the world to be as good as he is. God is an artisan or craftsman who shapes anarchy into goodness and order. Both Plato and the Bible describe a primordial state of chaos that a good God orders. Neither depicts God as creating from nothing; God must work with what is given. The Divine brings order to what seems chaotic and out of control. Plato goes on to argue that we too can bring goodness and order to the world by shaping our lives to reflect the good. The twentieth-century Platonist Iris Murdoch argues forcefully that even in a world without God, we can indeed shape our lives according to a moral ideal of the good.

While Plato holds up an eternal, unchanging realm of values as an ideal, we learn in chapter 3 that for Chinese thought, in contrast, change itself is fully real and good. The Way (the *Tao*) is expressed through the ever-changing cycles of nature. Human good furthers the moral virtues embodied in nature. However, there is a tension in Chinese culture between Confucian and Taoist streams of thought. While Confucians value civilization, rules of propriety, and assertiveness, the *Tao Te Ching* tells us that real strength is found in natural spontaneity, receptivity, and the feminine. The *Tao Te Ching* even values non-being over being, for non-being represents infinite potential. Anytime we value something in particular, we lose the vast field of possibility from which it springs. The text invites us to return to the uncarved block, the mysterious root of all change. By letting go of attachment to a fixed perspective, we can remain flexible and fluid. Thus we can attune ourselves to new situations as they arise. The process philosophy of twentieth-century philosopher and mathematician Alfred North Whitehead offers us a Western parallel to Chinese thought. All of nature is in process; the fundamental fact about the universe is its newness and creativity. Quantum physics has abandoned the notion of isolated atoms; physicists describe interconnected events or occasions, each of which exhibits novelty. Whitehead creates a bridge between science, philosophy, and religion; he maintains that what philosophers have called God is the principle that brings definiteness to random possibility. This perspective allows Whitehead to respond to the problem of evil. Evil, he argues, is the force of disintegration; it is by nature unstable. However, if there were only instability, the world could not survive. God is the force that brings harmony and integration. Whitehead sees an aesthetic harmony in scientific order that is akin to the beauty Chinese culture finds in nature.

In chapter 4 we learn that like the modern philosopher Whitehead, the medieval philosophers Augustine and Maimonides draw on both Plato and the Bible to express the relationship between God and the good. Both argue that every entity that exists inhabits a unique rung upon the great chain of being. Evil is lack of being, or privation; judging things to be evil reflects a limited, subjective point of view. Things appear to be evil because they are in conflict with one another, or because they interfere with our limited desires. However, if we look at things in the context of the whole, we see that indeed, the whole of being is greater than the higher things alone. If we saw all events in the context of the whole, we would achieve contentment and neither suffer nor harm others.

In chapter 5 we find that the Hindu scriptures known as the *Upanishads* maintain that the Absolute has qualities not only of being and goodness, but of awareness and joy. In fact, when we discover our true inner Self (*ātman*) we discover that it is one with the universal Spirit (*brahman)*, which is existence, knowledge, and joy. Like Plato, the *Upanishads* believe that knowledge has existential, transformative power. However, a popular Hindu devotional text, the *Bhagavad Gītā*, points out that to discover the Absolute by knowledge alone requires intense concentration. The *Gītā* thus sets forth two additional paths more accessible to the average person: continuing to act in the world while letting go of attachment to the results of our actions, and a relationship of devotion to a loving personal God.

Buddhism grew up against the background of Hindu thought and practice, as we learn in chapter 6. In contrast to the *Upanishads*, which posit an eternal Self, the Buddha denied the existence of any eternal principle or of a real entity that corresponds to our experience of a self. Buddhism denies, however, that it is nihilistic or pessimistic. Buddhist teachers argue that we find true freedom and flexibility when we let go of attachment to limiting definitions and labels. Instead, by realizing the ubiquitous nature of change, and the fact that there is nothing that has permanent, substantial identity, we discover the openness of reality, a way of being that combines wisdom, fluidity, and compassion. Enlightenment is a way of awareness—a way of seeing reality as it is—and a way to live in the world that is a gift to others.

In chapter 7 we focus on Aristotle, who, like the *Bhagavad Gītā* and the teachings of the Buddha, offers an earthy, practical path to human flourishing. His ethical works reflect the tension we see in the *Upanishads* and *Gītā* (and between monastic and engaged Buddhism) between the contemplative life of the philosopher and the active life that is engaged in society. Surprisingly, we find a bridge between these two paths in the notion of contemplation or study (*theōria*). Aristotle's use of the concept in varied contexts suggest we can find fulfillment through learning about every aspect of our world. Like the *Gītā*, Aristotle proposes that we can engage in a kind of contemplation in action. Charles Taylor, a contemporary thinker, shows us that the evaluations we make in our own lives reflect frameworks much like Aristotle's moral thinking.

Chapter 8 turns to the Islamic philosopher al-Fārābī, who tells us that the goal of philosophy is not to achieve fulfillment only for ourselves; a true philosopher is a teacher, someone who guides others to realization. Plato, too, had suggested that the philosopher must return to society, for this is a philosophical duty. Al-Fārābī goes further: he insists that our own happiness is not complete until we share it with others.

In chapter 9 we return to Maimonides, who suggests (like al-Fārābī, whom he read and greatly admired) that our knowledge of God will overflow into our lives with others—into teaching and embodying the qualities

God expresses in nature. Just as God's existence overflows to create a world, knowledge of God's attributes overflows into graceful human action.

In chapter 10 we come to the example of al-Ghazālī, a Muslim religious judge and teacher who at the height of his theological career was beset by a crisis that caused him to leave his position and retire into contemplation. Ghazālī testifies that it was in fact God who guided him to withdraw into seclusion and then return to teaching. What he discovered, he writes, was the true purpose and end of religious life: direct experience of the Divine. When Ghazālī was teaching theology and religious law from a solely intellectual point of view, God caused his tongue to dry up, and he went into retreat to study and practice with the Sufi mystics. He discovered that the Sufis were people of experience, not words, and that he could not attain their knowledge without actually traveling the path of mystical exercises culminating in direct experience. And yet the summit of his journey did not arrive with experience of mystical states. God just as surely told him it was time to go back and share with others what he had learned. Ghazālī expresses in a mystical context the Platonic motif of return to the cave—reentering society to share the fruits one has gleaned from vision of the truth. Thus the key to a person's journey may be found in inner aim and intention, irrespective of whether the journey externally appears to embody an active or a contemplative life. Ghazālī returned to the life of teaching with an entirely different motivation, one infused with the divine presence he had encountered. Ghazālī was called both to abandon and to return to an active life of teaching. His experience thus speaks to the power of knowledge gained in contemplation to transform action in the world.

Some comparative studies embrace what is known as a perennialist vision: the notion that in reality there is one universal truth that all cultures express from multiple points of view. This study, in contrast, explores many varied approaches to several fundamental questions of philosophy. My goal is not to present one truth, but to give the reader an appreciation of diverse ways of approaching these questions, each with its particular point of view, each expressing the integrity of its own system.

There is a conventional philosophical saying that every person is either an Aristotelian or a Platonist—that we share either Aristotle's passion for scientific investigation of our world or Plato's love for an ideal realm of pure eternal truth. In contrast, I would like to suggest that when we study Plato and Aristotle with sincerity and conviction we find each thinker's worldview compelling within its own framework. My aim in this study is to share that joyous process of discovery.

# I

# "God Saw That It Was Good"

## THE CREATION OF THE WORLD IN THE HEBREW BIBLE

### IS GOD OMNIPOTENT?

We are all familiar with the opening lines of the Bible, a foundational text for Western religious and philosophical reflection. But how many of us have considered why the Bible opens as it does, with an account of the creation of the world? The opening refrain is well known, although I will suggest a somewhat unconventional translation:

> In the beginning of God's creating Heaven and Earth, the earth had been without form and void. Darkness was upon the face of the deep, and a spirit of God was hovering over the face of the waters. God said, Let there be light! and there was light. God saw the light, that it was good, and God separated the light from the darkness. And there was evening, and there was morning, one day. . . . And God saw everything he had made, and indeed it was very good. And there was evening and there was morning, the sixth day. (GENESIS 1:1–3, 1:31)

Why does the Bible begin with creation? And does a real creation take place here? Western readers accustomed to thinking that the Bible teaches creation from nothing (*ex nihilo*) will find nothingness "in the beginning." However, if we read the text unadorned, bringing no previous assumptions, that is not exactly what we have here. When we look at the text carefully, we discover that there do seem to be elements present at the "creation" of the world: heaven, earth, void, darkness, and the deep, as well as the spirit of God. What then does creation mean for the Hebrew Bible?[1] And where does "good" fit into this picture?

Moreover, why were ancient Hebrews satisfied with a creation account that does not begin *ex nihilo*? Perhaps we should rather ask why we moderns see a problem. Influenced as we are by medieval philosophy and theology, we cannot imagine that this was not what mattered to the ancient mind. The ancients were concerned with the question of how our structured, orderly world came to be as it is, how the fearsome elements of darkness and chaos were overcome or tamed. They don't ask what Leibniz called the fundamental question of philosophy: Why is there something rather than nothing? Rather, they ask a different question: Why is there order rather than chaos?[2]

Genesis begins with an account of the ordering of our world. The Bible assures us that while the universe may be built upon primordial chaos, the world we inhabit in fact exhibits a beautiful order, including a sovereign Being in charge. But why then do *we* concern ourselves with a different question, the question of why there is something rather than nothing? The twentieth-century philosopher Henri Bergson suggests that this is in fact a second-order philosophical question. The concept of "nothing," Bergson argues, is not obvious. When we believe we are thinking from nothing, we—the thinker—are in fact present. We pretend to think ourselves away, but we nevertheless remain, the thinker posing the problem.[3] We cannot in fact abstract ourselves from the equation. Thus the fundamental question is not why there is something rather than nothing, but how we can make sense of the universe as it is. Our starting point must be the elements that make up our world, and not some fictitious nothing, devoid of any recognizable presence.

In the Mahayana Buddhist tradition, the most fundamental category of reality is "suchness" or "thusness" (*tathātā*)—the way things are.[4] Buddhism denies that we can assert a fundamental, eternal Being, Soul, or Source of the universe; there is no evidence to assert the existence of an abstract God, Creator, or indeed any reified reality. But we can see reality as it is; we can see the suchness of things. This is how things are. And the Bible, too, begins by describing reality as it is. It does so using a myth of origins, but the origin does not begin with a clean slate; it does not erase all of the world as we know it. The Genesis account believes there are certain elements without which we could not understand the world as it is.

Heaven, earth, darkness, deep. These elements are seen as primal by the ancient Biblical mind. Historical scholars of the Bible, who compare the

Hebrew account with those from other cultures of the ancient Near East, note similar and disparate elements. Echoes of these ancient Near Eastern stories are found in other texts of the Hebrew Bible such as Psalms, Isaiah, and Job. In these accounts, God battles personified forces of chaos and evil: the great fish Leviathan, the sea monsters, perhaps even the goddess of the chaotic waters Tiamat, whose slaying by Marduk in the ancient Babylonian epic *Enuma Elish* creates the world. Some scholars suggest that the Hebrew word for deep, *tehom*, echoes the name Tiamat.[5] From this perspective, the Genesis story appears to be a de-mythologized version of ancient Near Eastern accounts of the world's origin. However, what is notable is precisely what is lacking: the depiction of creation through combat and the overcoming of real foes. This pristine account is a new way of presenting the origin of our orderly world.[6] God merely speaks and the orderly world we know comes to be.

Moreover, the reader new to Genesis may be surprised to discover that there are actually two stories of creation here. The creation story in Genesis 2–3 is noticeably different from that in Genesis 1; the Bible juxtaposes two contrasting accounts side by side. In Genesis 1, God creates quietly, through the word. God says "Let there be light," and light is. There is no opposition, no real resistance. God simply declares God's intention, and God's word is carried out. Unlike the creation account of Genesis 2–3—in which God as it were gets God's hands dirty, forming a human being from the dust of the earth and blowing into Adam's mouth the breath of life—the account in Genesis 1 is stark, pristine, liturgical. It is a hymn of creation, much like the creation hymns we find in texts of other cultures, such as the Chinese *Tao Te Ching* and the Indian *Rig Veda*. Scholars suggest that this text may have originated in liturgical use, and there is evidence it was thus used in the time of the Second Temple, when it was recited by the priests on the sixth day. A remnant of this practice indeed may be found in the Jewish Friday evening Sabbath service, which to this day recounts the end of the story:

> The heaven and the earth were finished, and all their array. On the seventh day God finished the work that he had been doing, and he ceased on the seventh day from all the work that he had done. God blessed the seventh day and declared it holy, because on it God ceased from all the work of creation that he had done.[7]

Those who like to see the origin of texts within a living context (the technical term is *Sitz im Leben*, "situation in life") point to the fact that this text was recited in the Temple as evidence that the natural setting of this creation hymn is liturgical; it was recited or chanted as part of a religious ceremony, as were other creation accounts in the ancient Near East.[8]

Thus we find evidence of diverse approaches to creation in the Hebrew Bible. We have the stark, majestic, liturgical account of Genesis 1; the earthy, narrative human-centered story of Genesis 2–3; and the combat myths of Psalms, Job, and Isaiah. Why does Genesis begin in this way? Biblical scholars argue that from a historical perspective, the purpose of Genesis 1 is to assert a new kind of creation theology, to counter the older model of creation through combat. That is, the ancient Near Eastern mind saw the forces of evil and chaos as real and primordial. Moreover, they are ongoing, ever threatening to rise up once again and overtake the fragile created order, as we see in the narrative of Noah and the great Flood. From this religious perspective, the fact that God defeated these forces of chaos to create order is comforting, as it means that we, too, can beseech God to rise up once again and defeat these evil forces.[9]

We must note, however, that for the medieval mind sensitized by Greek philosophy, the very existence of such primordial elements is a challenge to God's sovereignty. Thus the ninth-century Jewish philosopher Saʿadya Gaon argues that if the material element of the universe were eternal—if there were a substratum in the universe that simply exists, without being created by God—it would not deign to listen to God's decree. This primeval, uncreated matter would argue, "I've been here just as long as you! Why should I listen to your command?"[10] However, despite Saʿadya's argument, we can see that Genesis 1 does seem to assert the existence of primordial elements. Perhaps the Bible shows a more subtle understanding of what it is to be dependent for one's existence on a greater being; even if these elements are as ancient as God, they do listen to God's word. The Bible does not need an overt myth of combat to assert God's status as absolute. While there may be elements of the world that are eternal and uncreated, it is God who asserts God's will and shapes them into an orderly cosmos. For the ancient Biblical mind, that is enough.

The first creation story as it now stands is capped by the declaration in Genesis 1:31 that God saw everything he had made, "and indeed it was good." This verse gives us a key to the story. It looks like the purpose of Genesis 1–2 is to tell us something about the goodness of the created order. Yes, we are aware of frightening dimensions to our world, and at times it may seem like our world is descending into pure chaos. But the world as a whole is not simply a mass of anarchic forces. At the heart of reality is goodness.

What is good about creation? God looks over all that has been created and is pleased; all is in place. The world is orderly and intelligible. Light and darkness, day and night, heaven and earth, sea and dry land—these distinctions and rhythms give comfort and intelligibility to the world we know. Anthropologists note that this is likewise the function of human ritual. Humans are uneasy with perceived chaos and disorder; ritual allays that discomfort, echoing and reinforcing our sense of balance in the world. Just as God creates order out of chaos by ordering the cosmos, humans create a ritual cosmos to reinforce our sense of an orderly universe. Rituals mark the comforting rhythms of nature, of the seasons, which God after the Flood promises will never be erased:

> Nor will I ever again destroy every living being, as I have done. So long as earth endures, Seedtime and harvest, cold and heat, summer and winter, day and night shall not cease.[11]

Good does not seem to have a moral connotation in the first Genesis creation story. Good means the way things are: balanced, harmonious, orderly, intelligible. The pairs of opposites in nature are not random or meaningless, but balanced and harmonious. Goodness is fundamental to reality.

We notice that the Bible is not concerned to say that God is the source of all the elements in the world: some things are simply present, even before God begins to work on them, shaping, ordering, and dividing. The Bible is asserting that there is a relationship between order, harmony, goodness, and God. There is an ontological goodness, a goodness built into the heart of reality. Reality is good because it works; it is structured and balanced. It is like a jigsaw puzzle, in which all the pieces are integrated in a harmonious whole.[12]

## IS GOD SURPRISED?

The phrase "God saw that it was good" Is nevertheless complex in its implications. Ancient rabbinic commentators in particular muse over the verse that expresses the divine response after the creation of humanity on the sixth day: "God *saw* all that he had made and *behold* (or *indeed*)—it was very good." What is the force of the word translated "behold" (*hinne*)? Was God surprised that all is good—is there doubt in God's mind as to the value of creation? Does God not know before creating that everything will turn out well? The image seems to be one of an artist or craftsperson pleased with his or her creation (one student suggested *voila!* as a translation for "behold," *hinne*).[13] Our expectations, shaped by medieval philosophy and theology, are thus foiled by the text itself. God is not portrayed here as omniscient, as knowing beforehand how this piece of work will turn out. The Bible portrays God as a divine craftsman, an artist looking at his or her creation and expressing satisfaction.

The Biblical God thus turns out to be very different from the omniscient, omnipotent God we moderns have inherited from medieval philosophy. God is not necessarily alone at the time of creation, but must contend with elements of an existing realm. God does not necessarily know the way all will turn out in this magnificent experiment. Nonetheless, the Bible is confident in asserting the goodness of creation.

What then does "good" mean in the original language of Genesis 1? Biblical Hebrew does not feature the similarity in sound and spelling between the words "God" and "good" that we find in English. Nevertheless, "God" and "good" are intimately connected in the Biblical text. To understand the meaning of Biblical terms, scholars often look at other ancient Near Eastern cognate words. The Arabic cognate term for good (Arabic: *tayyib*; Hebrew: *tov*) originally suggests "to be pleasant, delightful, delicious, sweet, or savory."[14] The connotation of the term "good" for the various stages of creation may be that each thing is excellent of its kind.[15] The created order, as it is, is a source of aesthetic and cognitive joy or delight. Just as the human experience of contact with the divine is described in metaphors of sensory delight—"taste and see that the Lord is good [*ki tov*]!" (Psalm 34:8)—so the created world possesses a sweetness that can be savored. Just as God's goodness can be "tasted" by humans, so is the world's goodness a source of delight to God.[16] God loves the created order as it is. God looks at each feature of the world, and cannot but declare how good it is (*ki tov*). God thus experiences the world as good. However, the text invites us to challenge this presumption, to ask the question posed by Socrates in the Platonic dialogue *Euthyphro*: is something "good" (originally: "pious") because God loves it, or does God love it because it is good?[17] Does God's pronouncement that the world is good make it good, or does God recognize an inherent goodness to creation?[18]

In Genesis 18, Abram (soon to become Abraham) argues that it is God's moral obligation to spare the destruction of the cities of Sodom and Gemorrah if there be found therein ten righteous individuals:

> Far be it from You to do such a thing, to bring death upon the innocent as well as the guilty, so that innocent and guilty fare alike. Far be it from You! *Shall the Judge of all the earth not do justice?*[19]

There are two possible interpretations of this verse. God may be the source of justice or the arbiter of justice; God may be said either to create moral standards or to recognize the morality he sees. In either case, God as steward of justice must live up to the moral demands of his system. Likewise, God in Genesis 1 may recognize the inherent quality of goodness that creation presents, or God's seeing it as good may make it good. In either case, the Genesis account suggests that God gives a divine imprimatur to the goodness of creation.

The God of Genesis 1 thus emerges as an artist or craftsperson refining creation until God gets it right. We find parallel images in ancient Greek philosophy; in the dialogue *Timaeus*, as we will see in chapter 2, Plato describes creation of the world by a divine craftsman. Creation is seen as an artistic product; there is an aesthetic as well as a moral purpose to creation.[20] Plato's craftsman is bothered by the chaotic state of a disorderly world and seeks to clean up the messiness, to separate out disparate elements. The God of Genesis, too, separates out pairs of opposites: day and night, darkness and light, sea and dry land. Historical-critical scholars attribute this account to a priestly source concerned with dividing, classifying, and ordering.[21] They likewise attribute much of the book of Leviticus (sometimes referred to in Hebrew as the "Instruction of Priests," *Torat kohanim*) to ancient priests seeking to distinguish the categories of creation: clean and unclean animals, what is permitted and what is forbidden. The anthropologist Mary Douglas has made sense of the Biblical dietary laws by arguing that the priestly mind is uncomfortable with lack of clarity. Animals classified as unclean are those that do not conform to one category:

> In the firmament two-legged fowls fly with wings. In the water scaly fish swim with fins. On the earth four-legged animals hop, jump, or walk. Any class of creatures which is not equipped for the right kind of locomotion in its element is contrary to holiness. Contact with it disqualifies a person from approaching the Temple. Thus anything in the water which has not fins and scales is unclean. (LEV. 11:10–12)[22]

From an anthropological point of view, there is a human unease with ambiguity. Both Genesis and Plato's *Timaeus* seek to resolve such ambiguity.

Looking at this confusing, complex universe, they assert that it is in fact founded upon order. Reflecting upon a world in which moral decisions are not clear-cut, they argue that the world only appears to be chaotic, when in fact it has been created by separating out and distinguishing confused elements. The most basic fact about this world is the binary opposites that shape primordial chaos into a comforting home.

What then does.the Bible mean by suggesting that God looked at all that he had made and saw that it was good? Rabbinic commentators observe not only that God "saw" and that the verse injects "behold," but that the verse includes the small particle "and," which seems unnecessary. Rabbinic interpretations center upon the notion that everything in this world has some measure of good, even those things we think of as evil or superfluous. Thus in the copy of the Torah of Rabbi Meir, a prominent Mishnaic sage of the second century CE, was found the interpretation of the words "and behold it was very (*me*ʾ*od*) good" as "and behold death (*mavvet*) was good."[23] This rabbinic investigation (*midrash*) plays on the word "very" (*me*ʾ*od*), which in its Hebrew orthography is similar to the word for "death" (*mavvet*). Even death, which we experience in our world as most evil and terrifying, has a distinct and vital purpose in the creative order. Other interpretations suggest that many things we think of as evil are actually good: sleep, suffering, the angel of death, punishment, the impulse to evil, the earthly kingdom.[24]

Each of these concepts reveals significant values in rabbinic theology. For example, the inclination or impulse (*yetser*) to evil is seen as good because without it, no one would build a house, get married, or have children. The *midrash* quotes Ecclesiastes 4:4: "Again I considered all labor and all excelling in work, that it is a man's rivalry with his neighbor."[25] The term translated as "impulse" (*yetser*) is not far conceptually from Spinoza's *conatus* ("will or drive") or Freud's *id* ("primal desire-nature"). The verb *yatsar* means "to form or fashion." The *yetser* is the source of fashioning, initiative, or drive in a human being. In the Biblical story of Noah, God sees that the inclination of humankind is evil from its youth: "Every imagination [*yetser*] of the thoughts of his heart was only evil, every day" (Gen. 6:5). At first, this is a source of despair for God; seeing the wickedness in the world, God chooses to destroy the world and begin again with the one righteous human being, Noah, and his family (Gen. 6:6). However, after the flood, when Noah sacrifices to God, God again sees that humans are evil from their youth and decides never again to destroy the world: "I will not again curse the ground for man's sake, for the imagination [*yetser*] of man's heart is evil from its youth" (Gen. 8:21). God sees that this is just the way human beings are—"humans will be humans"—and in an endearing way decides to keep us just as we are, adjusting divine parenting skills to human nature as it presents itself.

The *yetser* then is undifferentiated; it can be channeled in a positive direction, as an inclination to good (*yetser tov*), or in a negative direction, as an impulse to evil (*yetser ra*ʿ). Without a *yetser* or *conatus*, we would have no drive to create civilization. If there are negative dimensions to our drives, such as rivalry and competitiveness, it is our task to keep them in check and channel them productively. As the drive that creates civilization and keeps us striving toward excellence, the inclination to "evil" is actually a good.[26]

The dispensation of punishment is good because it is a source of justice, "measure for measure." Suffering is good because through suffering and chastisement we learn and grow morally, which leads to the world to come. *Gehenna* (a rabbinic term for "hell," a place of eschatological punishment) is good because it is fitting that there be justice for those who do evil as well as those who do good. Thus even the harshest of realities in our world can be seen to have some measure of good.

"God saw all that he had made, and behold it was very good." In the view of one rabbinic interpretation, this teaches that God created and destroyed many worlds before this one, saying, "This pleases me; these do not please me."[27] This *midrash* reinforces the image of God we discerned in both the Bible and Plato: God is portrayed as an artist or craftsperson who steps back after creating and is happy with the final product. There is no sense that this is an evil world. In fact, the word "evil" does not occur in the first chapter of Genesis; the word first emerges in chapter 3 in the image of the tree of the knowledge of good and evil. In Genesis 1 we find primordial darkness on the face of the deep and chaotic waters, but no evil. Everything in the world God has created is seen to be good. Genesis 1 suggests a holistic view of the created world: spirit and body, contrary human impulses, all are part of a good creation. There is no separate force of evil, and human beings are not seen as bad.

## GOOD AND EVIL IN THE GARDEN OF EDEN

What then do we make of the second creation account, beginning in Genesis 2:4, which culminates in the story of the Garden of Eden? Readers will notice that this story features a much more anthropomorphic God, a God who creates humans from the dust, blows the breath of life into them, plants them in a garden, and later walks in the same garden. This is not the majestic, transcendent God of Genesis 1, but an earthy, involved, human-like God.[28] Genesis 1 suggests an image of God as rational order, a principle appealing to the mind of an Einstein or Spinoza. In contrast, the God of Genesis 3—who walks in a garden park and asks Adam, "Where are you?"—is on the face of it a God rejected by the scientific mind.

However, let us consider Genesis 2–3 in a slightly different light. While Genesis 1 teaches that goodness is inherent in creation, Genesis 2–3 demonstrates that relationship is also a primal feature of our world. This belief is at the heart of the work of the philosopher and mathematician Alfred North Whitehead, who bases his theories on twentieth-century physics. All beings in nature, down to the tiniest subatomic particles, have an effect on each other; in Whitehead's language, every particle takes its neighbors into account.[29] Thus any knowledge we have of a particle requires that we understand something about its relationship to other particles. Moreover, without relationship, there can be no knowledge: "If anything out of relationship, then complete ignorance as to it."[30] The subatomic particle does not reveal its own identity until asked by the measuring instrument what it is; it defines itself in relationship to the question we ask of it. In our scientific sophistication, we argue that personality and relationship are purely human characteristics. The Bible asserts a different point of view, one echoed by Whitehead: relationship and personality are just as natural to the world as earth, sky, and water.

The notion that God is to be identified with the *impersonal* laws of nature—a perspective associated with the seventeenth-century philosopher Spinoza—is generally regarded as more scientific than the view that relationship is inherent in the natural world. Social scientists label as "primitive animism" the notion that rocks and trees have human-like feelings or qualities. However, there is another dimension of Spinoza's thought known as panpsychism that views the question differently. Philosophers such as Leibniz, Spinoza, Henri Bergson, and Alfred North Whitehead argue that those features of the world that we see as distinguishing humans above all else—consciousness, feeling, relationship—are simply more developed versions of facts that exist throughout nature.[31]

This discussion anticipates a theme we will explore in more depth below, when we turn to Whitehead. Here it is introduced simply to convey that the God of Genesis 2–3, the God who is intimately involved with humanity in personal relationship, need not be seen as a polar opposite to the transcendent, majestic God of Genesis 1, who suggests scientific order. To see relationship and relationality at the heart of the cosmos need not leave us with the naïve caricature of God as an old man who walks with feet and is ignorant of where the first human beings are hiding. The Bible clearly includes two creation stories side by side, each with a different perspective. While the first story portrays a transcendent God who creates by the fiat of the spoken word, the second story gives us a God inextricably connected with humanity.[32] The second story suggests that there is an aspect of divinity with which humans are in relationship, an aspect of the source of creation that is personal. From the Biblical perspective, it is as naïve to describe God exclusively as transcendent as it is to depict God as fully anthropomorphic. Our humanity is not a discordant element in an otherwise unfeeling, impersonal cosmos.[33] Plants cooperate in an ecosystem; animals may kill for food but they also tend their young. Love and compassion are as much features of the world around us as are the facts of life and death. Perhaps it is modern science that is naïve in thinking that one can simply bracket these features and study a brute world of impersonal cause and effect.

Keeping in mind these reflections on the nature of the personal God of Genesis 2–3, we can return to the story of good and bad presented in Genesis 3. For "evil" is too strong a word to describe the quality revealed by the tree: the plain sense of the Garden of Eden story does not include the figure of a devil or Satan, but a snake, who tricks Eve into talking about the tree and overcomes her objections to eating from it. Biblical scholars are divided as to the intent and purpose of the story. Some interpreters argue that God wanted humans to eat from the tree, and thus intentionally planted the tree so that human beings would have the chance to reach moral maturity.[34] Scholars also point out that the curses at the end of the story do not necessarily suggest punishment, but fact. The world is different now. For example, Eve is now capable of bearing children; she is a potential mother. It is not that she was able to bear children painlessly before and is suddenly cursed with pain in childbearing; the facts of her universe have inexorably changed.[35] The text is pointing out the way things are, rather than passing judgment. This parallels the approach of the creation story in Genesis 1, which is more interested in describing the way the world is than accounting for ultimate origins. Genesis 1 shows God shaping elements that are already present into the order we know now; Genesis 2–3 shows the human, moral dimension of our order. Both stories are concerned with the realities of life: darkness and light, pain in childbirth, the difficult toil by which we sustain ourselves on this earth.

The existentialist philosopher and exegete Martin Buber suggests that once human beings have gained free will, God shields them from the pain of having to live forever with the consequences of their actions. Since they have become capable of choosing evil as well as good, God now prevents them from eating from the tree of life as an act of compassion.[36]

However, the plain sense of the phrase "knowledge of good and evil" is not clear. Nahum Sarna suggests that it is the capacity for independent judgment, without divine command.[37] Some commentators through the ages have argued that it is sexual knowledge; immediately after the story Adam and Eve have sexual relations.[38] Others have ventured that there is nothing magical about the tree itself that confers knowledge of good and evil; it is the fact that they do what God has prohibited them from doing that *is* the knowledge of good and evil.

How can we get a better sense of what the phrase "knowledge of good and evil" meant to the Biblical mind? There is internal Biblical evidence for the way this phrase was understood. It seems to be a merism, a statement that includes not just the pairs of opposites, but everything in between. In II Samuel 14:17, we read that the king is like an angel of God discerning (lit. "hearing") good and bad. A few verses later, we are told that the king is wise according to the wisdom of an angel of God, knowing all things that are in the earth. This parallelism suggests that knowing good and bad is tantamount to knowing all things. The exact phrase "knowing good and evil" occurs again only in Deuteronomy 1:39: "your little ones who have been carried off, who do not yet know good from bad." This suggests "not having arrived yet at the age of moral discernment." The phrase in Samuel thus either could connote knowing all things—as the parallel verse in Samuel also suggests—or it could refer specifically to moral knowledge, as in Deuteronomy 1:39, the kind a king would need in order to rule.[39]

The beauty of the text lies in its ambiguity. The first human beings take independent action; their choice to act against God's prohibition in itself represents an awareness of good and bad. Independent action has consequences. Eating from a tree is not itself a moral evil. However, human beings who exercise their free will enter into a state in which life is difficult, actions have consequences, and certain wonderful boons such as childbirth are achieved only through pain and struggle. We generally do not judge children's actions to be good or evil; it is only once humans become responsible for their actions that we can speak of good and bad.

We have thus seen several different ways in which the term "good" is used in the Hebrew Bible to refer to God's creation. When God looks at all of creation, God sees that the entire creation is good. This does not mean that all of creation is pleasant, or even pleasing to God. But it is all meant to be there. It is the stage upon which the human historical drama will be played. All its parts are important and none initially displease God.

God sees that all of creation is good prior to the humans' eating of the fruit of the tree. One can look at this fact in two ways. One could say that God becomes disillusioned with humanity, as expressed later during the generation of Noah, and would no longer at that point say that it was all good. Or one could argue that the term "good" as used in Genesis 1 includes both good and evil. The whole of creation is good, including both what we would term "good" and "evil." As we will see below, Augustine and Maimonides, following Plato and the Neoplatonic tradition, identify good with being. Being itself is good, and God's bestowing of existence on other things is good. This is the realm of good in itself. Within this framework, all features of the cosmos—including suffering, death, and moral tragedy—may be considered good, valuable, and worthwhile. All are part of the cosmic drama. Within the framework of a good universe, acts of egregious evil may take place. But these do not take away from the overall goodness of creation.[40]

The midrashic interpretations we have examined are in consonance with this perspective, which is expressed in many rabbinic meditations on God's creations. Even things we find annoying or unnecessary, such as gnats, have a place in God's creation, and the rabbis enjoy searching for their purpose.[41] These meditations can be spiritual exercises designed to teach students to experience gratitude and appreciation for every dimension of experience, even the most difficult and painful. Even suffering and chastisements bring a share in this world and the world to come. It is the reality of this existence in all its joy and suffering that helps us grow. [42]

What then do we learn about God and the good in these two creation stories? At the heart of reality is a sovereign source who sees all as orderly and harmonious, a tapestry of rhythms that give aesthetic delight. This story is crowned by the creation of the Sabbath, the symbol of holiness built into the order of creation. The world is beautiful and holy. So why do we not see it that way? The element of evil seems to have entered our world with human free will. We do not see animals as evil; even earthquakes and floods are not in themselves evil. We consider things evil because we judge them from a moral perspective. And morality enters with free will and human responsibility. It is thus important for the Bible to establish that free will is not something that was thrust upon human beings against our wishes. Humankind chose to become moral adults. If we had remained within childhood, we would never be held responsible for our actions. But God gave us the gift of free will to use as we might. From the rabbinic perspective, we can raise ourselves to the level of angels or lower ourselves to the level of beasts.

Life is difficult; we no longer bask in the Eden of childhood. As adults, we must work for a living. The joy of having a family brings with it the pain of childbirth, sibling rivalry, family tension, and struggle. The Bible suggests that this is all as it is meant to be. Our human world is a realm in which we can learn and grow, one which offers the joys and pains of a fully engaged life.

2

# A Divine Craftsman Shapes All for the Good

## PLATO'S REALM OF THE FORMS

UP TO this point we have explored the connection between God and the good in the Hebrew Bible. We have seen that the Bible asks not about the origin of the cosmos as a whole, but about the origin of the ordered world in which we live. We find a fascinating parallel in Plato's dialogue the *Timaeus*, one of the few Platonic dialogues actually read by philosophers in the Middle Ages—Jewish, Christian, and Islamic. Moreover, Plato draws an explicit connection between God and the good.[1] Plato's language and world view are not as familiar to the average Western reader as those of the Bible; we nevertheless ask that the reader stay with us as we dive into the world of Platonic metaphysics, which also holds great rewards.[2]

> Let us, then, state for what reason becoming and this universe were framed by him who framed them. He was good; and in the good no jealousy in any matter can ever arise. So, being without jealousy, he desired that all things should come as near as possible to being like himself. . . . Desiring, then, that all things should be good and, so far as might be, nothing imperfect, God took over all that is visible—not at rest, but in discordant and unordered motion—and brought it from disorder into order, since he judged that order was in every way the better.

Why does Plato make the connection he does here between God and good? Since we have ventured out from the familiar world of the Bible, let us pause a moment to consider the relationship between the concepts of God and the good in the history of religious thought. We generally use the word "God" to describe an ultimate principle of the universe—the source of all existence, knowledge, and value in our world. Thus Hinduism describes the divine principle, *brahman*, as existence (*sat*), consciousness or knowledge (*cit*, pronounced *chit*), and joy or bliss (*ānanda*).[3] Similarly, historian of philosophy W. K. C. Guthrie suggests that in his concept of the Good,[4] Plato combines three notions. Plato's Good is at once:

1. the end or purpose (*telos*) of life—that is, the supreme object of human desire or aspiration (*value*, like *brahman's joy*);
2. the condition of *knowledge*, which makes the world intelligible and the human mind intelligent; and
3. the sustaining cause of what Plato terms the eternal Forms or Ideas—absolute values or templates of our world such as justice, piety, and courage. The Good is that which gives all Forms their *being*.[5]

Plato's Good is not, however, a personal God. The Good has no will, and the Good does not create the world or exercise any intentional effect on the world's existents. And yet as the supreme source of being, knowledge, and value, the Good is in many ways parallel to our notions of the divine. If we can judge anything in the world to possess value, it is because there exists an ultimate source or principle of value. This is not a nihilistic world in which there is nothing that gives our lives meaning; we look out at the universe and see significance. We are in awe at the beauty of existence.[6]

As we have seen, Leibniz termed this the fundamental question of philosophy: Why is there something rather than nothing? The essential object of our awe is the fact that there exists a universe at all; being itself is the supreme mystery. Plato takes this one step further. He speaks of contemplating the Forms, reflecting upon absolute values that inspire human awe. Plato insists that these objective values are embedded in the fabric of nature.

Why is there an orderly cosmos? Plato answers that it is because a divine artisan was good, and wanted to fill the chaos of the pre-creative state with goodness and order. Plato does not describe creation of the world from nothing (*ex nihilo*). As in the Biblical Genesis, creation is really an act of ordering chaos. Plato's ultimate intention in the *Timaeus*, then, may be to suggest that were it not for creative ordering through goodness, this world would be chaotic.[7] The presence of order is a testimony to the intelligence and goodness of the universe. Here the Bible and Plato show remarkable consonance.

## CREATION IN PLATO'S *TIMAEUS*

### The Two Realms

With this background in mind, let us trace the steps of Plato's argument. In *Timaeus* 27d, Plato posits two realms, or orders of reality: the intelligible realm, and the realm of Ideas or Forms (singular: *eidos* or *idea*), that which is *eternally the same* and *never becomes or changes in any way*. These are abstract concepts, unchanging truths, or moral absolutes—in other Platonic dialogues we find the examples of beauty, justice, the number two, the perfect triangle. They are grasped by thought or understanding (*noēsis*) with the aid of a reasoned account (*logos*). According to Plato, the Forms are in fact the sole genuine objects of knowledge. We can only be said to *know* that which is unchangeably real, that which is what it is eternally. We can *know* that two plus two equals four, always and forever.

This view of knowledge is so counterintuitive to students coming to Plato for the first time that we should pause a moment to think about it. For Plato it is only unchanging truths, such as the truths of mathematics, that are real and can be completely known; nothing in the changing world can claim the same degree of reality or provide such an immutable object of knowledge.

The second realm, then, is the realm we live in: the sensible realm, the realm of all that is visible, sensible, and tangible, that which becomes, changes, comes to be, and passes away. These are objects of belief or opinion (*doxa*—related to our words "orthodox" and "paradox") together with unreasoning sensation. For example, the sun looks to our eyes as if it is just beyond the horizon; our eyes cannot tell that it is actually millions of miles from the earth. Even reasoned judgments based upon sense-perception hold true only as long as the empirical facts hold true. In billions of years when the sun has burned out, these judgments of distance will no longer be accurate. Thus all judgments about the sensible realm are based upon belief or opinion; they do not constitute knowledge in the strict sense. The realm of Forms or Ideas can be known and is real; the realm of beliefs is subject to change and therefore not fully knowable and not as real. The world as a whole (*ouranos* or *kosmos*) belongs to the visible, sensible realm; it can be seen and touched and has a body. It is always changing, so it is grasped by belief or opinion based upon sense perception.[8]

Plato's next move is to argue that anything that becomes must have a cause that brings it into being.[9] He does not say whether he believes that something that is not in the realm of becoming can be self-caused;[10] Plato's assumption seems to be that that which always *is* needs no explanation for its existence. That which *becomes* needs a causal explanation to explain why it has come to be. Things do not become by chance. Movement and change require a causal explanation.

Since the changing world is visible or sensible and thus has come to be, it must have a cause that explains how it came to be. Therefore, the world must have a cause, a maker (*dēmiourgos,* or Demiurge, lit., "one who fashions, a craftsperson or architect"), although this being is difficult to find and nearly impossible to declare to all.[11] The maker fashioned the world on an eternal, unchanging model, that of the Form of a Living Creature.[12] The motive for creation is that the maker was good, rather than jealous. Desiring that all things should be like himself, he brought all that was in disorder into order (*kosmos,* the Greek word for "order").[13]

Now, does Plato intend this to be read as a real creation story, a depiction of events that actually took place in the historical past? From the time of the ancient Greek philosophers onward, one strand of interpretation of the *Timaeus* has suggested that Plato's creation account should be read metaphorically, as an allegorical depiction of the role of good and reason in ordering the world. This strand asserts that the story is a mythological way of suggesting that were it not for reason—which orders everything for the good—all we would have is chaos. The Demiurge could be a metaphor for the Form of the Good or Reason (*Nous*), whose existence imposes order on an otherwise chaotic universe.[14]

Whether or not we choose to read the story metaphorically, we find here central aspects of Plato's conception of the good. In the *Timaeus*, Plato associates good with order and God's lack of jealousy. This association finds a parallel in the *Republic*, where Socrates asserts that no one who spends time with the Forms—which are everywhere orderly and the same, and which neither hurt nor oppress—would have the desire to do injustice; the philosopher draws from his or her proximity to the beautiful, orderly realm of the Forms a great yearning to be like them.[15] Plato's notion of good thus combines a moral with an aesthetic vision. The realm of the Forms is orderly, always the same; God wanted our world to share in the ordered Being of the eternal realm and thus wanted this world to be orderly rather than chaotic.

We have seen that only that which is the same eternally can truly be known. Plato adds that it is the Good that enables things to be known; the Good is the source of intelligibility as well as order.[16] Chaos is disturbing, not only spiritually, but epistemologically; it confuses our sense of the rightness and order of things. We want a world that makes sense to us, a world we can understand. The Good not only provides moral and aesthetic grounding, but satisfies an intellectual need to comprehend the world.

## The Receptacle

Up to now, Plato has spoken of two realms, those of Being and of Becoming. Being is the realm of the Forms, the intelligible models, which are real and unchanging. The world we live in is the realm of Becoming, that which changes and is visible and tangible. In *Timaeus* 48e–49e, Plato finds it necessary to add a third element to make sense of our world. He calls this third element the Receptacle, or the nurse of becoming, something which "receives" the Forms, a site in which they can become.

Donald Zeyl offers the following example: let us say that we want to make a statue of Lincoln. We know the image of Lincoln that we want to represent, but it needs a medium in which it can be represented—perhaps marble or canvas.[17] If we have an eternal realm of models and a world of images, there must be a place or medium in which those images can appear. The Receptacle—in 52b called "space" (*chōra*)—provides a physical bridge between the eternal Forms and our changing, sensible world, a bridge never quite constructed in other dialogues in which Plato talks about the Forms, such as the *Republic*. Space, Plato suggests, is fundamentally different from time. Whereas time is created—he calls it the moving image of eternity—space simply is, a setting or stage on which our drama of becoming can unfold.

In 51d, he expresses the triad of world elements in more imagistic language. He calls *the Form* the "father," the model in whose likeness that which becomes is born. *That which becomes* is the offspring—all things in our visible, sensible world. The *Recipient* or *Receptacle* is the "mother," that *in which* all things become. Plato's description reflects ancient Greek notions of the birth of human children. The Greeks believed that the father's sperm held all genetic information; the child was thus the image or likeness of the model, the father.[18] The woman's womb was seen as a mere empty space in which the seed was planted. Thus the image of a nurse of becoming is a passive one; the mother simply provides a site in which growth and maturation can take place. Likewise, Plato presents the spacious Receptacle as an empty matrix.

Being needs a place in which its eternal ideals can be expressed, an empty canvas on which to paint images of the Forms.

In 51e–52d, he explains the threefold nature of reality further. He tells us that Forms themselves are inert; they don't receive anything into themselves or enter anything. They are pure unchanging ideals, objects of thought—uncreated, indestructible, invisible, imperceptible. In contrast, the sensible copies in our world are not static but dynamic. They are brought into existence, are perpetually in motion, come to be in a certain place, and vanish out of it. It is for this reason that we cannot be said to *know* the changing perceptible objects of our world. We are aware of them through sense perception, but they are fleeting, and thus not suitable objects for knowledge. Plato describes sensible objects as objects of *belief*, involving unreasoning sensation. We can only *know* that which is eternal. And then there is the third element—what he calls here space (*chōra*). Space provides a situation (lit. "fixed site, seat") for all things that come into being. We do not perceive space directly; rather it is grasped without the senses by what he calls "a sort of bastard reasoning." We will examine below what Plato might mean by this.[19]

Why does Plato feel it necessary to add this mysterious Receptacle to his account of the world? The later example of Aristotelian metaphysics offers an interesting parallel. In order to account for the possibility of change, Aristotelian metaphysics introduces the concept of prime matter—a neutral stuff devoid of characteristics that receives all forms and qualities.[20] Plato at times speaks as if the Receptacle is something like Aristotle's prime matter—a moldable substance like clay or wax out of which all things in our world are made. On the other hand, at times Plato speaks as if the Receptacle is simply an empty space into which things in our changing world are poured, a "where" in which all change can take place.

Plato describes the Receptacle using disparate and perhaps even contradictory images, one of which is that of gold. We can point to a piece of gold jewelry and ask what it is. Rather than answering that it is a ring, a bracelet, or a necklace, it is safer to say "gold," since these things change even as we assert their existence—they decompose, and can be remolded into other shapes.[21] The same is true of the nature that receives all bodies; while it accepts all things into itself, the Receptacle never takes on the character of things it receives. It is a characterless matrix for everything; it only seems to be changed by what enters it. The fundamental elements—earth, air, fire, and water—make it *appear* different at different times. But the Receptacle is never really watery or fiery—Plato seems to depict it like a screen or mirror on which are projected likenesses of Water in itself and Fire in itself, that is, the non-physical Forms. The things that "enter" and "leave" it are imitations of the Forms—"imprinted after their likeness in a marvelous way that is hard to describe" (50c). Similarly, reflections appear to enter a mirror, but the language of entering is metaphorical; reflections don't properly enter a space inside a mirror. This may be one reason he compares our knowledge of space to that of dream images (52b).

Kenneth Seeskin argues that the image of gold is misleading; it can lead us to believe that Plato thinks of the Receptacle as a material substratum out of which all things are made.[22] But we have seen that Plato goes on to qualify his remarks: he is emphatic that while the Receptacle receives all bodies, it never takes on the character of the bodies that enter it. The Receptacle does not literally change into other shapes the way gold does when it is molded into diverse forms of jewelry. The point of the metaphor, rather, is that the underlying character of the Receptacle remains the same amid diverse and fluid changes; its character is unaffected by the shapes that come and go.[23]

Plato uses two additional material metaphors—those of perfume and of wax. When mixing a fragrance, one must be certain that the base contains no fragrance of its own. Similarly, when taking an impression in a soft substance like wax, one must be certain that the original substance is completely smooth. Likewise, that which receives the likenesses of eternal and intelligible things must in its own nature be free of all characteristics. Thus the mother and receptacle of all sensible things must not be called earth, air, fire, or water, or any of their compounds, but rather "a nature that is itself invisible and characterless, all-receiving, partaking in some very puzzling way of the intelligible and very hard to apprehend. That part of it which has been made fiery appears at any time as fire; the part that is liquefied as water"[24] (51b).

Donald Zeyl offers an ingenious resolution to the tension between these material images and Plato's language of space. He reconciles these diverging images by suggesting that the Receptacle may be *filled space*—and since the original receptacle contains moving particles, it can be both space and that which moves around in that space, like a filled container of water. One piece of the container could move around another part; water would be both "the room to move around in" and that which is moving—both space and stuff.[25] This suggests a curiously contemporary image: where is the universe? It is not itself anywhere. It is a container that holds itself, like the fluid container of a fluid universe. Particles of earth, air, fire, and water can move around and themselves constitute the space in which they move.

Nevertheless, the most puzzling element of this account remains—the relationship between eternal Forms and the images or reflections that appear in the Receptacle. As Seeskin points out, Plato's Forms are not efficient causes; they don't do anything.[26] They do not create or choose to project themselves into a material, as the sculptor imprints the image of Lincoln in marble. How then do their traces, vestiges, or reflections appear in our world? The fourth-century philosopher Plotinus interprets the Receptacle as a mirror in which images are temporarily reflected and then pass out of existence.[27] Along the same lines, perhaps we can think of it as a screen on which images are projected. But why should there be *sensible* images of the *intelligible* world? At the heart of the text we have a problem that has plagued both ancient and modern philosophers: the relationship between spirit and matter, mind and body, the realm of ideas and the realm of the senses. How are ideas or spiritual ideals expressed or reflected in our world?

Plato introduces space, the matrix of becoming, as the link between the two, which itself cannot be perceived, except indirectly. Perhaps what Plato means is that it must be inferred by deduction from the other elements. Given that there are stable objects of knowledge and changing sensibles, there must be a medium in which the eternal ideas are reflected, a "where" in which they appear.[28] Plato's words here echo the Socratic language of crafts; the carpenter needs a blueprint or model and a site in which to carve an impression. Whether or not the receptacle is actually a material substance, it provides a place in which the model can appear. The image of Lincoln needs a medium in which we can either carve or reflect that image.

We have seen that in the *Timaeus*, Plato tells us explicitly that the images are imitations of the things that always are, "imprinted after their likeness in a way that is hard to describe" (50b). In other dialogues, such as the *Republic* and *Phaedo*, he uses the language of participation; the concrete things we see in our world in some way participate in the intangible Forms. In the *Timaeus* Plato bridges the intelligible and the sensible in a more concrete way than in his other works. He brings in the Receptacle as a tangible bridge, for it belongs to the sensible, visible world, as do the images or traces of the Forms.

## The Craftsman Who Orders Chaos

We must consider another piece of information, one to which Plato alludes several times. Plato tells us that images, vestiges, or traces of the Forms were together in a chaotic state before the divine craftsman ordered them, using the Forms as a model. In that pre-creation era, things were in the state one would expect of something absent of divinity. The allusion to pre-creation chaos can lend itself to either a real or a metaphoric interpretation. Plato does tell us that whereas space is uncreated, time is created as "a moving image of eternity" (37c–38c). The plain sense of Plato's myth suggests that he envisages an era before time is created, in which elements moved about chaotically in a Receptacle that was itself in motion—a depiction not unlike the opening of the Bible's first creation story.

The image he uses here is that of a winnowing basket. Before Heaven came to be there were Being, Space, and Becoming. The Becoming, the nurse, was made watery and fiery and received the characters of earth and air. It took on diverse appearances as it acquired the properties that come with these characters. These elements were swaying and shaking, and the Receptacle was shaken by them and in turn shook them. The four elements were separated and carried in different directions as in a winnowing basket—thus were earth, air, fire, and water separated into distinct realms. With deity absent from them, they were in a chaotic condition, without proportion or measure. God gave them a distinct configuration by means of shapes and numbers. God fashioned these four kinds to be as perfect and excellent as possible, when they were not so before. In the next section, the speaker Timaeus goes on to explain that the primary constituents of reality are not earth, air, fire, and water but triangles, and these triangles combine in different proportions and configurations to make all things.

Thus the historical reading suggests that God, looking to the Forms, imposed order upon chaos—separating out earth, air, fire, and water as distinct elements in distinct regions. Another way to read the text is metaphorical, whereby Plato's creation story functions as a myth—that is, a metaphor in story form.[29] The ordering of chaos by a rational God is meant to tell us that in the absence of Reason—here personified as a deity—all elements in our world would be mixed together in confusion. This reading does not posit that there was a *historical* pre-creative era. Moreover, there is an additional evocative way that Plato speaks of the creation of the world: as the persuasion of Necessity by Reason.[30] Here too we are confronted by a deep metaphor. There are aspects of our world that are simply given; Plato seems to believe space is one of them, as well as the four physical elements. Space has no why; it simply is. There is no way to account for its being. What we can explain is the way Reason or order takes elements that are given and arranges them for good.

Even if we take Plato's creation story as real rather than metaphorical, it is nevertheless clear that we do not find here a God who is omnipotent, who has ultimate triumph over nature. Like the Bible, the *Timaeus* features already-present aspects of the world with which God must contend. Space, as well as particles of earth, air, fire, and water, simply are—reason can, at best, persuade or tame them. As Seeskin suggests, Plato is more interested in the structure of the world than in how it got to be this way.[31] Plato presents a gestalt vision, a wholistic view of the world not reducible to its parts; what we can do as philosophical readers is to ask whether that vision is coherent. Perhaps the contradictory images of the Receptacle reflect the fact that Plato is not certain how the realm of ideas and the realm of sensible reality interact. When talking about the sensible world, all we can give is a likely account; we are dealing with the realm of belief, based on sensation.[32]

Plato is attracted to the ideal of a pure conceptual world in which all is perfectly ordered and harmonious. And yet we find ourselves in a world far from perfect, a world seemingly in disarray, in which physical things wither and decay and moral values can be uncertain and compromised. On the other hand, this world is not one of pure disorder; we would have no concept of harmony, beauty, and perfection if there were not some trace of moral ideals in our world.[33] Thus comes the creative vision of Plato. The goal of philosophers as stewards of the Forms is to paint the canvas of our world with ideals, to look to the eternal Forms as models and imitate them as best we can. The legislator seeks to shape human nature in accordance with the divine image by creating laws that bring out moral ideals. We as individual philosophers can come closer to the divine image by imitating the Forms.[34]

Students are often tempted to contrast Plato's God with the allegedly omnipotent God of Western monotheism. But the latter view of God is actually a medieval theological creation—a hybrid of Greek and Biblical thinking. As we have seen, recent scholarship suggests that the Bible's account draws upon ancient Near Eastern mythology; many Biblical passages describe God's creative act as a taming of chaotic forces of nature, natural powers with which God must contend in an ongoing way. Like the *Timaeus*, the Biblical creation story describes not creation from nothing, but the ordering of chaos—a forceful persuasion, as it were, of reason over necessity.

## God and the Good in Genesis and *Timaeus*

We have seen that for Plato it is good that undergirds the created order. If there must be sought a reason for this world to exist as it does, it is that God wanted to share and express divine goodness. Thus there is a natural conversation between Plato's *Timaeus* and the Genesis narrative in the Hebrew

Bible. In both accounts, we find a pre-creation state of chaos, which a good God decides to order. The Hebrew Bible does not tell us God's motive for creation, but after each stage of creation, God looks at creation and sees that it is good. The *Timaeus* tells us emphatically that the motive for creation was that the divine craftsman wanted the world to be as good and ordered as he was.

Both Plato's *Timaeus* and the Hebrew Bible portray a God who is not completely sovereign, who did not create all from nothing, but simply shaped chaotic elements into habitable order. We as heirs of the medieval tradition may find ourselves profoundly uncomfortable with the notion that God is not completely in charge of the universe, that there are elements beyond God's control. How could it be that there are features of the cosmos that are simply present, coexistent with God? How is God then God? And how can the Hebrew Bible accept a God who is not completely sovereign?

Historical critical scholars of the Bible argue that in fact monotheism developed only gradually among the ancient Israelites. Some argue that even the credo of Deuteronomy 6:5, "Hear O Israel, the Lord our God, the Lord is one," may express not full-blown monotheism, but at best monolatry, the assertion that one God is most deserving of Israel's absolute loyalty and devotion. It is not that there are no other divine beings (for example, the Israelites proclaim at the Red Sea: "Who is like You, *among the gods* [*elim*]?"),[35] but that Israelites should worship this God alone, the God they know through their own experience. For this is the God who brought the Israelites out of Egypt, the God to whom Israel owes devotion. Faithfulness to this God is a natural response to God's loving acts of commitment to the patriarchs and matriarchs, and to the entire nation whom God liberated from Egyptian slavery.[36]

The notion that there are elements that preexist God is unsettling to us today; why was this not so for the ancient Israelites? Israel Knohl argues that the creation story of the first chapter of Genesis is meant to answer the question of theodicy. If God creates everything, then God is responsible for evil. However, if the evil, chaotic elements preexist God's creative action, then God is not responsible for them. Everything God created is "very good"; the dimension of evil is precisely that which God did not create.[37] The notion that the world was created from something preexistent is even known to the rabbis. It is expressed by the midrashic rabbi Bar Kappara, who proposes that the unformed void (*tohu va-vohu*) from which God created is something preexistent. However, other rabbis deem this view unseemly—as if God would set God's creation upon a pile of dung.[38] Perhaps the Genesis account itself suggests that it is more important that God's goodness be protected than God's sovereignty.

The first chapter of Genesis simply does not answer the question of how the primordial elements of darkness, water, the deep, and the unformed void got here. The rabbis are also comfortable asserting that God created and destroyed many worlds before this one; Genesis 1 tells us only about the creation of the ordered world *we* live in.[39] By setting forth this interpretation, the rabbis indicate that there may be mysteries to creation not explicitly accounted for in our Bible. They leave room for philosophers, mystical thinkers, and generations of readers to ponder the ultimate origin of the universe.

In contrast to the Genesis account—in which preexistent elements might threaten the sovereignty of God—the Biblical book of Isaiah presents us with full-fledged monotheism. "I am the Lord, there is none else; beside me, there is no god."[40] "I form good, I create darkness, I make peace, and create evil. I the Lord do all these things."[41] For true monotheism, there is nothing outside the sphere of God, even evil. Evil is not a split-off entity, a power that can challenge or threaten God.[42]

It seems that the pre-creation state of Plato's *Timaeus* functions precisely the way the pre-creation state functions in the Bible. That is, the question on Plato's mind may be: if God is good and wanted the world to be good, why are there nevertheless elements of chaos and disorder in our world? Plato's answer in the *Timaeus* is that God is not omnipotent. Creation is the victory of reason over necessity. The Greek term "necessity" (*anankē*) does not suggest determinism, but rather those things over which one has no control—brute fact, things that simply are.[43] Reason takes the things that are and forms them into an orderly universe.

Unlike the God of the Hebrew Bible, Plato's Demiurge is given no role in sustaining the cosmos; the Demiurge simply shapes the chaotic elements into order. The divine craftsman is confronted, like the Biblical God, with primeval realities. In the Platonic image, these include the eternal Forms, space, and particles of earth, air, fire, and water, moving randomly in space. The work of the divine craftsman is to look to the Forms, to look to the random motions, and as best he can, to mold the random particles into the image of divine perfection, through the persuasion of reason. This looks very much like what Plato describes in the *Republic* as the goal of philosophical legislators: to look to the Forms as they legislate, creating laws that will shape the characters of citizens so that they may resemble the divine image.[44] Forms or ideals such as justice and temperance give us models for our aspirations. Plato acknowledges the existence of brute facts or givens in the world, but he also affirms the presence of reason, which does its best to gently guide these irreducible facts toward their natural *telos*, their purpose and aim.

We have seen that scholars disagree whether the Demiurge is meant by Plato to represent a real figure, or to serve as a metaphor for the role of reason. That is, the entire creation story may be a way of saying that were it not for the presence in the universe of ordering intelligence, all we would have is chaos.[45] In this view, the story is not meant to suggest an actual temporal act of creation or shaping. Just as the *Republic* portrays the features needed for an ideal state by symbolically creating one from scratch, the *Timaeus* teaches us about the elements of our world through what looks like a temporal creation story.[46]

What are the elements needed to make sense of our world? First of all, reason itself must be seen as a feature of the universe; even modern scientists would agree. Whereas at the quantum level we find randomness, uncertainty, and lack of definition, somehow at the macrocosmic level, there is coherent order. While the nature of a packet of light is only a possibility until it is asked a question by an instrument of measurement—it might be a wave or it might be a particle—and while its speed and location cannot both be specified, we can rely on the fact that we have light.[47] The molecules in a table may have only potential location, and theoretically could dissolve. And yet as an empirical fact, tables do remain tables and chairs chairs. There is order; there is intelligibility. We need not speak of intelligent *design*, as if an intelligence designated things to be this way, but there is order, and that might be just what Plato is interested in pointing out. The Forms may represent conceptual order, and the Demiurge, the shaping of chaos by patterns that cohere. Plato also seems to think that space is primeval, that events must take place somewhere. Without space, there would be no setting for the events of history.

## The Language of Number

We have seen that space, or the Receptacle, represents Plato's attempt in the *Timaeus* to create a bridge between the intelligible and the sensible realm, between the world of Being and the Forms and the world of Becoming. Before leaving the *Timaeus*, we should note an additional dimension of this bridge: the language of mathematics. Plato's affinity for number may give us a clue to the way we as moderns can understand Plato's vision of the Forms.

Plato's later thinking seems to have moved increasingly in a Pythagorean direction.[48] Both in late dialogues such as the *Timaeus* and in what has been called the "Unwritten Doctrine"—reflected in his letters and the testimony of writers such as Aristotle—the Forms may have evolved into numbers. The numbers exist in the world Soul; from the Soul the four dimensions are projected upon matter in combinations of basic triangles, forming the elements earth, air, fire, and water.[49] Aristotle asserts that in addition to the Forms, Plato believed in "Mathematicals," or "objects of mathematics." These differ from the Forms because there can be many the same and combinable; that is, there is not just a Form of the mathematical "two," but also "one plus one." In addition, Aristotle asserts that for Plato, the "world soul" is the place (*topos*) of the Forms. Plato may have believed that the world soul receives the Forms into itself and transforms them into mathematicals, which it then projects upon matter to form the physical world.

In *Timaeus* 35a, Plato describes the construction of the world soul; this description also appears in *Laws* X. The human soul is a microcosm of the world soul; it seems to function as a mediator between the intelligible and the physical realms. It is at the level of soul that the four primal numbers take on their mathematical aspects of point, line, plane and solid; the soul receives influences from the intelligible realm and passes them on in extended form to bring about the creation of the sensible world.

Thus Plato has a mathematical answer to the question we have been asking: what is the relationship between spirit and matter, the intelligible and the sensible? In the *Phaedo* and the *Republic*, he uses the language of imitation and participation. Late in his life, he seems to have arrived at a mathematical solution, one with parallels to the thought of early modern rationalists such as Descartes, Leibniz, and Spinoza, as well as modern Platonists such as Alfred North Whitehead and Paul Davies. The equations of geometry provide a template for the three dimensional reality of our world. Plato's conception is comparable to that of Spinoza, for whom thought and extension are simply two ways of describing one reality, like a proposition expressed in the sentences of two different languages.[50] The language of mathematics is the aspect of thought; the language of physics is that of extension. Similarly, Plato's Forms or Ideas are the mathematical blueprints for the reality of our world.

How are these equations expressed in our world? Here Plato uses the image of the Receptacle as a mirror that receives the Forms and translates them into the sensible reality we know. In his description of the initial chaotic state of the Receptacle, Plato asserts that what was present were traces of earth, air, fire, and water, but in the chaotic, mixed state one would expect in something absent of deity. God ordered them by giving a "distinct configuration by means of shapes and numbers."[51] Thus triangular configurations are the means by which chaotic, random motions are given order. Plato's model might find a modern scientific parallel in the complex configuration of tiny sub-atomic particles, or the double-helix structure of DNA, by which genetic information is encoded. If there were no order—which Plato likens to divinity or divine Mind—we would have simply random, chaotic motion.

Plato's teleological order is thus not as naïve as we might think at first glance. In *Phaedo* 97b, Plato portrays his spokesperson Socrates expressing delight at discovering that the pre-Socratic philosopher Anaxagoras taught that all had been created by Mind. He thought that he would find in these teachings teleological explanations of why things are the way they are. Since Mind would direct all things for the good, he thought Anaxagoras would teach whether the earth was round or flat and why it was so, i.e., why this was the best possible way for it to be. Socrates is dismayed to discover that Anaxagoras made no real use of Mind as a causal explanation, but used the ordinary mechanical efficient causes:

> That seemed to me much like saying that Socrates' actions are all due to his mind, and then in trying to tell the causes of everything I do, to say that the reason that I am sitting here is because my body consists of bones and sinews . . . I no longer understand or recognize those other sophisticated causes, and if someone tells me that a thing is beautiful because it has a bright color or shape or any such thing, I ignore these other reasons—for all these confuse me—but I simply, naively and perhaps foolishly cling to this, that nothing else makes it beautiful other than the presence of, or the sharing in, or however you may describe its relationship to that Beautiful we mentioned, for I will not insist on the precise nature of the relationship, but that all beautiful things are beautiful by the Beautiful.

Socrates thus abandons physical explanatory causes for a more abstract notion of what makes a thing what it is. He goes on to argue that something is made bigger by participation in Bigness. Since the *two* can be made in many different ways—for example, by adding one to one or subtracting eight from ten—we cannot say that it is the eight that makes *the two* or the one that makes *the two*, but rather its participation or sharing in *twoness*. Things are what they are by sharing in essential qualities. This can help us understand Plato's concept of the Forms. Water is wet by the presence of wetness in it; likewise things are good due to the presence of goodness.[52]

## GOD AND THE GOOD IN PLATO

### Plato's Absolute

With this understanding of the role of Forms for Plato, how can we make sense of his ultimate Form, the Form of the Good? We have seen that Plato's Good fulfills some of the functions of God in the Bible. The Form of the Good is the source of absolute value. The Demiurge looked to the Forms as models for creating this world; the Good is that in which all the Forms participate. The Forms owe their being and their truth to the Good.

What does this mean in practical terms? Plato believes that values are as fundamental to the world as facts.[53] To know what it is to be a chair, one must know what it is to be a *good* chair.[54] In the words of David Ross, the Forms are Forms of Excellence.[55] They are Ideals and not just Ideas; they are paradigms of what it is to be a thing or to hold a quality.[56]

Goodness is that which makes things what they are; this is the essence of Plato's teleological view of the world. The appeal to teleology was criticized by thinkers such as Spinoza for presuming that the world is designed for *human* ends. But that is not Plato's view. Plato believes that the world is like an organism in which every part contributes to the whole. Everything has a function in the world. The virtue or excellence of a knife is to cut well; the virtue of a leader is to lead well. The virtue of a human being is "doing well," which is tantamount to "living well" and "living happily."[57] A thing is good or excellent insofar as it fulfills its function. A human being is not a genuine human being if he or she is not exhibiting what it is to be human. Thus it is goodness or the fulfilling of function that makes a thing what it is.

Let us look at this question from another angle. In his classic lectures on Plato's *Republic*, R. N. Nettleship explains that the Greek term "the good" (*to agathon*) meant to both philosophers and ordinary Greeks the object of desire, that which is most worth having, that which we above all seek. We all aim at a good or goal, a *telos*. That we are goal-directed beings is inherent in the Greeks' conception of reason. For Plato, all of nature likewise expresses an immanent reason or teleology, which is parallel to the intentional teleology of the human being. In any complex object or being, each of the parts performs a function with respect to the whole. Thus the science of biology is fundamentally teleological; it sees every natural organism as a whole and each part serving a function in the organism.[58] Even inorganic nature is analyzed with a view to the way elements act with respect to one another in an ordered whole.[59]

This recognition can help us understand Plato's conception of the Form of the Good, which he may also have understood as the one, or unity. To perceive an immanent reason throughout nature is simply to posit that everything has a good, what it is meant to do or to be.[60] The world order holds together because in every being of any complexity there is a unity that brings together parts into a coherent whole; it is this unity that makes the being intelligible. The principle of unity makes things both intelligible and good, for it enables them to be what they are meant to be. It thus stands to reason that in Plato's enigmatic "Lecture on the Good"—in which students were disappointed that he discoursed on mathematics rather than ethics—Plato seems to have identified the Good with the one.[61] The Good is the oneness that binds things together into a unified, coherent whole.[62]

Goodness, or unity, is thus the binding force that holds together all things in the cosmos.[63] It is this teleological order that Socrates thought Anaxagoras would recognize in teaching that Mind directs all things for the good. Unfortunately, he discovered that Anaxagoras was just like other thinkers who seek materialist explanation for all things in the cosmos. These thinkers do not seek truly teleological explanations:

> As for the power of things being now placed as is best for them to have been placed, this they do not look for, nor do they consider [that power] to have any divine force, but they believe they will somehow discover a stronger and more immortal Atlas to hold everything together more. And the good that is actually necessary both to bind together and to hold together all things, this they do not consider at all.[64]

Materialist thinkers look for a material principle to hold the earth together, an external cause that can replace the mythical Atlas and account in a physical way for why things are the way they are.[65] Socrates himself is looking for a deeper principle of explanation. He believes things are where they are because of an inner teleological principle, a capacity for being in the best place they can be. Plato describes this immanent principle by playing upon two senses of the Greek term *to deon*, which can refer both to that which literally binds things together—like ropes or chains, or as we would say, a kind of glue—and, by extension, to that which is binding, needful, and proper. He thus alludes to a cosmic principle that both literally binds things together and binds them to be necessarily what and where it is proper for them to be. The Good is the glue that holds things together properly. For Plato, there is no gap between the "is" and the "ought"; things are naturally as it is proper for them to be.[66]

Perhaps now we can make sense of Plato's enigmatic remark: "the objects of knowledge not only receive from the presence of the good their being known, but their very existence [*einai*] and essence [*ousia*] is derived from it, although the Good is not essence [*ousia*], but is still beyond it in dignity and power."[67] The Good is the principle of reason and unity within each thing; a thing can be known insofar as it participates in Goodness, that is, intelligible order. All objects of knowledge *are* insofar as they are coherent wholes bound together by unity.[68] Plato's enigmatic statement thus becomes intelligible. All things *are* insofar as they are good or unified; the Good is thus ontologically "superior" or logically prior to being. Things *are* by participating in Goodness.[69]

How then does the Form of the Good sustain the other Forms? The Form of the Good gives the other Forms their coherence and order, just as individual things are given coherence and order by the Good.[70] Moreover, since the Forms are forms of excellence—exemplars of what it is to embody a certain quality, to be a good or perfect example of a thing—what they share in common is goodness. It is thus the Good that gives the Forms their being or essence.[71] The Good can be thought of as a kind of intelligible light or radiance that shines through all the other Forms, revealing their coherence and value.[72]

This view of the Good has practical implications. How can it be helpful for us to possess a talent or virtue, if we have no conception of its goodness or benefit?[73] The Form of the Just tells us what it really is for an action to be just; in order to truly act with justice, we need to know why it is good to do so. Indeed, we have all seen people who possess talents, but do not know how to use them well. In order to make the most of our gifts, we need more than to possess the virtue or talent; we need also to understand what makes it a virtue, that is, what its good or excellence is. This is precisely why Socrates argues in the *Meno* that virtue is a form of wisdom. Wisdom ensures that we will use our physical and spiritual gifts well. A person may be fearless, but without wisdom, such fearlessness may deteriorate into rashness; wisdom turns fearlessness into courage. A person may be gifted with attention to detail; without wisdom, this can deteriorate into mere obsessiveness. Wisdom—the knowledge of how to use our talents well—can turn the obsessive prober into a gifted scientist. All of the Forms must thus participate in the

Form of the Good. The Good gives them their being; courage owes its being to goodness, for without goodness, it is merely recklessness.

Goodness is thus fundamental to existence. From Plato's point of view, Anaxagoras missed an opportunity to see that Mind would direct all things to the good, that the true understanding of things is rooted in understanding their purpose, what they are good for. In fact, the term virtue (*aretē*) simply means excellence. The virtue of a knife is to cut well; that is its purpose or function. Plato's worldview is teleological, not in the sense that things are moving toward a goal, but in the sense that everything in the world has a purpose and function. The world is intrinsically ordered, and ordered for the Good.

## Human Virtue and Happiness

Our discussion of Plato has thus moved from the question of God, the Good, and creation to the question of human virtue. This is a fitting coda for our examination of God and the good in Plato, as it parallels our discussion of the Bible. The first chapter of Genesis asserts the ontological goodness of creation: all beings are good, as they are all created by God. The second creation account shifts to the human sphere; human beings must achieve moral goodness through intentional moral action.

From Plato's perspective, human virtue is in one sense not that different from the excellence of anything in the universe that is fulfilling its function. And yet there is a difference, because we human beings can consciously strive to fulfill our function and achieve excellence (*aretē*). Plato has his character Socrates express the conviction that virtue is a form of knowledge or wisdom, and that virtue is the key to happiness. In what follows, we will examine some of Plato's key discussions of virtue and happiness from the *Protagoras*, *Meno*, and *Gorgias*.

In the *Protagoras*, Plato presents Socrates in dialogue with Protagoras, a Sophist. The Sophists are teachers who groom wealthy young men for public office. They claim to be able to teach young men *aretē*. The term *aretē* originally meant masculine virtue; in Homer and elsewhere, it has the connotation of prowess on the battlefield and other manly arts, and it probably retains this flavor for the Sophists. The Sophists are like latter-day public relations consultants, teaching young professionals how to win friends and influence people—in other words, how to succeed in public office.

Protagoras is known for his teaching that "man is the measure of all things," that all values are relative. Good is what is good for me; what is good for me is what I as an individual deem to be good. Socrates has a different view of *aretē*; he shifts the focus of virtue from external success in the public sphere to internal traits of character—justice, self-mastery, courage. These traits may express themselves in virtuous actions, but the key to lasting virtue is the character we develop. In his early dialogues, Plato teaches the unity of the virtues as well—that is, if a person possesses one virtue, he or she possesses them all.[74] Virtue is a unified state of character, and the key to that state of character is wisdom. Moreover, in contrast to the Sophists, Socrates is not a moral relativist. Protagoras believes that whatever the individual thinks to be good *is* good for him or her. Socrates believes that there is an objectively good life and that a person can achieve it or, through ignorance, fail to achieve it.

In the *Protagoras*, Socrates gives an overview, in a polemical form, of an argument he will make in earnest in the *Gorgias* and *Meno*. In the *Protagoras*, Socrates' interlocutor Protagoras upholds a form of hedonism. Socrates thus makes an ad hominem argument, an argument directed specifically to Protagoras on the basis of the hedonistic assumption. Socrates seems to argue that good is just a matter of maximizing one's own pleasure. In the *Gorgias* Socrates argues vigorously against the hedonist thesis; there he draws a clear distinction between pleasure and the good. In the *Protagoras*, however, he argues that even if we maintain that the good is simply a matter of maximizing our own pleasure, we need to give forethought to that which will give us the greatest degree of pleasure.

Thus he answers the question of why we do things that we know will harm us. We are blinded by a kind of optical illusion: the pleasure of the moment looms large, blinding us to the fact that it will have painful and perhaps even dire consequences in the long run. We break a promise to ourselves, giving in to the tempting extra drink or forsaking fidelity to the one we love, because the pleasure of the moment is so great. In the *Protagoras*, Socrates argues as if virtue is simply a matter of maximizing pleasure; we should measure pleasures against pains, and determine what will give us the greatest degree of enjoyment. He argues that we must learn not to be blinded by the optical illusion of immediate gratification; we must calculate more accurately what will in fact give us most pleasure—that which is genuinely good for the soul (in Greek, the *psyche*).

In *Phaedo* 69b, we see a corrective to the perspective of the *Protagoras*: there Plato argues that it is improper to simply exchange pleasures for pleasures and pains for pains; the only genuine medium of exchange is wisdom. It is wisdom alone that is the key to the virtues of moderation, courage, justice, and piety, and that will create for us a genuinely balanced, virtuous, and happy state of being.

In *Protagoras*, Socrates argues vigorously that knowledge is strong enough to overcome any desire; he rejects the notion that knowledge is a slave, dragged around by the senses. This passage is quoted by Aristotle, who deduces from it that Socrates rejects the concept of weakness of the will (*akrasia*), the notion that if we fail to do good, it is because we do not have the willpower to do the right thing. Socrates seems to believe that knowledge is all-powerful, that if we are aware of what is good, we will necessarily do it, and that knowledge is so strong that it cannot be overcome by even the greatest desire.

Such a view seems to be contradicted by our experience. Socrates appears to speak here as if the soul is purely rational, as if there is no battle between the part of us that knows we should not take that extra drink and the part of us that desires it. It is precisely such a struggle that we see in book 4 of the *Republic*, which leads Plato to divide the soul into three faculties—the rational, the spirited, and the desiring—and to describe an ongoing battle between the faculties.[75] Justice in the soul—the goal of the *Republic*—consists in achieving the proper balance, so that reason guides desire with the aid of the spirit or will.[76] In the *Phaedrus*, too, Plato describes the soul as divided; he paints the image of a chariot driven by one good, disciplined horse and one that is wild and unruly. Here, too, it seems that the driver of the chariot would be reason, as in the tripartite soul described in the *Republic*.

The image of a *psyche* that struggles to make peace between its conflicting impulses is familiar to us, makes intuitive sense, and harmonizes with our common experience. Can we defend Socrates' contrasting view, expressed in the *Protagoras*, of the sovereignty of knowledge? This seems a key to the so-called Socratic paradox—the notion that virtue is a form of knowledge, and that no one does evil against his or her will.[77] We can certainly find many counterexamples to this paradox, instances in which we seem to act against our better judgment. However, we can also find evidence to defend Socrates' claim. For example, it is true that an alcoholic can lose years of his or her life in a seemingly hopeless struggle, time and again losing the battle with addiction. Moreover there is a physical component to addictions that makes them even more intractable. And yet miraculously, there are courageous individuals who do manage to overcome even the most unyielding problem. How do we account for this fact? The phenomenon commonly known as "reaching rock bottom" supports Socrates' thesis. A person may lose partner, job, and family, everything that seems to matter most, and still not be able to overcome the desire to drink. And yet there may occur a moment—perhaps it is losing custody of children, or looking into the eyes of a beloved childhood friend and realizing we have totally lost his or her trust—that suddenly brings the realization that we must change. It is this kind of insight or realization, the transformative "aha" moment, which suggests that knowledge can, indeed, be powerful enough to overcome the senses. This is not theoretical knowledge but existential knowledge, knowledge of what is genuinely good for our soul. Suddenly the desires of the moment pale against the deeper understanding attained by our *psyche.*

Plato is convinced that everyone wants what is genuinely good—to live a healthy, fulfilling, and balanced life. The problem is that people are ignorant of what will make them genuinely happy. He articulates this view most clearly in the *Gorgias.* Here he draws a sharp distinction between pleasure and the good. To achieve pleasure is a kind of knack, a hit-or-miss proposition, like the talent for pastry baking. To achieve good, in contrast, requires wise forethought about what is genuinely best for our soul. To achieve the good is like the craft of medicine; it requires knowledge, skill, and planning.

Everything we do, Socrates argues in the *Gorgias*, is for the sake of some good; like Aristotle in the *Nicomachean Ethics*, he argues that the good is the aim of all our actions.[78] For example, when we take medicine, we seek the good that will be achieved, i.e., health. Every action we undertake aims at some good we think we will attain. Even pleasure, he argues, is for the sake of the good, not good for the sake of pleasure. He can argue thus because he believes that there is an overall objective good for the soul, and that there are some pleasures that are harmful, in that they will not help us achieve this desirable state of the soul.

Socrates goes on to argue that we are good when we have an excellence (*aretē*) present in us, and that the key to excellence is organization, craftsmanship, and order. Thus, again anticipating Aristotle, Plato argues that the key to human good is the organization of our soul.[79] The key virtue is self-control or self-mastery (*sōphrosynē*), and a self-controlled soul will do what is appropriate with respect to both divinity and to human beings.[80] The self-controlled soul thus possesses the five cardinal virtues: he or she will be just, temperate, courageous, pious, and wise. Such a person is completely good, does well and admirably whatever he or she does, and is blessed and happy, while the undisciplined person does badly and is miserable.[81] We who cannot make priorities for ourselves, who can't discipline ourselves to go to sleep on time so that we will have enough energies for our activities the next day, cannot create the kind of happy, productive lives we seek, nor be there for friends in our lives. Socrates thus goes on to offer a passionate encomium in praise of the disciplined life and an argument against lack of discipline. The undisciplined person "cannot be a partner, and where there is no partnership there is no friendship." He goes on:

> Yes, Callicles, wise men claim that partnership and friendship, orderliness, self-control, and justice hold together heaven and earth, and gods and men, and that is why they call this universe a *world order* [*kosmos*], my friend, and not an undisciplined world-disorder.[82]

We are thus brought back to themes of the *Timaeus*. God created order from chaos because he discerned that order was in every way better. As in the *Republic*, Plato articulates the view that organization or justice in the soul is the harmonious balance of various forces, each one singing its own part in the choir.[83] Justice in the individual soul is a microcosm of justice in the city (*polis*), in which each citizen does his or her part without encroaching on the tasks of others.[84] Finding the correct balance among our own conflicting drives enables us to enter into genuine partnership and friendship with others. If we are ruled by our desires of the moment, we cannot truly be open to others; if we put the selfish drives of our souls first, we cannot achieve the more expansive potential for giving to others of which we are capable.[85] When our own souls are orderly and balanced, we are integral parts of a balanced world-order, the *cosmos* created by God from *chaos*, or disorder.

Plato articulates this view of human fulfillment in the closing speech of the *Timaeus* itself. We must devote ourselves to the tendance (*therapeia*) of the rational, divine soul within us, making it well-ordered (*eu kekosmēmenon*).[86] In this passage, Plato plays on the etymology for the Greek word for happiness: well-being (*eudaimonia*) is achieved by keeping in good order the divine spirit (*daimon*) within.[87] Earlier, Timaeus asserted that the rhythm of the human soul was thrown out of kilter at birth; the goal of human life is to realign the revolutions of our souls with those of the cosmos as a whole. By aligning our souls with the harmonious and proportional motions of the spheres, we attune the divine faculty of understanding to the cosmos it seeks to understand.[88] The *kosmos* is a beautifully proportioned, mathematically ordered organism, and when we have attuned ourselves to it, like an instrument in a choir, we achieve human virtue and well-being (*eudaimonia*), the most excellent life offered to humankind by the gods.[89]

Socrates argues in the *Meno* that the key to achieving human virtue is knowledge. However, it seems clear that Socrates describes virtue as a form of knowledge or wisdom not because he believes—as Aristotle wrongly supposed—that theoretical deliberation alone makes one wise. Rather, Socrates emphasizes that wisdom is what can discern what is genuinely good for our soul. In the *Apology, Crito*, and *Republic*, Socrates argues that what is crucial in any life decision is whether the action we are undertaking is good or bad, whether it is just or unjust, and whether it will make us a good or a bad person. The goal of each person's life is to live well, to create the best possible state of our soul, and to be true to our goals in every action we undertake:

> We should attach the highest value not to living, but to living well . . . and [we still hold] that living well and honorably and justly are the same thing.[90]

> You are wrong, sir, if you think that a man who is any good at all should take into account the risk of life or death; he should look to this only in his actions, whether the things he does are right or wrong, and the acts of a good or bad man.[91]

> For I go around doing nothing but persuading both young and old among you not to care for your body or your wealth in preference to or even to so great an extent as for your soul, that it should be as excellent as possible, as I say to you: "Virtue [*aretē*] does not come from wealth, but wealth comes from virtue [*aretē*], and so too all the other goods for human beings, both individual and collective."[92]

> The just person "puts himself in order," is his own friend, and harmonizes the three parts of himself like three limiting notes in a musical scale—high, low, and middle. . . . Only then does he act . . . he believes that the action is just and fine that preserves this inner harmony and helps achieve it.[93]

> And from all these things he will be able, by considering the nature of the soul, to reason out which life is better and which worse and to choose accordingly, calling a life worse if it leads the soul to become more unjust, better if it leads the soul to become more just, and letting everything else go. We have seen that this is the best way to choose, whether in life or in death.[94]

Let us summarize the evidence we have gathered thus far. The creation myths of the Hebrew Bible and Plato describe the ordering of the cosmos from a pre-creation state of chaos; both the God of the Bible and Plato's God associate order with goodness. The Genesis account suggests that human beings find evidence of order in the regularities of nature: day and night, darkness and light, the cycles of the seasons.

As the Biblical tradition illustrates, humans mark these cycles of nature through the comforting rhythm of ritual; rituals order the human experience of time. Ritual, or rite, gives us a sense of the rightness and order of the world. The sphere of ritual provides an expressive outlet for the human desire for goodness; it represents one human effort to balance ourselves—to create a just and harmonious order in both our inner and outer worlds. Plato is likewise interested in finding ways to balance our desires, pleasures, impulses, and will to create a moral and fulfilling life.

We have seen that Socrates' discussion of virtue and happiness has brought us back to the concept of goodness as order. To order the universe is God's motive for creation; by ordering our own soul, we achieve both virtue and happiness.

## A MODERN PLATONIST: IRIS MURDOCH AND THE SOVEREIGNTY OF GOOD

Is Plato's moral philosophy of merely antiquarian interest? Can we as modern people continue to draw moral inspiration from Plato's notion of the good? We have already mentioned modern scientific Platonists such as Alfred North Whitehead and Paul Davies, who uphold Plato's concept of eternal ideas, whether as objects of mathematics or as qualities needed to make sense of our varied universe. Iris Murdoch takes inspiration from Plato not as a mathematician or scientist, but as a moral philosopher. *Metaphysics as a Guide to Morals*, published in 1994 to critical acclaim,[95] is an extended meditation on moral philosophy. We will focus here on the more systematic treatment of these topics found in her earlier essays "On 'God' and 'Good'" and "The Sovereignty of Good Over Other Concepts," where she offers thoughtful critiques of trends in moral philosophy, both analytic and existentialist.

For the purpose of her study, Murdoch assumes that the traditional God does not exist, or at least is not available as an inspiration to the modern moral agent. She nevertheless believes we can rescue key features of the concept of a traditional God, and that something very much like Plato's Idea of the Good can inspire our moral choices. God, she argues, "was (or is) a *single perfect transcendent non-representable and necessarily real object of attention*." Her approach to ethics is to retain all aspects of this conception without assuming a traditional personal God.

To explain what she means by an object of attention or contemplation, Murdoch offers a universal, non-theistic illustration. When we are in love, we orient our entire being to the object of our affection. At times, we realize this love is not working and that we must fall out of love. How do we achieve this? We must consciously focus our attention in new directions.[96] "Human beings are naturally 'attached,'" writes Murdoch, "and when an attachment seems painful or bad it is most readily displaced by another attachment, which an attempt at attention can encourage." This shows that something like prayer can be directed to an impersonal ideal like Plato's Form of the Good. Good, like God, can be the focus of meditation, attachment, and love; the disciplines of prayer and meditation can be reimagined in non-theistic ways. Most of us have had the experience of falling in love with an idea, a pursuit, or a goal as surely as we have fallen in love with a person. A person can shift his or her entire sense of identity based on love for a form of dance, dress, and music; we seek inspiration from a charismatic entertainment figure or political leader, from a political or musical ideal. Just so, the idea of Goodness can genuinely inspire our moral striving. And this, she suggests, is the purpose of traditional meditation and prayer: "God, attended to, is a powerful source of (often good) energy"; likewise virtuous people, great art, and the idea of goodness itself can inspire us to moral greatness.[97] What is it that inspires civil rights leaders or concentration camp survivors to ennobling acts of self-sacrifice? Commitment to a moral ideal. And like modern Humanists, Murdoch reinvents traditional forms of religious life to suit a path of moral striving free of theistic imagery.

Murdoch thus argues that just as God was the focus of traditional religion, the Good can be an object of concentrated attention and an inspiration for moral growth. But why should the Good be single, and why must there exist one unifying source of value? Murdoch acknowledges that it may be "consoling" to believe that there is one grand meaning of life, that all things make sense in light of one supreme value. But she argues time and again that we should guard carefully against ideas that are simply consoling. Like the ancient Buddha and the modern thinker Jiddu Krishnamurti—with whom Murdoch conducted a series of engaging recorded interviews[98]—Murdoch is a ruthless seeker-after-truth; her aim is to see things as they are, not as we would like them to be, to describe honestly what is, however challenging or unlovely.

Nevertheless, Murdoch argues that we can indeed discern a unifying moral center. It is not just that it is natural for the human mind to seek unity, and that the notion of one unifying virtue happens to be consoling. When we reflect on the nature of goodness, we discover that there is a natural relationship between the moral virtues. The courage of a person in a concentration camp is "steadfast, calm, temperate, intelligent, loving";[99] likewise, to understand justice, we need to understand its relationship to courage, self-mastery, and wisdom. This is precisely what Plato posits in the *Protagoras*, *Meno*, and *Republic*: the individual virtues are unified in virtue or excellence (*arête*) as a whole, and excellence is unified in an all-embracing idea of the Good. Like Plato, Murdoch argues for a kind of moral monism.

The Good is thus a unitary principle not only in that it is single, but also in that it unifies many diverse aspects of morality. The Good can inspire courage, compassion, originality in scholarship, and fearlessness in dramatic art. It is important to reflect on the varied virtues that the Good brings together; this diversity points to its power and dynamism. Murdoch argues for the Good as an overarching principle that can inspire our passion for growth in many spheres—political, interpersonal, aesthetic—giving unity and integrity to our moral lives.[100]

Thus far she has established the Good as a *single object of attention*. How does she adopt the notion of transcendence, without the concept of a personal God? Murdoch argues against two contemporary depictions of transcendence. One strand of moral philosophy relegates good to a "transcendent" realm precisely because it is thought that goodness cannot be discovered empirically. Values cannot be found in the world of facts, it is argued, and therefore they "transcend" the world of fact. On the other hand, Marxists suggest that we are alienated from our own values, which are depicted as transcendent. Contemporary sociologist Peter Berger analyzes this phenomenon in less value-laden terms; we project our values outward, where they then confront us as if they had a transcendent life of their own.[101]

Murdoch goes against these strands of modern philosophy by using the language of transcendence to argue for moral realism—the notion that there are genuine moral qualities to reality, and that moral statements are not merely subjective and relative. Murdoch insists that there is something objective and transcendent about the moral deed and moral values. Genuine morality, like great art, is not a private, romantic fantasy; it is not the creation of the individual agent. The genuine artist sees reality as it is; what we admire in Shakespeare is not his private vision but the truth he shows us about the human condition. Moral realism is thus parallel to great art. To carry out a genuine act of kindness we must respond to the other person's true needs, not our projection of what the person needs. Genuine morality requires that we let go of our desire for moral self-aggrandizement in order to respond to the persons with whom we are in relationship and the true needs of the present moment.

Murdoch therefore seeks to rescue Plato's Form of the Good from a romantic vision, and argues that this moral realism leads directly to the notion of transcendence. What Murdoch means by transcendence is a dimension that is permanent and untouched by time; she thus offers a defense of the Platonic notion of an eternal Form or Idea. For example, when we reflect upon a moral action, we discern an element that is lasting, even after the action itself has passed. It is true that moral transcendence is more difficult to discern than the transcendence of beauty, because beauty itself is at least partially perceived by the senses. We are dazzled by the brilliant color of a majestic flower; the flower withers and fades, but something of its beauty lives on. In contrast, when we witness a selfless act of compassion, it is more difficult to put our finger on the quality of goodness that moves us. And yet there is clearly transcendent power to a truly good act.

While that quality of transcendence is not perceivable by the senses, as it partially is in the case of beauty, it nevertheless imparts a kind of certainty that Murdoch suggests cannot be reduced to psychological terms alone. One dimension of transcendence lies in the certainty and power of an absolute standard of goodness, which she insists cannot be reduced to the mind consoling itself. Despite all the suffering and evil we see in the world—or perhaps because of it—we are certain that there is a timeless standard of goodness, an ideal by which we judge the real.[102]

The other dimension of transcendence is the notion of perfection—an absolute standard that motivates us in a way no partial standard can. "One cannot feel unmixed love for a mediocre moral standard," Murdoch writes, "any more than one can for the work of a mediocre artist."[103] She notes the psychological danger of comparing ourselves to an unattainable ideal, but turns the caution on its head. Rather than despairing that we cannot meet our ideal, we can note that the ideal represents a part of us we can love and strengthen. Perfection functions as a moral asymptote, an ideal to which we can aspire, while at the same time recognizing that no finite human being can achieve perfection. An artist tries to capture his or her vision on canvas or in words, but must accept that the complete vision cannot be represented in a finite medium. Nevertheless, the artist is not free to desist; the vision calls to be realized.[104] Likewise, an absolute moral standard can spur us to growth as we strive to realize our moral ideal. If a human being were "perfect," how could we grow? The ideal of a person who can truly respond to what the moment demands can inspire growth toward health, balance, and integration. Plato's Idea of the Good functions for Murdoch like an Aristotelian final cause, a purpose that draws us to realize it; the Good inspires our love, awakening our passion to realize the ideal, however imperfectly.

The idea of perfection thus holds a kind of authority; we are responsible to this vision. When we act responsibly as an artist or writer, we cannot let ourselves convey less than the truth; the reality of the situation, the truth of the data before us holds an authority. The scholar, too, feels a responsibility to the truth he or she strives to convey and transmit. Truth and perfection hold an authority for the agent.[105]

Murdoch thus translates the religious concept of transcendence into the moral realm. Moral ideals possess permanence, certainty, perfection, and absolute authority. Murdoch argues further that these dimensions of transcendence lead to the concept of *necessity*; she thus seeks to retrieve in the moral realm the well-known ontological proof for the existence of God. The ontological proof, made famous by the medieval monk Anselm, argues that God is a concept of absolute perfection, the concept of a being than which there is no higher. Existence is a perfection; therefore this being necessarily exists. The proof argues from an idea of God that includes existence to the notion that God must necessarily exist. Another way to state this is that God is a being in whom essence and existence are one—God's essence includes existence. A third way to look at necessary existence is that Being simply is and always will be; there is no possibility that it will fall out of existence, as its existence depends on nothing.[106]

Murdoch points out that the ontological proof is really not a philosophical proof but an assertion of faith: one has the certain conviction that behind this changing, variegated world there stands a Being whose existence is certain. The proof is thus certain only for those already convinced; Anselm himself utters it as a prayer, which arises in his meditation on the psalms: "The fool says in his heart there is no God." Murdoch expresses this conviction as psychological fact: "My conception of God contains the certainty of its own reality. God is an object of love which uniquely excludes doubt and relativism." Or even "The desire for God is certain to receive a response"; and likewise, "We must receive a return when good is sincerely desired." We might add the statement of Confucius: "I desire goodness and lo! Goodness is there."[107] Her argument is that the idea of good possesses the same degree of certainty as the idea of God.[108]

What follows is an inspired defense of Plato's moral realism. The Form of the Good is compared to the sun because it genuinely sheds light on our world. The Good allows us to see things as they are. To look through the light of the Good is not to look at the world through rose-colored glasses; it is to look through a clear lens. We do not deny the evil, painful dimensions of reality; we see them as they are, for a good person must know things about the external world in order to respond appropriately. The Good sheds light on the extent to which things in this world do not live up to ideals; it shows where there is work to be done.

In this context, Murdoch argues that creating art can itself be a spiritual exercise, an exercise of the will, "the checking of selfishness in the interest of seeing the real."[109] Even though individual artists put their own creative stamp on their art, they reveal to us something not just about their inner world but about our common objective world, which they reveal "with a clarity which startles and delights us simply because we are not used to looking at the real world at all."[110] Murdoch stresses the impersonal, objective, and detached quality of art. Detachment means setting aside the selfish pursuit of our own needs; we refrain from seeing an object from the perspective of how we can *use* it, so that we can see it as it is in itself. Beauty, she writes, attracts such attention: "unsentimental, detached, unselfish, objective attention."[111] This same exactness, she argues, is required in moral life. We need a form of the Good because we do not see situations objectively; we are too accustomed to bringing our self into a situation in which the self has no place. And that is why Murdoch agrees with Plato that the realism required for goodness is "a kind of intellectual ability to perceive what is true, which is automatically at the same time a suppression of self,"[112] or at least the narrowness of the self's partial vision.

Murdoch thus offers an original explanation of the necessary character of the Good: Good possesses the kind of necessity involved in seeing the reality of what is. But how does seeing clearly inspire us to act morally? When we see that people are different from us, that they have unique, objective needs, it is harder to treat a person as a thing. Art helps us see people as having claims as demanding as our own; the form of the good invites the same realism.[113] Murdoch presents the Good as a "transcendent magnetic center"; or, in the words of David Tracy, as a magnet "forcibly drawing one to itself despite oneself, attracting us by its beauty, its objectivity, and its goodness."[114]

What then are the non-theistic substitutes for prayer that might attune us to the magnetic force of goodness? First for Murdoch stand the love and detachment of great art and the contemplation of beauty in nature, which have the ability to lift us out of our self-absorption. She notes that Plato, too, held up the arts and sciences (the *technē*) as possessing great power to discipline and refine the soul. Plato's favorite example is mathematics, the training par excellence that philosophers receive in the *Republic*. For the non-mathematically inclined, Murdoch offers the discipline of learning a language. Here we are confronted with an authoritative structure that commands our respect. Attention is rewarded by knowledge of reality. Love of the language takes us away from our self-absorption toward something objective outside of ourselves that makes real demands upon us. Learning a language requires the same honesty and humility as all scholarship, in which we must admit what we do not know and give up our treasured theories in pursuit of truth as it reveals itself.[115]

Moral dilemmas operate in the same way. We must give up the limited lens of our individual perspective to objectively contemplate the reality of the situation. Thus Plato uses the image of the sun, which sheds light on all things but which itself can hardly be perceived. "It gives light and energy and enables us to know the truth. In its light we see the things of this world in their true relationships. But looking at the sun itself is very difficult and unlike looking at those things it illuminates."[116] And while in Plato's well-known allegory of the cave the ascent toward the sun seems to leave the world of particularity for unity, the descent and return to the cave must embrace ever-increasing detail and particularity, such as goes into our moral decision-making. This involves a fine art of intuiting unity among the diversity of details; for example, a mother has to consider every member of her family in making a decision that affects the family as a whole.[117]

Thus she suggests that honesty is much the same virtue in the parent, the mathematician, the chemist, the historian, and the artist. And it is much the same virtue when one is trying to perceive the real state of one's relationship with another person. If we aim to be both serious scholars and also morally good persons, we must evaluate the place of art or scholarship in our life as a whole. The understanding required to make a decision about the place of scholarship or art in one's life is greater than the understanding of art or science or even human relationships in general.[118] And while excellence in one area is no guarantee of excellence in another, "the concept Good stretches through the whole of it and gives it the only kind of unachieved shadowy unity which it can possess."[119] Thus whereas Aristotle was careful to separate theoretical from practical virtue, Plato proposes that the concept of Good unifies them, and Murdoch follows this unifying vision.

In her inspired modern interpretation of Plato's allegory of the cave, she offers a cautionary warning. It is difficult to look at the sun. The lines of our search, she suggests, converge at a magnetic center. "There are also false suns, easier to gaze on and far more comforting than the true one . . . It is easier to look at the converging edges than at the center itself."[120] This, for Murdoch, is the meaning of the fire in the allegory. When the people chained turn around, they can see the fire, which they have to pass in order to get out of the cave and behold the genuine source of light, the sun. The fire, she speculates, represents the self, a great source of energy and warmth. "Before they were motivated by blind selfish instinct; now they can see this clearly. They see the flames that threw the shadows, and they see the puppets that they used to take for real. They don't dream that there is anything else to see."[121] The prisoners have achieved the kind of self-awareness that we today find so absorbing.[122]

This, she argues, may be why Kant went to such lengths to draw attention away from the empirical self, why he so wanted people to focus upon duty rather than happiness. The psyche and its power to cast shadows is powerful and fascinating; recognition of its power may be a step toward escape from the cave, but it is not an end in itself. It is too easy to mistake the fire of our selves for the sun, to get caught up in endless self-scrutiny rather than goodness. She argues too that not everyone who escapes from the cave needs to spend much time by the fire of self; perhaps the "virtuous peasant" escapes the cave without even noticing the fire. In valorizing the virtuous peasant, Murdoch suggests that intellectuals are so involved in discovering how bad we are and seeking virtue that we fall in love with the quest itself rather than what is really demanded to be virtuous—not to endlessly scrutinize how bad we are, but to forget ourselves in the moment, to lose ourselves in the reality of what the moral situation demands of us.

Not only are we as individuals mesmerized by the hypnotic pull of the self; religions and ideologies too are prone to substitute the self for the true object of reverence. But that does not mean we should abandon the quest to attune ourselves to an absolute source of guidance:

> There is a place both within and outside of religion for a sort of contemplation of the Good not just by dedicated experts but by ordinary people: not just the planning of particular good actions but an attempt to look away from self towards a distant transcendent perfection, a source of uncontaminated energy, a source of new and quite undreamt of virtue. This attempt is a turning away from the particular, and may be the thing that helps most when difficulties seems insoluble, and especially when feelings of guilt keep attracting the gaze back towards the self. To look at the good, the objective good of the situation, and to take oneself out

> of it. This is the true mysticism which is morality, a kind of undogmatic prayer which is real and important, though perhaps also difficult and easily corrupted.[123]

For Murdoch, morality is the true mystical attunement; to seek objective, unbiased guidance is the highest form of prayer. Genuine prayer is a gaze at the transcendent goodness, a source of illumination that can shed objective light on the situation in all its complexity. Should we put our elderly parent or aunt into assisted living? Everyone wants to be at home, but can we properly care for her, given the demands of our nuclear family? These decisions in the real world are not as simple and beautiful as mathematical equations; it is only by looking at the facts in the light of the Good that we can have any hope of seeing the complexity of the situation and the good of all concerned. That is why religious traditions encourage us to pray not just for what we personally seek, but for what we as individuals cannot easily discern—what is genuinely good for all. Whether or not there is a personal God, to surrender oneself to the light of silent contemplation can bring clarity in our complex, troubled world.

Murdoch argues at length that good is indefinable; the closest one might come to a definition is love. However, she argues that good and love should not be identified:

> Good is the magnetic center toward which love naturally moves.[124] False love moves to false good. When true good is loved, even impurely or by accident, the quality of the love is automatically refined, and when the soul is turned towards the Good the highest part of the soul is enlivened. Love is the tension between the imperfect soul and the magnetic perfection which is conceived of as lying beyond it.[125]

We realize we are imperfect; while we can strive for the perfection we sense, we can never fully achieve it. Perhaps Plato's metaphor of the imperfect imitation striving to achieve an ideal is an apt description of our state in this world.[126] Love is the magnetic force of attraction toward the good. And when we imperfect beings strive to love what is imperfect, "our love goes to its object via the Good to be purified and made unselfish and just," as the mother who loves her special needs child or her aunt with Alzheimer's. While love can be selfish and grasping, when it is refined "it is the energy and passion of the soul in its search for the Good, the force that joins us to Good and joins us to the world through Good. Its existence is the unmistakable sign that we are spiritual creatures, attracted by excellence and made for the Good. It is a reflection of the warmth and light of the sun."[127]

In other words, love is what both attracts us to goodness and shows our affinity to the good. Any love and kindheartedness we express is a reflection of the Good itself. Without the hypothesis of a creator God in whose likeness all beings exist, Murdoch is nevertheless not without an Absolute. Like Plato, Murdoch identifies Goodness as the transcendent object of attention whose radiance awakens love and transforms the moral self.

Charles Taylor, a modern upholder of the Aristotelian tradition, acknowledges his great debt to Murdoch, the great modern Platonist. As we have noted, Taylor points to the ways we are still motivated by moral frameworks for understanding the world, even if we cannot explain precisely the view of reality that underlies them. Images and myths continue to have moral power, even if we have abandoned their philosophical and religious roots. And while we may not be ready to substitute a new ontology for the one underlying the ancient myths, "the old images nevertheless have the power to inspire us. Perhaps they even point toward a moral source, something the contemplation, respect, or love of which enables us to get closer to what is good." He points to Murdoch's theory of the "sovereignty of 'good'" as an illustration:

> No one today accepts Plato's metaphysical theory of the Ideas as the crucial explanation of the shape of the cosmos. Nevertheless, the image of the Good as the sun, in the light of which we can see things clearly and with a kind of dispassionate love, helps define the direction of attention and desire through which alone, she believes, we can become good.[128]

The force of Murdoch's argument is that Good is more absolute than God. In *Metaphysics as a Guide to Morals*, she writes: "Nietzsche's 'God is dead' seems to announce the end of moral as well as religious absolutes. But we continue to recognize moral absolutes just as we continue to use ordinary language. . . . We can lose God, but not Good."[129]

# 3

# Change and the Good

## CHINESE PERSPECTIVES

UP TO this point, we have discussed the tradition of Plato and that of the Hebrew Bible and its rabbinic interpreters. We have seen that the quest for God and the good expresses a yearning to find order, comfort, and safety in our world, as well as the sense that ordering and balancing our conflicting impulses is the key to a fulfilling life.

When we turn to Chinese culture, we find a tradition in which it is not clear whether we can actually speak of a creation or even a shaping, as in Plato and the Bible. We find here instead a web that has no weaver, creation without a creator. Moreover, Chinese culture is somewhat unique in that it not only recognizes but fully accepts change as fundamental to reality. Hindu and Greek thought posit that only that which is eternal is fully real. For Plato, the realm of Being is more real than the realm of Becoming. The realm of Becoming is the realm of appearance; the Real is that which is eternal. For Aristotle, both the heavens and God are what they are eternally. For Hindu thought, as we will see, *brahman* is the Real—eternal being, knowledge and joy. Our world of changing appearance is less than fully Real; it is not as real as the eternal realm of the divine.

For Chinese thought, in contrast, the changing world of nature is conceived of as the essence of reality. What is eternal is the Tao, the Way, but that Way expresses itself through the interplay between the ever-changing elements of *yin* and *yang*.[1] These complementary forces of nature—conceived of as a feminine and a masculine principle—are expressed through the cycles of nature: darkness and light, summer, fall, winter, and spring. For the Chinese philosophical tradition, the only thing that is eternal is change itself. There is no escape from the cycle of change. Even death is merely the transformation of energy: the body returns to the earth, decomposes, feeds the earth, and changes form.

This notion of nature could be morally problematic, as it suggests that the polarities in nature are morally neutral. For it is not simply the case that all things have their opposites, but that opposites are necessary and complementary. Moreover, opposites merge and interchange with one another.[2] Night becomes day, hot becomes cold. Are good and evil likewise complementary forces that arise, merge, and interchange qualities? Perhaps good and evil each have a complementary place in the universe, and all morality is relative or irrelevant. To the contrary, in the view of modern scholar of Chinese philosophy JeeLoo Liu, Chinese thought conceives of the universe as deeply moral. Morality is embedded in the fabric of the universe, and human morality is patterned on nature, as we shall see below.

## THE *I CHING*

According to the *Book of Changes* (*I Ching*), a foundational text of classical Chinese thought, natural reality embodies moral virtues. Heaven exemplifies creativity and steadfastness. The sun models warmth, kindness, and impartiality. Wind shows gentle penetrating power; fire radiance and clarity; and water humility and continuity. Heaven and the sun are said to have moral attributes in themselves; other natural phenomena are seen as models for human behavior, rather than themselves possessing the attributes.[3]

Human beings are an integral part of the universe—in particular, the triad of Heaven, Earth, and humanity. Humans have a duty to carry on the moral work of Heaven and Earth.[4] Thus although Heaven is not necessarily a personal God, it does embody a kind of morality, albeit in an impersonal form.[5] It is the duty of humans to pattern our own morality on the morality of Heaven and Earth. These absolute values are deeply ingrained in nature; they are not good simply in relation to human situations or perspectives. Human good models itself on natural good. We read in the *Appendices* to the *I Ching*: "Heaven creates divine things; the holy sage takes them as models. Heaven and Earth change and transform; the holy sage imitates them."[6]

The *Appendices* to the *I Ching* suggest that good is what follows from and continues *Tao*, the way:

> The reciprocal process of yin and yang is called the Way. That which allows the Way to continue to operate is human goodness, and that which allows it to bring things to completion is human nature. The humane see it and call it humaneness (*ren*) and the wise see it and call it wisdom. It functions for the common folk on a daily basis, yet they are unaware of it. This is why the Way of the noble person is a rare thing![7]

Human good is an extension of the rhythms of Heaven and Earth; these rhythms of nature simply *are* and *are good*. Insofar as we harmonize with the natural balance and assist it, we are in tune with the natural good and can carry on its task. Liu writes:

> Since *Yijing* defines the "Good," on the basis of *Dao*, which governs the whole universe, this is *Good* in the absolute sense. To aid others in their fulfillment of life's potentials is not relative to individual or cultural perspectives; it is simply *good* in and of itself. This . . . became the theoretical foundation for Confucian ethics.[8]

From the perspective of Western moral philosophy, thinkers since David Hume in the eighteenth century have been suspicious of deriving ideas of what *ought to be* from what is, of deriving human ideals of moral goodness from nature. The *I Ching* does not see this problem. For this text and some branches of Confucian ethics, the way of nature is the way things ought to be, and human beings should pattern their actions on the workings of nature. These thinkers see the natural world as one that achieves a balance of conflicting forces and manifests harmonious change.[9]

Another moral value patterned on nature is the principle of reversal. Once a pattern reaches an extreme, it gives rise to its opposite; nature balances *yin* and *yang* in a state of dynamic equilibrium. We work too hard and push ourselves to an extreme degree; our bodies tell us that we need rest. Thus the mean is not a simple midpoint, but rather a state of homeostasis or balance between extremes. Things change and the harmony is disturbed; equilibrium is the virtue of restoring balance, of dynamically responding to change. We may achieve the mean before and after any disequilibrium. It is the natural state of things; all disturbances return to this intrinsic state of balance. The Way of the world is not static; rather, forces continually change, but balance is restored. Liu compares this process to a cosmic pendulum that maintains a consistent flow; the consistent movement is harmony or equilibrium. A development toward one end does not necessarily violate the principle of the mean, as long as the development eventually returns to the mean, the state of balance.[10]

The thesis that human nature originally possesses equilibrium and harmony is elaborated in the opening of one of the Confucian classics, the *Doctrine of the Mean*:

> What Heaven imparts to humanity is called human nature. To follow our nature is called the Way (*Tao*). Cultivating the Way is called education. The Way cannot be separated from us even for a moment. What can be separated from us is not the Way. . . . Before the feelings of pleasure, anger, sorrow, and joy are aroused, it is called equilibrium (*chung*, centrality, mean). When these feelings are aroused and each and all attain due measure and degree, it is called harmony. Equilibrium is the great foundation of the world, and harmony its universal path. When equilibrium and harmony are realized to the highest degree, heaven and earth will attain their proper order and all things will flourish.[11]

What we find articulated in the philosophy of the *I Ching* and the *Doctrine of the Mean* is the view that human nature is naturally good, as it comes from Heaven. To follow our nature is to "continue" *Tao*; thus, for human beings to be good entails following our nature. Within our inborn nature we find emotions such as pleasure, anger, sorrow, and joy. Before these emotions are aroused, we are in a state of equilibrium; once our emotions are aroused, we need to moderate them so that they are in a state of harmony. When humans maintain equilibrium and harmony within ourselves and extend these to the world of Nature, the task of Heaven and Earth is completed.[12]

## THE *TAO TE CHING*

With this background in Chinese cosmology, we can turn to the *Tao Te Ching* (*Classic of the Way and Its Power*, said to have been written by Lao Tzu), another foundational text within Chinese thought.[13] As we have noted, here it is not clear whether we can actually speak of a creation or even a shaping, as in Plato and the Bible:[14]

Something unformed and complete
Before heaven and earth were born
Solitary and silent
Stands alone and unchanging[15]
Pervading all things without limit
It is like the mother of all under heaven
But I don't know its name
Better call it *Tao*
Better call it great. (*Tao Te Ching*, CHAPTER 25)[16]

Here we have an ontological principle—a principle or pattern of all that is—that is not itself a personal being. It has no will, it has no personality, and yet in some sense it is the source of all. It is like the mother of all things. It is called the Way; it has no name. A name fixes and limits a thing; that which pervades all things cannot be limited in any way. It can have no fixed identity.

*Tao* called *Tao* is not *Tao*
Names can name no lasting name
Nameless: the origin of heaven and earth
Naming: the mother of ten thousand things
Empty of desire; perceive mystery
Filled with desire, perceive manifestation
These have the same source, but different names
Call them both deep
Deep and again deep
The gateway to all mystery. (CHAPTER 1)

At the heart of the universe is an eternal mystery, the source of all. It is not a personal being, but a Way. It has no personality or will, but if spoken of at all, it is described metaphorically as feminine, the mother of all things. It is their source and their progenitor. However, it is not clear whether we can speak of creation in the *Tao Te Ching*:

*Tao* engenders One
One engenders Two
Two engenders Three
Three engenders the ten thousand things. (CHAPTER 42)

Reversal is *Tao*'s movement
Yielding is *Tao*'s practice
All things originate from being
Being originates from non-being. (CHAPTER 40)

These passages can be interpreted in diverse ways. One could argue that a real creation takes place; all proceeds from the *Tao*.[17] However, these lines may simply portray the ongoing process of coming-to-be, or they may teach us about the relationship of all things to the *Tao*, which is logically prior to them. One "engenders" two in the sense that the two, three, and ten thousand things all depend on the One for their being or vitality.[18] Some classical commentators have interpreted the passage to suggest that the One is what is called in Chinese thought the Great Ultimate, from which flows the *yin-yang* principle of the Two, the Three that embraces *yin* and *yang*, and then the ten thousand things, meaning all the beings in existence.[19]

However, this may also simply represent the scheme of dependence of the world: the many depend ultimately on the One. Several modern commentators focus on this scheme not as a creation myth, but as an analysis of the way all things come into being in our own world of experience. The *Tao Te Ching* is interested in the emergence of the formed from the unformed, and especially the magical interface between non-being and being—in the words of Benjamin Schwartz, "that mysterious region where the world of non-being comes to relate to the world of the determinate, the individuated, and the related, or perhaps literally in Chinese, to the world of the 'there is' (*yu*)."[20]

Thus the *Tao Te Ching* conceives of the *Tao* as an uncarved block, the "undivided"; when you cut it up, you get names and divisions.[21] Whenever we focus our attention on one aspect of the whole, we value it as foreground, and the background recedes. The *Tao Te Ching* bids us to value the background that we have ignored, the unhewn block from which all definite, determinate things emerge. In the words of Brook Ziporyn, we should "attend to the beginning, the transitional border between not-yet-intelligible and intelligible, and privilege the former."[22] This entails being alert to the moment when, out of pure potentiality, definite forms emerge. If we overvalue these realized entities, we will lose touch with the vast spaciousness of pure potentiality that is their source.

Ideas, for example, begin inchoate, unformed. We come up with a brilliant theory, which we express in a beautiful sentence. If we fix upon this sentence and become attached to it, we are unable to let it go when we realize that in fact it does not fit naturally with the context or situation. We must keep one foot firmly planted in potentiality, possibility; if we become too attached to any actuality that has emerged, we are not aware when it is no longer appropriate to the situation. The *Tao Te Ching* thus encourages us to value what has previously been devalued: non-being, openness, the feminine, humility, patience. We can act with assertiveness and creativity, but we must always be attentive to the context in which we act. Following the *Tao*, we aim to stay attuned to the signals of those around us; this enables us to succeed with a quiet graciousness and dignity. We will ultimately engender greater value in the world if we respond with openness to the evolving situation than if we become attached to a fixed purpose.[23]

## THE WAY OF NATURE

The *Tao Te Ching* describes the *Tao* as the Way of nature, the eternal principle that embraces and undergirds all. The *Tao* is a loving, compassionate presence that embraces all beings as a mother does her children. Nothing is left out, nothing is despised in creation. Nature is perceived as beneficent; there is no aversion to the things of this world:

> Bears them without owning them
> Helps them without coddling them
> Rears them without ruling them
> This is called original *Te*. (CHAPTER 51)[24]

*Te* is the potency, force, or efficacy carried by those who are attuned to the *Tao*. Since *Te* is that which enables individuals to express the *Tao*, the *Te* is sometimes regarded as the individualizing force within the *Tao*; it is that which gives individuals their particular efficacy as singular beings. Thus we see the correct relationship of one who wants to live in accordance with the *Tao*:

> *Tao* bears them
> *Te* nurses them
> Events form them

Energy completes them
Therefore the ten thousand beings
Honor *Tao* and respect *Te*
*Tao* is honored
*Te* is respected
Because they do not give orders
But endure in their own nature
Therefore,
*Tao* bears them and *Te* nurses them
Rears them
Raises them
Shelters them
Nurtures them
Supports them
Protects them (CHAPTER 51)

Although this is not a personal being, the images that emerge here are nurturing and protective. The universe is benevolent; when we are in touch with the goodness at the heart of creation, we find ourselves sheltered and protected. When beings honor their source, they are supported by the *Tao*; living in accordance with the Way creates a sheltering context within which to flourish. Moreover, by honoring the principle from which we have emerged, beings find our proper place within nature.

All beings are also supported by the *Te*, the expressive, potent energy of the *Tao*.[25] *Tao* expresses itself as *Te* through individuals:

*Tao* is honored
*Te* is respected
Because they do not give orders
But endure in their own nature (CHAPTER 51)[26]

By enduring in one's own nature, one allows the *Tao* to express itself through one as *Te*. To bring out the full potential of one's own nature is to honor the creative principle of the universe:

Reversal is *Tao*'s movement
Yielding is *Tao*'s practice

All things originate from being
Being originates from non-being. (CHAPTER 40)

The creative order of nature is to reverse and to yield. Day gives way to night, winter gives way to summer. To yield is to be powerful, to give way makes one strong to overcome, like water that washes away the rock. As A. C. Graham emphasizes, this is a reversal of the ordinary scale of values: the *Tao Te Ching* values the weak over the strong, the feminine over the masculine, what is not over what is.[27]

In Western ontology, we think of Being as supreme. Taoist ontology sees being as originating from the vast field of non-being, from spacious emptiness. Non-being is absolute potential; it has the capacity for infinite transformation. It is the hub of the wheel that gives power to the spokes; it is the empty space that makes a window open to a vista. A cluttered room has no space for use; a cluttered mind has no space for new thoughts. Emptiness and spaciousness give birth to infinite possibility. The *Tao* engenders One, the One engenders Two, the Two engenders three, and then the infinite realm of possibility.[28]

For Taoism, non-being is not simply a void; it has the positive character of pure potentiality. Like "Einsteinian space-time, which is nothing, yet directs the motion of particles," for Lao Tzu non-being is the substance of the *Tao*.[29] The *Tao* is non-being in the sense that being is something definite: finite and defined. *Tao*, in contrast, is the unlimited; like Plato's form of the Good, which is superior to being in beauty and power, the *Tao* transcends the realm of being.[30] Lao Tzu thus stresses the mystery at the heart of the universe. It is not clear what is our Source or origin.[31]

Western philosophy must go out of its way to articulate the principle of negative theology, the notion that we know nothing about the Absolute and thus can only speak of the mysterious One by means of negation. In the *Tao Te Ching* it is clear that what is not said is more than what is said. The language of the text is poetry; it is not even clear what the *Tao* "is." Lao Tzu alludes rather than spells out; the poet's aim is to foster an intuitive sense of the reality behind the poetic images.

The *Tao* is primordial; it is older than the oldest known spirit in the world.[32] We do not know its origin. Western philosophy expresses this with the concept of a Necessary Existent, the fact that Being eternally is.[33] The *Tao Te Ching* does not say that the *Tao* is necessary—just that it is, deeply subsistent, an underlying presence that simply exists. Like water, it blunts sharp edges, and becomes one with this lowly, dusty world. It is not grand, glorious, exalted, and transcendent, but small, lowly, silent, and humble. And yet that is its power, to seep into the interstices of reality.[34]

## FROM UNKNOWING TO NON-INTERFERING ACTION (*WU-WEI*): *TAO* AS A WAY OF LIVING IN ACCORDANCE WITH THE *TAO*

The goal of philosophical Taoism is to transcend distinctions; Taoism is a critique of key Confucian values. Confucianism extols human-heartedness and righteousness, learning and ritual; Taoism pokes fun at these classical Confucian values:

Great *Tao* rejected:
Benevolence and righteousness appear
Learning and knowledge professed:
Great hypocrites spring up.
Family relations forgotten:
Filial piety and affection arise.
The nation disordered:
Patriots come forth. (CHAPTER 18)

Banish learning, discard knowledge:
People will gain a hundredfold.
Banish benevolence, discard righteousness:
People will return to duty and compassion . . .
Look at plain silk; hold uncarved wood.
The self dwindles; desires fade. (CHAPTER 19)

The Taoist Chuang Tzu records a fictional conversation between Confucius and his favorite disciple Yen Hui. Yen Hui says he has made progress: he has forgotten human-heartedness, righteousness, rituals, and music. "I have abandoned my body and discarded my knowledge. Thus I become one with the Infinite. This is what I mean by sitting in forgetfulness." Confucius answers: "If you have become one with the Infinite, you have no personal likes and dislikes. If you have become one with the Great Evolution [of the universe], you are one who merely follow its changes. If you really have achieved this, I should like to follow your steps."[35] Chuang Tzu thus articulates what the Western mystical tradition has called the way of "unknowing." Contemporary scholar Fung Yu-lan notes that this is different from the unknowing of a child, who is naïve and has never had knowledge. It is an unlearning of the knowledge we have acquired, abandoning the acquired distinctions to return to the mystical ultimate beyond all distinctions.[36]

The world has a source: the world's mother
Once you have the mother,
You know the children.
Once you know the children,
Return to the mother (CHAPTER 52)

Realizing the source of all things puts the differentiated universe in perspective. If we know that the source of all individual things lies in the undivided, we see things in their largest context—the context of the whole. Knowing the mother (the One, the undivided), we know the children (the many). Once we know the children, we can return to the mother. Thus there is a continual dialectical interplay: by returning to the source, we can investigate how all things are related to the whole. Living in the world of the many, we learn to experience it as continually pervaded by the *Tao*. We act always with the awareness of the whole of which we are a part. We then realize:

Your body dies
There is no danger . . .

Seeing the small is called brightness
Maintaining gentleness is called strength.
Use this brightness to return to brightness (CHAPTER 52)

The *Tao Te Ching* thus expresses paradoxical values. Gentleness is actually the source of strength, the soft overcomes the hard. The small and humble is the strong, which is close to the *Tao* and ultimately endures.

Best to be like water
Which benefits the ten thousand things
And does not contend.
It pools where humans disdain to dwell
Close to the *Tao*.

The small, the quiet, the lowly, and the unobtrusive are closest to Nature. It is the hidden and unmanifest that is the real power in the world. We can see how Taoism provided fertile ground for the transplantation of Buddhism from India; both traditions have a deeply developed sense for the power of the seemingly empty:

*Tao* is empty
Its use is never exhausted.
Bottomless
The origin of all things
It blunts sharp edges
Unties knots
Softens glare
Becomes one with the dusty world
Deeply subsistent
I do not know whose child it is
It is older than the Ancestor. (CHAPTER 4)

The most powerful way to act in the world is to imitate the *Tao*, which acts by spontaneous, non-interfering action (*wu-wei*). *Wu-wei*, though often translated "non-action," should not be confused with passivity; *wu-wei* is to act non-intrusively, to act without imposing one's will on the natural world. One must be aware of the context; situations are more complex than we think. We should not superimpose our preconceived views on a situation, but rather be aware of the interconnectedness of mutually defining apparent opposites:

Recognize beauty and ugliness is born
Recognize good and evil is born.
Is and isn't produce each other.
Hard depends on easy.
Long is tested by short
High is determined by low
Sound is harmonized by voice
After is followed by before

Therefore the Sage is devoted to non-action
Moves without teaching
Creates ten thousand things without instruction

Lives but does not own
Acts but does not presume
Accomplishes without taking credit
When no credit is taken
Accomplishment endures.

The way of *wu-wei* entails recognizing the subtleties of circumstances; it sees the *yin* in the *yang*, that which underlies seeming polarities.[37] Thus we can sense deeply the rhythms of the situation, and accomplish not by imposing our will, but by discerning what the situation invites.[38] When we practice non-interfering action, the natural order is not disrupted.[39]

Following the *Tao* means returning to simplicity, the uncarved block of wood, knowing the masculine way of assertion, but aligning ourselves fundamentally with the feminine way of receptivity:

Know the male, maintain the female,
Become the channel of the world
Become the channel of the world,
And *Te* will endure
Return to infancy
Know the white, sustain the black
Become the pattern of the world
Become the pattern of the world
And *Te* will not falter.
Return to the uncarved block.
Know honor, sustain disgrace
Become the valley of the world
And *Te* will prevail.
Return to simplicity.
Simplicity divided becomes utensils
That are used by the Sage as high official.
But great governing does not carve up. (CHAPTER 28)

The way to govern effectively is by subtlety and humility—by disgrace, rather than honor, by being a channel, a child in infant simplicity. When one becomes a valley or channel, what prevails is true power or virtue, the talent all beings naturally possess to be what they are and express themselves effectively in the world. The sage sees himself as very different from others:

dull, like a child, wayward. Of course such statements are probably made in irony: true wisdom looks like foolishness.[40]

## THE CONFUCIAN WAY AND THE WAY OF LAO TZU

From this understanding of Taoist values, we can see a genuine difference between Confucian and Taoist notions of *Tao, Te*, and *wu-wei*. The term *Tao* originally means road, and thus way or method. As a verb, it can also mean "to point out the road" and thus "to tell." Over time *Tao* therefore came to have a sense of a "course of conduct," a doctrine of moral principles.[41]

The Confucian *Tao* is thus a moral method, a guiding course that enables humans to achieve Confucian virtue.[42] The "Taoist" *Tao* in contrast, does not prescribe a specific course. It is no longer the Way as a specific doctrine guiding us along the moral path. The Way that is truly constant for Lao Tzu is the unnamed, non-prescribed Way, returning to the nameless, the non-defined. Brook Ziporyn thus characterizes Lao Tzu's use of the term *Tao* as ironic. True moral guidance comes not by inculcating prescribed values, as in Confucian thought, but by returning to the state of pure potentiality and following the natural course that emerges.[43]

Philip J. Ivanhoe traces this distinction further through the notions of *Te* and *wu-wei*. The Confucian sage exhibits the moral force or authority of *Te*. "One who rules through *de* ('moral charisma') is like the Pole Star, which remains in its place while all the myriad stars pay homage to it" (*Analects* 2:1). This image brings to mind the rare teacher who commands authority and respect from his or her students; no student would dare come to this teacher's class unprepared.[44] Moral charisma is subtle and invincible. "The *de* of the cultivated individual is like the wind. The *de* of the petty person is like grass. When the wind blows upon the grass it is sure to bend" (*Analects* 12:19). The *de* of the Confucian moral sage is awe-inspiring and brings others to yield to it. The Confucian sage rules by the power of ethical authority, just as exemplary teachers command respect from their students not by threats or coercion, but by the power of moral dignity.[45]

Ivanhoe points out that in contrast to the Confucian model, the *Te* of the Taoist sage inspires from below rather than above, from a position of lowliness rather than commanding authority. The *Tao Te Ching* bids us to be like water, which dwells in lowly places—to be a valley to the world. The Taoist sage attracts us not by commanding respect, but by inviting comfort. "For Laozi," writes Ivanhoe, "the draw of *de* is not the awesome power of the Pole

Star or the wind, but the natural tendency of things to migrate down toward low, safe, and inviting, terrain. The *de* of the Daoist sage is welcoming, accommodating, and nurturing—not awe-inspiring like that of Confucius's sage. The Daoist sage 'shines but does not dazzle.' "[46]

What is the effect of the Taoist sage on others? One who is in harmony with the *Tao* has cast off cleverness and artificiality. He or she expresses without self-consciousness the nature of the *Tao*—to be spontaneous, self-so (*tsu-jen; ziran*).[47] The Taoist sage walks through life with the ease of effortless action (*wu-wei*); the sage's tranquility creates what Ivanhoe calls a "therapeutic effect" on others, inviting all those in his or her presence to shed their social masks and artificial striving as well.[48] Ivanhoe sees this effect as akin to a natural phenomenon: "Laozi believed that whatever is 'still' naturally has the *de* ('power') to settle and govern that which is agitated or restless. For example, 'Restlessness overcomes cold; stillness overcomes heat. Limpid and still, One can be a leader in the empire.' "[49] In any interaction of natural forces, it is the stronger—that is the softer, quieter, more tranquil—that wins, calming any restless agitation. This can be extended to our ordinary interactions with others; it is the calm, tranquil, self-reliant person who quietly wins the day.

The Confucian sage inspires people to develop into responsible ethical agents through moral self-cultivation. The Taoist sage, in contrast, inspires people to abandon the mask of cultivated virtue, returning to natural, spontaneous, and unselfconscious action, which in his eyes is a more authentic form of virtue.[50]

## PROCESS AND BEAUTY: THE PHILOSOPHY OF ALFRED NORTH WHITEHEAD

We have seen that Plato finds the key to human happiness in harmony, self-mastery, and balance. Chinese thought also aims at harmony and balance. The *Tao Te Ching* adds an ironic twist: we can best attain balance by emphasizing values that we usually reject: softness, rather than rigidity; receptivity, rather than forthright action; emptiness and openness to possibility rather than glorying in achievement.

Like Plato, Chinese thought sees goodness and value built into the fabric of the universe. As JeeLoo Liu observes, in the naturalistic cosmology of the *Tao Te Ching* and the *I Ching* there is no distinction between the *ought* and the *is*. What is is the way the world ought to be. The moral attributes of the universe are what humans ought to emulate. When morality is grounded in an objective moral reality, it is simply part of the fabric of the world. Liu observes that "this is a form of moral realism, which asserts objectivity and reality in moral values. What is good is not what God commands, what social conventions decide or what human reason prescribes. Good is what is seen in Nature; it is what is manifested by natural phenomena. Moral standards are derived from observation of the external world, and the world is conceived differently from a mechanistic, physicalist universe."[51]

Chinese thought has a modern Western parallel in the process thought of Alfred North Whitehead, who also sees values as intrinsic to nature.[52] Nature itself realizes values. While we have thus far focused on premodern thinkers and texts, Whitehead gives us a good window into the modern quest for God and the good. Whitehead is famous for his statement that all of Western philosophy is a series of footnotes to Plato. Thus the perspective of Whitehead is a fitting component of our Socratic investigation.

In the medieval world, the goodness of nature and the human place in the universe were taken for granted. Human beings saw themselves as part of a rich theatre of sight, sounds, qualities, and colors. It wasn't until Descartes that we began to see ourselves as disembodied subjects that project qualities onto nature. Modern science and philosophy, beginning with Newton and Locke, distinguished between primary and secondary qualities. For these early modern thinkers, primary qualities, such as length and width, actually inhere in nature. Secondary qualities, such as colors, sounds, and fragrances, are projections of the human mind onto the world. The universe itself is silent, cold, and heartless—without objective value or spirit. The human self is radically alone in this universe. No wonder, then, that Descartes could imagine himself a disembodied subject looking out onto the world, that he could locate the human self in a being that simply thinks and is aware.

Whitehead seeks to correct this tragic modern view of the human condition with a new metaphysic based upon quantum physics. In fact, he argues, qualities very much inhere in nature. Feeling, taking one's environment into account, values, and aesthetics are a part of the natural world, even the quantum world. Amoeba perceive their environment and respond to it. Quantum forces take other quanta into account; they respond to their environment, behaving either as waves or as particles. To respond or behave is not an anthropomorphic metaphor; we think it is because we mistakenly think that all experience is conscious. However, conscious experience is only the most developed form of experience; all events in nature experience in varied ways. The entire universe is an interconnected fabric, in which every part responds to other parts. A particle behaves in a certain manner; it shows certain properties and reveals itself in distinct ways, depending upon its context. Nothing exists without a context.

Perception is based upon relationship, and all parts of the universe stand in relation and perceive at some level. Again, we do not have to attribute conscious perception or subjectivity to a particle. However, when I look at a blue carpet and see it as green because of the way the light hits the carpet, or when the sound of a fire engine bends as it passes me because of the Doppler effect, we can see that there is a transaction or interaction between beings that together creates perceived reality. More dramatically, the path a quantum particle "chooses" is actually affected by my choice as an observer to perceive and measure it.

The universe itself is a feeling universe. Values are embedded in the fabric of nature. The cooperation between particles and, on a larger scale, between all beings in the ecosystem embodies a value of harmony and mutual cooperation. It is true that some evolutionary biologists emphasize "the selfish gene," which seeks its own survival above all others. However, if there were only selfishness, the ecosystem could not survive; the cosmos works because there are also elements of cooperation and harmony.[53]

Whitehead terms the fundamental ingredients of the universe *actual events* or *actual occasions*.[54] We are not separate atoms or substances traveling alone in the universe, isolated from one another. In fact, modern particle physics shows that there is no "thing" or substance that can exist completely independently, and no instant of time not thickened by an awareness of the past and a moving toward the future. The continuity between moments—the fact that a table retains its identity over successive moments of time—in itself represents the most primitive embodiment of memory.[55] Thus Whitehead sees the universe as a living fabric of actual occasions, which at every moment choose to renew themselves and establish values in the world.[56] The universe is not a static fabric of "things," but a dynamic happening of interrelated *occasions* of experience. At a microcosmic level, the quantum particle is an occasion of experience; likewise, every part of a human body grows through physical events, and through our conscious choices, each human being becomes an interrelated nexus of events.

Whitehead's metaphysics is somewhat like that of Plato in that he recognizes an equivalent to Plato's Forms—what he calls eternal objects, qualities that are potentially to be realized in the world. However, for Whitehead it is only when potentials are actualized, when they become something in particular, that value is achieved. Actuality is the ground of value.[57] The greatest paper conceived in my head has no value until I have actually committed myself to the first word. Then, although the realization may be "less" than the potential I had envisaged, it is nevertheless more, because it is real.[58] Thus unlike Plato, Whitehead sees the world of actuality as of greater value than the world of eternal Forms or Ideas, which are pure, but also purely potential.[59]

Good is realized here on earth. God, for Whitehead, is that ground of being who envisages all potentials and inspires actual events to enable our realization.[60] God inspires us to make our choices within the underlying creative energy of the universe. In fact, Whitehead sees the urge toward creativity as the most fundamental fact of the universe. The creative pulse runs even through God. Things in our universe happen; the universe exhibits genuine novelty. Every moment is new and original. However, if there were just the pulse of creativity and unlimited potential, the universe would have no pattern or direction. God is that being who not only envisages all possibilities, but lures our choices into an actual harmonious whole. While every entity has free will to become whatever it chooses to be, God inspires choices that will blend with the creative order.

The energy of creativity is purely potential until it is actualized. Indeed, Whitehead makes the startling statement that *no value* can be ascribed to this underlying energy of realization apart from the matter of fact events of the real world.[61] In the terminology we have seen in the *Tao Te Ching*, the value of the Tao—the underlying energy of realization—can only be determined in the *Te*, that which the individual being receives or expresses of the Tao. We are a vital part of the creativity of the universe. God needs us to express divine potential.

For Whitehead, the universe exhibits harmonious order—aesthetic, as well as moral—and we are an integral part of that order. "The religious insight," he writes, "is the grasp of this truth:

> That the order of the world, the depth of reality of the world, the value of the world in its whole and in its parts, the beauty of the world, the zest of life, the peace of life, and the mastery of evil, are all bound together—not accidentally, but by reason of this truth: that the universe exhibits a creativity with infinite freedom, and a realm of forms with infinite possibilities; but this creativity and these forms are together impotent to achieve actuality apart from the completed ideal harmony, which is God.[62]

God is the master artist, who inspires a creative uniting of the purposes of all beings in the universe.

Is Whitehead's vision of moral order realistic? It is beautiful, but does it describe the world as we know it? Whitehead's goal is to develop a metaphysics that reflects developments in quantum physics; he maintains that his vision is true to our new understanding of the way events in the world interact. For example, Whitehead claims that he introduces God because without a principle of definiteness, we would have only random possibilities. God has one foot in actuality and enables potentialities to become concrete and actual.

We thus see that Whitehead is responding to many of the same questions addressed by the Hebrew Bible and Plato. Why is there order rather than chaos? Why do events hold together? Given our discoveries about the randomness of events on the quantum level, it would seem miraculous that tables do remain tables from moment to moment. God, for Whitehead, is that principle that allows things to hold together, that makes it possible for an event to choose to be something in particular.

As much as Whitehead stresses the harmony and goodness of the world order, he does not deny evil; evil is that which seeks to destroy rather than create, that tears apart rather than integrates within a harmonious whole. Whitehead argues, however, that evil is by its nature unstable. The continued working together of the universe is the best argument for the existence of a divine energy. There is an aesthetic beauty to the working together of nature that is akin to the beauty Chinese thought sees in the *Tao*.

Whitehead thus grounds the Chinese vision of a changing world of events in the most current conceptions of Western science. Taoism shows us a way to live within this changing world; Whitehead offers a vision of the universe that aims to harmonize with science as well as to inspire.

# 4

# The Harmony of Reason and Revelation

## AUGUSTINE AND MAIMONIDES ON GOOD AND EVIL

WHITEHEAD, THEN, sees nature as a realm in which values are realized. God sees potentials; the universe is built upon an underlying energy of creativity, which God can help make actual by inspiring us in our creative choices. But without us—the community of actually existing beings—there is no good. We are the medium by which good is realized. In the book of Genesis, we have seen, God creates and declares all of creation good. How then do we make sense of the presence of evil?[1] Western thought has struggled to make sense of the reality of good and evil in this world. We have seen some of the Biblical approaches; we will now look at two medieval approaches, those of the Christian thinker Augustine of Hippo (354–430 CE) and the Jewish thinker Moses Maimonides (1138–1204 CE).

The medieval world assumed two sources of truth—reason and revelation. They identified these respectively with Greek philosophy and Biblical tradition, and worked hard to reconcile these two sources of truth. When medieval religious thinkers come upon apparent contradictions, they search for ways to resolve such inconsistencies through philosophical interpretation.[2] Thus, although Augustine is a fourth-century Christian and Maimonides a twelfth-century Jew, their approaches to the nature of good and evil draw upon a common Biblical and philosophical tradition and come to similar conclusions. Each addresses both the problem of moral evil and the problem of metaphysical evil. These problems entail two questions: first, the moral question, why would God give human beings free will, allowing humanity to perpetrate such horrific moral indignities? And second, the metaphysical or ontological question, the question of the existence of evil itself: if the world is created by a good God, how does the very fact of evil and suffering enter our universe? Let us then investigate how these thinkers wrestle with two faces of the problem of evil.

## AUGUSTINE ON THE PROBLEM OF EVIL

In fashioning their response to the problem of evil, Augustine and Maimonides draw upon a common philosophical tradition, that of Neoplatonism, although Maimonides is strongly influenced by the Aristotelian tradition as well. Plotinus, the third-century founder of Neoplatonism, builds his philosophy upon a transcendent first principle he terms the One. Plotinus describes the world as emanating from the One like water from an overflowing fountain. This is not a temporal process; as long as there is One, being radiates from it just as a blossom gives off fragrance. The One is beyond being and non-being; all emanates from the One. Plotinus also terms the One "the Good." Everything, insofar as it *is*, is good, for its being derives from the Good; being is goodness.[3] The farther things descend from their origin, the less goodness they have, until we arrive at matter, which Plotinus identifies with evil and lack or privation.

We have seen that the identification of the One with the Good may go back to Plato.[4] Plotinus assumes that all complexity must originate from something simpler, and thus that the world as a whole—including the world of Intellect—must originate in a principle that is absolutely simple and prior to all being.[5] Plotinus is thus the first thinker to formalize an idea adopted by both Augustine and Maimonides: that of the great chain of being. This is a hierarchical chain, with ultimate value at the top and nonexistence at the bottom. Every being along this chain has value in creation. In the infinite variety of Forms, each has a unique value. Being is itself of value; every realization of being is a realization of value. In the monotheistic expressions of Augustine and Maimonides, God wants to realize as much good as possible, to realize every rung possible on the chain of being; this is known as the principle of plenitude.[6]

In this light, even things we might characterize as evil are not really so. As Augustine articulates the idea, what looks like evil is simply the fact that beings are at variance with one another; the life and purposes of one being seem to interfere with those of another.[7] For example, bears enjoy their own existence, but interfere with human enjoyment of camping. Bacteria benefit the ecosystem, but may damage human health. Conflict is the apparent dissonance of contrasting values, but conflict is not evil as such. Everything has a place when seen within the larger Gestalt of being; the realization of more rungs on the chain of being is greater than would be the existence of "higher" types of good—such as the angels—alone. Both Augustine and Maimonides derive support from the verse in Genesis that reads, "And God saw *all* that he had made, and indeed, it was *very good*." When looked at in the context of the whole, all things can be seen to be good.[8]

We have noted that Augustine deals with evil on two levels: metaphysical or natural evil, and moral evil. Metaphysical evil is the existence of evil as such, as a natural property of our world—the problem of why there are hurricanes and floods, why innocent children suffer. Metaphysical evil, explains Augustine, is simply negation. Anything that has being is good. Evil is due to corruption, that which deprives something of its being or goodness. Evil is not a positive force in nature but a deprivation of being and goodness. Things begin intact; evil is what deprives them of being or corrupts their goodness.[9]

What about moral evil? At an early stage in his spiritual journey, Augustine was attracted to the solution proposed by Manichean dualism, which posited the origin of evil in the will of an evil divine principle. Augustine comes to deny that perspective. "When I will," he asserts, "I am conscious that I am willing. I am the source of the evil I do; the source of the evil I do is my own will. The will that God gave me is free; I corrupt my will by turning away from eternal things one cannot lose to temporal things that are shifting and that one can lose."[10] Goodness and true happiness lie in contemplating eternal values in the mind of God. Augustine thus weds Biblical Christianity and Platonism; he places Platonic Forms in the mind of God. These Forms are the source of eternal happiness. My will is corrupted when I allow myself to crave things that pass away and can never satisfy an eternal desire.[11]

Augustine likewise identifies our own free will as something we cannot lose. We see here a Stoic strain in Augustine's thought. The Stoics taught that no matter what our circumstances, the attitude we hold toward our situation lies firmly within our control. Thus in the end we are in control of our experience—not what happens to us, but how we respond to it. We can rejoice in our own good will, no matter what the external circumstances of our lives.[12]

In a larger sense Augustine also sees evil as an inheritance from Adam and Eve. It was the first man and woman who turned from the eternal to the corruptible; all of humanity inherits the sin of the first human beings. We in later generations can be held responsible for our own actions, as each of us reenacts the sin of Adam and Eve in turning from contemplation of eternal truths to the corruptible things of this world.[13]

Augustine finds consolation rather than despair in the fact that he does evil of his own free will, for he therefore no longer needs to see the source of evil in God or in a Manichean principle of evil.[14] And yet the problem of how evil crept into the world continues to trouble him. God is not only good, but Goodness itself.[15] All things are good; if something ceased altogether to be good, it would cease to be.[16] This brings us to the second kind of evil, metaphysical evil. Evil is not a substance but a diminishing of substance.

Augustine originally envisaged God as a vast sea infusing all of creation; he pictured creation as a sponge thoroughly immersed in the ocean of God.[17] He revises this view of God when he realizes that all things are in God as a ground of being, not a physical substance. God does not materially pervade the universe; God's infinity is not one of extension.[18] God's infinity is of a different order than mathematical time and space. God's eternity is not a very long time, nor is God's infinity the extension of all space and time.[19] God dwells in eternity; God's Being is a necessary foundation for our existence. What brings Augustine to this new awareness is a personal religious experience. In this vision, he sees God coming to him as a supernatural light, different from any light he has experienced in this world. Realizing that God has no physical extension or limits, he ponders, "Is truth then nothing at all, simply because it has no extension in space, with or without limits?" His answer comes from a new intuitive understanding of Exodus 3:14: "I am the God who IS."[20] Finite things are in God not as a sponge immersed in water, but as beings grounded in Being itself:

> I looked at other things too and saw that they owe their being to you. I saw that all finite things are in you, not as though you were a place that contained them, but in a different manner. They are in you because you hold all things in your truth as though they were in your hand, and all things are true insofar as they have being. Falsehood is nothing but the supposed existence of something which has no being.
>
> I saw too that all things are fit and proper not only to the places but also to the times in which they exist, and that you, who are the only eternal Being, did not begin to work only after countless ages of time had elapsed, because no age of time, past or still to come, could either come or go if it were not that you abide for ever and cause time to come and go.[21]

Augustine thus realizes that all things exist in God not as a sponge immersed in water or any physical substance, but as ideas exist in Truth, and beings in Being. Moreover, God, being eternal, exists outside of time and did not wait countless eons to create; God is rather the eternal ground and witness of temporal becoming, like the eternal witness of a temporal drama. God sees the entire historical drama at once.[22]

Augustine likewise realizes that wickedness is not a substance "but a perversion of the will when it turns aside from you, O God, who are the supreme substance."[23] The will that wills good is purely good. It is only when it desires that which is outside itself that it turns away from God to inferior things. This is the source of evil. The soul that desires inferior things is miserable. As Plato and Aristotle note, the tyrant is actually tyrannized by his or her own desires.[24] Goodness and peace of mind go hand in hand.[25]

## MAIMONIDES ON GOOD AND EVIL

With this understanding of Augustine's fusion of Biblical and Neoplatonic traditions, we can turn to explore Maimonides' somewhat more complex view. Maimonides addresses the question of good and evil at the opening of his *Guide of the Perplexed*, in the context of a philosophical interpretation of the Garden of Eden story. For Maimonides, the original nature of humanity is one in which human beings do not see good and evil, but only true and false. Maimonides explicates his position most clearly in *Guide of the Perplexed* 1.2, responding to an exegetical problem. It cannot be that human beings were given the gift of reason, the crown of human faculties, as a consequence of disobeying the word of God. Thus the knowledge of good and evil humans gained after eating the fruit of the tree of knowledge of good and evil must be of a lower quality than the cognition with which they were born.[26]

Beyond this exegetical problem, Maimonides sees moral knowledge as inferior to knowledge of true and false. The categories of good and evil are not absolute categories; they arise from our subjective imaginings and desires.[27] They cloud our cognition of the world; we see the world through the filter of our own distorted needs and perceptions.[28] The goal of Maimonides' *Guide* is to bring us back to that pure apprehension, cognition of the truth, which will bring about an end to enmity, hatred, and oppression.[29] Thus Maimonides is a proponent of Socratic intellectualism, the notion that knowledge of the truth brings about human transformation, that to know the good is to live it.[30] For Maimonides, of course, the Truth is ultimately God; knowledge of God brings about—or is identical with—human salvation.

## The Aristotelian and Neoplatonic Strands

In recent years, through detailed and beautiful exegesis, scholars have demonstrated a strong Aristotelian strand in Maimonides' discussion of the good. In the following discourse, I would like to focus on a strand of thought more prominent in the Platonic and Neoplatonic traditions, which brings out another dimension of Maimonides' philosophical sensibility.[31] The dialogue between these two strands will show us the complexity and artistry of Maimonides' own thinking on God and the good.

First, the well-known Aristotelian strand. Maimonides observes that "in the language of human beings," we use the term "good" to describe that which conforms to our purpose.[32] We also use the term "good" to describe that which achieves a noble aim.[33] From these two statements about the way we use the term "good" in ordinary human language, we learn that when Genesis 1:31 tells us that God looked at the world and saw that it was "very good," the Bible is informing us that the world conformed to God's purpose in giving beings existence. As Sara Klein-Braslavy expresses it, reality, as conforming to the divine intention, is the absolute good.[34]

So far Maimonides echoes language we find in Aristotle, who opens the *Nicomachean Ethics* with the statement that every action, art, or investigation seems to aim at some good; thus the good has been well defined as that to which all things aim.[35] In *Guide* 3.10–12, however, Maimonides expresses himself in language we find more prominent in Plato and the Neoplatonic tradition. In *Guide* 3.12 he sets out to counter the views of those who believe that the world contains more evil than good. To the contrary, argues Maimonides, in the view of adherents of the truth, God is the absolute good, and everything that proceeds from him is indubitably an absolute good.[36]

In fact, he reiterates, God's bringing us into existence is absolutely the great good.[37] All of God's actions are an absolute good, for God only creates being, and all being is good.[38] The true reality of the act of God in its entirety is good, for it is being.[39] He says several times that the ultimate intention is to bring into being as much existence as possible, for existence is indubitably a good. This is the principle of plenitude we have seen in Plotinus and Augustine; the great chain of being is a complete expression of every degree of being and goodness possible.[40]

What does it mean for Maimonides to say that God is the absolute good, and that everything that proceeds from him is an absolute good? To fully understand these statements we must delve into Maimonides' complex view of religious language. Maimonides' sense of God's transcendence is so absolute that he holds we cannot make any positive statements about God's essence. God's being is utterly unique and mysterious; God is beyond what any human being can know. Echoing language of both Plotinus and the Islamic mystics, he writes:

> All people, past and future, affirm that God cannot be apprehended by the intellects, that none can apprehend what He is but He alone, that apprehension of Him consists in the inability to attain the farthest limit in apprehending Him. Thus all the philosophers say: We are dazzled by his beauty, and he is hidden from us because of the intensity with which he becomes manifest, just as the sun is hidden to eyes that are too weak to apprehend it.[41]

God is unlike any other being in the universe because God's existence does not have a cause; it simply is. In technical language, God's existence is necessary—that is, independent of any other being—while the existence of every other being in the universe is contingent—that is, dependent—upon God. We are like waves on the ocean of God; the waves are dependent on the existence of the ocean, while the ocean does not depend on the existence of waves.[42] Stated more simply, God exists whether or not the world exists; the world is dependent on God, not God on the world.[43] This is Avicenna's concept of God as Necessary Existent, which Maimonides articulates boldly at the opening of his code of Jewish Law (*Mishneh Torah*):

> If it could be supposed that he did not exist, it would follow that nothing else could possibly exist. If, however, it were supposed that all other beings were non-existent, he alone would still exist. Their non-existence would not involve his non-existence. For all beings are in need of him; but he, blessed be he, is not in need of them nor of any one of them. Hence, his real essence is unlike any of them.[44]

In the *Guide of the Perplexed*, Maimonides offers a version of Avicenna's proof for this Necessary Existent. All beings in the world other than God are only possible or contingent; their existence depends upon prior causes. If it were not for a particular chain of causes, any one of us might never have come into existence. God's existence, in contrast, does not depend upon any cause; God simply *is*. The fact that there is an Existent who eternally *is* ensures that being as a whole will never cease.[45]

However, how can we speak at all about a God whose essence we can never know? Speech about God must be translated into language appropriate to a Being who is transcendent and unknowable. If we say that God is "good," we mean not only that God is not evil, but also that God is not good in any sense we know of—that God is beyond qualities of both good and evil.[46] When we say that God is living, knowing, and powerful we mean that God is not inanimate, but also that God lives "without life," knows without knowledge, and that God is not incapable; God's existence suffices to bring into existence many beings from God's overflow.[47] In other words, there is a Being who simply is, and from this Being overflow all the beings we see in creation, like water overflowing from a fountain.[48]

In other contexts—specifically, when explaining the qualities ascribed to God in the Bible—Maimonides speaks of God's attributes of action; these are qualities that describe God's relationship to the created world. Since we cannot know God's mode of existence directly, we cannot, strictly speaking, assert that God is good or merciful in essence. What we can say with confidence is that the results of God's actions are beneficial.[49] We look at the created world and see that embryos are provided all the nourishment they need; we can thus say that the Being from whom they have sprung is a source of goodness, or acts in ways that human beings do when we have qualities of goodness.[50] In this way, we do not overstep the bounds of our knowledge of a God who must always remain in some sense mysterious. We can infer qualities of our Creator by contemplating the beauty of this universe. However, we do not truly know the essence of a Being who is the condition of everything in this created order.[51]

Another reason we cannot ascribe any qualities to God's essence is that to do so would be to introduce multiplicity into God's nature, which is absolutely one and simple. Any statement of the form "God is . . ." has already introduced multiplicity into the absolutely unified nature of the divine.[52] Monotheism for Maimonides means not only that there is only one God, but that God must be utterly one, a being who is absolutely simple and unified.

## On God and Good

With this understanding of Maimonides' complex view of language about the divine, we can return to our question: What does it mean for Maimonides to say that God is the absolute good, and that his bringing us into existence is the absolute good? One way we can understand Maimonides is as follows. As the Necessary Existent and source of the universe, God is the ultimate source of existence, truth, and value.[53] God is the creator of every being in the universe.[54] In *Guide* 3.11, Maimonides suggests that if we have a clear perception of this fact, we will not treat any being with less than ultimate respect, since every creature is an embodiment of the source of worth. Every creature is of intrinsic value as an expression of the one God.[55]

For Maimonides, then, "good" is an equivocal term; it has very different meanings when applied to God and to creation; "good" is likewise different when applied to humanity in its ideal state and in its actual state.[56] We can understand this best by examining what Maimonides says about evil. On the one hand, things we think of as evil are only evil from our individual, subjective point of view. From the perspective of an individual person, death is an evil, for it deprives him of his own life, which is precious to him; still worse, death deprives a person of those he or she most dearly loves. But when looked at in the context of the whole, death is necessary, for it ensures that the planet will not be overpopulated; it allows room for succeeding generations to also enjoy the gift of life.[57] Thus nothing is truly evil when examined within the context of the whole. This entire universe is one living organism, and every creature and event has a unique place within the whole.[58]

Maimonides, like Augustine, must grapple with two kinds of evil: metaphysical evil and moral evil. Like Augustine, he argues that metaphysical or ontological evil is simply privation or lack. If the greatest good is being, then evil is a lack of being, and evil that is inflicted is anything that deprives another of its being.[59] Natural evils such as earthquakes and floods simply happen; they are an unfortunate by-product of the fact of material existence.[60] The immaterial infinite One chose to create a finite world. If the Divine had chosen not to create, we would not be here to rail against the problems of finite existence, but neither would we be able to enjoy its benefits. Thus if we wish to enjoy the splendors of existence, we must come to terms with its limitations. Anything that is not God is finite; finitude entails privation or lack. We as physical, material creatures lack some of the perfections of the divine. Being finite, we will die; being finite we are subject to physical and emotional suffering and deprivation. But we should not therefore deny all the good in existence, because a good existence by necessity also entails evil and suffering. Would the lack of a world be a better solution? God could have enjoyed eternal unchanging perfection forever. Instead, God chose to share some of God's good. The absolute Being shares existence; this act of endowing us with being is the greatest good.[61]

What of moral evil? What can we say about a depraved soul that knowingly and willingly inflicts suffering and harm upon others? Maimonides suggests that infliction of harm can only be a result of another form of deprivation—the deprivation of knowledge. Anyone who has a true perception of reality—knowledge of God—would be unable to inflict harm. Thus moral evil, too, can ultimately be understood as a consequence of privation or deprivation.[62] Evil is a lack of being and not a positive entity or substance that vies with the sovereignty of God.

## The Garden of Eden

Returning to the Garden of Eden, we recall that Maimonides argues that the knowledge of good and evil acquired after eating the fruit of the tree represents a *deprivation* of true knowledge. How can we understand Maimonides' exegesis, given that elsewhere in the text he makes the Platonic identification of being as the absolute good? Maimonides must be using the terms "good" and "evil" in two ways.[63] From an absolute standpoint, evil is not a positive substance or quality to be known; it is a lack. Those who see evil are seeing something that is not actually present. Whatever is is good. Evil has no real existence; it is that which is not.

The good *is*; being and the conferring of being are good. But this use of the term "good" makes it a synonym for the "true." Truth is that which is; falsehood is that which is not.[64] "Evil" too is that which is not. On an absolute level, then, good is that which is and evil is that which is not. This is the absolute, ontological sense of good and evil known by humanity in its ideal state in the Garden of Eden. However, in our actual state, we choose relative good and evil. Relative good is what pleases a person according to his or her subjective desires, when he or she has lost sight of the absolute good. Relative, subjective good is thus not truly good. In humanity's ideal state—represented by Adam and Eve in the Garden—the term "good" represents humanity's objective end of knowing absolute Truth, of knowing God. In our actual state, we use the terms "good" and "evil" to describe our subjective aims, clouded by our individual desires. In fact, these relative "goods" can be seen from an absolute standpoint as "evil" in that they turn us away from the absolute Good or Truth. Thus Maimonides sees all human morality as relative, a function of our relative purposes.

However, there is also an absolute "commandment" of God: to see only the false and true, to realize our objective, divine end of knowing Truth, that is, God.[65] In our hypothetical ideal state, before eating of the "tree of knowledge of good and evil," humanity knew the absolute Good or the True. In our actual state, the terms "good" and "evil" characterize the shifting sands of human morality clouded by our imaginings and desires.

## AUGUSTINE AND MAIMONIDES

Both Augustine and Maimonides see God as the absolute Good. Augustine is a more conscious Platonist, and so Augustine's God comes across as a personal embodiment of Plato's Form of the Good. Maimonides absorbed Platonic elements through Neoplatonic metaphysics. In describing God as the absolute Good, in the case of Maimonides, or as Goodness itself, in the case of Augustine, each thinker weds the Biblical and Platonic worldviews. Augustine's God, however, is a personal God, a God he can describe as Sweetness, a God to whom he can talk. Maimonides' God is at first glance more austere, more like the Aristotelian God who is "thought thinking itself," or the unknowable Neoplatonic One. However, we have also seen that for Maimonides, God can be known through God's attributes of action in creation, such as loving kindness, justice, and righteousness.[66]

Both thinkers see God and Good as tied to Being, and see evil as a lack of being. Metaphysical evil is simply the lack of being or reality. For Augustine, moral evil is corruption of the original goodness of our will; for Maimonides, moral evil is a result of deprivation of the knowledge of God. Maimonides is thus more Socratic: to know the Good or God is to act in accordance with it. For Augustine, humanity fell by listening to the suggestion of the snake, thus corrupting our originally pure will. The snake itself is the Devil—an angel who fell from pure contemplation of God. How then did the Devil himself fall, so that he might go on to tempt humanity? The mind contemplates eternal truths but can also become aware of itself as a changeable soul. When it becomes aware of itself it realizes that it is not the same as God, and that it can be something pleasing aside from God. This is pride—taking pleasure in oneself and one's own power "in a perverse imitation of God." We can love God and the Good in a pure state, or we can be full of pride for awareness of ourselves as souls that can contemplate these eternal verities. The pride of the Devil was to want to be like God; the Devil then tempted humanity to want to be like God as well.

For Augustine then, the fall is indeed a historical occurrence; every human being inherits a soul corrupted by the sin of the first human being. Since we all were descendents of the original ancestors, we share in their sin and inherit its effects. For Maimonides, in contrast, the Garden of Eden is an allegory. Every soul is born with free will and on its own volition turns from eternal Truth to judging good and evil. For Augustine, good and evil are real. Souls have genuinely sinned and forfeited their original goodness. For Maimonides, the reality of the relationship between humans, God, and good is Truth; good and evil are subjective judgments human beings add when they leave their state of contemplation.

In *Guide* 3.12, Maimonides quotes Psalms: "All the paths of the Lord are mercy and truth to those who keep his covenant and testimonies." He comments that those who keep the covenant are those who "keep to the nature of that which exists; they thus keep commandments of the Law, and know the ends, apprehend the excellence and true reality of the whole." Rémi Brague has suggested that Maimonides gives the verse from Psalms an ingenious philosophical interpretation: the philosophical covenant with God is to see reality as it is in truth.[67] The greatest commandment (*mitsvah*) is to see what the Buddhists call the "suchness" of things, to simply see Reality as it is.[68] The passage thus suggests a Spinoza-like element in Maimonides—a way in which Maimonides anticipates Spinoza's view that God is equivalent to the scientific system of nature. Does Maimonides thereby devalue the traditional content of God's covenant—the positive and negative commandments of the Law? One need not read the passage as antinomian, as denying the authority or value of the active commandments of God—the "thou shalts" and "thou shalt nots." For Maimonides maintains that God's commandments of action are also part of the wisdom and excellence of God; they are the way God has instructed us to live in this excellent reality.[69] Thus, just as someone who knows the true reality of God will not hurt or oppress others, so he or she will keep the commandments of the Law. One who knows the Truth will live the Truth; for Maimonides the Torah is truth, and one who knows it will live it.[70]

# 5

# You Are the Absolute

## PHILOSOPHIES OF INDIA

We have noted that like Greek philosophy, Indian thought affirms a realm of eternal self-subsistent Being. When we turn to the worldview of two formative repositories of Indian religious thought—the Upanishads and the *Bhagavad Gītā*—we thus find a surprising coincidence of themes we have heretofore explored.

A brief introduction to Indian thought will orient us. The Indian religious tradition, called Hinduism by moderns, arose out of a complex interaction of two civilizations: the civilization of the Indus Valley in northwest India and Indo-European Vedic culture. Excavations in the Indus Valley have uncovered evidence that an urban civilization thrived in northwest India from about 2500 until 1500 BCE. While we have not yet deciphered the civilization's script, we do have artifacts of its material culture. For example, many female figurines have been found, suggesting that goddess worship may have been prominent, as it became in later Hindu tradition. There are also seals of a horned male figure surrounded by animals, seated in what might be a yoga pose. Some scholars suggest that the early images on these seals are reflected in later imagery of the Hindu god Shiva, the great yogi and lord of the animals. Phallic-shaped stones have also been found, reminiscent of the *liṅga*, the phallic representation of Shiva. Thus Hindu civilization appears to have drawn elements from this early indigenous culture, which came to an end around 1900 BCE.

At around the same time, a group of Indo-Europeans seems to have migrated to the Indian subcontinent from Central Asia on horse-drawn chariots. They called themselves *ārya*, "noble"; this is termed by scholars the Aryan migration.[1] Nineteenth-century European scholars hypothesized that a military invasion of these Central Asian tribes destroyed the thriving Indus Valley civilization and brought in Vedic Aryan culture. More recently, scholars have come to think that the civilization came to an end on its own at the same time waves of Europeans were migrating to the subcontinent. Others believe that Aryan culture developed from within the Indus Valley civilization rather than being brought from without. Linguistic evidence suggests that elements of both views are true—that we find in Hindu culture a complex blend of indigenous and Indo-European elements.[2]

Hinduism finds its earliest source of sacred inspiration in hymns dating from about 1500–1200 BCE, collected in a text called the *Ṛig Veda*. The language of these hymns was Sanskrit, from the term *saṃskṛita*, "well-formed." The term "Veda" means "body of knowledge"; the *Ṛig Veda* was the "body of knowledge concerning verses of praise [*ṛig*]."[3] The Vedas are also known as *śruti*, "that which is heard";[4] they are considered the most sacred of Hindu scriptures, an authorless eternal text revealed directly from the cosmos or the Divine.[5]

The hymns of the *Ṛig Veda* include speculation on the source of the universe. In one famous hymn, all is said to arise out of That One—an impersonal being, neither existent nor nonexistent, from which even the gods arose. This early hymn thus anticipates the notion of an impersonal underlying essence to the universe, which will develop into the central concept of *brahman*. Another hymn describes the universe arising out of the sacrifice of a cosmic Person (*puruṣa*). [6]

Sacrifice was indeed central to the Vedic worldview. The Vedic hymns were chanted by priests as they made sacrifices to the gods. The priests officiating at such sacrifices were known as Brahmins; the later exegetical portions of the texts were known as Brāhmaṇas. These texts set forth both the technical rules of the sacrificial ritual and an explication of its hidden meaning and purpose; they identify mystical correspondences between the sacrificial ritual and the cosmos, and assert that it is the ritual itself that maintains the cosmic order.[7]

The composers of the Vedic hymns were known as seers (*ṛishis*), those who had the gift of seeing into the truth. The texts thus had the status of revelation; they were "seen" or heard—that is, perceived—by direct inspiration from the cosmos.[8] In the Vedas, the creative power by which the seers discovered and expressed this truth was known as *brahman*, and the hymns themselves were said to hold this power of *brahman*, the power of the sacred utterance.[9] They were more than simple hymns of praise; it was the chanting of the hymns themselves that made the sacrifice efficacious. The hymns thus came to function as *mantras*, ritual formulas accompanying the sacrifice that made the sacrifice work. The *mantras*, expressed in Sanskrit, were formulations of the truth in sound. Just as a painting captures the truth of a visual image, *mantras* were not arbitrary symbols but aural expressions of the essence or reality of things; they thus had sacred, magical power. *Mantras* expressed both the unique qualities that make beings in the universe distinct and their underlying unity.[10]

The role of the Brahmin priests was to protect *brahman*, the reality underlying the sacred mantras and the sacrifice. Gradually, at the end of the Brāhmaṇa period, in texts known as the Āraṇyakas, there arose in priestly circles the view that the universe had been created by the sacrificial action of the gods, and that it was sacrifice itself that sustained the cosmos.[11] Since sacrifice preserved the cosmos and *brahman* was the power of the sacrifice, *brahman* was the power or essence that sustained the universe. Thus while in the Brāhmaṇas the term *brahman* refers to the power of the sacrificial ritual "apart from which there is nothing more ancient or brighter,"[12] gradually the concept evolved from "the power of sacred word and the sacrifice" to encompass "the essential underlying reality of the universe."[13]

We have seen that the Brāhmaṇa texts, priestly commentaries on the sacrificial rituals, provided knowledge of *brahman*, key to the success of the sacrifice.[14] By the end of the Brāhmaṇa period (800 CE), it came to be believed that since knowledge was the key to the sacrificial ritual, the ritual no longer needed to be performed externally; one could perform the ritual simply by chanting the *mantra* internally, as described in the Āraṇyakas. The key to connection with *brahman* was no longer external performance of the sacrifice, but the sacrifice performed within; a person could become one with *brahman* by internal knowledge alone.[15] The individual Brahmin, practicing the ritual internally, was identified with the cosmic reality, even independent of the external sacrificial ritual. The human individual who embodied the inner reality of the sacrifice was identified with the cosmic Person (*puruṣa*), who is described in the *Ṛig Veda* as bringing forth the cosmos through his own self-sacrifice at the hands of the gods.[16] The search thus began for the essential human person, who by knowledge alone could become one with the universal *brahman*, the reality at the very heart of being.

This led to Upanishadic speculation on the ultimate human self—or what in Sanskrit is termed *ātman*, the inner core of the individual who could come to know and become one with the universal *brahman*.[17] In the

Upanishads—the body of secret teachings that came to speculate increasingly on metaphysical matters—*brahman* came to be understood not just as the power of the sacred word or the key to the sacrifice, but as the one Spirit underlying the entire universe. In the *Chāndogya Upanishad*, the ultimate identification is made: *ātman*, the Self, is described as one with *brahman*, the universal Spirit.[18]

With this prehistory of the concepts of *ātman* and *brahman*, we can begin to explore Hindu metaphysical speculation as it comes to be expressed in the Upanishads. While there is a great diversity of views in these texts, we do find an underlying assumption that the Upanishads share with Greek thought, particularly that of Plato: the positing of an eternal Reality that is the truly real. In the *Chāndogya Upanishad*, for example, the sage Uddālaka asserts that all things come from Being, which is the underlying Reality or truth of all.[19] Just as all things made of clay are in essence clay, so all manifestations of Being are in essence Being alone; individual modifications of the underlying Reality are mere differences of name and form.[20] In the beginning, Being was one alone, without a second; all things evolved from and will return to Being. All rivers eventually return to the sea; in the great ocean, they do not have the awareness "I am this one" or "I am that one." Just so, when all beings return to their source, they merge with the Self of which they are a part.[21] Beneath the phenomenal self—the thoughts, feelings, sounds, colors, and sensations we experience—is an underlying Reality that does not change; uniting all things, this Self is an island of peace in a stormy sea. We saw that Chinese thought examined all of reality and recognized that things are constantly transforming. Upanishadic thought asserts that underneath the turbulence we experience as the great drama of creation unfolds, there is in fact an eternal unchanging Self. "That which is the finest essence; this whole world has That as its soul. That is Reality. That is *ātman*. And that art Thou! [or 'thus are you!' 'that's how you are!']."[22]

Like Augustine, the Upanishads find peace and ultimate happiness in discovery of the divine reality. If we discover our eternal home and abide there, no sorrow can find us.[23] However, unlike Augustine, the Upanishads assert that we ourselves are not separate from that eternal unchanging Being. That which we seek is not outside ourselves; we are a part of that divinity. Of course, the Upanishads are not monolithic; in the Upanishads we hear many voices and find diverse images of the relationship between the One and the many, *brahman* and the world.[24] What they share is the notion that knowledge of ultimate Reality is the key to happiness. This is not merely cognitive knowledge, knowledge one can find in a book or even that a teacher can transmit to a student. This is truth as lived—existential, transformative knowledge, the kind of profound understanding that turns our world upside down. We discover we are no longer who we thought we were; we experience the universe and ourselves in a completely new way. This is the kind of knowledge that makes us into new beings.

According to some Upanishadic teachers such as Yājñavalkya, knowledge that we are the nondual Self causes us to become that Self; we experience ourselves and the world in a unified state of awareness.[25] While for Yājñavalkya the closest analogue to this state is the state of deep sleep—which might seem to be unconscious—others emphasized that this unified state is beyond the dichotomy of consciousness or unconsciousness; it is a fourth state beyond waking, dreaming, and dreamless sleep.[26] Building upon the thought of the Upanishadic sages, the later Advaita Vedānta tradition teaches that this is not simply a state of consciousness, but who we essentially are; we never lost identity with our eternal Self. What is needed is not a long process of transformation, but a realization of what we have always been; we realize that the nondual Self has always lived within.[27] It is only ignorance and desire that keep us from realizing who we are; these cause us to mistakenly identify ourselves with the body in which we temporarily reside. Our true self is not our body, not our personality, not our changing thoughts and sensations. Behind what we think we are—the temporary person with an individual history—lies who we really are, the eternal Self within our heart.[28] Here are the words of the disciple in a later Vedāntic text who has realized his oneness with the All:

> The ego has disappeared. I have realized my identity with *brahman* and so all my desires have melted away. I have risen above my ignorance and my knowledge of this seeming universe. What is this joy that I feel? Who shall measure it? I know nothing but joy, limitless, unbounded!
>
> The ocean of *brahman* is full of nectar—the joy of the *ātman*. The mind cannot conceive of it. My mind fell like a hailstone into that vast expanse of *brahman*'s ocean. Touching one drop of it, I melted and became one with *brahman*. And now that I return to human consciousness, I abide in the joy of the *ātman*.
>
> Where is this universe? Who took it away? Has it merged into something else? A while ago I beheld it—now it exists no longer. This is wonderful indeed! Here is the ocean of *brahman*, full of endless joy. How can I accept or reject anything? Is there anything apart or distinct from *brahman*?

> Now, finally and clearly, I know that I am the *ātman*, whose nature is eternal joy. I see nothing, I hear nothing, I know nothing that is separate from me.[29]

The path of knowledge might at first glance appear easy—simply wake up and realize who you are. In fact, the path of knowledge is a steep path associated with ascetic renunciation of action and rigorous, disciplined meditation; it is by and large neither practical nor accessible to the average person. In addition, by the time of the early Upanishads there had developed a factor that complicated the search for liberation: the notion of cycles of death and rebirth (*saṃsāra*) controlled by one's own action (*karma*). In the *Bṛihadāraṇyaka Upanishad* it is expressed as a secret teaching; in later texts, it is taken for granted. Yājñavalkya explains that good actions make us good and ensure a good rebirth; bad actions have the opposite effect.[30] In an earlier period, the cyclical nature of life was embraced in a joyous and life-affirming spirit, and the end that was hoped for was arriving at the world of the ancestors or the world of the gods. The only end to be feared was re-death after one had arrived at the afterlife, and certain ritual actions were prescribed to prevent this prospect.[31] Gradually—it is not clear how—there developed the notion of *saṃsāra,* a cycle of death and rebirth into this world. Transmigration of the soul was seen not as an opportunity but an entrapment in an endless cycle, an inexorable burden from which the soul desired to be liberated.[32]

There thus developed a tension between two competing ideals: *dharma* (sacred duty) and *mokṣa* (liberation). In its broadest sense *dharma* is the action that maintains the world order.[33] Codes such as the *Laws of Manu* set forth in great detail the duties incumbent upon human beings to fulfill their responsibility to society and uphold the cosmic order. By fulfilling the sacred duty appropriate for one's stage of life (*āshrama*) and social class (*varṇa*), a person would achieve two goals: one would both uphold the order of the world, and achieve for oneself good *karma* and the prospect of a good rebirth. Nevertheless, a good rebirth is but a finite goal, not a permanent release from the cycle of birth and death. And thus there remained to some extent an uneasy tension between the world-affirming ideal of fulfilling *dharma* and the world-renouncing goal of liberation (*mokṣa*) from the wheel of birth and rebirth.[34]

The *Bhagavad Gītā*, a popular devotional text, offers a doctrine designed to resolve this tension; at the same time, the *Gītā* sets forth diverse but complementary paths, perhaps for individuals of different abilities and temperaments. The *Bhagavad Gītā* also represents various metaphysical streams—not only Upanishadic monism, but Sāṃkhya dualism and its practical analogue, Yoga practice. Sāṃkhya dualism analyzes the world differently from the teachings of the Upanishads. For many teachers of the Upanishads, reality is one seamless whole, and the soul is not really trapped in the phenomenal world. If our soul realizes its essential identity with *brahman*, we can achieve liberation and not return to a body after this life; we return to *brahman* itself. Sāṃkhya philosophy views the situation in a different way. There are two metaphysical principles in the world: Spirit (*puruṣa*) and nature (*prakṛiti*). Nature is the phenomenal world; it is not simply matter, but anything experienced, including our thoughts and ego-mind. *Puruṣa* is Spirit; it is the subject rather than the object of experience. When *puruṣa* begins to desire the objects of consciousness, it takes on the illusion of being trapped in nature.[35] It must thus engage in the arduous process of separating itself from nature and reconnecting itself to spirit. Yoga texts offer meditation techniques to effect that process of yoking or binding together one's mind and senses and freeing the Spirit from nature.[36]

Sāṃkhya metaphysics is not only dualistic; it is pluralistic. There are many *puruṣas*, many individual spirits. In fact, in early Sāṃkhya teaching we find many spirits, but no God. In the later philosophy of Yoga—a school related to Sāṃkhya, but exhibiting some distinct features—there exists as well a supreme Lord, who is Spirit and separate from nature. We find here a genuine personal God who can become the object of our worship. However, this is not a Lord who created the world, but simply a model of the practitioner of Yoga, the *yogin*, who is eternally separate and has never mistaken himself for the object of experience.[37]

While the *Bhagavad Gītā* reflects both Sāṃkhya metaphysics and Upanishadic monism, Sāṃkhya dualism seems to predominate.[38] The *Bhagavad Gītā* is engaged in a polemic—a revolutionary redefinition of many of the old Brahmanical ideals—and responds to the challenge of sectarian movements such as Buddhism and Jainism as well.[39] The setting of the text is a battlefield; Arjuna, the great archer of the warrior class, turns to Krishna, his charioteer, seeking wisdom moments before the battle is to begin. Arjuna is engaged in a clan war, torn between his duty (*dharma*) as a warrior to fight the battle and his duty to his family not to kill his own kin. Arjuna knows Krishna simply as his charioteer; as the text progresses, Krishna reveals that he is in fact an incarnation of the god Vishnu. At play are two ideals. The older ideal is one of ascetic renunciation, the steep path of knowledge and realization of identity between *ātman* and *brahman*; the new ideal entails a new definition of *karma yoga*, the discipline (*yoga*) of work or action (*karma*). The original context of the term *karma* was Vedic sacrifice; the path of action (*karma-mārga)* entailed offering of the prescribed sacrifices.[40] The *Bhagavad Gītā* creates a new path of *karma yoga*: action without attachment to result, desireless action (*niṣkāma karma*).[41] This is linked with the *yoga* of devotion, in which we dedicate all our actions to the object of our devotion, Lord Krishna.

The *Bhagavad Gītā* in fact teaches three practical paths to realization.[42] The first is the discipline of knowledge (*jñāna* or *sāṃkhya yoga*). As Krishna presents it in the second teaching of the *Gītā*, this is knowledge that our Self is separate from nature and does not perish.[43] Arjuna need not fear killing his kinsmen, since the soul does not die when the body dies. Arjuna must fulfill his sacred duty (*dharma*) as a warrior and fight the good fight, a righteous battle for the protection of virtue.

The second path is the path of action, *karma yoga*. The old ideal of renunciation is illusory; we are in danger of deluding ourselves that we have renounced our desires and attachments when in fact we are still very much possessed by them. If we sit in meditation preoccupied by sense objects, desires, anger, hatred, and jealousy, we have not achieved the goal of renunciation.[44] The idea that we can give up action is also a delusion. Everyone acts. Krishna himself acts; he has nothing to accomplish, but continues to act for the sake of the integration of the world. He must act as a role model, lest everyone cease to act and society disintegrate.[45] It is our nature as phenomenal beings to act. What we should realize is that it is simply the elements of our natural constitution that in fact perform action; we need not identify with the action that our nature undergoes. The *Gītā* teaches that nature is like a chain composed of three strands (*guṇas*): lucidity (*sattva*), passionate activity (*rajas*), and dull inertia (*tamas*).[46] When we engage in action, we should simply acknowledge that the senses act upon their sense objects and these strands act according to their nature.[47]

This is one facet of *karma yoga*; another is to let go of attachment to the results of action. Our goal is liberation from the cycle of rebirth (*saṃsāra*); what keeps us trapped in the cycle of *saṃsāra* is the results of our actions. All actions, including good actions, produce consequences. The Upanishadic path of renunciation sought to minimize our karmic inheritance by severely limiting our actions. A more effective way, argues the *Gītā*, is to not identify ourselves as the doer and thus to renounce the reward of the action. If I am the witness and not the doer, and if I let go of attachment to any reward, the action ceases to be *my* action. I accrue no *karma*, and thus do nothing to chain myself to the cycle of rebirth.[48] This teaching entails a radical redefinition of renunciation. True renunciation, argues the *Gītā*, is not to renounce all action, but to renounce all rewards—to remain in the world, unaffected by one's actions.[49]

The third discipline or yoga creates an even more radical revolution. This is the discipline of devotion (*bhakti yoga*), a path that opened the way for a broader, egalitarian ideal.[50] No longer does one need to be a Brahmin, practicing an arduous ascetic path of renunciation or the steep, elite path of learning the Vedas and realizing oneness with the All. Any offering to Krishna—be it as simple as a flower or a fruit—will be accepted.[51] Krishna is a personal deity who grants grace to his devotees, even overcoming the law of *karma*.[52]

The path of devotion is thus linked in the *Gītā* to the path of action. Not only can we renounce the results of our actions; we can dedicate them to the personal God Krishna.[53] Knowledge is similarly redefined, from knowledge of the identity of *ātman* and Brahman to knowledge of the personal god Krishna.[54] The *Gītā* goes so far as to argue that the personal God is higher than the Unmanifest *brahman*. It is relationship with a personal God that brings supreme happiness; the *Gītā* raises this personal relationship over impersonal knowledge of the All that is so highly valued in Upanishadic culture. It eschews the path to the Unmanifest *brahman* as needlessly steep and arduous.[55] Why pursue the elite path of knowledge of the Unmanifest, when there is a personal Lord who will rescue us from the ocean of sorrow?[56]

How can we summarize the teachings of the Upanishads and the *Gītā* in light of our theme of God and the good? For both the Upanishads and the *Gītā*, the goal to be pursued in life is liberation from *saṃsāra*, the cycle of birth and death. In the early Upanishads, liberation is attained through knowledge of the identity of one's inner self, the *ātman*, with the cosmic principle, *brahman*. In the later Upanishads, there develops a devotional theism to a personal God. Liberation is then redefined to mean abiding with the object of our devotion.[57]

The *Gītā* reflects this devotional ideal. The *Gītā* is engaged in a redefinition of older Upanishadic models that stressed renunciation of engagement in the world. The new ideal of *mokṣa* is not achieved by striving to accrue no *karma* through inaction. Rather we may be engaged actors who maintain our stance as a nonattached witness. Liberation in the *Gītā* is thus portrayed as being in the world, but not of it.[58] We act, fulfilling our responsibility to maintain the social order, but realize at the same time that we are not in fact the doer. We identify with the eternal witness, seeing the qualities of nature acting upon one another:[59]

> Abandoning attachment to fruits of action, always content,
> independent
> He does nothing at all, even when he engages in action. (4.20)

This way of looking at the human self is quite foreign to modern Western consciousness. We are used to identifying ourselves as the agent of action; the concept of nonattachment strikes us as a way of being uninvolved with the world. There is a strand of modern Hindu thinkers who read the tradition in a different way. They look to Mohandas Gandhi as a model of *karma yoga*, someone very much involved in this world and yet looking to Lord Krishna's teachings in the *Bhagavad Gītā* for inspiration. This is illustrated well in the following anecdote about Gandhi:

> For me, Gandhi is the perfect example of the statement that a person filled with the love of god, practicing the presence of God, never acts at all. Once when I went to Gandhiji's ashram, as I walked about in the neighborhood of his little cottage, I saw the unending stream of political leaders from Britain and India who came to him throughout the day. I was wondering how he was able to bear the pressure of these significant interviews which would change the relations of two great countries, and in the evening, I expected to see a tired, irascible, very impatient man coming out. Instead I saw a smiling figure who looked as if he had been playing bingo with children all day. I could not believe my eyes, because I was used to the idea that if we work eight hours we should be tense and ready to be irritated by anybody who tries to be nice to us. But he was completely untouched by his action.
>
> Every day in our work, as long as it is not at the expense of others, we can learn to avoid tension and pressure when attending to us the most challenging tasks that life may bring us. For most of us, tension has become a badge of action. In fact, we usually expect someone who has engaged in intense action during the day to complain about his ulcer. Tension need not accompany action; we can act free from any tension, any movement in the mind, any ripple of consciousness. Once Gandhi was asked by Western friends, "Mr. Gandhi, you have been working fifteen

hours a day for fifty years for these helpless millions of India. Why don't you take a long holiday?" Gandhi replied, "I am always on holiday."[60]

The *Gītā* thus suggests that when we let go of attachment to the results of action, and especially when we surrender them to the divine, we are freed from the karmic bonds of our actions and can even achieve liberation through our actions.[61] Similarly, we are used to identifying with our joys and sorrows. The *Gītā* asks us to step back and discover a joy that is deeper than elation. It suggests that elation and depression are mutually entailing pairs of opposites, whereas the goal of the practitioner of *yoga* is to find a joy that transcends these distinctions. When asked whether he was excited about the prospect of his upcoming presidency, John F. Kennedy was reputed to say, "Excited? No. Interested? Yes."[62] The mature, reflective way of living suggested by the *Gītā* is to take intense interest in our lives, while at the same time taking the stance of Krishna: I am the actor who never acts.[63] We can be fully engaged and interested, while not suffering from the intense dramas of pleasure and pain.

The *Gītā* is thus engaged in a redefinition of *yoga*. Whereas the earlier tradition associated yogic discipline with the renunciation of action, sitting in certain postures, and meditation, the *Gītā* introduces the revolutionary discipline of *karma yoga*, defining *yoga* as evenness of mind and skill in actions.[64] The *Gītā* thus argues that evenness of mind toward success and failure is actually the most effective way of acting.[65] When we are involved in the action itself rather than the results, we lose ourselves in the action and begin to act with the effortless ease described by the *Gītā* as *karma yoga* and the *Tao Te Ching* as *wu-wei*.[66]

The Good for the Hindu tradition is *mokṣa*, freedom or liberation, which is defined in various ways. Liberation is depicted either as achieving unity with the All, or as eternal abiding with Krishna or any personal God with whom we are in loving relation. The Good may be achieved by an integrated path of disciplines, including deep, existential knowledge of who we really are, meditative practice, disciplined action, and purity of devotion.

# 6

# Compassion, Wisdom, Awakening

THE WAY OF BUDDHISM

BUDDHISM GREW up against the background of the culture of Hinduism. In the sixth century there was much discontent with the old Brahmanical system. Economic prosperity produced wealthy priestly and warrior classes; camps of teachers known as *śramaṇas* were set up along the Ganges River, and these were the scene of lively debates on philosophical and religious questions. One prominent group, the Jains, taught that every living being contains a *jīva*, a soul or life principle, that undergoes a round of birth and death. Jainism emphasized stringent austerities such as fasting, pulling out one's hair, vegetarianism, and complete nonviolence, so that no negative *karma* would be created. It is from among this religious, social, and economic ferment that Buddhism arose.[1]

## EARLY (THERAVADA) BUDDHISM

Prince Siddhartha ("One who achieves his goal"), who would become the Buddha, was a prince of the Shakya clan and hence known by the honorific *Śākyamuni* ("sage of the *Śakyas*"). Western and Indian scholars date his life to 566–466 or 563–483 BCE, while according to Sri Lankan and East Asian Buddhists he might have lived a much earlier (624–544 BCE), and Japanese scholars, using Chinese and Tibetan texts, date him later (448–368 BCE). He lived in a kingdom in what is now Nepal.[2]

The legend of his birth and early life tells that astrologers predicted that he would be either a great king or a great religious teacher. His father, the king, wanted to prevent his becoming a spiritual leader and world renouncer and thus tried to shield him from the problems of the world. He secluded him in a palace, where he grew up amid worldly pleasures and delights. At the age of twenty, Gautama (the prince) became discontent and curious about the outside world, and ventured on four chariot rides, during which he beheld what are known as the four visions or sightings. On the first ride out, he saw an old person for the first time, and was told by his charioteer that old age befalls everyone. On the second ride, he saw a sick person. On the third journey, he saw a corpse. In this way he learned of the great ills of the world: old age, sickness, and death. On the fourth chariot ride, he saw a wandering religious ascetic, and took this as a sign that he should leave the worldly life of luxury in search of spiritual liberation.

Siddhartha left his wife and child and over the next six years engaged in the religious practices of his time, including fasting and asceticism. When he became so hungry that he could not meditate, he decided that asceticism is self-defeating. He ate some rice and, seating himself under the *Bo* or *Bodhi* tree (the tree of Awakening), awakened to a new vision of existence. He thus became the Buddha—the one who is awake. Freed from *karma*, he was no longer subject to rebirth. His initial impulse was to remain silent, as he doubted whether others would understand the profound truth he had witnessed. And yet out of compassion for those suffering, he chose to reveal his teachings to others, who became his disciples, the beginnings of the Buddhist community (*saṅgha*). From this arose the three jewels or treasures of Buddhism, affirmed in three "refuges." To become ordained as a Buddhist monk or to acknowledge one's faith as a Buddhist lay person, one asserts "I take refuge in the Buddha; I take refuge in the *dharma* (the Buddhist teaching); I take refuge in the *saṅgha* (the community of Buddha's disciples)."[3]

Buddhist teachings were at first transmitted orally and formulated in teaching devices. Certain core sermons attributed to the Buddha were transmitted in what came to be known as the Four Noble Truths—actually, the four truths for nobles (*ārya*)—and they taught what are known as the three marks of existence.[4] The first truth is that all of life is *dukkha*. Conventionally translated as "suffering," the term conveys much more: unsatisfactoriness, frustration, impermanence. The image used is a wheel off its axle, or a bone dislocated from its socket. Things are just not quite right. The second truth is the arising of *dukkha*. Unsatisfactoriness is caused by desire (lit. "thirst"; *taṇhā*) or craving. The third truth is the good news: there is a cessation, extinction (*nirodha*) of suffering. The image is the extinguishing of a flame. The fourth truth is the path or way (*mārga*): the eightfold noble path, whose components are right understanding, right thought, right speech, right action, right livelihood, right effort, right mindfulness and right concentration. The path is also divided into the three disciplines: ethical conduct (*sīla*); mental discipline (*samādhi*); and wisdom (*paññā* or *prajñā*).[5]

What is the connection between the first and second truths? Why does unsatisfactoriness lead to thirst or craving? The three marks of existence flesh out the understanding of *dukkha*. The first mark of existence is impermanence (*anitya*; *anicca*). All things are constantly changing, eluding our grasp. We become attached to things, people, and pursuits that we love, but they change. The person we love develops new interests; the pursuit that gave us such joy no longer holds our attention. All of us are subject to old age, sickness, and death—no one escapes the continual process of aging and change. And that is why thirst or craving leads to suffering. There is a curious phenomenon about desire: whenever we satisfy a desire, we create a desire; desire and disappointment go hand in hand. The nature of desire is to trick us: it gives us a strong message that if we just satisfy the desire of the moment—to buy that new device of technological wizardry, to attract the attention of the new person in whom we are interested, to find the book or film we have so assiduously been hunting—we will be happy. But if we observe our response carefully, we notice a slight sense of disappointment the minute our desire is fulfilled—a sinking feeling that this was not the promised deliverer of the happiness we crave.

Desire always leads to disappointment. Even if we experience joy at the initial fulfillment of desire, the delight doesn't last. All things change; our feelings change. And our desire nature therefore must seek new and greater objects to fulfill its quest. Thus the first mark of existence, impermanence, leads to the second: frustration (*dukkha*). Frustration is the nature of existence because all things are impermanent and changing; we crave and grasp, but no sooner do we grasp something than we discover that the happiness we seek still eludes us.

Finally, all things are characterized by the lack of a permanent identity—literally "no self" (*anatta; anātman*).[6] To understand this last mark of existence—the most challenging teaching of Buddhism—we return to the Upanishads. Buddhism shares much with its parent tradition of Hindu thought.

Both traditions describe all phenomenal reality as changing. However, Upanishadic thinkers posited that behind this changing phenomenal world is an eternal, unchanging reality, *brahman*, which is the Self (*ātman*) of the universe. Notice that "self" here is not only a quality of human entities; *brahman* is known as the Real of the real, the self of all entities and indeed of the universe itself.[7] And this Self, we have seen, is described by three qualities: existence, awareness, and joy. Teachers in the Hindu tradition insist that there is something that can bring us permanent, abiding joy—discovery of the *ātman*. As Śaṅkara's disciple said: "Now finally and clearly, I know that I am the *ātman*, whose nature is eternal joy. I see nothing, I hear nothing, I know nothing that is separate from me."[8] The discovery of our true divine nature brings abiding joy because joy is the very nature of our being.

The Buddha agrees with Hindu thought that all things in the phenomenal world are impermanent and changing. He differs from the Upanishads in one key view, however: he suggests that the Self or *ātman* posited by the Hindus is just another attachment—a concept created by the mind to give humans comfort.

How does such a concept arise? The Buddhist analysis of the human being gives us a clue. In a conversation with a wandering monk, King Nāgasena offers the example of a chariot. A chariot cannot be analyzed into any of its several components: it is not the seat, nor the wheel, nor the body alone; rather, all these components working together give the illusion of something called a chariot.[9] Similarly, we arrive at the notion of a person from the interaction of our various activities. The Buddha termed these *skandhas*, "bundles of energy": bodily phenomena, feelings, labeling or recognizing, volitional activities, and consciousness.[10]

What we notice immediately is the different analysis and evaluation of consciousness. For Hindus, consciousness is independent of the body; it is pre-bodily. The mind is an instrument or tool of consciousness; consciousness sees through the eyes, hears through the ears, thinks through the mind, but can do all this without the bodily organs. That is why the Upanishads call the *ātman* "the ear of the ear, the eye of the eye."[11] It is consciousness that sees, hears, and knows; the mind can only think because the light of awareness shines through it, like a store manikin that comes to life when the energy of electricity gives it animation. We are animated not only by *prāṇa*, the vital breath or life force, but by the *ātman* itself, which, being *brahman*, is existence, consciousness, and joy. Joy and awareness are our very being.

Not so for Buddhism. Buddhists maintain that consciousness is simply one of the five aggregates, bundles of energy (*skandhas*) whose interaction gives us a sense of self. However, when we analyze these interacting streams of energy, the mysterious self we think ourselves to be is nowhere to be found. Just as the chariot is not the wheel, the seat, or the axle, so we are not our thoughts, our feelings, our bodily sensations, or even our consciousness. In fact, Buddhism analyzes consciousness as arising with its objects. When light hits the organ of the eye, there is visual consciousness, when sound hits the ear, there arises auditory consciousness. There may even be a basic sense of being aware that coordinates these various conscious sensations. Nevertheless, consciousness is conditioned by its objects.[12] For Buddhism—as for many contemporary cognitive scientists—consciousness is an epiphenomenon, a by-product of the body-mind complex, and not something independent or transcendent.

Consciousness is in fact merely one link in a complex chain of causation. What gives us the sense of a self is a chain or circle of causal continuity. All things in the world, according to Buddhism, are interdependent and mutually caused. The Buddha refused to answer questions about the beginning of world, or whether the world is eternal. Rather, he described all things as mutually conditioned. (1) Our ignorance of the truth of the way things are leads to (2) our volitional actions or *karma* formations, which lead to (3) the arising of a new individual "consciousness," which gives rise to (4) a new body-mind complex of mental and physical phenomena, which leads to (5) the basis of sensing, which conditions (6) sense impressions, which condition (7) conscious feelings or sensations, which condition (8) craving (desire, "thirst"), which leads to (9) clinging or grasping for things, which leads to (10) the process of "becoming" (the drive to be reborn), which leads to (11) rebirth, which leads to (12) decay, lamentation, pain, old age, and death, which lead back to (1) ignorance, and the circle continues. The good news is that the teachings of Buddhism allow us to break through this circle of causation. Through (1) cessation of ignorance, (2) volitional actions and *karma* formations cease, which allows the (3) body-mind complex to cease, and so on. *Karma* ceases; decay, lamentation, old age, and death cease; suffering is eliminated.[13]

Consciousness is thus mutually conditioned by matter, sensation, perceptions, and mental formations and cannot exist without them. What we call "I" or "the self" is only a convenient label or name given to the working together of these five bundles. One thing conditions the appearance of another in a chain of causes and effects, but there is nothing permanent underlying these events that can be called a self. When these all work together, we get the idea of an "I" or a self. This idea of self is itself just a concept or mental formation. Buddhists don't deny that we experience ourselves as selves, nor do they deny our everyday experience of causal continuity. Fishes don't wake up one day as elephants; there are patterns of causal connectedness. That is what persons are: patterns of regularity. We habitually respond to the world in certain ways; this gives us the sense of being the kind of person we think we are. But in fact, they argue, if we analyze our experience, we discover that there is no single self to whom all these experiences refer. There is a continuity between the self you were in high school and the person you are today, but there is no permanent unchanging essence to whom all these experiences happen.[14]

The sense of self is so basic to our Western culture that this is a hard concept for Westerners to grasp. The writings of American Buddhist teacher Pema Chödrön can help us understand the teaching of no-self in contemporary terms. Chödrön traces her awakening to Buddhism to the day her husband came home and with no warning, unceremoniously informed her that he was having an affair and wanted a divorce. She writes:

> I remember the sky and how huge it was. I remember the sound of the river and the steam rising up from my tea. There was no time, no thought, there was nothing—just the light and a profound, limitless stillness. Then I regrouped and picked up a stone and threw it at him.
>
> When anyone asks me how I got involved in Buddhism, I always say it was because I was so angry with my husband. The truth is that he saved my life. When that marriage fell apart, I tried hard—very, very hard—to go back to some kind of comfort, some kind of security, some kind of familiar resting place. Fortunately for me, I could never pull it off. Instinctively I knew that annihilation of my old dependent, clinging self was the only way to go.[15]

Chödrön sheds light on the teachings of no-self and the three marks of existence. Introspection led her to realize that nothing is static; our moods shift, life goes up and down. The noble truths teach us that it is not because we are getting things wrong; this is simply the way things are. The problem is only that we resist the facts of life. Once we accept that we win some and we lose some, that everyone gets older and loses the physical vibrancy of youth, that aging, sickness, and death are inevitable, our experience of life's changes is no longer as frustrating. We soften toward life when we realize that this is just how life is.[16]

The second mark of existence, no-self, she calls egolessness. We needn't think of this as a saintly ideal. Rather, we should notice how much we lose from the fixed ideas we hold of ourselves. We cling to an old, outworn self-image: the "shy one," "the socially awkward one," "the athlete," "the computer geek." When new abilities and impulses awaken in us, we ignore them, tied as we are to the illusion that our self is static, fixed, and unchanging. Buddhism, she writes, teaches:

> The fixed idea that we have about ourselves as solid and separate from each other is painfully limiting. It is possible to move through the drama of our lives without believing so earnestly in the character that we play. That we take ourselves so seriously, that we are so absurdly important in our own minds, is a problem for us. We feel justified in being annoyed with everything. We feel justified in denigrating ourselves or in feeling that we are more clever than other people. Self-importance hurts us, limiting us to the narrow world of our likes and dislikes. We end up bored to death with ourselves and our world. We end up never satisfied.[17]

No-self or egolessness, then, is really about a flexible identity. We can be more fluid in our sense of who we are; the understanding of no-self can manifest as "inquisitiveness, adaptability, as humor as playfulness. It is our capacity to relax with not knowing, not figuring everything out, with not being at all sure about who we are—or who anyone else is either."[18] When new identities knock on our door, we can open ourselves to them—unlike the man who was so sure his son was dead that he refused to believe the boy knocking on his door was indeed his lost son. So, when growth and change surprise us, we can allow ourselves to evolve and grow.[19]

The third mark of existence is dissatisfaction (*dukkha*), the suffering we experience when we resist the impermanent, changing nature of reality. We suffer when we expect life to be regular and predictable. We forget to expect the unexpected. We suffer when we think that we are one, unchanging essence:

> We insist on being Someone, with a capital S. We get security from defining ourselves as worthless or worthy, superior or inferior. We waste precious time exaggerating or romanticizing or belittling ourselves with a complacent surety that yes, that's who awe are. We mistake the openness of our being—the inherent wonder and surprise of each moment—for a solid, irrefutable self. Because of this misunderstanding, we suffer.[20]

We become so used to avoiding suffering that we become unable to tolerate the least amount of discomfort. And thus begins a vicious circle:

> What begins as a slight shift of energy—a minor tightening of our stomach, a vague indefinable feeling that something bad is about to happen—escalates into addiction. This is our way of trying to make life predictable. Because we mistake what always results in suffering for what will bring us happiness, we remain stuck in the repetitious habit of escalating our dissatisfaction. In Buddhist terminology this vicious cycle is called *saṃsāra*.[21]

Thus *saṃsāra* is not just the never-ending cycle of birth and death: it is also the experiential treadmill to which we consign ourselves. The good news is that seeing the three marks of existence has the paradoxical effect of freeing us. When we stop resisting the changing nature of reality, "we can stop harming others and ourselves in our efforts to escape the alternation of pleasure and pain. We can relax and be fully present for our lives."[22]

Chödrön thus translates the Buddhist vision into terms contemporary readers can understand. No-self is no longer primarily an ontological teaching about the nature of reality, but a practice, a different way of living in the world. It is a softening of the perception of what it is to be a human being. When we become less attached to a fixed, permanent identity, we can relax into a softness of being, a fluidity much like what we saw in the tradition of the *Tao Te Ching*.[23]

Chödrön interprets *saṃsāra* as the never-ending cycle of frustration in which we find ourselves. What then is *nirvāṇa*? Notwithstanding its adaptation as a word in contemporary English, *nirvāṇa* is a difficult concept for Westerners to grasp. It will be important for us to explore the concept in its ramifications in early and later Buddhism, for it is the key to understanding the Absolute and the good in Buddhist tradition.

First of all, we must realize that for the Buddhists, no-self is a universal characterization of reality. It is not just that humans do not have a permanent, fixed nature: nothing in the world has an independent, permanent identity. From an early sermon of the Buddha, we hear:

> The body, *Bhikkhus* [monks], is selfless. Were the body self, the body would not be subject to disease, and it would be possible in the case of the body to command: "Let my body be thus, let not my body be thus." . . . sensation is selfless, perception is selfless.[24]

Here we may hear a refutation of a notion in the Upanishads that the self is an inner controller. Our body is not in control of its own perceptions, therefore it is not a self. Consciousness too is subject to disease, he argues; we are not in full control of our consciousness. None of the five *skandhas* is a self, a permanent fixed identity that is in control of itself; all are subject to growth, decay, and death.[25]

The Buddha extends this analysis to all existents in the world:

> To what extent is the world called "empty," Lord?
>
> Because it is empty of self or of what belongs to self, it is therefore said: "The world is empty." And what is empty of self and of what belongs to self? The eye, material shapes, visual consciousness, impression on the eye—all these are empty of self and what belongs to self. So too are ear, nose, tongue, body and mind (and as above for the eye); they are all empty of self and of what belongs to self. Also that feeling which arises, conditioned by impression on the eye, ear, nose, tongue, body-mind, whether it is pleasant or painful or neither pleasant nor painful—that too is empty of self and of what belongs to self. Wherefore is the world called empty because it is empty of self and of what belongs to self.[26]

In early Buddhism, this vision led to the analysis of all reality into momentary events of existence called *dharmas*.[27] All of reality is an interconnected web of these momentary events.

What then is *nirvāṇa*? The image given by the Buddha is that of a flame. What fuels the fire of our existence is our desires. When the flame of existence is no longer fueled by our desires, the fire of existence goes out. This extinguishing of the fire of existence is *nirvāṇa*, extinction, cessation.[28] Indeed, in his very first sermon the Buddha taught that all is burning: "the eye is burning, visible forms are burning, the mind is burning. With what? Burning with the fire of lust, the fire of hatred, the fire of delusion, burning with birth, aging and death, with sorrows, with lamentations, with pains, with grief, with despair."[29]

Perhaps with this metaphor in mind, Richard King argues that the *skandhas*, the five bundles of energy into which the Buddha analyzed what we call "self," are actually an allusion to the bundles of fire sticks brahmanical priests used in the administering of their five ritual fire sacrifices. The Upanishads had already begun to allegorize the sacrifice as the internal experience of the human being: fire had become associated with the five breaths, and the fire sacrifice was interpreted by some as an inner process of control of the five breaths.[30] The Buddha, in contrast, denies that these inner processes constitute a human self. Thus the Buddha taught that we should declare with respect to each of the five bundles of energy: "This is not mine. I am not this, This is not my self." The five *skandhas* themselves are continuously transforming and thus do not represent an unchanging abiding self. In the Buddha's statement denying that the *skandhas* are the self, we may hear a refutation of the famous statement of the *Chāndogya Upanishad*: "That is Reality. That is the Self. And that's what you are!" To which the Buddha replies: "This is not mine. I am not this. This is not my self."[31]

What then is *nirvāṇa*? We can just as easily ask: where does a flame go when it goes out? If there were a fire in front of us, would we know it? Of course, and we would know what makes it burn: the fuel of grass and sticks. If it were put out we would also know why. Since the fire burns because of the fuel of grass and sticks, when it receives no more sustenance in the way of grass and sticks, lacking sustenance, it goes out. However, if we were asked in what direction the put out fire had gone—to the east, west, north, or south, it would be harder to answer. Where does a flame go when it goes out? The term "where" does not apply.[32] Just so, when someone has "*nirvāṇa*-d," extinguished or ceased, the question of where he or she goes or arises simply does not apply. But neither does "not arise" apply, nor both "arises" and "does not arise," nor neither "arises" nor "does not arise." When the fuel of existence is no longer fed by the fires of desire, greed, hatred, and jealousy it simply goes out.[33]

Is this a doctrine of nihilism or annihilation? The Buddha's words suggest otherwise. Some of his language is, to be sure, negative: "all material shapes, feelings, perceptions, constructions, consciousness by which a Truth-finder might be made known have been destroyed by him, cut off at the root, made like the stump of a palm-tree, so utterly done away with that they can come to no future existence. A Truth-finder is freed of the denotation of 'body,' and so on; he is profound, measureless, unfathomable, even like unto the great ocean."[34] The first part of the Buddha's statement seems entirely negative. All the bundles of energy that make up what we know as self have been destroyed; there is nothing to give fuel to future sensations and perceptions, when our desire, and greed, and grasping nature have been stilled. But is there simply nothing left—the complete snuffing out of the flame of existence? Note that the Buddha ends on an affirmative note: "A Truth-finder is freed of the denotation of 'body,' and so on; he is profound, measureless, unfathomable, even like unto the great ocean."

The Buddha goes further. At the end of the Pali canon there are recorded several inspired utterances regarding *nirvāṇa*. Here is one:

> There is, O monks, the unborn, ungrown, and unconditioned. Were there not the unborn, ungrown, and unconditioned, there would be no escape for the born, grown, and conditioned. Since there is the unborn,

> ungrown, and unconditioned, so there is escape for the born, grown, and conditioned.[35]

And another:

> There is, monks, a domain where there is no earth, no water, no fire, no wind, no sphere of infinite space, no sphere of nothingness, no sphere of infinite consciousness, no sphere of neither awareness nor non-awareness; there is not this world, there is no other world, there is no sun or moon. I do not call this coming or going, nor standing, nor dying, nor being reborn; it is without support, without occurrence, without object. Just this is the end of suffering.[36]

We see then that there is a positive dimension to the Buddha's statements about *nirvāṇa*, and that we must carefully distinguish between the several senses of *nirvāṇa* that emerge. Rupert Gethin points out that when English translations of Pali and Sanskrit texts have "he attains *nirvāṇa*," the Pali or Sanskrit idiom is usually a simple verb: he or she *nirvāṇa*-s, or *parinirvāṇa*-s. Gethin thus teases out three meanings of the term *nirvāṇa* in early Buddhist texts.

1. The first level of *nirvāṇa* is the event, the moment of awakening, what happens when the fires of greed, aversion, and delusion are blown out. This event is what happens when a person *nirvāṇa*-s or *parinirvāṇa*-s.
2. *Nirvāṇa* is also spoken of as the content of an experience, what the mind knows at awakening.
3. Finally, *nirvāṇa* is spoken of as the state or condition enjoyed by awakened beings after death.[37]

We have examined the first, the event of ceasing to fuel the flames of desire and delusion. After the defilements of greed, desire, and delusion have been rooted out, the Buddha continues to live in the world as other people do. However his or her "thoughts, words and deeds are completely free of the motivations of greed, aversion, and delusion, and motivated instead entirely by generosity, friendliness, and wisdom."[38] This stage is called *nirvāṇa* with remainder or residues. Eventually, when the remainder of life is exhausted, the person will die and "*parinirvāṇa*," or enter into final *nirvāṇa*, *nirvāṇa* without residues. Since there is nothing more to feed the flame of existence, the person will not be reborn.[39]

What is known at the moment of awakening, what is the content of the experience of *nirvāṇa*? Perhaps it is the unconditioned realm described in the inspired utterances. The Buddha refused to call *nirvāṇa* a state of existence, but also refuses to say it is non-existence. It is what one sees when one sees the four noble truths. Gethin writes:

> Thus in the moment of awakening when all craving and attachments are relinquished, one experiences the profoundest and ultimate truth about the world, and that experience is not of "a nothing"—the mere absence of greed, hatred, and delusion—but of what can be termed the "unconditioned."[40]

In refusing to characterize *nirvāṇa* as either existence or nonexistence, the Buddha refrained from putting forth a positive ontological doctrine. He sought to follow a middle path between annihilationism—the view that ultimate reality is a nothing, a void—and eternalism—the view that there is some reality that abides eternally, like the Hindu *ātman*. Thus the Buddha refused to answer the wanderer Vacchaggota's ontological questions: Is there a self? Is there not a self? The Buddha stood silent, so that he would side neither with the eternalists nor with the annihilationists. He could not answer that there is a self, because it was not in accordance with his knowledge that "all things are not-self." But if he would have answered that there is not a self, this would have confused him. "Was there not a formerly a Self for me? There is none now."[41]

The Buddha's teaching is thus subtle; he refuses to assert a positive view. He seeks to push his hearers to "see" the nature of reality as he himself has seen it. He similarly refuses to answer questions about whether the world is eternal or created, finite or infinite. These questions, he said, are not profitable. He has come simply to declare what is suffering, the cessation of suffering, and the method for the cessation of suffering.[42]

We have now outlined the views of early Buddhism. What can we assert with respect to the quest for God and the good? First, while Buddhists acknowledge the existence of "gods," these gods are much like the *devas* of Hindu tradition: phenomenal beings, who neither abide in nor have insight into the unconditioned realm of *nirvāṇa*. They too are in need of the insight into reality that the Buddha brings.

One of the most startling features of Buddhist teaching is that, like Taoism, Buddhism does not acknowledge a supreme God. But is there an Absolute? *Nirvāṇa* is unconditioned, and while the Buddha refuses to say that *nirvāṇa* exists, he also refuses to say that it does not exist. He is adamant that one not deny the reality of *nirvāṇa*. For if there were not an unborn, ungrown, and unconditioned, there would be no escape from the born, grown, and conditioned. *Nirvāṇa* is. It is not produced; it simply is.[43] Nor does *nirvāṇa* represent the annihilation of self, because there is no self to annihilate; it is the annihilation of the illusion of self. In the words of Walpola Rahula, *nirvāṇa* is "freedom from all evil, freedom from craving, hatred and ignorance, freedom from all terms of duality, relativity, time and space."[44]

Thus although early Buddhists do not talk about goodness per se nor use terms such as "Divinity" or "Absolute," Buddhism articulates a clear vision of the Good. What we would term the Good for Buddhism is *nirvāṇa*: a way of life characterized by flexibility, openness, wisdom, and compassion. One is no longer trapped by unending desire, hatred, and greed, fueled by the illusion that there is an unchanging self that can grasp onto permanent sources of happiness. From the Buddhist perspective, the Hindu teaching that there is an eternally abiding self is unhelpful and leads to all the evils in the world. The view that I am a "self" leads directly to selfishness; indeed, the notion of self is but an aspect of selfishness. I want to hold onto some part of the universe and grasp it as my own. We are all like the two-year-old who, having first learned the word "mine," uses it constantly to assert his or her possession of some part of the world. The toddler asserts a newfound sense of identity: mine, mine, mine!

When I discover and carve out an identity for myself, I have a desire to expand it to aggrandize myself: I am a student, a teacher, a folk dancer, a spiritual seeker or atheist, punk or Goth, athlete or social outcast. And this leads to my fear that not only my material possessions but my very sense of identity will be taken from me; I may even be driven to acts of violence to protect my persona. The notion of self is the cause of all our problems. As Steven Collins suggests and Gethin echoes, "the goal of the Buddhist path is to become a truly 'self-less person.'"[45]

But this need not mean being self-effacing and meek. Empirical accounts from the Buddha's time suggest that disciples of the Buddha radiate wisdom, compassion, and a sense of presence:

> When asked why his disciples, who lived a simple and quiet life with only one meal a day, were so radiant, the Buddha replied: "They do not repent the past, nor do they brood over the future. They live in the present. Therefore they are radiant.[46]

Buddhists assert that the illusion of self is distorting; when human beings discover who they really are—or are not—they radiate a presence and loving kindness that testifies to the truthfulness of this teaching, however difficult it may be to grasp theoretically.

*Nirvāṇa* is then a mode of being, but it is also an absolute; it functions the way concepts of both God and Good function in other cultures. Although the indescribable condition of *nirvāṇa* might seem far from the personal God of Western theism, we must remember that we also find highly nuanced concepts of God that share features with the unconditioned, unborn realm of *nirvāṇa*. Just as the Maimonidean believer awakens to a vision of a Necessary Existent that cannot fully be known—a vision that gives rise to love and awe—so the Buddhist seeker awakens to a vision of the unconditioned, which brings abiding peace.[47]

## MAHĀYĀNA VISIONS

Thus far we have set forth the view of what we can call early, or Theravada, Buddhism, the Buddhism that grew up in India and moved to Southeast Asia. The second step in our exploration is to look at the phenomena of Mahāyāna Buddhism. Theravada Buddhism exists today in the Southeast Asian countries: Vietnam, Sri Lanka, Thailand; Mahāyāna flourishes in East Asia: China, Japan, and Korea. Tibetan Buddhism is a third type, Vajrayāna, which shares some features with Mahāyāna. We will also look at the Engaged Buddhism developed by Thich Nhat Hanh, a Vietnamese Zen monk who teaches extensively in the West.[48]

Teachers of Mahāyāna, "the Great Raft," referred to early Buddhism by the pejorative term "Hinayāna"—"small or narrow raft." There are several related dimensions of the Mahāyāna school we will explore. First is the doctrine of Emptiness; second is the figure of the *Bodhisattva*.[49]

In early Buddhism all of existence is analyzed into droplets of experience known as *dharmas*. Early Buddhism asserts that all reality is constantly changing, and that each little droplet of experience flashes into and out of existence. Thus causality is analyzed as sequences of moments that give the illusion of causal continuity. Patterns of causality are just that—patterns of regularity: "this being, this arises." But there is no first cause; everything is mutually interconnected. This is known as the circle of conditioned genesis.[50]

Early Buddhist sutras describe reality using the language of emptiness:

> Suppose a person who was not blind beheld the many bubbles on the Ganges as they drove along. . . . After he had carefully watched them and examined them they would appear to him empty, unreal, and unsubstantial. In exactly the same way does the student of the Buddha behold all corporeal phenomena, sensations, perceptions, moods, and thoughts. . . . He watches them, examines them carefully; and, after carefully examining them, they appear to him empty, void and without a self.[51]

The Mahāyāna Perfection of Wisdom literature develops this insight. Even the teachings of Buddhism must be seen to be ultimately empty. Early Buddhism sought to free us from attachments, and thus urged us to see reality as a kaleidoscope of changing events, lacking all permanent identity. But of course with any ontological analysis, there is the danger of getting attached to the conceptual model itself. Whitehead called this the "fallacy of misplaced concreteness": we mistake our theories for actualities.[52] The Perfection of Wisdom literature applies this insight to all views, opinions, conceptual constructs, including those of Buddhism. Thus the Heart Sutra teaches that form is emptiness, emptiness is form.[53] Those who seek *nirvāṇa* are to be laughed at.[54] Even the insights of the Buddha—the four noble truths, the eightfold noble path—are true only on a conventional level; on an ultimate view they are empty. They are views, models, but we should not think that they point to an ultimate, self-existent reality. The ultimate reality of things is their emptiness.[55]

In the second century CE, the Indian Buddhist monk Nāgārjuna drew upon these insights to develop the theory of *Mādhyamaka*, the way of the Middle, showing that the theory of dependent origination is equivalent to emptiness. If all *dharmas*, the tiny moments of experience, arise in dependence on each other, then none can be said to have independent identity. All things are mutually causing; there is no self-established cause on which all else depends. However, Nāgārjuna notices that this analysis causes a problem for the notion of interdependent origination. How can one thing be dependent on another if that thing itself is dependent on another? If everything is empty of independent existence, we can't truly talk about dependence on another. First we must abandon the notion that anything (a *dharma*) possesses its own existence. Then we must abandon the view that it is dependent on another. Finally, we must be careful not to cling even to the notion of the emptiness of existents. We shouldn't speak as if Emptiness is a self-existent ontological reality; Candrakīrti compares this to someone who, when told that a merchant has nothing to sell, asks if he can buy some of that nothing. Emptiness—that's what I want! Emptiness, like the Upanishadic Self—becomes another substance to cling to.[56]

Nāgārjuna's caution is not just ontological; it has important consequences for our lives. The Buddhist path depends on the idea that we can change, that we can genuinely relieve our suffering. He argues that those who analyze reality into *dharmas* and claim that *dharmas* ultimately exist in themselves deny the possibility of change. For if a *dharma* exists in and of itself, it could never change; it would be itself forever. But if it was affected by something else, then it would cease to be itself.[57] In contrast, when we realize that things are empty of ultimate, self-existent identity, we realize that we have opened the door to true freedom: "everything is possible for someone for whom emptiness is possible."[58]

There are two points here: one about language, another about ontology. To say that something exists implies that it exists in and of itself forever. Thus we cannot assert things exist. Moreover, to assert that something exists dependent on another implies that that other thing is self-existent. Therefore the theory of interdependent origination ultimately implies emptiness; to speak of what exists or what does not exist is to err. The best is to do as the Buddha did—to use language and silence so that one does not assert an erroneous view of one's own.

But does this imply the emptiness even of the concepts of the Buddhist path? On a certain level, yes:

> There is no difference between *saṃsāra* and *nirvāṇa* and there is no difference between *nirvāṇa* and *saṃsāra*.[59]

Thus, Nāgārjuna establishes on a theoretical basis some of the paradoxical statements we find in Mahāyāna Buddhist texts:

> All things are the perfection of being, infinite perfection. . . . All things are enlightenment, for they must be recognized as without essential nature—even the five greatest sins are enlightenment, for enlightenment

> has no essential nature and neither have the five greatest sins. Thus those who seek for *nirvāṇa* are to be laughed at.[60]

How do we arrive at this insight? If all things are empty of substantial existence, there is nothing keeping us from *nirvāṇa* right now. The entire project of early Buddhism is thus recast. Early Buddhism suggested that this world of suffering is *saṃsāra*, the wheel of birth and death, and our goal is to achieve *nirvāṇa* and ultimately *parinirvāṇa*, final *nirvāṇa* after death, in which we do not need to be reborn. Indeed the Buddha himself has gone into final *nirvāṇa*.

But if all things are empty and we can realize *nirvāṇa* at any moment, there is no real difference between *saṃsāra* and *nirvāṇa*. *Nirvāṇa* is not another realm to which we need to escape to be freed from suffering. Rather, *nirvāṇa* can be realized in the here and now: *nirvāṇa* is a different way of experiencing this world. When we see the way things are, we have *nirvāṇa*-d; *nirvāṇa* is a different way of seeing.[61]

This leads us to perhaps the key doctrine of Mahāyāna Buddhism: the doctrine of the *Bodhisattva*. The ideal of Theravada Buddhism is the ideal of the *arhat*: the person who hears the teaching of the Buddha, practices it, and enters into *nirvāṇa*. There was an understanding, however, that even the historical Buddha *Śākyamuni* did not simply become enlightened in one lifetime and enter into *nirvāṇa*. Rather, he had become enlightened and took a vow to stay in *saṃsāra* and perfect his wisdom over many lifetimes. This path of vowing to stay in *saṃsāra* to work on the perfection of one's being is known as the *Bodhisattva* ideal. In Theravada Buddhism, it was seen as the exception to the rule; in Mahāyāna Buddhism, it became the noble aim to which all should aspire.[62]

The Mahāyāna vow goes further: one vows also to stay in *nirvāṇa* to work for the enlightenment of all beings. One does not forgo one's own enlightenment; one achieves enlightenment. But knowing that there is no ultimate difference between *saṃsāra* and *nirvāṇa*, one realizes that there is no rush to leave this world for *parinirvāṇa*. Through deep compassion, one can work for the enlightenment of all beings, realizing at the same time that there is no one to be enlightened, that all already are Buddha nature:

> A *Bodhisattva* resolves: I take upon myself the burden of all suffering . . . I do not turn or run away, do not tremble, am not terrified . . . do not turn back or despond. And why? . . . I have made a vow to save all beings.[63]

On the other hand:

> The Lord said: Someone who has set out in the vehicle of a *Bodhisattva* should think in this manner: "As many beings as there are in the universe of beings—egg born, born from a womb, moisture-born, or miraculously born—all these beings must I lead into that Realm of *nirvāṇa* which leaves nothing behind. And yet, although innumerable beings have thus been led to *nirvāṇa*, in fact no being at all has been led to *nirvāṇa*."[64]

The *Bodhisattva* thus realizes the emptiness of all things, that "all things are enlightenment, for they must be recognized as without essential nature. . . ."[65] One thus enters the path of the *Bodhisattva* knowing that all beings are already enlightened. Wisdom and compassion inspire the vow to help all beings realize this fact.

## ZEN BUDDHISM

One form of Buddhism that has become very popular in the West is Zen, a school of Mahāyāna Buddhism that arose in China, where it was known as Ch'an—a term derived from the Sanskrit *dhyāna*, which means "meditation"; the term "Zen" is its Japanese equivalent.

The traditional Buddhist account traces the Ch'an school back to *Śākyamuni* Buddha, who held up a flower before an assembly of his disciples. No one said a word until one student, the venerable Kashyapa, smiled. The Buddha saw that he had understood, and thus entrusted to him the transmission of the true teaching, the Buddhist *dharma*:

> A special tradition outside the scriptures
> No dependence upon words and letters
> Direct pointing at the human heart
> Seeing into one's own nature and the attainment of Buddhahood.[66]

Following the traditional account, the true *dharma* was transmitted for twenty-eight generations in India until Bodhidharma brought it to China in 520 CE and became the first patriarch there. The transmission continued to Hui-neng (638–713 CE), the sixth patriarch, whom we hear of in the Platform Sutra. Many historians doubt the existence of Bodhidharma, but recently scholars have discovered there was a somewhat later person named Bodhidharma, during the years 420–479 CE, who practiced meditation and taught Buddhist teachings based on the *Laṅkāvatāra Sūtra*.[67]

Scholars situate such a figure among the Buddhist meditation masters who wandered throughout China at that time.[68] While these early practitioners were wandering ascetics, during the time of the fourth and fifth patriarchs Ch'an meditation practitioners began to gather in monastic communities combining appropriation of Ch'an meditation with day-to-day household and agricultural work.[69]

According to Ch'an tradition, the Platform Sutra of the sixth patriarch tells the story of the split between the Northern and Southern schools of Ch'an, which was the result of their two conceptions of human nature and the nature of enlightenment. As Southern tradition portrays it, the Northern school conceived of ordinary human nature as defiled; thus a gradual meditation practice is needed to polish the mirror and restore its pristine purity. A representative of the Northern school, Shen-hsiu expressed this in his verse:

> The body is the *bodhi* tree [tree of enlightenment].
> The mind is like a bright mirror's stand.
> At all times we must strive to polish it
> And must not let dust collect.

Hui-neng, the representative of the Southern school, disputed this view through a sharply contrasting verse. The earliest texts of the Platform Sutra actually contain two versions of the verse:

> *Bodhi* originally has no tree.
> The mirror also has no stand.
> The Buddha-nature is always clean and pure
> Where is there room for dust?

. . . . . . . . .

> The mind is the *bodhi* tree.
> The body is the bright mirror's stand.
> The bright mirror is originally clear and pure.
> Where could there be any dust?

Later versions mediate between the two verses and add an even more striking third line:

*Bodhi* originally has no tree.
The bright mirror also has no stand.
Fundamentally there is not a single thing.
Where could dust arise?[70]

Ch'an tradition explicates these verses as illustrating the debate between gradual and sudden approaches to enlightenment. In contrast to Shen-hsiu's verse, which presents enlightenment as a gradual attainment achieved through active self-cultivation, Hui-neng depicts enlightenment as a total, instantaneous transformation. There is no substantial mind to be sullied and defiled; all is Buddha nature, always clean and pure. Rather than depicting mind as a mirror stand gathering dust, Hui-neng prefers the metaphor of a sun temporarily covered by clouds. The mind shines brightly even if we don't see it.[71]

These teachings may appear to be very abstract, but they led to quite concrete methods of practice. According to a traditional depiction presented by contemporary Zen teacher Thich Nhat Hanh, Ch'an Buddhism arose in response to what it perceived as a scholasticism that had pervaded Chinese Buddhism, which saw the rise of multiple new scriptures, complex metaphysical theories, and a growing distance from experience.[72] If we look at the progression of Buddhist thought, we can thus discern a series of critiques. Hindu thought posited an eternal *ātman*; Buddhism protested that the notion of an eternal Self is just another attachment of the mind, which finds terrifying the notion of an ever-changing reality, with nothing stable. Buddhist logic, in contrast, analyzed the basic constituents of reality as *dharmas*, tiny drops of experience. The Mahāyāna school responded that Buddhist logicians had simply created a new reified entity, once again trying to escape the fact that nothing in the world is permanent. Finally, the Ch'an/Zen movement, while considered a school of Mahāyāna, offers its own critique of Mahāyāna metaphysics. The goal of Zen is to get back to the experiential basis of Buddhism.

Thich Nhat Hanh is somewhat unique as a contemporary teacher of Zen; while the majority of Southeast Asian Buddhists belong to the Theravada tradition, he is a Vietnamese Zen monk. Exiled from Vietnam since 1966, he teaches what he calls Engaged Buddhism, originally in Vietnam and now in the West. In *Zen Keys: A Guide to Zen Practice*, he suggests that the Buddhist teaching of no-self was not meant to establish a view or doctrine of its own; it arose in response to the Hindu teaching of a permanent self or *ātman*. He describes even the central teaching of no-self as a teaching tool, what is known in Buddhist terminology as skillful means (*upāya*), a thunderclap meant to wake us up. "This self of which you speak, whether it is the great self or the small self, is only a concept that does not correspond to any reality."[73] The Buddhist teaching of no-self represents a critique of the Hindu notion of consciousness. Buddhists see blissful states arrived at in meditation as manifestations of the ordinary mind; they are "mind-created, mind-produced, mind-conditioned (*saṃkhata*)."[74] From the Buddhist point of view, one should not mistake blissful meditative states for a permanent divine self. The joy that Hindus call *ātman* is just another passing state, like other pleasant meditative experiences.

Zen encourages awakening, but awakening to what? To the reality of the present moment, says Thich Nhat Hanh. Enlightenment is not a mysterious state. He acknowledges that we can learn to realize the identity of ourselves and everything around us—when we drink tea, to become one with the tea. But true enlightenment is also to be able to see the wonderful variety of reality as it is:

> An awakened person lives in the material world the same as everyone else. When she sees a rose, she knows that it is a rose, like everyone else. But she is neither conditioned nor imprisoned by concepts. Concepts now become marvelous skillful means in her possession. An awakened person looks, listens, and distinguishes things, all the while being perfectly aware of the presence . . . that is the perfect and non-discriminative nature of everything. She sees deeply the nature of interbeing.[75]

Many Zen stories playfully poke fun at the seriousness with which so-called spiritual or pious people take themselves. Zen turns on its head spiritual goals such as getting rid of one's anger and desires.[76] One gets the sense in these iconoclastic tales that the goal of Zen is to fully experience what it is to be a human being. In Hinduism, we hear about *mokṣa*, a state of permanent liberation and bliss. In contrast, Zen teachers speak of moments of insight or enlightenment that are continually deepened by ongoing practice.[77] The goal is to continue to live as an ordinary person, but with a heightened sensibility and sensitivity:

> Before practicing Zen, rivers were rivers and mountains were mountains. When I began practicing Zen, I saw that rivers were no longer rivers and mountains were no longer mountains. Now I see once again that rivers are rivers and mountains are mountains.

The goal is to return to ordinary perception but with the freshness and clarity of the awakened mind.[78] A monk told Joshu, "I have just entered the monastery. Please teach me." Joshu asked, "Have you eaten your rice porridge?" The monk replied, "I have eaten." Joshu said, "Then you had better wash your bowl." At that moment the monk was enlightened.[79] The enlightened life is one in which every action is done with a heightened awareness and sensitivity. Before enlightenment, chop wood and carry water. After enlightenment, chop wood and carry water.

Zen is known also for its unorthodox teaching techniques, including the use of *kōans*, paradoxical riddles meant to jar us from habitual ways of thinking. What is the sound of one hand clapping? Does a dog have Buddha nature? What was the shape of your face before your parents were born? *Kōans* were traditionally given in private meetings between a master and student; after long periods of pondering the riddle, the student would return with his or her answer. The answer might be given by the student not in the form of a conceptual statement but a phrase or gesture indicating that the student has transcended the dualistic way of attacking conceptual problems. The answer to the *kōan* lies not in the riddle but in the student.[80] Zen masters are known also to shout at or beat their students with sticks to awaken their understanding.[81]

Zen is sometimes irreverent, even toward the concepts of Buddhism. This is because one can become overly attached and cling to Buddhist concepts such as emptiness and no-self.[82] To attach oneself to these concepts is to miss the point, which is to live life *directly*, rather than through the filter of complex metaphysical assertions. Enlightenment is not a discourse on the subtleties of fine tea, but drinking the tea with pleasure and awareness. Enlightenment is a way of seeing and living everyday life.[83]

There is also another way that Mahāyāna teachers, including those of the Ch'an/Zen school, talk about enlightenment; they refer to Buddha nature or Buddha mind, the mind of awakening in which we all participate. Thus while on the one hand, Zen masters insist that enlightenment is simply a way of seeing everyday reality, on the other, they at times speak of Buddha mind in ways reminiscent of an absolute like the Hindu *ātman*:

> Buddhas and living beings participate in the same pure and unique mind. There is no separation concerning this mind. Since time immemorial this mind has never been created or destroyed; it is neither green nor yellow; it has neither form nor aspect; it is neither being nor non-being; it is neither old nor new, neither short nor long, neither big nor small. It

> transcends all intellectual categories, all words and expressions, all signs and marks, all comparisons and discriminations. It is what it is; if one tries to conceive it one loses it. Unlimited like space, it has no boundaries and cannot be measured. This mind is unity and thusness. It is Buddha.[84]

However Thich Nhat Hanh insists—contrary to what might appear at face value—that "true nature, or true mind, is not what we would call an idealistic, ontological entity. It is reality itself."[85] The true nature of reality is not a world built of concepts or discovered by the conceptualizing mind: "The only way to realize this mind of unity and thusness, which is also called true mind, is to return to ourselves and see into our true nature."[86] To discover our true mind is simply to see with clarity. Buddha nature is just the way things are; all beings have the capacity to attain enlightenment.

What then is the Good in the Mahāyāna and Zen traditions? The Good is to realize our original Buddha nature and to live from this awakened state. It is to live with wisdom and compassion, and to see clearly with an awakened mind. Finally, the Good is to share this wisdom and compassion by dedicating oneself to the awakening of all beings.

# 7

# The Good Is That to Which All Things Aim

## ARISTOTLE ON GOD AND THE GOOD

WE HAVE said that the Upanishads resemble in certain respects the philosophy of Plato, while the *Bhagavad Gītā* resembles that of Aristotle, who, like the *Gītā*, lays out a practical road of moral virtue. Thus students of Aristotle's *Nicomachean Ethics* usually walk away aware of the doctrine of the mean, the notion that the path to happiness is one of following the middle way between extremes. However, this practical aspect of Aristotle's *Ethics*, while it certainly takes up the bulk of his discussion, is only one dimension of Aristotle's thought. In fact, there is a deep divide in Aristotle between the practical, social realm of ethics and the call of the contemplative life. This cuts to the heart of Aristotle's conception of who we are as human beings, our role in the universe, our highest aspirations, and how we can live these aspirations in our everyday earthly life.

In short, the key question of Aristotle's *Ethics* is this: is the goal of life the active, engaged life in society, or the contemplative ideal of the scholar? And if contemplation is our purpose in life, should all our endeavors be aimed toward it? Or should contemplation be balanced and integrated within a life of action? Another way of articulating the question is this: Does complete happiness lie in developing *all* our potential, or is there some one dimension of life that is so important that it should color our whole lives? Is the ideal life a completely focused life, or an exquisitely balanced life? Our discussion of Aristotle will aim at exploring and resolving this tension.

## ARISTOTLE'S NOTION OF THE GOOD AND THE MORAL LIFE

As we have seen, Plato's ideal is the Form of the Good; knowledge of the Good is the ultimate aspiration of the philosophical life. In contrast to Plato's wholly abstract, metaphysical Form of the Good, Aristotle's good in the *Nicomachean Ethics* appears to be concrete and this-worldly.[1] He denies that there is one universal good that is held in common by all arts and sciences. Every human pursuit has its own form of excellence. A good is that to which each thing aims; the good of a thing is not an abstract quality of excellence but its own unique goal. A carpenter seeks excellence in carpentry; a cobbler seeks excellence in the craft of making shoes. There is not one art of the good that extends to every human pursuit.[2]

While there is not one single good for all endeavors, human beings do share a common trait on which their good is based—reason. Human beings thus have a good unique to ourselves that arises from the quality that makes us specifically human. Since it is reason that differentiates us from all other species, our unique excellence must stem from this specific difference.[3] However, we can exercise reason in two domains. We have a purely theoretical intellect, one that has the capacity to think about the unchanging principles of nature—the principles of mathematics, biology, physics, and metaphysics.[4] But reason also has a practical dimension. To understand these two aspects of reason, we must grasp Aristotle's psychology. For Aristotle, the human being is a hylomorphic unity, that is, an integrally connected unity of body and soul. The soul has a nutritive aspect, which it shares with plants. This part is present even when we are asleep; our autonomic nervous system continues to function. Our heart beats, we breathe, the blood in our veins continues to circulate. Our soul also has an aspect that we share with animals; we desire things, we have appetites for food, drink, sex, and general pleasure.[5] The pleasure-seeking principle is present in animals; it can even be argued that plants have a tropic principle, growing toward the sun.

When we look at the human rational function, we find two dimensions. While there is an aspect of our reason that is purely theoretical—directed to abstract principles of nature—there is also an aspect that is turned to our human condition. The desiring part of our soul, the part that we share with animals, can also respond to reason. It is debatable whether a hungry dog or cat can tame its desire for food or drink. As humans, we can learn to defer gratification, to train our body and emotions to act according to what is in harmony with our values.[6] Our physical and emotional natures can respond to what our mind decides is good for us.

Along with theoretical intellect there is thus also a practical, moral intellect, and alongside intellectual virtues stand moral virtues. Intellectual virtues aid us in our purely mental pursuits; we are aided in our intellectual creativity and achievement by originality of thought, the capacity to deduce conclusions quickly, depth of insight, and sound judgment.[7] Moral virtues are of an entirely different nature. Moral virtues have to do with training our habits of feeling and responding; morality pertains to how we habitually respond to certain stimuli and situations. If we find ourselves in an unfamiliar context, do we respond fearfully or with courage? When asked to go out on a limb for a colleague, do we do so grudgingly or with a willing heart? Do we respond to someone who has wronged us with a desire for vengeance, or with compassion and forgiveness? These responses may seem automatic; in fact they can be nurtured and developed.

Socrates argued that virtue is a matter of wisdom. Courage is knowing what is and is not to be feared;[8] generosity is a matter of knowing what is appropriate to give. How then does one account for someone who knows what is good and fails to act upon it? Does knowledge automatically lead to doing the right thing? Aristotle argues that it does not, that we have stubborn patterns of behavior that don't necessarily respond to simple insight. What is needed is behavioral training. Thus the Socratic approach is akin to insight-oriented psychology, while Aristotle's approach is that of behaviorists, who insist that change comes only with practice. The good news is that actions create our character; we become what we do.[9] If we force ourselves to practice an action, however difficult or challenging, the habit becomes fixed in our character. We become a compassionate person by practicing deeds of loving-kindness.

The overall principle of morality is the rule of the mean. But this is not an arithmetic mean. We cannot simply calculate a midpoint in any situation and assume that this is the ideal. The mean is situational, and it is constantly moving.[10] Aristotle derives his view of the mean both from nature and from art. The successful work of art is one in which there is neither too little nor too much. Nature too knows just the right proportion.[11] Is this simply a truism? Perhaps Aristotle is actually introducing a subtle teaching about sensitivity and awareness. Aristotle wants us to become aware of the virtues we saw alluded to in the *Tao Te Ching*: knowing when to stop, sensing just how much to give, intuiting when to move forward and when to hold back. Morality is a precious art of attunement, rather than a science.[12]

I suggested that Aristotle's philosophy in certain ways resembles that of the *Bhagavad Gītā*. In the *Gītā*, each of the *yogas* aims at the goal of reaching liberation or abiding with Krishna. What is the ultimate aim in the philosophy of Aristotle? Aristotle asserts that all would agree that the human good or aim is *eudaimonia*, although people disagree on what this means. The Greek term is often translated as "happiness," although that word may mislead us. Some contemporary scholars render the term as "well-being," or "human flourishing." I sometimes suggest "human fulfillment," because this phrase captures two aspects of *eudaimonia*. Aristotle believes that to be truly fulfilled as human beings, we must realize our moral, intellectual, and spiritual potential. We will always feel vaguely dissatisfied if we know that we have not fulfilled our promise. Gnawing at us is a sense that we could have lived more creative and compassionate lives, that we could have more fully grasped the beauty of the world and expressed our unique vision. Aristotle's notion of fulfillment is related to his nuanced view of pleasure, to which we will return. It is the deep satisfaction that we have made the most of what we have been given.

This is in keeping with Aristotle's teleological view of the universe—the notion that all things in nature aim at some *telos*, or end—and what has been called his moral perfectionism, which can be defined as follows.[13] Aristotle believes that all beings have an intrinsic, essential nature that makes them what they are; all natural beings have a specific function or work (*ergon*) and a purpose (*telos*). It is the *telos* of an acorn to become an oak tree; the purpose of the oak tree is to flower as the most perfect oak it can be. For Aristotle, although the universe is uncreated, purpose pulsates throughout. Within the seed lies the potential to flower. It is bursting with natural creativity; it wants to fully realize itself as a natural being. Nature is alive with purpose; purpose is not something imposed from the outside by a creating God or Platonic Demiurge, nor is it superimposed by human reason.[14] Aristotle, ever the empirical scientist, examines natural beings and sees them as manifesting a natural desire to grow, develop, and perfect themselves.[15]

Aristotle sees human beings, too, as fundamentally biological entities, although crowned with reason. In book 1 of the *Ethics*, he thus asks plaintively: does everything in nature have a purpose and human beings lack one? He answers that we, too, must have a *telos* based on who we are as natural entities. Our purpose must be based on our essence, that which makes us essentially human. It cannot be simply the life of nutrition and growth—the life of plants—or the life of sense-perception, which characterizes animals. It must be that which makes us specifically who we are as human beings. Since Aristotle believes that our essence as human beings is our capacity to reason, he sees our function as the life of activity (*energeia*) of the reasoning part of the soul. Our good as human beings is the activity of our soul expressing its unique human virtue or excellence.[16]

Aristotle thus insists that the human good, well-being, or flourishing is an *activity* of living and not a capacity or a state. The real gift of humanness lies in our ability to project an aim and to work toward it, to envision for ourselves a good and to become it. Virtue is a capacity to act in ways we value and find appropriate; our happiness lies in activating that capacity. The ethical life thus involves training ourselves to be in a receptive state, so that when a critical situation arises, we can respond as we would like. Our partner wakes us in the middle of the night not feeling well. Have we trained ourselves to respond in caring and helpful ways, even though we would rather go back to sleep? If we have practiced acts of generosity and kindness, it will be second nature for us to do the right thing. Aristotle sees training in virtue as a matter of building character traits that will be there for us when we need them. Courage, resilience, optimism—such virtues can give us the strength to survive crisis and tragedy, breakdown of health, loss of loved ones, and loss of ideals.[17]

*Eudaimonia* is thus neither a capacity for virtue nor a static state of fulfillment; *eudaimonia* is a way of living creatively. It is only when a person's life is complete that we can judge whether the life was *eudaimon*; flourishing is, for Aristotle, a quality of *lives*, rather than people.[18] It is like a drama or film; we cannot know whether a film is a successful piece of art until we have seen it to completion. Just so, we don't know what a character has made of him- or herself until we can see that life as a whole. A person may redeem herself after having abandoned her children; she may find them later in life and repair the broken relationship. A businessperson may leave a successful but unhappy career to find true expression as an artist; a world-weary politician may discover that the thing he values most is home and family. It is only by contemplating the entire life that we can answer Aristotle's key question: did the person become an authentic human being?

Aristotle thus offers a rich account of human moral promise. Since *eudaimonia* is an activity, it is not something that is achieved once for all; it must continually be renewed and strengthened. Human well-being lies in responding creatively to the challenge of each situation. Aristotelian *eudaimonia*, as described in the middle books of the *Nicomachean Ethics*, is clearly a way of living actively, with responsiveness and creative purpose.[19]

## HAPPINESS AS *FOCUS* OR *BALANCE*?

When we come to the end of the *Nicomachean Ethics*, however, we may be jolted by what seems to be an abrupt turn-around. The earthy concerns of life in community recede, and suddenly we seem to find ourselves in the territory of Plato, contemplating eternal, unchanging principles of the universe.

Aristotle spends eight books discussing engaged life within society; he seems to have genuine regard for moral intelligence and the virtues expressed in community—sometimes even in contrast to the abstract virtue of theoretical wisdom. For example, in his discussion of moral wisdom in book 6, he mentions the pre-Socratic philosophers Anaxagoras and Thales, commenting with a touch of irony that while their knowledge is extraordinary, amazing, and divine, their wisdom is worthless, because they cannot take care of themselves.[20] Moreover, in book 1, he notes that moral virtue is even more enduring than knowledge of the sciences.[21]

However, he gives us hints throughout the work and particularly in book 1 that ordinary moral virtue is not the ultimate goal of human life, that there may be a supreme human perfection, which in book 10 he goes on to identify as intellectual. In a key passage in book 1, he tells us that the good for a human being is activity of the soul in conformity with excellence or virtue; if there are several virtues, then activity should be in conformity with the *best and most complete* (or *perfect*) (1098a16–18). And he summarizes: happiness is a certain activity of the soul in conformity with *complete* (or *perfect*) virtue (1102a5–6). For the best activities encompass all these attributes, and it is in these, *or in the best one of them*, that we maintain happiness consists (1099a29–31).

The term we have translated here as "complete" is *teleion*, from *telos*, literally "end-y," related to an end or goal (*telos*). It can have the connotation of being complete or of being perfected, and these different nuances give rise to significant differences in interpretation.[22] Thus it is not clear from book 1 whether Aristotle believes that happiness consists in fully perfecting all one's virtues, both moral and intellectual, or simply in fulfilling the potential of one supreme virtue—which in book 1 he does not identify, but in book 10 he defines as intellectual virtue. In book 1 he argues that there are three competing ways of life: the life of pleasure or sense-gratification, the active political life within community, and the contemplative life. He dismisses the life of pleasure as not worthy of consideration, but the political life and the contemplative life are both serious competing possibilities for the best way of life (*bios*) (1095b–1096a).

When we turn to book 10 we find he fills in the gap he left in book 1. He writes that if happiness is activity in conformity with virtue, it is to be expected that it should conform with the highest virtue, and that is the virtue of the best part in us (10.7 [1177a12]):

> It is the activity of this part [when operating] in conformity with the excellence or virtue proper to it that will be *complete happiness*. That it is an activity concerned with theoretical knowledge or contemplation has already been stated. It follows that the activity of our intelligence constitutes the *complete happiness of man*, provided that it encompasses a complete span of life; for nothing connected with happiness must be incomplete [1177b24]. . . . A further indication that *complete happiness* consists in some kind of contemplative activity is this [1178b7]. . . . Consequently happiness is *some kind of study or contemplation* [1178b32].[23]

What leads him to this conclusion? Shouldn't complete happiness be found in developing *all* our potential—moral, artistic, intellectual? Or is there some one form of virtue that is so important that we should develop it at the expense of other parts of ourselves? Scholars discuss this question in the following way. Is *eudaimonia* meant to be a *dominant* end—one in which the activity of one, supreme virtue predominates in one's life? Or is *eudaimonia* meant to be an *inclusive* end, where the most successful life is one in which we engage in activity of the soul expressing many, diverse virtues?[24] Is the ideal life a completely focused life, or an exquisitely balanced life?

Aristotle's argument in book 10 seems to be that there is one part of us that is not merely human but represents our divine potential. For Aristotle this is our theoretical intellect, our ability to contemplate the highest beings and unchanging principles in the universe. This is what the gods do. The gods don't deliberate about contracts or economic justice; they think about purely divine unchanging things (1178b10). Some scholars have hypothesized that at a certain period in Aristotle's thinking, he made what he considered a crucial discovery: that there is a part of the human mind that is divine, that comes to us from without, and is thus separate from what he calls the compound, the body-mind complex.[25] But if a part of our mind is divine, then it would seem that one virtue *is* supreme, and should be cultivated above all else. Why choose a lesser form of happiness, the happiness of being a mere human, when we can choose the supreme felicity of developing the part of us that is divine?[26]

But did Aristotle actually mean to suggest that we should develop this part of ourselves *exclusively*? Did he believe that since contemplation is the development of the highest part of ourselves, it should be the *predominant* feature of our life (the *dominant* view)? Alternatively, perhaps Aristotle wanted to suggest that while ultimate happiness must include the supreme fulfillment enjoyed by the gods, a flourishing life will also allow for development of diverse virtues and their varied forms of expression (the *inclusive* or *comprehensive* view).[27]

We can investigate this question more thoroughly through the study of key passages. Perhaps we can find Aristotelian texts in which the active and contemplative lives are more integrated.

## THE ACTIVITY OF CONTEMPLATION

First, we should note a point of terminology: the distinction between *activities* and *lives*. As we have seen, Aristotle distinguishes between three *lives*—the pleasure seeking, the political, and the contemplative—rather than three activities (seeking pleasure, political involvement, and contemplation).[28] In pondering the crucial choice Aristotle presents between active and contemplative lives, we should not compartmentalize the activities of these lives completely; we should look rather for the target or organizing principle of each way of life, the ultimate good at which each life aims. For it is not true that the contemplative philosopher will engage in no moral actions. As a human being, living with other citizens, he or she will certainly express acts of moral excellence. But in Aristotle's view, philosophers don't make moral virtue their raison d'être; they don't seek ultimate fulfillment through acts of moral virtue. Political actors, however, do seek fulfillment through grand acts of nobility. Thus when we are choosing a way of life, we are choosing a dominant goal of that way of life, a goal that will give an orientation and focus to all that we do.[29]

Second, we should note that to describe the problem as a tension between active and contemplative lives is inaccurate. Aristotle believes that the life of contemplation is in fact the most active way of life. In a well-known passage in *Metaphysics* 12.7–8, Aristotle describes God's contemplation as the paradigm of the active life. To understand this passage, we must briefly clarify Aristotle's notion of divinity. Aristotle's God is not the monotheistic God of the Bible or the Qurʾān who creates a world and gives human beings moral guidance. Aristotle's God must also be distinguished from the pantheon of Greek gods, whose existence he acknowledges but belittles. The God of Aristotle is the philosophers' God, a being whose existence he establishes by means of philosophical demonstration.

In the *Physics*, Aristotle argues that since there is motion in the universe, there must be a substance that is the ultimate source of all movement. Motion involves a change from potentiality to actuality, and there cannot be an infinite regress of such motion; it must be grounded in a substance that is fully actual. Aristotle's God is thus an "unmoved mover," the ultimate source of all movement in the universe. In Aristotle's universe, the heavens consist of concentric spheres, each moved by an immaterial "mover." The Unmoved Mover is the ultimate source of celestial motion. However, it moves the universe not through physical, mechanical motion, but through desire: it arouses desire in the outermost sphere of the heavens to move in circular motion, in imitation of its perfection. It is full actuality, the source of all potential motion.

In the *Metaphysics*, Aristotle further defines this God as mind (*nous*), as thought thinking itself:

> Such, then, is the first principle upon which depend the sensible universe and the world of nature. And its life is like the best [life] that we temporarily enjoy. It must be in that state always (which for us is impossible), since its actuality [*energeia*] is also pleasure. (And for this reason waking, sensation, and thinking are most pleasant and hopes and memories are pleasant because of them.)
>
> And thought in itself deals with that which is best in itself, and that which is thought in the fullest sense with that which is best in the fullest sense. And thought thinks itself because it shares the nature of the object of thought; for it becomes an object of thought in coming into contact with and thinking its objects, so that thought and object of thought are the same.[30]

Aristotle's God is thought thinking itself, and Aristotle believes that this is the most intense and continuous mode of activity. When we think, we too engage in this active way of life. The activity of thinking, of processing reality, is a participation in God's fully realized existence. Aristotle argues that this is the most dynamic and fulfilling life:

> If, then, God is always in that good state in which we sometimes are, this compels our wonder; and if in a better [state] this compels it yet more. And God *is* in a better state. And life also belongs to God; for the actuality of thought is life, and God is that actuality; and God's essential actuality is life most good and eternal. We say therefore that God is a living being, eternal, most good, so that life and duration continuous and eternal belong to God; for this *is* God.[31]

While we can think only sometimes, God can engage in thinking all the time; thus God is in a better state than we. Life belongs to God not because God is a biological entity, but because the activity of thinking is in Aristotle's view life par excellence.

What does it mean to *live*? Aristotle equates living with actuality and full expression. For beings other than God, to live is to grow, to become; a being that is alive realizes potential, it actualizes itself. It is clear that our human potential is actualized only as a result of a long, arduous process. A pianist, for example, strives for years to master Chopin's *Études*; then she may go on to Scriabin and Shostakovich, ever striving to realize her artistic talent. A physicist will ponder string theory and struggle for decades to refine an inelegant equation. God, in contrast, is at every moment completely realized; as a thinker, God is actually thinking all thoughts possible. God is fully realized being; the actuality of thought *is* God's life. Aristotle's God does not "do" anything; Aristotle's God does not create the world, or even shape it in the manner of Plato's Demiurge. It simply thinks eternally; it is the pure energy of creative thought. For Aristotle, this is the fullest expression of life.[32]

However, it appears that for Aristotle divine thought is purely theoretical. Is this who *we* truly are as human beings or even as understanding minds (*nous*)—a purely abstract thinking about thinking? Even in book 10 of the *Ethics*, where he speaks of our essence as pure intellect, Aristotle acknowledges that we are also embodied humans, living in society with other human beings. Contemplative philosophers thus choose to do activities expressing virtue and need external goods for living a human life.[33] This is what distinguishes us from gods: "It is traditionally supposed that the gods more than anyone are blessed and happy: but what sorts of actions ought we to ascribe to them? Just actions? Surely they will appear ridiculous making contracts, returning deposits . . . Brave actions? Do they endure what they find frightening and endure dangers because it is fine? Generous actions? Whom will they give to? And surely it would be absurd for them to have currency or anything like that."[34] These are, after all, the heavenly immortals. They do not live in the *polis,* in political community; they are not involved in human society, in which the life of moral virtue is appropriate (1178b). Complete or perfect happiness seems to be the activity of contemplative study, in which the gods are perpetually engaged.

The human life of contemplation is likewise portrayed in 10.7 as a life disengaged from society; the philosopher seems to be in an ivory tower studying, not participating in just actions in community. Aristotle asserts that this is a divine form of happiness, while activities such as just and brave actions constitute a secondary, human kind of flourishing. Moral actions are the virtues of the mind-body compound, of humans as embodied, social animals. We have the temperament—tied to the body—of being just or courageous; thus the life of engaging in noble social and political deeds constitutes a lower, human form of happiness. However, the virtue of pure understanding (*nous*) is separate from this mind-body complex. Insofar as we contemplate the eternal and unchanging beings in the universe, we are, as it were, like God or the gods; we participate in the divine life. And insofar as we are divine, we can almost separate from our bodies—for those moments. But of course, we must then come down from our lofty philosophical speculations and rejoin our human compatriots.[35]

Thus while it is clear that according to Aristotle, to actualize our intellect is to fulfill our divine potential, the middle books of the *Ethics* compel us to recall our human potential as well. Is the virtue of theoretical wisdom (*sophia*), then, the only virtue that is important? There is evidence that it is not, that Aristotle conceives of wisdom as simply one part of the total complex of virtue whose activation constitutes human fulfillment. For example, in the *Nicomachean Ethics*, he writes:

> Wisdom [*sophia*] thus produces happiness, not in the way that medical science produces health, but in the way that health produces [health]. For since wisdom is a part of virtue as a whole, by having it and exercising it, a person is made happy. (6.12 [1144A])[36]

This passage suggests that the flourishing of *all* our human virtues makes us happy. Anthony Kenny argues that Aristotle would not have gone out of his way to tell us that *sophia* makes us happy as a part of virtue as a whole unless he believed that full, complete *eudaimonia* must include not simply abstract, theoretical wisdom but the activity of moral virtue as well.[37]

The point made by Kenny with respect to *Nicomachean Ethics* book 6 is more explicit in another work of Aristotle's, the *Eudemian Ethics*, which will be discussed further below:

> Life may be complete or incomplete, and virtue likewise may be either whole or partial.[38]

> And as physical well-being is made up of the excellences of the several parts, so too the virtue of the soul [is made up of the several virtues], insofar as it is an end [or: "complete whole, full realization"; *telos*].[39]

Inclusivists argue that Aristotle conceives of theoretical wisdom as a part of a virtuous life, but not all of it.[40] The content of pure theoretical wisdom is, to be sure, beings that do not change, "beings of a far more divine nature than human beings, most evidently, the constituent parts of the universe (the sun and the stars)" (*NE* 1141b). Thus it would seem that theoretical wisdom is—as he suggests in book 10—of a more exalted and divine nature than practical wisdom (*phronēsis*), which makes decisions about how we should live our lives. Nevertheless, after asserting that we are not the highest subject of study in the universe, Aristotle goes on to make the striking statement we mentioned earlier about Thales and Anaxagoras:

> Theoretical wisdom comprises both scientific knowledge and understanding about what is by nature most honorable. That is why people say of Anaxagoras or Thales or others of that sort that they are wise [*sophous*] but not possessed of practical judgment [*phronimous*] when they see that they are ignorant of what benefits themselves. And so they say that what they know is extraordinary, amazing, difficult, and divine, but useless, because it is not human goods that they look for. (*NE* 1141B)

Aristotle is clearly aware of the problem of the philosopher or natural scientist caught up with things extraordinary and divine, yet unable to tie his or her own shoes.[41] Surely, we would think, intellectual and moral virtue must be integrated in some way in the perfectly realized human being.

## AN INTEGRATED LIFE: ARISTOTLE'S *EUDEMIAN ETHICS*

The *Nicomachean Ethics* is not Aristotle's only ethical treatise; another, the *Eudemian Ethics,* presents a more integrated ideal. It is true that the majority of scholars see the *Eudemian Ethics* as an earlier work of Aristotle, and regard his views in the *Nicomachean Ethics* as representing Aristotle's mature, considered perspective. However, a minority—Anthony Kenny being the most articulate—regard the *Eudemian Ethics*, too, as a mature work of Aristotle. In either case, scholars agree that the work offers us a fascinating portrait of an alternative Aristotelian view. The *Eudemian Ethics* portrays an integrated ideal, a life that includes both contemplation and action—an ethical model that strikes our modern sensibility as a more balanced way of life. Let us look then at some of the evidence from the *Eudemian Ethics.*

In *Eudemian Ethics* (henceforth, *EE*) 2.1 (1219a), Aristotle asserts that it is the function of the soul to make things live; the soul is the animating principle, the living part of us. The function of the soul when it is at its excellence is a good life, and the excellence of the soul is to create a good life. Thus, human happiness is the activity of a good soul creating a good life. Happiness, he continues, is agreed to be something complete (*teleion*). In the context of the *Nicomachean Ethics*, it is not clear whether Aristotle uses this word *teleion* to signify that which is at the top of the ladder of virtue and all by itself is perfectly complete, or to signify that which is comprehensive, including all the other goods.[42] In the *Eudemian Ethics*, Aristotle makes it clear that the term is inclusive, for he states that happiness was agreed to be something complete, and life may be complete or incomplete. If it is incomplete, it would seem to lack something, while if complete, it would seem to include all the virtues. He adds that the activity of what is incomplete is itself incomplete; thus happiness must be the activity of a complete life in accordance with complete virtue (*EE* 1219a35–39). He remarks, too, that nothing incomplete is happy, as it does not form a whole (*EE* 1219a35, 1219b8). Throughout this passage, it is evident that Aristotle here conceives of happiness as complete, inclusive virtue—not just excellence of one part of the soul, the part that studies, but the whole soul, including the part that engages in moral actions.

We have seen that in 1220a, he adds that as physical well-being is made up of the virtues of the several parts (of the body), so too is the virtue of the soul made up of the several virtues, insofar as it is a fully realized whole (*telos*). Just as all the parts of one's body have to function well to create physical health, so too all the virtues must function together to create an excellent soul, the end (*telos*) of a flourishing human being. Again, Aristotle suggests that to express true excellence of soul, we must develop not only theoretical virtue but also moral virtue.

Finally, at the very end of the *Eudemian Ethics*, we hear that we need to live by reference to what Aristotle terms "the governing thing." In book 9 of the *Nicomachean Ethics* Aristotle suggests that what is sovereign in a human being is reason. Here in the *Eudemian Ethics* he writes:

> But since a human being by nature consists of a part that governs and a part that is governed, and [since] each person should live in accordance with their governing principle—but this [principle] is twofold: for medicine is a governing principle in one way, and health in another, for the first is for the sake of the second—it holds true in this way also, then, for the faculty of contemplation [*theoretikon*]. For the god is not a governor in the sense of one who issues commands [or: "prescribes, arranges things"], but it is that for which practical wisdom prescribes (but that for

> which is of two sorts, which have been distinguished elsewhere) since the god is in need of nothing. (*EE* 1249B)[43]

There are several difficulties with this passage. First, Aristotle says that "it holds true in this way also for the faculty of contemplation," but the antecedent of "this" is not clear. Is the faculty of contemplation like health, that for the sake of which all is done? Or is the faculty of contemplation twofold, like the two meanings of governing principle (*archē*)? Second, the mention of "the god" seems rather abrupt. Aristotle is speaking about the faculty of contemplation, and suddenly he turns to "the god." Is this the Unmoved Mover—thought thinking itself, the being we have met in the *Metaphysics*? The abruptness of the shift from the faculty of contemplation to "the god" has led some scholars to argue that "the god" here refers to the governing part of the mind, the theoretical faculty, which is that for the sake of which practical reason prescribes.[44] Pursuing the analogy of health will help us clarify Aristotle's meaning.

Aristotle explains that human beings consist of a part that governs and a part that is governed. We would ordinarily think this means that there is a rational part of the soul that governs and an irrational part that is governed. However, he then goes on to qualify: the notion of a governing principle (*archē*) is twofold. Health is a governing principle in one way: it provides the standard or template by reference to which the art of medicine prescribes. The medical art is a governing principle in another way: it prescribes the particular treatment plan by which health is achieved.

The contemplative faculty is also twofold. For the god, like health, is not a governor that issues commands. Health is a state to be achieved; health does not itself command, for it does need us to achieve healthiness. Just so, the god does not need anything; the god has no need to issue commands. The god, like health, is that for the sake of which practical wisdom prescribes. The god is a governing principle by serving as a model or template; like the physical state of health, contemplation is a state we seek to realize. The theoretical faculty looks to the divine state of contemplation it wants to emulate; practical wisdom prescribes the way of life that will make this state of contemplation possible. The god, like health, does not itself organize a way of life. The god provides a template according to which the art of medicine or practical wisdom spells out what should be aimed for.[45]

Thus our own practical wisdom prescribes those things that make theoretical contemplation (*theōria*) possible. When we are deciding how much time we should spend with family or friends or alone with work, our practical wisdom should consider what will make possible our ultimate goal of divine contemplation:

> So whatever process of choosing and acquiring things good by nature—whether goods of the body or wealth or friends or the other goods—will best bring about [or: "produce, conduce to"] contemplation [*theōria*] of the god, this is the best process, and this the finest standard [or: "criterion"]; but whatever process, whether through deficiency or excess, hinders service [or: "attending to"; *therapeuein*] and contemplation of the god, is poor. This holds so for the soul, and this standard for the soul is the finest—perceiving as little as possible the irrational part of the soul, insofar as it is irrational.

The phrase "contemplation of the god" has been read in different ways. The plain sense of the text appears to refer to our thinking about the god; we should orient our life so we can spend as much time as possible contemplating the divine. The alternative way some scholars have read the passage takes "the god" as the governing part of our mind; we should do everything to allow our governing part—our mind—to contemplate. They have suggested that "the god" can signify the immanent reason within our soul; divine contemplation is something our mind can engage in. On either reading, whatever allows us to do the most contemplative thinking allows the sovereign part of us to flourish. Thus when we think about how to divide our time, whatever allows us to contemplate is the best, and this is what we should pursue. Our ultimate *telos* is to devote ourselves to divine service and contemplation.

But what exactly could divine service mean for Aristotle? One sense of the verb *therapeuein* is "to serve the god in a ritual setting." However, Aristotle's conception of the god is not personal, so he cannot be referring here to ceremonies of worship. An extended meaning of *therapeuein*, however, is "to tend or attend to," as a servant takes care of a master, or one takes care of one's own body or person. In this sense, in Greek as well as English, one can serve or attend to one's health. Just so, one can attend to the god by making possible the conditions for contemplation.[46]

Aristotle may also have in mind several key Socratic statements. For example, the pivotal dramatic moment of Plato's dialogue *Euthyphro* is a question Socrates poses to Euthyphro: What is that excellent aim the gods achieve using us as their servants? Socrates hints that perhaps true service of the god is found in performing just actions.[47] Aristotle may also have in mind Socrates' articulation of his goal of service in the *Apology*:

> Know well that this is what the god bids [me to do], and I believe no greater good ever came to pass in the city than my service to the god. For I go around doing nothing but persuading both young and old among you not to care for your body or your wealth in preference to or even to so great an extent as for your soul, that it should be as excellent as possible, as I say to you: "Virtue [*aretē*] does not come from wealth, but wealth comes from virtue [*aretē*], and so too all the other goods for human beings, both individual and collective."[48]

Thus Aristotle may mean that we serve God when we contemplate noble moral ideals, or even that we serve God through performing just actions. For in the exercise of just actions, we achieve the flowering of who we are as human beings. Our essence or form as a person is to be a rational animal; when we express our excellence—whether through noble moral deeds or through contemplation—we perfect our human form. Since everything in the universe is striving to fulfill its purpose, when we fulfill our *telos*, we are serving the divine order. We can imitate divine perfection through engaging in contemplation and its approximation, noble moral action. To fulfill our essence and purpose is true service of God.[49]

Like the celestial spheres, human beings are ultimately moved by love for divine perfection. When we perfect our being, we fulfill our natural purpose, and thus become akin to the perfection of the Unmoved Mover.[50] Our ultimate good is to devote ourselves to contemplation of this divine ideal, and to express in action the complete realization of our *telos*: moral perfection in our relation with fellow beings, and intellectual perfection in our contemplation of God.[51]

## *THEŌRIA* AND INTEGRATION IN THE *NICOMACHEAN ETHICS*

We have seen that action is fully integrated into the notion of complete happiness in the *Eudemian Ethics*, even while there too contemplation (*theōria*) is ultimately presented as an orienting principle. Is there evidence for the integration of contemplation and action in the communal moral life of the *Nicomachean Ethics*? Can we bridge Aristotle's discussion of contemplation in book 10 with the discussion of the moral life in the middle books?

To do so, it may be useful to distinguish between the activity of happiness proper (*eudaimonia*)—which Aristotle at times seems to define as purely intellectual in nature—and the happy (*eudaimon*) life, the life in which *eudaimonia* prevails.[52] *Eudaimonia* is the activity of expressing who we are as human beings. We can excel in many domains: artistic, scientific, literary, spiritual. We have the capacity to relate to human beings around us in creative ways. We have the potential to write great works of literature, to create striking and innovative works of dance or music, to advance the pure sciences, to make great medical discoveries. When we express our gifts, we experience a unique sense of human fulfillment; we fulfill our function as human beings, and fulfill—that is express and actively exercise—our many potential forms of human excellence.

These are the activities of a happy life, activities in which our soul fully expresses itself. The *eudaimon* or successful life is one in which we are able to fulfill our purpose. In some lives, severe physical and economic challenges tragically deny us the opportunity to express our gifts. Aristotle thus recognizes that we need some natural goods to enable us to fully become who we are. While Aristotle delineates two primary kinds of excellence, moral and intellectual, in book 10 he expresses a clear preference for the life of intellectual excellence over the political life and moral expression. However, even given Aristotle's preference for intellectual excellence in book 10, we can make an argument rooted in the *Nicomachean Ethics* that the activity of supreme, intellectual *eudaimonia* need not be divorced from moral action. As Gabriel Richardson Lear has argued, we can exercise a kind of contemplation in action.[53] To support this argument, let us turn to some compelling evidence brought by David Roochnik that there is a continuum to *theōria*, that even the exalted contemplation Aristotle discusses in book 10.7 need not be divorced strictly from moral deliberation (*phronēsis*). *Theōria* is best understood in the broadest sense as the actualization of our capacity to know, and this activity can take place in every domain of our lives.

Scholars generally acknowledge that the verb *theōrein*, "to study," is used throughout the Aristotelian corpus for a broad range of activities. The term originally means to "look at" (cf. the Latin "*speculari*"); *theōria* is the activity of looking at the world. Whereas animals look at the world only through the physical eyes, humans take pleasure in looking at and making sense of the world through the intellect as well. *Theōria* is the process of actively engaging our capacity to know. There is a debate whether *theōria* is a process of investigation and research, or simply a process of reflection upon truths already known; in either case, the key is that one is actively engaged in cognition.

The prime exemplar of *theōria* is God. Now we may ask whether God's cognition is a good model for us, as God does not know through a process of investigation; Aristotle's God is pure activity, and thus God's knowledge in no way proceeds from potentiality to actuality. One might thus imagine that God's contemplation is an eternal reflection on truths already known. Roochnik argues, however, that even in the case of God, creative engagement in thought comes closer to capturing the meaning of *theōria* than passive contemplation of knowledge.

To understand the active nature of *theōria*, let us look at a key passage in *De Anima*. In 412b5, Aristotle distinguishes knowledge (*epistēmē*) from theorizing (*theōria*). "Knowledge," he writes, means "having but not actively using," while *theōrein* means "actively engaged in or working with" (412a26). He gives two examples: arithmetic and knowledge of letters. When actually engaged in mathematical computation, we are "theorizing." Similarly, when actually using our knowledge of letters in spelling, we are "theorizing."[54] Reflecting on the example of arithmetic, Roochnik asks whether the activity of *theōria* is more like contemplating the proposition 7 + 5 = 12 or working on the more complex algebraic problem 369 + 3x = 1215. Since the textual evidence points to the notion that *theōria* is actively engaging in using one's knowledge, he argues that we do this to a more significant extent when we work out a complex algebraic equation than when we reflect on a simple proposition such as 7 + 5 = 12. Thus *theōria* seems more like active *study*, rather than thinking about knowledge already acquired, the connotation of our English *contemplation*.[55]

The Unmoved Mover is said to be perpetually engaged in *theōria*. Now it is true that since the Unmoved Mover is fully actual, it cannot proceed from not knowing to knowing; its knowledge is always fully realized. But the divine—like certain human prodigies, notably autistic savants—can "see" the answer to 369 + 3x = 1215 with the immediacy that ordinary human beings see that 7 + 5 = 12. And *theōria* is, after all, an intellectual kind of "seeing."[56] Thus *theōria* can signify intellectual engagement and active use of knowledge even for God, whose knowledge is always fully actual.

Roochnik acknowledges that he is not the first scholar to notice that Aristotle uses the verb *theōrein* throughout the corpus for mundane as well as exalted modes of knowing. However, most have argued that the *theōria* of *Nicomachean Ethics* 10.7–8 is confined to theoretical wisdom (*sophia*), the theorizing of exalted, eternal, changeless beings, and that there is in fact no *theōria* of the contingent, that is, things that are not eternal and necessary.[57] Roochnik's textual evidence, however, points to a continuum between the various kinds of study, one which compels a rethinking of *NE* 10.7–8. In short, he argues, the *theōria* of *NE* 10.7–8 is simply the most exalted form of the study in which we engage all the time as active, thinking beings. We look at and describe the world as it is.[58]

*Theōria* applies when one is actually using one's knowledge. And there is pure delight in the active use of our faculties, just as the athlete loves to run and the musician delights in playing music. "Actualization is pleasure," Aristotle writes in *Metaphysics* 1072b, and God's mode of being is pure activity. When we engage in *theōria*, then, we engage in a kind of "imitation of God." However, "participation in God" would probably be a more apt term, for this is not simply imitation; we are ourselves enjoying for those pure moments of thinking the eternal pleasure that is God's mode of being.

This gives us a clue to Aristotle's conception of *eudaimonia*, and may help bridge the gap between book 10 of the *Nicomachean Ethics* and the middle books. Aristotle writes in book 1 that *eudaimonia* is the activity of the soul expressing excellence, and if there is more than one form of excellence, expressing the best and most complete or perfect. In book 10, he harkens back to that initial formulation: "If *eudaimonia* is activity expressing excellence, it is reasonable for it to express the supreme virtue, which will be the virtue of the best thing." The best, he says, is understanding (*nous*), and thus complete happiness will be *its* (understanding's) activity expressing its proper virtue, and this activity is the activity of *theōria*.

It is true that the purpose of *theōria* is not to decide how to live the best life or engage in the best action, but to reflect with pleasure on the world around us and on making sense of that world. However there is no reason that we cannot engage in the philosophical life while in action. If *theōria* need not be confined to objects that are eternal and unchanging—as Roochnik's evidence suggests—we can also make sense of our world by reflecting on our own actions, thoughts, and lives. All of life can partake in the philosophical life in the sense that Socrates suggested: that the unexamined life is not worth living for a human being.[59] We do not need to be professional philosophers to live the philosophical life. We can choose to be—in the words of Martha Nussbaum—professional human beings.[60] We can engage in contemplation in action.

All human beings by nature desire to know; we love to investigate every aspect of our world.[61] *Theōria* is thus a part of the engaged moral life as well as of the abstract, scientific life. *Eudaimonia* is the activity of fulfilling our potential; when we express our potential we are engaged in the most active lifestyle. God is pure activity, and when we actualize our capacities we are like God. Moreover, we feel we are fulfilling our purpose in life; pleasure completes the activity. Pleasure is the experience of actualizing our talents and bringing them to fruition.[62] When we exceed our personal best in running, write a brilliant line of poetry or prose, or create an innovative work of art, we are bringing into activity the latent treasures within. We feel most alive when we are becoming who we are capable of becoming.

Aristotle thus offers a naturalistic account of pleasure; pleasure is simply the subjective experience of a being expressing its potential. The seed pushes out of the ground; it bursts into bloom. The toddler no longer wants to crawl, but desires to walk; she derives pleasure from realizing her natural capability.

The life of philosophy is the most active life, and as such represents the full flowering of our humanity. John Cooper may therefore be correct that for Aristotle complete, perfect happiness is the activity of study; reflection, for Aristotle, represents the peak of our humanness. We learn to be moral by habit; we then develop the ability to deliberate well about human action. But the purest pleasure is the activity of thinking about thinking. This kind of thinking does not proceed from a state of not understanding to understanding; it is the mature exercise of the abilities we have developed. A musician once began her studies playing scales, and now ascends the stage to perform a concerto she has mastered. We witness the fruits of her success, the triumphant performance of the virtuoso. A concert documentary shows the preliminary preparations for the tour, the backstage jitters, and the culminating performance; everything for which she has primed herself now comes to fruition.[63]

Aristotle suggests that contemplation is not for the sake of anything else; it has no utilitarian value. This is a mark of its sublimity. Perhaps as moderns we can best grasp this notion through our appreciation for the arts. Beethoven's *Eroica* symphony is beautiful simply because it is; a work of art is a pure expression of the sublime. Now it is true that Aristotle himself categorizes art, or *poiēsis*, as an act of making; in artistic creation, a product exists apart from the act of creativity, and thus the making is not an end in itself. A better analogy for Aristotle's view of *theōria* might perhaps be improvised music or dance, or—as Aristotle suggests in book 10—play. In all these examples, the activity is a pure expression of joy. There need be no product after the experience itself—no sand castle, no recording—just the simple expression of one's soul. This is the way Aristotle sees *theōria*. Aristotle took sublime delight in thinking about the universe; Aristotle's God, as *nous*, *is* that sublime delight.[64]

## INTEGRATED *THEŌRIA* AND ITS REPERCUSSIONS FOR THE *ETHICS*

Aristotle believes the activity that expresses the full flowering of our humanity is understanding the universe. When we are engaged in understanding, we are self-sufficient; for those moments of pure understanding, we need no external goods—neither people, nor wealth, nor even food or drink. Yes, we must return to our human bodies and our workaday lives; we cannot remain in pure thought as long as we are human beings. But at those moments of pure understanding we are like gods, almost separate from our bodies and our humanity.[65]

Indeed, in the *Politics*, Aristotle describes the philosophical way of life as that of "an alien cut off from the political community."[66] And he asks the question we have seen in the *Ethics*: which life is more choiceworthy, the one that involves taking part in politics with other people in a city-state, or the life of a stranger cut off from the *polis*?[67] Aristotle does not give a clear-cut answer. He seems to argue that *eudaimonia* is the life of activity, but that study and thought too are forms of activity; in fact, they are pure activity for its own sake and thus may represent the most active form of life.

In the *Nicomachean Ethics*, he suggests that complete or perfected *eudaimonia* is found in pure study: complete immersion in understanding the universe.[68] But even if we acknowledge that supreme fulfillment is found in thinking, we cannot engage perpetually in the highest form of thought—contemplating the eternal principles of nature. God is simply thinking on thinking; we human beings can only engage in such moments sporadically. At other moments, we must take care of our bodies, interact with our fellow human beings, and participate in moral activity.

Must we be continually frustrated in such moments, and should we aim for a life that limits everyday human interaction to a bare minimum?[69] If we see *theōria* as the broad activity of understanding, we find a bridge between the life of study and the life of political action. Even Pericles, in making political decisions, was engaged in *theōria*.[70] We observe and study the actions of virtuous friends, because we can see them more clearly than our own, and thereby learn about human excellence.[71] Book 9, which depicts a person living in community and involved with virtuous friends, points to a life of actively engaging our minds. We learn about virtue, about the best modes of life. We practice virtue, first from habit, and then from understanding, and we observe our friends and fellow citizens. Every moment of our lives we can be immersed in a kind of human flourishing.

The question is, which represents the supreme fulfillment in our lives: is it moments of pure contemplation, or those moments when we learn as we engage in moral or political action? Aristotle shows a clear preference for purely intellectual pursuits. He believes our purpose here is to comprehend the universe, to fulfill our capacity for complete knowledge. Since it is absurd to think that we humans are the highest beings in the universe, human moral understanding is not the supreme form of knowing. The apex of our knowledge is to understand the stars and heavens and the eternal principles by which nature is governed. Ultimately, we want to engage in the activity of the Unmoved Mover, who is thinking about thinking.[72]

That is our divine potential. Clearly, not everyone in the polis can be perpetually engrossed in such pure study. Our human fulfillment—in contrast to divine fulfillment—flowers when we express moral excellence through acts of political engagement. And as rulers, we can cause many others to engage in noble action.[73] Thus it might seem that the political life causes the greatest degree of actualization, and should be supreme. Nonetheless, Aristotle adds a caveat:

> It is not necessary, as some suppose, for a life of action to involve relations with other people, nor are those thoughts alone active which we engage in for the sake of action's consequences; the study and thought that are their own ends and are engaged in for their own sake are much more so. For to do or act well is the end, so that action of a sort is the end too. And even in the case of actions involving external objects, the one who does them most fully is, strictly speaking, the master craftsman who directs them by means of his thought.[74]

He thus plants the suggestion that pure thought is also activity, and perhaps the supreme, most creative form of activity.[75]

How then can we bridge the supreme form of flourishing with ordinary human happiness? Gabriel Richardson Lear has argued that moral action is a kind of approximation of contemplation. Study aims for truth in understanding; moral activity aims for truth in action. Moral virtue is thus a kind of contemplation in action, and therefore partakes in the good of the supreme end.[76] By performing morally virtuous actions, we express our love for the ultimate *telos* of contemplation; moral virtue is loved both for its own sake and for the sake of the supreme good.[77] Richardson Lear makes a convincing case for the place of moral virtue in Aristotle's philosophical life. The truth of our situation is that we are embodied beings, and thus we cannot spend every moment of our lives in study. Even if moments of pure understanding represent the acme of human life, maximizing those moments does not necessarily maximize our good.[78] To neglect our human needs does not do justice to the truth of our situation. If we neglect our bodies, we get sick; if we neglect our human needs, we become spiritually unhealthy. If every natural being must fulfill its *telos*, then our human perfection as physical and emotional beings cannot be neglected.[79] The function of our human, moral reason must be to perfect ourselves as humans, while aiming toward our ultimate divine perfection. One might even argue that our divine perfection *requires* care for the human parts of ourselves. True, one can be a useless Thales or Anaxagoras, who excels in divine wisdom but knows nothing of practical affairs. However, it seems clear that the person who does not fully understand the human dimensions of the cosmos has a blind spot in his or her *theōria*.[80] Mastering the human would seem to be an integral part of ultimate devotion to the divine, the principle of perfecting every natural aspect of the world.

There is thus a profound truthfulness in accepting the human dimension of our nature. Plato's philosopher contemplates the Forms—the true, eternal verities that give fundamental value and goodness to our world. But such contemplation may make it all the more difficult to accept the flawed, imperfect nature of the world we live in. As Julia Annas points out, while Plato is sometimes seen as utopian or idealistic because of his focus on a perfect world of eternal truth, in fact there is also a strain of pessimism regarding the ability of our world to come close to that ideal.[81] Andrea Nightingale suggests a different reading of the *Republic*; in her view, Plato suggests that the actual living philosopher—in contrast to the idealized philosopher of the cave analogy—must ever shuttle between the perfect world of the Forms and our flawed reality, in order to create a just republic here on earth, modeled on the perfect Forms.[82]

Aristotle, it has always been said, is the more earthy and realistic thinker. He engages with the realistic empiricism of a natural scientist investigating every dimension of the universe as it is. As a moral theorist, too, he begins with human nature as it is. And while he urges us to develop and perfect our divine nature, he cannot ignore the reality of our humanness. So while ultimate *eudaimonia* for Aristotle will consist in the activity of our *nous*—that part of us that at moments transcends the human—he recognizes that, in Hume's phrase, at times the philosopher must come down from the attic, dine, play backgammon, and make merry with his or her friends.[83] If our purpose is to soar the cosmos in wonder, we also return and land in our human hearth. To aim for Stoic *apatheia* and self-sufficiency, the complete denial of our human passions and needs, seems to Aristotle profoundly unwise and unrealistic. While supreme contemplation is the end of life, living according to the mean of virtue is the most realistic way to achieve it. Balance between divine contemplation and human action may be the most realistic way to achieve our *telos* as beings who have immortal potential.

There is another way to look at the philosopher's need for moral virtue. The philosopher—even more than other people—needs moral virtue to mediate the tension between the divine and human dimensions of who we are. The philosopher is at moments fully immersed in divine reason, contemplating the eternal. But everyone must return to the body, and how does one do this gracefully? Recall the poignant words of Plotinus:

> Often I have woken up out of the body to myself and have entered into myself, going out from all other things; I have seen a beauty wonderfully great and felt assurance that then most of all I belonged to the better part; I have actually lived the best life and come to identify with the divine; and set firm in it, I have come to that supreme actuality, setting myself above all else in the realm of Intellect. Then after that rest in the divine, when I have come down from Intellect to discursive reasoning, I am puzzled how I ever came down, and how my soul has come to be in the body when it is what it has shown itself to be by itself, even when it is in the body.[84]

How do we mediate pure intellect and the human, flawed beings we are as embodied humans, as compounds? We need moral virtue. It is those who have developed patience, courage, and resilience who can walk gracefully in both worlds.[85]

Thus the classic way of posing this problem—the paradox of the morally flawed contemplative—may be only partially accurate. True, there are scientists who are vicious human beings. But the person who wants to experience the true joy of contemplative *eudaimonia* must build up the fortitude and realism to accept his or her humanness.

Aristotle may have felt poignantly the conflicting pulls of the human theorizer. Plato's Socrates would lure contemplators back to the cave with a reminder of their civic duty: since it is the *polis* that has nurtured them and enabled them to pursue the vision of Truth, they owe it to the *polis* to come back and reveal to others what they have discovered.[86] Aristotle suggests that by developing the moderation of moral virtue, we will have an anchor to guard us against the impulse to dedicate all our energy to the divine activity of *theōria*, thus neglecting our human context.[87] Perhaps the life of moral virtue develops those character traits that both enrich the life of the *polis* and make possible a genuine philosophical contribution.[88] Thus moral virtue might be a prerequisite both for the development of intellectual virtue and for its balanced, healthy expression.[89]

If we reflect back upon the ethics of Plato and Aristotle, we find a paradox. We think of Aristotle as the more grounded, realistic, earthy thinker; the departure in *Nicomachean Ethics* 10.7–8 seems like a Platonic move. However, the picture is more complex, as Nightingale has shown. She points out that Plato's model actually suggests a fluid movement between *theōria* and *praxis*, between contemplation of eternal values and putting those values into action. Plato would bid philosopher-rulers to look toward the Forms and then toward existing laws; they can thus paint constitutions that would encourage the development of the divine form and image in human beings.[90] He believes that we should model laws on the eternal values that we want to develop in citizens. Moreover, he argues that no one who spends time with the eternal Forms would want to hurt or oppress people.[91] Contemplation of the ordered realm of beauty—of mathematics and eternal values such as justice and piety—shapes human character. This assertion owes much to Socrates' conviction that intellectual investigation of our values can change us; understanding has the power to transform.

Aristotle seems skeptical about the power of pure understanding to transform human nature. Socrates had spoken of virtue as a craft (*technē*)—the art of living well. Aristotle carefully distinguishes between theoretical contemplation, moral decision-making, and craft. Socrates is certain that if you convince someone that an action does not aim at their good, they will be able to refrain from doing it. Plato does not tell us just how contemplation of eternal verities transforms character; he believes in the power of pure awe. Aristotle is perhaps a more realistic moral thinker; he gives us a road map of virtue.

So while we are disappointed in Aristotle's total divorce of theoretical contemplation from *praxis*—and particularly in his aristocratic disdain for practical work—we also recognize his moral realism. The value of knowing is intrinsic, he suggests; we should not necessarily expect it to transform us morally. However, if we have carefully done our moral work, we can enjoy the fruits of our labors and enjoy pure learning for learning's sake. He values the nobility of doing the good for the sake of the good, but even beyond that he values the pure joy of understanding. However, it is Richardson Lear's insight about living the truth that appeals to us most as moderns searching for moral guidance. We want to believe in the power of study to transform us, and the resources are present in Aristotle for such a moral vision. If we are committed to the truth we study, we need to live the truth as well. Our commitment to the truth—even abstract, philosophical truth—will overflow into living true lives.

Our investigation of Plato and Aristotle has shown us that Whitehead's view of the history of philosophy is apt: while no one philosophy will contain all of truth, each offers a perspective that is integral to the whole. We need both Plato and Aristotle for a synoptic moral vision. When we turn to al-Fārābī and Maimonides, we will find an integration of these two moral visions with that of scriptural monotheism. This integration will bring the knowledge gleaned from contemplation into action.

## MODERN ARISTOTELIAN REPERCUSSIONS: ALASDAIR MACINTYRE AND CHARLES TAYLOR

The Aristotelian tradition is by no means dead. It is true that much modern ethical thinking draws its inspiration from the Enlightenment and the monumental achievement of Immanuel Kant, and modern Aristotelians formulate their views against this tradition. Kant's moral philosophy centers on the value of human autonomy—the dignity of a moral agent who obeys no law except that which he or she also gives.[92] Kant opens the conclusion of *Critique of Practical Reason* with this thought: "Two things fill the mind with ever new and increasing wonder and awe, the oftener and the more steadily we reflect on them: starry heavens above me and the moral law within me."[93] During the eighteenth-century Enlightenment, human beings threw off the shackles of turning for moral answers to the external authority of God and scriptures. We find the moral law within, in our conscience, the ability of our own independent reason to discover the absolute moral law. Thus Kant writes that when the Biblical Abraham was confronted with the voice of God telling him to sacrifice his beloved son Isaac, he should have resisted and responded (to paraphrase Kant's words): "Voice, I don't know who you are. But I do know that the moral law within my own reason tells me that I cannot commit murder, let alone kill my own son."[94]

The key to Kant's ethics is that moral principles must be capable of being universalized. The categorical imperative—a moral imperative that can never be abrogated—states that we must be able to act in a way that any rational being in this situation would act. Our act must be able to be formulated as a universal moral law.[95] Morality is not dictated by my individual, subjective needs and desires, but by universal moral principles. Aristotelian and Kantian ethics differ on just this point. Aristotle believes that our individual contexts and relationships do affect our moral obligations, while Kant believes they do not. Thus Aristotle believes we have greater obligations to our family and community than to the world at large, whereas Kant conceives us as purely rational beings whose obligations are universal. Aristotle situates us in a particular human community and context; Kant disembodies us as agents of a universal moral reason.

This contrast is reflected in contemporary ethical debates between modern Kantians and Aristotelians. John Rawls' monumental *Theory of Justice* draws inspiration from Kant's vision of a moral agent abstracted from particular concerns and ends, from individual visions of the good life. He suggests that the way to ensure a just society is to imagine that we are all placed in "an original position," formulating the laws of a potential social framework behind a veil of ignorance. We do not know who we will be in this society: cook or sanitation worker, dancer or teacher, parent or orphan, able bodied or facing a serious health challenge. It is only from behind such a veil of ignorance, abstracting from our own concerns and needs, that we can be certain of constructing a system of justice fair to all.[96]

Communitarians such as Michael Sandel challenge the wisdom of holding up the disembodied Kantian self as an ideal. Communitarians argue that we can never fully abstract ourselves from our context; our selves are constituted by our relationships and commitments. We make moral decisions from our context as friend, parent, member of a particular community and nation with individual perspectives and concerns.[97]

Alasdair Macintyre pushes the critique in another direction. He points out that we make moral decisions from within a tradition of practice. But there is more: we cannot truly understand a virtue such as justice without an overall conception of the purpose of our human lives as a whole. Kant and Rawls suggest that justice requires abstraction from any particular end, from any overall conception of the good life that would be held by a factory worker or an administrative assistant, by one particular moral agent in contrast to another. Rawls thus holds up justice as the supreme virtue—defending justice, rights, and moral obligation is more important than defining a good, an individual goal in life. In contrast, Macintyre argues that a conception of the overall purpose of our lives is key for organizing other values in a hierarchy—including the virtue of justice. Moreover, there are certain virtues, such as consistency and integrity, that can only make sense within the context of an overall life orientation, an overarching good.[98]

Charles Taylor has undertaken an equally ambitious working out of a modern Aristotelian vision. In *Sources of the Self*, he argues against what he calls the naturalism of modern ethics. The modern ethical tradition models itself on the empiricism of natural science, arguing that we can make moral decisions objectively, that we can discover what is moral by taking the stance of a neutral observer, independent of subjective conditions and concerns.[99] He responds to this viewpoint in the spirit of Aristotle. Aristotle pointed out that his *Nicomachean Ethics* was written only for those whose moral responses were nurtured by moral training from an early age. Likewise, Taylor argues that "moral argument and exploration go on only within a world shaped by our deepest moral responses."[100] He calls this moral world in which we live a framework, or a background picture. Taylor goes further still: he argues that we cannot make ordinary moral judgments about our lives without what he calls a moral ontology. Why does he suggest that this is a radical statement? Taylor is arguing against the neutral stance presupposed by the modern tradition; he argues that all of us make decisions about our lives against a picture of what we hold up as most important.[101] The waitress at a café who treasures weekend time at the local club has a sense of what is most significant in her life, as does the parent who is devoted to family outings and the rap artist who wants to pursue his or her craft.

Taylor identifies three values that modern people universally hold up as central. The first of these is that we moderns universally value human life—we don't accept that certain lives are discardable, that slavery is acceptable, that certain ethnic groups have lesser worth.[102] And yet we do so on diverse grounds. Some of us inherit this intuition from the religious traditions in which we were nurtured growing up. Others value human autonomy, believing that each of us has a right to choose our goals in life. The point is that each of us acts against the backdrop of a larger moral framework than we normally acknowledge. Even Kantian liberals, who argue that they are making decisions independent of any particular commitments, are in fact operating from a supreme commitment—to the overriding virtue of neutrality and justice. Kant and Rawls are as passionate and eloquent about this moral vision as the most dedicated Aristotelian. We have seen that Kant begins his moral magnum opus, the *Critique of Practical Reason*, with an homage to the moral law. Rawls ends his with a modern secular vision of an eternal moral value, the beauty of true objective justice:

> The perspective of eternity is not a view of a transcendent being; rather, it is a certain form of thought and feeling that rational persons can adopt within the world. And having done so, they can, whatever their generation, bring together into one scheme all individual perspectives and arrive together at regulative principles that can be affirmed by everyone as he lives by them, each from his own standpoint. Purity of heart, if one could attain it, would be to see clearly and to act with grace and self-command from this point of view.[103]

Taylor sees this Kantian vision as itself a moral framework; his project is to begin to articulate those frameworks that go largely unacknowledged. Like Macintyre, he argues that none of us can live without the view of an overall purpose in life, one that makes sense of other goods in a hierarchy of values. That is why day-to-day decisions are often so wrenching for us. Should we spend more time with our partner, or devote our weekend to our pet hobby or catching up on work? Which part of our identity ultimately defines us? Is it our commitment to a religious practice or community, or is religious identity something we can easily discard? Answers to this question may change over the course of our lives, as young couples often discover when they decide to have children. How we define ourselves and who precisely we feel ourselves to be changes over time, but we cannot escape that we have a self with a sense of commitments. That is what it is to be human. Further, Taylor maintains, this is precisely what Aristotle means when he argues that we are fundamentally rational; to be rational is to have a *telos* and commitments. And this is a very difference sense of what it means to be rational than the rationality of the Kantian tradition.

Taylor thus stresses three axes of modern moral thinking:

1. A sense of respect for and obligations to others;
2. An understanding of what makes for a fulfilled life, a life of meaning;
3. A sense of human dignity.[104]

This dignity is how we view ourselves in the public square. It is this sense of dignity that is threatened when we lose a job, a relationship, our physical health, or even the youthful appearance of our body. We feel our very identity threatened in a fundamental way.[105]

Taylor notes that frameworks are threatened today in a way different from what was true in previous eras. Eric Erickson sketched a compelling portrait of Martin Luther, arguing that Luther was beset by a crisis of identity. Taylor points out, however, that Luther's crisis is fundamentally different from what we call a crisis of identity today. Today we are threatened by a sense of meaninglessness, a sense that we have lost all framework or moral compass, that we are stranded in a vast, meaningless universe. Luther felt rejected by a religious and moral order that still had absolute authority in his world; he was not beset by a crisis of meaning. We today choose our structures of meaning, our frameworks; they do not confront us as absolute and unquestioned.[106] Nevertheless, frameworks are as important today when they are chosen by the individual as when they were universally shared and monolithic.

In sum, Taylor argues that we as human beings cannot exist without an orientation to the good. A self is not an objective, neutral entity that can be studied like other objects of empirical scientific research. Selves are inextricably orientated toward goals and overall values around which we structure our lives.[107] Moreover, love for the good is itself among the most powerful motivators for moral action. Hence Socrates' notion that the unexamined life is not worth living; the articulation of our most deeply held moral values inspires not only love for philosophy but love for the good itself and for expressing the good in action.[108]

Taylor thus offers a robust defense of Aristotle's ethical vision, expressed in the opening of the *Nicomachean Ethics*: every craft, activity, and action aims at some good. In Aristotle's teleological universe, this includes the natural world, but all the more so the human. To be human is to have a function that sets us apart from nature: to use our reason to consciously direct us toward ends we choose. Alasdair Macintyre and Charles Taylor argue that this vision holds as true for moderns as it did for ancients. Moderns have gone astray in locating the sphere of morality narrowly in the question of rights and obligations, of what we ought to do. Macintyre and Taylor argue that ethics is most properly concerned with who we are, of how we orient our lives toward the good.

# 8

# The Philosopher as Teacher

## AL-FĀRĀBĪ ON CONTEMPLATION AND ACTION

AL-FĀRĀBĪ, A ninth-century Islamic philosopher, develops the political dimension of Aristotle's thought. To understand the trajectory from Aristotle to al-Fārābī, we should note the social context of Aristotle's work. Aristotle's time saw the emergence of the new discipline of philosophy, and Aristotle was asking a compelling social-political question: Which is the best life—a life cut off from the political community, simply engaging in philosophy, or one committed to political participation? In the *Politics*, he dismisses the notion of being completely cut off from the community, since the book is about choosing the best political order, and the question of complete political disengagement is simply not relevant to an essay on politics. The question then remains whether to engage in the life of philosophy within the political community, and here he answers some relevant criticism: that it is not an active life. He answers that intellectual engagement is, indeed, as significant an activity as political action.[1]

In the *Nicomachean Ethics*, Aristotle argues that the most complete form of happiness is engaging in contemplative study, and he asks rhetorically: Why settle for mere human happiness, when we can fulfill our divine potential? Aristotle recognizes that even the contemplative philosopher lives among other people and so will engage in moral action. Thus here, too, he does not consider the hypothetical alternative he mentions in the *Politics*—that one could disengage oneself totally from society in order to pursue a purely contemplative life. He does raise the question of whether this life is too exalted for a human being, but seems convinced that we can live, at least nominally, in a human community and still pursue this exalted end. And this is what he suggests in the *Politics* as well, that the purpose of wartime is to promote peace and leisure, and the purpose of leisure is to be able to pursue the supreme goal of the human quest—to participate in the divine activity of understanding.

Al-Fārābī takes this integration one step further. Drawing upon the Platonic ideal of the philosopher-king, al-Fārābī asserts that the supreme human goal is to govern. However, in his view, governance need not involve legislating politically but may consist in sharing teachings that will lead other human beings to happiness. Al-Fārābī's view suggests a model for integrating the active and contemplative lives, one that Aristotle might have chosen. That is, Aristotle could have seen himself, like Socrates, as a public intellectual who expresses contemplation in action by awakening others to a reflective life. Aristotle seems not to have thought of himself in this way; it was left to medieval thinkers such as al-Fārābī and Maimonides to make this conceptual leap. Al-Fārābī speaks in many voices on the question of the end of human life. Miriam Galston has brought together this varied testimony in an illuminating way for exploring the question of theory and practice, contemplation and action. Let us examine the evidence she sets forth.

Al-Fārābī defines practical philosophy as the study of things from the perspective of attaining human happiness.[2] Our goal here is genuinely practical: we actually want to become happy.[3] However, if we consider the broad sweep of al-Fārābī's writings, we seem to find three visions of happiness, which are parallel to views we have seen in Aristotle. The first vision is that of a purely theoretical life, consisting of contemplative study alone—the view many scholars see in *Nicomachean Ethics* 10.7–8. The second image is of an engaged, political life in community, such as we see in the middle books of the *Nicomachean Ethics*. Finally, we find a comprehensive or inclusive view, in which theoretical contemplation and political activity are both necessary dimensions of a flourishing life; this is the view we have seen in Aristotle's *Eudemian Ethics*.

The opinion that human happiness consists in political activity alone—that there is no happiness except political happiness—was reportedly contained in one text of al-Fārābī's that unfortunately has not survived: his commentary on Aristotle's *Nicomachean Ethics*. This is reported by the Islamic philosopher Ibn Bājjah, who thinks it does not represent al-Fārābī's mature view. The Islamic philosopher Ibn Tufayl transmits al-Fārābī's statement that there is no afterlife, but not the additional notion that the only form of happiness is political happiness.[4] So it seems that one view of al-Fārābī's is that happiness is to be found in an active life in community, perhaps because there is no higher goal of afterlife joy that contemplation might promise.

But there is another aspect to al-Fārābī, a strong voice for the purely contemplative life. In three works al-Fārābī describes happiness as purely intellectual—an exalted view far beyond that expressed by Aristotle. In the first of these, *The Opinions of the People of the Virtuous City,* al-Fārābī teaches that happiness refers to a human soul's attaining a perfected state in which we can live without a body or any form of material support. Happiness thus consists in our becoming what he calls a separate substance, a transcendent being who can live in pure thought, with no need for a body.[5] This ideal represents an extension from the views of Plato and Aristotle, a contemplative path forged by Plotinus and the Neoplatonic tradition. Al-Fārābī goes on to assert that happiness is the ultimate end, the good sought for its own sake, never for the sake of anything else. Moral virtues and noble actions are good only as a means to an end; they are beneficial because they bring happiness.[6] The purpose of practical, moral reason is to make possible theoretical reason; the sole purpose of theoretical reason is to bring us to happiness.[7] The whole purpose of our lives is to attain a transcendent state of pure thought, which al-Fārābī identifies as the ultimate human joy.

On the one hand, we can see that al-Fārābī is developing an exalted view of contemplation that is already present in Aristotle's *Nicomachean Ethics* 10.7–8. But we find in al-Fārābī something quite new: the claim that through theoretical contemplation, a human being can achieve the transcendent afterlife state of becoming an intellect completely separate from the material world.[8] We have no hint of this in Aristotle.[9] Nor is there a clear statement in Aristotle that the rational soul—which is simply the form or animating principle of the body—can survive physical death. If it is difficult for modern readers to accept Aristotle's claim that the happiest life is a life of pure contemplation, it is even more difficult for us to understand al-Fārābī and Maimonides' claim that activating our intellect is literally the key to eternal life.

We find this view articulated again in al-Fārābī's *Political Regime*; in several passages, al-Fārābī suggests that the ultimate human goal is to reach the highest degree of perfection by becoming a separate intellectual substance. This is the attainment of ultimate happiness: actualizing one's own intellect, becoming a fully intelligible being.[10] In the *Selected Aphorisms*, al-Fārābī attributes this view—that happiness is a matter of pure contemplation—to Socrates, Plato, and Aristotle. He ascribes to them the teaching that there are two forms of perfection. The first perfection is to acquire moral virtue and to express virtue in action, but this is only a means to the final perfection. The final perfection is the ultimate happiness and the absolute good; it is desired and chosen for itself and not for the sake of anything else. This is the happiness of the afterlife.[11]

The view I would like to focus upon represents a third facet of al-Fārābī's vision—not the purely political or the purely contemplative ideal, but his comprehensive or inclusive portrait of happiness, which shares certain features with Aristotle's *Eudemian Ethics* but also introduces a new twist. Al-Fārābī offers a sustained exposition of this view in *The Attainment of Happiness*. Here he makes the surprising claim that *theoretical* perfection itself includes not only metaphysics, but also knowledge of human ethics and politics. Theoretical perfection begins with metaphysical knowledge of the beings that constitute the universe and their relation to the divine. However, it goes on to include the study of humanity and the purpose for which we have been made—that is, the perfection we are here to achieve. Theoretical study tells us how we as both individuals and nations can achieve supreme happiness; what remains for us as human beings is to realize and express this theoretical knowledge in action.[12]

In the final section of the work, al-Fārābī addresses the question of whether someone who has achieved perfection in theoretical knowledge should go on to develop practical virtues and abilities. Given that theoretical knowledge includes the science of human happiness, is it genuinely desirable for us to turn from the contemplative life and use our knowledge of human happiness to benefit others? If we have attained happiness, should we return to the cave and assist others to achieve freedom as well? This question has followed us from Plato onward, and al-Fārābī's answer is bold and refreshing. He distinguishes between genuine philosophy and several types of false philosophy. Theoretical philosophy is defective when a philosopher does not know how to use it to benefit others. He suggests that the greater our ability to share learning—to make theoretical knowledge accessible to students, and to use our practical knowledge to help others—the greater our own ability to philosophize, and by extension, the greater our own happiness.[13] The genuine philosopher must be a teacher; the genuine contemplative must share the fruits of his or her contemplation. Otherwise contemplation is for naught. The false philosopher is someone who gains theoretical knowledge, but does not know how to share it with others. Another type of illusory philosopher—the philosopher "in vain"—learns theory, but does not perform acts of virtue. Illusory philosophers thus fail to recognize the purpose for which philosophy is pursued: philosophy enables us both to practice virtue in action and to share our theoretical knowledge with others, to bring others to happiness.[14]

This is a remarkable statement. It is what we have been looking for all along: the notion that true theory must be expressed in practice. Philosophy is about discovering how to live our lives, to achieve human fulfillment and flourishing. If a person has not achieved happiness, he or she cannot truly be called a philosopher. But philosophy is not only about achieving happiness for oneself. A true philosopher is a teacher, someone who can guide others to spiritual fulfillment. If true fulfillment is to be found in theoretical contemplation, then we must help others achieve this ideal as well. But there is more here: our own theoretical virtue is not complete until we have shared the fruits of our understanding.

Why is this so, for al-Fārābī? In brief, the answer is that in the medieval Neoplatonic worldview, perfection must overflow. Divine goodness and bounty are so great that they overflow to create a universe. Likewise, when human beings discover the key to flourishing, we cannot help but share it; understanding is not complete until it has spread and benefited others. God's goodness overflows to create a world; the prophet's understanding expands outward to create a religious community with a Law or to call others to live by such a Law. The teacher receives the first teaching and then shares it with others. True knowledge must be expressed; contemplation cannot be separated from action.[15] [16]

In the *Selected Aphorisms*, al-Fārābī brings the hypothetical case of someone who has mastered theoretical and practical philosophy and yet behaves immorally; he then compares such a person to someone who acts morally but is ignorant of philosophy. The moral person who is ignorant of philosophy is closer to being a philosopher than the immoral person who is an expert in theory. How can this be? He defends his view by explaining that philosophy consists in a human being achieving theoretical understanding, and in all his actions conforming to what is noble (*jamīl*). Philosophy is a comprehensive whole, including both theoretical and moral virtue. Although true virtue is ultimately grounded in theoretical knowledge, the proof of one's knowledge is in one's action. Only a person who behaves morally can be said to be a true philosopher.[17]

We see a new expression of the integrated ideal in the *Virtuous City*, where al-Fārābī equates prophecy with the highest degree of happiness. This suggests a comprehensive portrait of happiness, one that includes action as well as contemplation, since in al-Fārābī's view prophecy overflows from theoretical understanding into practical affairs. The goal of prophecy is not primarily to predict events, but to teach human beings how to live. The prophet represents the most perfect level of humanity and the highest degree of happiness. He or she knows the actions by which we can reach genuine fulfillment, and is able to lead people along the right path toward the attainment of happiness. We saw earlier that the *Virtuous City* described happiness as becoming a self-sufficient separate intellect. However, in this passage of the same text, the philosopher-prophet is held up as an alternative, integrative model of happiness, for the prophet is a teacher, active in the community.[18]

We find a similar description of the prophet in *The Political Regime.* Here the person is described as the recipient of revelation (*waḥy*); revelation follows from a person's union with the transcendent intellectual realm and gives rise to the ability to discern and teach the path toward happiness.[19] A person who receives revelation is the true ruler; those who are guided by this rulership are described as virtuous, good, and happy.[20] However, it is not stated explicitly that the ability to legislate and guide others to fulfillment necessarily enhances a prophet's own happiness.[21]

Al-Fārābī's novel idea is that the true philosopher is one who governs, whether as a legislator in a state, as a leader of a religious community, or simply as a public intellectual who, through teaching and writing, shares knowledge about how to live the good life and attain happiness. That is, the true ruler does not need to rule over land or territory; one can exercise the art of governance even over future generations, by teaching them the art of human flourishing. However, al-Fārābī seems conflicted about whether ultimate fulfillment consists in actualizing our intellects and becoming purely intelligible beings, or whether it is enhanced by sharing with others the knowledge of how to attain happiness. Is the highest fulfillment that of the purely contemplative philosopher, the head of a religious community, or the prophet? Al-Fārābī insists that all of these comprise one idea.[22] However, the view he presents in some contexts that happiness consists in becoming a purely self-sufficient intellect seems to conflict with the model of the engaged prophet, teacher, and leader.[23]

Al-Fārābī is also innovative in his classification of the arts and sciences. He includes practical knowledge within the theoretical, and insists that a thinker who does not have the ability to share his or her wisdom with others is not a genuine philosopher. Thus overflow to others—engaging in what we might call community outreach—seems to be intrinsic to the philosopher's calling. Galston notes the way al-Fārābī's language of overflow with respect to the human philosopher parallels his language about the transcendent divine intellect he calls the Active Intellect, which brings human intellects from a state of potentiality to actuality. While the Active Intellect is not depicted as a personal God, it does seem to have a kind of intent. The Active Intellect looks out to perfect all beings; it overflows intelligible light to bring them to knowledge and thus fulfillment.[24] The philosopher-prophet similarly shares his or her knowledge of the Good or the One with humanity, bringing human beings to flourishing. The prophet-philosopher is thus depicted as a kind of human version of the divine Active Intellect. Moreover, al-Fārābī's depiction of the Active Intellect offers a model of engagement in helping others; it is not simply a self-sufficient separate substance.

A passage in the *Treatise on Logic* further clarifies the intertwined nature of theory and practice in this comprehensive model. Al-Fārābī writes that in Aristotle's view the philosopher is the person who has attained the end of the two parts of philosophy, the theoretical and the practical. The goal of theoretical philosophy is simply truth and knowledge. The end of practical philosophy is making good choices when we choose one thing over another. Human beings do not attain the end of the practical part through their own insights, but through knowledge of practical philosophy that precedes or accompanies action. However, when a person attains knowledge of practical ethics without acting, that knowledge is in vain.[25] Just as the person who has achieved theoretical knowledge will not be a philosopher until he or she attains the end for which inquiry and investigation exist—which is setting forth intellectual demonstrations—so the person who possesses practical knowledge will not become a philosopher until he or she, too, attains the end of practical philosophy, which is to act virtuously.[26] Here knowledge and action are both integral parts of philosophy. Theoretical wisdom attains its end when it is put to use in demonstrations; practical wisdom attains its end in actions. If practical philosophy stops short of action, it is not truly philosophy.

Finally, al-Fārābī rejects the traditional identification of theoretical philosophy with theoretical reason and practical philosophy with practical reason. In the *Treatise on Logic* he does not, with Aristotle, identify practical philosophy as what is subject to human craft or will; rather, he defines it as the study of what brings human happiness or misery. Some sciences traditionally classified as theoretical will therefore be part of practical philosophy or political science if their purpose is to bring human happiness; moreover, only the theoretical faculty can attain real knowledge of what constitutes happiness.[27] Thus we find the following striking statement of the integration of theory and practice in the *Selected Aphorisms*:

> Wisdom then acquaints one with true happiness, and practical wisdom acquaints one with what must be done to attain happiness. These two then are the two ingredients in the perfecting of man, so that wisdom is that which gives the ultimate end, and practical wisdom gives that by which the end is attained.[28]

In short, al-Fārābī has brought together theoretical and practical philosophy, active and contemplative pursuits, in new ways we did not see in Aristotle. These innovations will in turn furnish Maimonides with a rich conception of the ultimate goal of human life.

# 9

# The Imitation of God

## MAIMONIDES ON THE ACTIVE AND THE CONTEMPLATIVE LIFE

### MAIMONIDES ON HUMAN PERFECTION: MORAL OR INTELLECTUAL?

Maimonides, like his predecessors Aristotle and al-Fārābī, struggles to reconcile the contemplative and the active ways of life. Maimonides accepts Aristotle's assertion that the essence of a human being is intellect; through it a human being is human.[1] He asserts that the purpose of the Torah's system of religious law is to bring about human perfection, which he defines in various ways: he speaks of the welfare of the soul and the welfare of the body, as well as the perfection of both the soul and the body.[2]

Lawrence Kaplan explains well what Maimonides means by these terms. "Welfare of the soul" and "welfare of the body" are communal, social-political categories, whereas "perfection of the soul" and "perfection of the body" pertain to the individual. "Welfare" refers to the well-being of the community;[3] welfare of the soul enables the community to acquire the truth about God and metaphysical matters. Welfare of the body improves the ways people live together; this is accomplished by creating a society in which citizens do not oppress one another. Thus it is in the community's interest for people to develop moral qualities useful for life in society; we can think of this as welfare of the body politic.[4] However, Maimonides states explicitly that the purpose of developing physical and moral qualities is for the welfare of the soul. In other words, he does not see morality as an end in itself, but as a means for human beings to acquire intellectual perfection. The purpose of morality is to create a society in which human beings can become enlightened by knowledge of the truth.

The perfection of the body consists of individuals' being healthy and in the best bodily state. However, individuals cannot achieve this state alone; thus we must ensure that everyone in society receives a just measure of physical provisions. The perfection of the soul, for Maimonides, is perfection of the rational soul, the mind: to actualize our intellectual potential, to understand all the ideas it is possible to conceive. In his technical, medieval, philosophical vocabulary, Maimonides explains that this is becoming "an intellect *in actu*," that is, an actualized intellect.

We see here a development of Aristotle's notion that human beings flourish by actualizing our human potential. Both Aristotle and Maimonides believe that the essence of humanity lies in what sets us apart from other species, which is our reason; thus the highest human perfection is to actualize our intellect. For Maimonides, physical and moral perfection are purely instrumental. We cannot achieve our intellectual potential if we are hungry or in great pain. Society's purpose is to create conditions that provide for human flourishing, and specifically, the flourishing of philosophical wisdom.[5]

Many readers are taken aback by Maimonides' bold statement that the perfection of moral qualities exists only for the purpose of intellectual perfection; in fact, he writes in *Guide* 3.27 that the ultimate perfection does not include moral qualities at all. We tend to think that the development of a just, compassionate, kind, and loving nature is the highest human aim. In order to understand Maimonides' intellectualism we must recognize that for Maimonides what lives on of the human soul is the rational soul, the intellect. It is the intellect that can achieve immortality. We are more familiar with the Platonic view of the soul; for Plato the soul is by nature immortal. For Aristotle and the medieval Aristotelians, in contrast, the human rational soul is pure potential at birth; it is up to us to actualize this intellect by developing our thinking capacity. Maimonides inherits this Aristotelian view. The ultimate human goal is immortality, but immortality must be achieved by the human being. We have work to do in this world: to actualize our intellectual potential so that our rational soul might live on, contemplating God in the afterlife.[6]

Although Maimonides does find some intrinsic value to morality,[7] he nevertheless insists that the development and practice of moral wisdom is not our ultimate human aim, for moral character is not what we take with us when we die. Since it is the intellect alone that achieves immortality, to actualize our intellect is the highest human aim; morality is only a stepping stone. We actualize our minds by acquiring purely rational virtues, learning true views on divine or metaphysical matters.[8]

Is Maimonides' ideal, then, a purely rational one? And is this ideal one we can accept—do human beings really aspire to be austere, disembodied intellects contemplating God and metaphysical truths? Is this the model Maimonides draws from al-Fārābī—the aspiration to be a disembodied intellect, separate from matter? What about all the other parts of the human being—our senses of love, compassion, and justice? Are these really of no intrinsic value, are these merely means to an end?[9] These virtues seem so central to the Biblical tradition Maimonides inherits and embodies; it would be a radical break with tradition for Maimonides to dismiss them as purely means to an intellectual end.

It is certainly true that Maimonides places a great deal of emphasis on a purely intellectual state, which culminates after death in the knowledge of God and metaphysical truth. However, the final chapter of the *Guide* suggests that human realization is not a matter of intellectual contemplation alone. Modern students of Maimonides take heart in the integrated ideal of human perfection we find at the end of the *Guide*.

## THE END OF THE *GUIDE*: KNOWLEDGE OF GOD'S ACTIONS, EXPRESSED IN ACTION

Maimonides sets forth his ultimate, integrated ideal in *Guide* 3.54 by bringing together the Bible with philosophy. He correlates terms in a passage from the book of Jeremiah with four perfections spoken of by "the philosophers."[10] Jeremiah 9:22–23 reads: "Let not the wise person glory in his wisdom, let not the rich person glory in his wealth, let not the mighty person glory in his might, but let he that glories glory in this: that he understands and knows me, that I am the Lord, who exercises loving-kindness, justice, and righteousness in the earth, for in these things I delight, says the Lord." Maimonides correlates the philosophers' perfection of the body with Jeremiah's "might" and the perfection of possessions with wealth. He identifies the perfection of moral qualities with wisdom—which he thus identifies as moral wisdom—and the perfection of rational virtues with knowledge of God, which is the "true science."[11]

However, he notes that the verse in Jeremiah does not end with the assertion by God: "Let him who truly glories glory in this, that he understands and knows Me—that I am One," or "that I have no body." Rather the verse goes on to add "that I am the Lord who exercises loving kindness, justice, and righteousness, in the earth, for in these things I delight, says the Lord." These attributes describe God's actions in relation to the created universe. This is the ultimate mystery: God did not remain in eternal hiding, but chose to create a world. We recall from our discussion of Maimonides' views on negative attributes that we cannot know God's essence—God before or apart from creation. Nevertheless, we do see God's traces in the world; we see God's "loving-kindness, justice, and righteousness, *in the earth*."

For Maimonides, this means God's actions are apparent in the lawfulness of the natural order, the laws that govern the universe.[12] Maimonides describes these qualities as attributes of action, descriptions of the way God governs nature—or in more scientific terms, the way the natural world reflects divine order or governance. Thus God's loving kindness is reflected in the fact that embryos are given everything they need for their physical development.[13] God's graciousness is seen in the fact that there is a universe at all. We have no inherent right to be here; God's creation and sustenance of the universe are signs of God's gracious granting of life.[14] God's justice is reflected in the fact that there is an overall balance in the occurrence of relatively good things and relative calamities.[15]

Maimonides' ultimate stance is that the highest human ideal lies beyond what he identifies as the fourth perfection, the perfection of rational virtue; it is found in the overflow or expression of rational perfection, our embodiment of God's attributes of action, expressed in the world in which we live.[16] The human ideal entails knowing that there is an intimate connection between God and the world, that God does exercise governance in creation. Our ultimate aim is thus to achieve an awareness of God and the way God governs the earth. However, such knowledge is not purely theoretical; it must be expressed in action. The way of life of such a person will always have in view loving-kindness, righteousness, and justice through participation in God's attributes; our awareness of God will be expressed in all we undertake. Just as God's existence overflows to create a world, knowledge of God's attributes can overflow into graceful human action.[17]

Modern Neo-Kantians such as Hermann Cohen and Steven Schwarzschild see in this last expression of Maimonides a turn to the ethical.[18] They argue that there is an ethic of human practice and habituation, just as in Aristotle's process of developing moral habits. But there is also a higher ethic in Maimonides that flows from knowledge of God. Here we are not simply habituated to ethical action; our actions flow from our assimilation of God's attributes.

Other scholars describe the *telos* of human beings for Maimonides as political activity, or as practice of the commandments.[19] It seems to me that Maimonides includes all of these dimensions of human *praxis* in the imitation of God. He speaks of God's actions in two spheres: we can study God's actions as expressed in nature or as expressed in the divine law.[20] When we see God's graciousness in the fact of created existence, in the way God provides embryos with all they need, we see a model for our own deeds of loving kindness. As a leader, each of us will model ourself on God's dispassionate action, taking care to govern according to the needs of the people around us, not as an outburst of our own passions. Like the Stoic or Buddhist sage, we will simply see the truth of the situation and act accordingly.

Maimonides also speaks of the Torah's laws as God's actions. Thus we begin by practicing the commandments out of habit, but through our knowledge of God come to understand their wisdom, and practice them with a deep understanding of the way God's attributes are manifest therein. As Menachem Kellner has shown, Maimonides uses the verse "You shall be holy, for I the Lord your God am holy" to suggest that we emulate God's attributes by becoming sanctified through the commandments.[21] Maimonides, however, does not confine imitation of God to knowledge through the Torah or actions commanded by the Law. In several works, Maimonides suggests that *all* our actions should be for the sake of God.[22] In *Guide of the Perplexed* 3.51, Maimonides suggests that the patriarchs and Moses were able to practice contemplation even when engaged in mundane affairs, for their every action was directed to creating a community that would know and love the divine. When we act from our knowledge of God, all our actions—whether duties sanctified by the Law or actions of everyday living—are transformed by emulation of God's attributes. We see God not only through the prism of the Torah, but also through the prism of the magnificent way the world is put together.[23] Scientific study is a means by which we see God's traces in creation, and the divine qualities we find in the natural order provide a model for our own endeavors.

We have seen that religious law and the natural order provide human beings with ethical models; several passages in the *Guide* in addition reflect Socratic and Platonic ethics. If we truly had knowledge of God, Maimonides asserts in *Guide* 3.11, we would not oppress one another. Oppressive actions are the result of ignorance; knowledge of the truth produces virtue.[24] Thus knowledge of the way God acts in the world necessarily results in assimilation of those qualities. As we have seen, this notion of *imitatio Dei* can be traced back to Plato. In the *Republic*, Plato asserts that one who spends time contemplating the Forms would surely not want to act oppressively, since the Forms themselves are perfectly harmonious, neither oppress nor harm others, and do not overreach, but play their own role perfectly. Likewise philosophers who spend their time contemplating this eternal intellectual order will assimilate these qualities.[25]

In the *Theaetetus* Plato asserts this ideal as a desideratum: in the divine there is no evil, and the human goal should be to assimilate oneself to the divine.[26] Of course, Jewish thought also has a tradition of *imitatio Dei*, tracing back to the verse in Leviticus: "You are to be holy, just as I the Lord your God am holy" (Lev. 19:2). Jewish sources tend to enjoin imitating God's *actions* rather than God's being.[27] Maimonides reflects this tradition in *Guide* 1.54; he suggests that while we cannot know God's essence, we can strive to imitate God's deeds of loving-kindness by acting in kind ways. So, too, in *Guide* 3.53, we see God's kindness in creating a world, and we emulate this in our own deeds of compassion.[28]

## THE PURPOSE OF LIFE: INTELLECTUAL PERFECTION OR ACTION IN THE WORLD?

Do these passages redeem Maimonides' philosophy from intellectualist solipsism—from a person seeking the perfection of rational virtues "for you and for you alone"? Before we close our discussion, we do need to take into account one counterargument. Warren Zev Harvey points out that according to the medieval hierarchical paradigm, an individual's intellectual perfection is a self-contained end, not needing to be expressed through giving to others. This principle would explain Maimonides' strong statement in *Guide* 2.11 that "the higher does not exist for the lower"; that just as God does not exist for the sake of the world, higher intellects do not exist for the sake of those below. On the basis of this passage, Harvey argues that for Maimonides, Moses' ultimate perfection is rational perfection; Moses' governance is simply a by-product of his rational perfection, which naturally overflows in acts of guidance. "Moses exists to know God," Harvey writes, "not to guide the multitude."[29]

We encountered earlier a variation of this principle. God exists whether or not the world exists; the world is dependent on God, not God on the world.[30] This is Avicenna's concept of God as Necessary Existent, which Maimonides expresses boldly at the opening of his code of Jewish Law (*Mishneh Torah*):

> If it could be supposed that he did not exist, it would follow that nothing else could possibly exist. If, however, it were supposed that all other beings were non-existent, he alone would still exist. Their non-existence would not involve his non-existence. For all beings are in need of him; but he, blessed be he, is not in need of them nor of any one of them. Hence, his real essence is unlike any of them.[31]

In that light, God's giving of existence is not necessary, but an act of pure graciousness. Harvey notes that Maimonides extends this principle of overflow to prophetic governance, in a passage that echoes al-Fārābī and Avicenna's notions of prophecy:

> Sometimes something comes from [the divine overflow] to a certain individual and . . . renders him perfect, but has no other effect. Sometimes . . . the measure of what comes to an individual overflows from rendering him perfect toward rendering others perfect. This is what happens to all beings: some of them achieve perfection to an extent that enables them to govern others.[32]

Some scholars argue that Maimonides' turnaround at the end of the *Guide* suggests that the purpose of life is political leadership.[33] Harvey puts it differently: political leadership is an overflow from knowledge of God, just as creation is a gracious overflow of the divine being. Or in Harvey's felicitous phrase, only the rich can be philanthropists.[34]

Al-Fārābī and Maimonides thus offer a possible resolution to the tension between the contemplative and the active life in the quest for God and the good. Al-Fārābī and Maimonides—like the Upanishads and *Bhagavad Gītā*—insist that the ultimate goal of human life is apprehension of the Divine. Each of these sources maintains that when human beings attain this perception, we find ultimate fulfillment, and that any actions we undertake will reflect our apprehension. What is the content of this understanding? For Maimonides, it is first and foremost that the one Necessary Existent overflows to create a universe. The Divine expresses itself in a natural universe governed by a perfect system of laws, which give beings all they need for sustenance and the means to attain fulfillment. Such knowledge attained by a human being will likewise flow into action; we will express our understanding in acts of kindness, governance, and guidance. As God's self-knowledge has overflowed to create a universe, our knowledge will flow into acts imitating the divine. We have seen this notion in the *Tao Te Ching* as well. One who is in touch with the *Tao* embodies the Way of nature in his or her action and very being, having a therapeutic effect on all around him or her.[35]

Of course, such knowledge must not simply be cognitive; this is existential, transformative knowledge. In our discussion of Socrates, we pointed to moments of understanding that can truly turn human lives around. Many people, however, find that in order to attain this kind of knowledge, we need a spiritual path, including a moral program and a system of meditation or worship. Worship of the divine may facilitate understanding and may also flow from understanding. For example, in Ibn Ṭufayl's parable *Ḥayy Ibn Yaqẓān* ("Alive, son of Awake,"), a medieval version of the Robinson Crusoe story, the young man who discovers Truth for himself on a desert island chooses a system of worship—circumambulation, imitating the circular motions of the spheres.[36] Ibn Ṭufayl here harkens back to Aristotle, who suggests that the spheres revolve in imitation of the perfection of the Unmoved Mover; the young, self-trained Ḥayy Ibn Yaqẓān, too, circles in imitation of the heavenly order. Avicenna and Maimonides likewise portray the heavenly spheres as engaged in eternal worship of their Creator; both thinkers enjoin human beings to emulate this heavenly praise.[37]

For Maimonides, God has given human beings the perfect system of divine worship, one that allows for and expresses intellectual apprehension; Maimonides maintains that this is embodied in the commandments of Jewish law. The commandments take on an aspect of preparation in the stage of ascent to knowledge of the Divine; in the stage of descent after knowledge, they are an expression of this awareness and love for God.[38] Maimonides even presents the traditional regimen of Jewish prayer as a system of meditation that can induce what Buddhists call mindfulness—awareness of the sublime in every dimension of life. We can see morality in the same way: in the stage of ascent, we engage in moral actions as a means to knowledge of the divine; in the stage of descent, our actions flow from our newfound understanding.[39]

We have seen Krishna argue in the *Bhagavad Gītā* that although he has no need to act, he continues to do so for the preservation of the world; therefore human beings, too, are enjoined to act in the world, without attachment to results.[40] Likewise, Maimonides suggests that one who truly loves God acts with no thought of reward, although happiness will of itself follow.[41] For each of these sources, when human beings apprehend God and the Good, actions and desires fall into place; we express this understanding in our words, in our gestures of gratitude and thanksgiving, and in our lives.

Only the rich can be philanthropists. But what philanthropists! The more a person learns, the more he or she has to share. We can thus understand Aristotle's emphasis on pursuing the contemplative life. Human beings need to continually return to their Source in order to perceive the understanding that sheds light on every facet of reality, including human action. As al-Ghazālī says of the Sufis: "All of their movements and rest are drawn from the light of the niche of prophecy; and beyond the light of prophecy, there exists no source of light from which illumination may be drawn."

# 10

# The Dance of Human Expression

## AL-GHAZĀLĪ AND MAIMONIDES

ABŪ ḤĀMID al-Ghazālī (d. 1111) was a Muslim religious judge and teacher who at the height of his theological career was beset by a crisis that caused him to leave his position and retire into contemplation.[1] His autobiography *Deliverer from Error* in fact narrates several crises. In the account he narrates, as a young man, Ghazālī experiences a skeptical crisis when he realizes that Jews, Christians, and Muslims are all brought up to accept religious doctrines with unquestioning reliance (*taqlīd*). How then can he know that the Islamic doctrines he was taught not to question are objectively true? If he had been brought up as a Jew or Christian, he would have been infused with unquestioning faith in Jewish or Christian teachings rather than those of Islam. Unquestioning acceptance is therefore no indicator of objective truth.[2]

Like Descartes several centuries later, Ghazālī reasons that he can only find certainty by submitting all he believes to the sword of doubt. Ghazālī doubts his sense-perception, intellect, and reasoning powers. His doubt is resolved not by a process of logical deduction, but by a light God casts into his heart that unveils for him the truth, granting him understanding through direct, intuitive witness.[3]

Ghazālī interviews representatives of the major approaches to Islamic thought: theologians, philosophers, Ismā'īlīs who believe in the infallible Imam, and finally Sufi mystics. In his youthful crisis, skepticism was resolved by the light of intuition that God cast into his heart. Likewise, at the next stage of his journey, Ghazālī discovers that it is direct experience that gives him the resolution he seeks. As an intellectual, he finds the theoretical study of Sufi texts easiest. However, he realizes that what is most distinctive in Sufism cannot be apprehended by theoretical study alone, but by direct experience, what the Sufis call taste (*dhawq*). A doctor may know theoretically the difference between drunkenness and sobriety; he or she may know the scientific causes of the intoxicated condition. But there is a world of difference between this theoretical knowledge and the actual experience of being intoxicated. Just so, Sufi manuals can discourse at length on the subtleties of various mystical stages and states, but to master a theoretical understanding of the mystical path is not to walk the path. Ghazālī knew that to progress he needed to abandon his worldly life and practice mystical exercises—to actually walk the Sufi path.[4]

On his own he did not find the courage to take this radical step; it was a second crisis that prompted his withdrawal. An objective analysis might suggest that he underwent a physical or emotional illness; Ghazālī describes this as a gift from God. He had reached the pinnacle of teaching in the Muslim world as a religious judge; now God dried up his tongue. He entered the classroom and could not speak. For Ghazālī, this was a signal from the divine that it was time to leave behind teaching from theory alone. It was time to actually walk the path.[5]

What he discovered was that it is the Sufis who actually embody the religious teachings that the intellectual elite—philosophers, theologians, jurists—merely study and expound. None of the knowledge garnered by intellectuals could improve the way of life of the Sufis, for all their movements and restings draw inspiration from the light of prophetic revelation, the only true source from which illumination may be received.[6] As in his earlier crisis, Ghazālī discovers that true insight is gained through illumination, an understanding that transcends the creative workings of the discursive intellect—that is, through experiential, existential knowledge. However intuitive insight is not simply non-rational, for it also sheds light on and completes intellectual understanding.[7] It is the Sufis who truly understand prophetic revelation, while for others, "prophecy" is a mere word, devoid of experiential content.[8] This assertion of Ghazālī's suggests that the orthodox sources of Islamic knowledge—Qurʾān, *ḥadīth*, the consensus of the community, legal reasoning—are not fully understood by scholars of these disciplines without illumination from the divine that reveals them in their full light.

Ghazālī goes on to describe a path of mystical ascent. The first level brings mystical experiences with content: revelations and visions, including beholding angels and the spirits of the prophets, and receiving verbal instruction from them. Then adepts ascend to levels beyond that of beholding forms and figures; these are levels that cannot be described in language, and if one tries, one utters what is erroneous. Ghazālī thus describes mystical experiences with form and content as leading to the highest level of ascent, experiences which defy definite form.[9]

We have mentioned that Ghazālī's narrative of ascent is highly stylized. Eric Ormsby points out that the autobiographical narrative is shaped by the theme of illness and cure, both spiritual and intellectual.[10] Note that there are also correspondences in the levels he sets out. Mystical experiences that are without content and that transcend language correspond to the levels that the Sufis reach in which all movement and rest emerge from and are illuminated by the lamp of prophetic revelation. These levels also find a parallel in the supra-intellectual light Ghazālī himself received in his heart that healed him of his doubt, and to the experiences he achieved in his ten-year sojourn with the Sufis.

One cannot accurately describe these ultimate states by the terms "inherence," "union," or even "connection." Those who do so utter what is erroneous; they make unfounded ontological inferences from their experience.[11] The terms "union" or "connection" suggest either that the individual can achieve unity with the Divine or that there are actually two entities in the universe to be joined, whereas Ghazālī believes that there is only one divine Reality. These unfounded inferences caused Sufis like al-Ḥallāj to utter phrases such as "I am the Truth," or Bisṭāmī, "There is nothing in this robe I am wearing save God." Rather one should allow the experience to be what is, and not attempt to give an account of it.

Ghazālī asserts that those who have not tasted these experiences know no more of prophetic revelation than the name. Those friends of God who have direct experiences are touching what is in truth the beginning of the prophetic path.[12] There is thus a continuum between Sufi and prophetic experience. This was a dangerous teaching of Ghazālī. To suggest a continuum between prophets, friends of God (pl. *awliyāʾ*; sing. *walī*), and Sufis puts Ghazālī dangerously close to the Neoplatonic philosophers, for whom prophecy and religious experience are achievements of the individual rather than divine gifts.[13] For Ghazālī, however, the light of prophetic revelation is a genuine self-disclosure of a willing, personal God.[14]

Ghazālī stylizes his notion of stages of ascent in one additional context. He writes that children first develop the sense of touch, then sight, hearing, and taste; then discernment (*tamyīz*); and then intellect (*ʿaql*). Beyond intellect, there is another stage at which an inner eye is opened, which allows one to see things beyond the level of the intellect-judge. Others might dismiss the existence of this level, just as someone blind from birth would scoff if told about colors and shapes. But none of us are truly in the position of that blind person, since we have been given a certain hint of the prophetic inner eye. We all have something analogous to the faculty of prophecy in the dream state. If we heard about the dream state, in which one falls into a dead faint and sees things that one cannot apprehend in the waking state, we would scoff at it. But just as intellect is a stage in which there is an eye that sees various types of intelligible objects, so is prophecy a stage in which there is an eye endowed with light such that in that light the unseen and other supra-intellectual objects become visible. The proof of prophecy is simply its existence and the existence of knowledge that we could not attain in any other way; this knowledge is attained by divine inspiration and assistance from God. The meaning of prophetic revelation is that there is knowledge that cannot be apprehended by the intellect alone. But that does not exhaust the meaning of prophecy. There are other qualities and properties of prophecy, which can be apprehended only by immediate experience (*dhawq*). But the property of giving knowledge we could not attain any other way is one that we can understand by analogy from the dream state.[15]

What do these accounts of the mystical ascent teach us about the quest for divinity and goodness? We have seen that Ghazālī testifies that it was God who guided him to withdraw into seclusion and later to return to teaching. What he discovered was that the true purpose and end of religious life is direct experience of the Divine. When Ghazālī had taught theology and religious law from a solely intellectual point of view, God caused his tongue to dry up, and he went into retreat to study and practice with the Sufis. What he discovered was that the Sufis were people of experience, not words, and that he could not attain their knowledge without actually traveling the path of mystical exercises culminating in direct experience. And yet Ghazālī's journey does not end with experience of mystical states. God just as surely tells him that it is time to go back and share with others what he has learned. Ghazālī expresses in a mystical context the Platonic motif of return to the cave—re-entering society to share the fruits one has gleaned from vision of the Truth. And yet he assures the reader:

> Although I have gone back, I have not gone back. Previously, I had been teaching knowledge by which worldly success is attained; I had called others to it by word and deed, and that was my aim and intention. But now I am calling others to the knowledge whereby worldly success is given up and its low place on the scale of real worth is recognized. This is now my intention, my aim, my desire; God knows that this is so. It is my earnest longing that I may make myself and others better. I do not know whether I shall reach my goal or whether I shall be taken away while short of my object. I believe, however, both by certain faith and by direct witness (*mushāhada*) that there is no power and no might save with God, the high, the mighty, and that I do not move of myself but am moved by Him; I do not work of myself but am used by Him. I ask Him first of all to reform me and then to reform through me, to guide me and then to guide through me, to show me the truth of what is true and to grant of His bounty that I may follow it, and to show me the falsity of what is false and to grant of His bounty that I may turn away from it.

Thus the key to a person's journey may be found in inner aim and intention, rather than whether the journey externally appears to embody an active or a contemplative life. Ghazālī returned to the life of teaching with an entirely different motivation, one infused with the presence of the God he has met. Ghazālī was called both to abandon and to return to an active life of teaching. His experience thus speaks to the power that the knowledge gained in contemplation holds to transform the active life.

## THE END OF THE *GUIDE:* THE FRUITS OF CONTEMPLATION EXPRESSED IN ACTION

Ghazālī's dialectic between activity and contemplation can perhaps shed light on Maimonides' vision. Recent scholarly discussion has raised the question whether the true end of the *Guide of the Perplexed* is to be found in the integrated ideal we have examined in *Guide* 3.54—that of return to the community, expressing God's attributes through our lives. Perhaps, rather, the true aim of the philosopher's ascent is the state of contemplative worship we read about in *Guide* 3.51, in which alone on our bed at night, we silently contemplate abstract spiritual truths. Or perhaps the goal is the state of Abraham, Isaac, and Jacob depicted in 3.51; although engaged in agricultural work, the minds of these leaders were immersed in the Divine, and the purpose of all their actions was to found a religious community that would know and worship God.

David Shatz has pointed out a paradox here; the patriarchs performed these actions "with their limbs alone," the precise opposite of the state of worship depicted in the same chapter, in which human beings are enjoined to worship with full concentration, not merely with "limbs alone."[16] This raises an interesting question. Is Maimonides' ideal one in which life with other human beings involves a mere going through the motions, while one's intellect and heart are with God? Or should interaction with people be more like worshipful communion with the Divine, in which we act not with our limbs alone, but with our entire being?

The resolution for Maimonides may lie in the human being's level of awareness. If a person realizes that every being has been given existence by God, that each of us is a divine spark and *in potentia* a loving servant of the Divine, there is no necessary tension between the active and the contemplative life. This realization can bring us to express God's attributes in relation to all those around us, to emulate God's overflowing kindness and graciousness in giving existence to all beings. According to Maimonides, the patriarchs and Moses knew how to maintain a balance between the inner and the outer, so that actions could flow as a natural expression of contemplation. It is true that Moses, Aaron, and Miriam died with a kiss, in the pleasure of their contemplation of the Divine; they looked forward with eager anticipation to complete return to the divine Source.[17] But this did not lead them to hasten leaving the community of this world; Moses, we know, longed ardently to stay on earth and lead his people into the Promised Land.

Ehud Benor suggests a resolution between action and contemplation in Maimonides' thought that is parallel to the resolution we found in our study of Aristotle. We noted that Aristotle suggests degrees of *theōria*; study may not be divorced from the world of human action. The most exalted degree of *theōria* is to contemplate pure thought, the divine thought itself; however, we can also theorize beings in this world. Given that Maimonides holds that we cannot know the divine essence, Aristotle's exalted *theōria* may not work in his system. Thus, Benor argues, for Maimonides the object we contemplate is precisely this world—a common object of our knowledge and of divine knowledge.[18]

In our study of both Aristotle and Maimonides, we have found that human beings are part of the teleological order of nature. Given that the world displays a wisdom and beauty in the way it is put together, we must recognize that human beings are also part of that wisdom and beauty. Just as we contemplate nature and its purposes, we can reflect upon human beings and our purposes. Study of the divine wisdom in nature will thus include anthropology and psychology—the deep understanding of humanity. This kind of wisdom would seem to express itself most naturally in compassionate action, just as the divine fountain overflows to express divine goodness throughout nature.

The deepest contemplation of God and the good may thus be inextricably connected with action. Or as Maimonides expresses his Socratic ethic, "The truth has no other purpose than knowing that it is truth. Since the Torah is truth, the purpose of knowing it is to do it." [19]

# Conclusion

What have we discovered in the course of our study? The book began by examining the relationship between God and good in the creation accounts of the Bible and Plato. We discerned a strong connection between God and goodness in both the Bible and Plato. In the Bible God creates and sees that all is good. Creation is not from nothing but from a preexisting chaotic state. Similarly, Plato's Demiurge takes a preexistent chaotic mix of earth, air, fire, and water and shapes them into an intelligible order, on the model of the Forms. Creation is the shaping of chaos into order.

What is good about order? The Hebrew Bible sees beauty in the orderliness of nature. This world may be built upon chaos, but has become an orderly cosmos. And it is so because there is a Sovereign Being who has fashioned the messiness of what simply is into a beautiful, meaningful whole. The Bible does not begin with a sheer void, but with the basic elements without which we could not make sense of the world as it is. And although there is some chaos underlying all, at the heart of reality is goodness. The creation myth of Genesis 1 does not tell the story of a primordial battle between the forces of chaos and those of order, but of a quiet ordering and the satisfaction of seeing how good and beautiful is our world. This is ontological, not moral goodness; the world is structured, balanced, and whole, and it works. While moral decisions are complex and the world can sometimes seem to be a frightening place, the Genesis story tells us that the rhythms of nature are constant and signal a deeper order at work in reality. The rabbinic tradition goes further and asserts that even evil is part of the goodness of creation. Even the elements of reality that seem negative or superfluous offer a benefit to the goodness of the whole, including the human inclination to evil. In the first creation story, everything that is created is good; the words "bad" or "evil" do not appear in Genesis 1.

Genesis 2–3 shows a different image of God and introduces the word "evil" in the story of the tree of the knowledge of good and bad. The second creation story introduces a God who is in relation to human beings—not a majestic, transcendent sovereign but a God who interacts with humans. The Biblical text suggests that God is not simply an impersonal artist who creates the laws of nature, but also a personal being—that love and compassion are as much a part of the cosmic order as the laws of physics. The second creation story also tells the tale of humans' acceptance of responsibility for their actions. Humans must have had free will in potential, otherwise they could not have eaten from the tree, disobeying the express command of God. But the story tells us that we chose freely the freedom to choose, growing away from the innocence of childhood in the process, and that as a result, life is difficult, and actions have difficult and steep consequences. But being adults is also wonderful; it is thus that we come into deeper relationship with ourselves, one another, and our creator. It is reality in all its complexity that enables us to learn and grow.

In Plato's *Timaeus*, too, we hear of a process of creation of order from a preexisting chaos. Random elements of earth, air, fire, and water were moving about chaotically in a Receptacle until a craftsman, the Demiurge, looked to the Forms and shaped the chaos on the model of the Forms. Since the earliest interpreters, there has been a question of whether this is meant to be a literal creation story or a figurative account. Perhaps what Plato wants to say is that were it not for the presence of reasoning Mind, all would be chaotic. Some scholars suggest that the Demiurge represents the Forms themselves or the Form of the Good. What is fascinating is the parallel to the Hebrew Bible; both cases may reflect a theodicy, an explanation of why there is evil in the world. Both accounts suggest that a good God ordered the world for the good. The reason there is evil in the world is that God operated under some constraints; God did the best God could given the materials that were present to work with. The world is both good and orderly; God's motive for creation was to make the world as beautiful as the eternal realm of

Forms. God's motive for creation is wanting to share in goodness, from God's lack of jealousy. The goodness of the world is also related to its intelligibility; the Good allows the world to be known.

Plato paints a portrait of a world that is neither pure chaos nor pure order. Our goal as philosophers is, like the Demiurge, to shape our world in accordance with the moral ideals at the heart of reality. Modern scientists also see patterns of order structuring our world: the double helix of the DNA structure, the laws of physics. And Plato's thought moved in an increasingly mathematical direction; he saw the Forms patterned upon number. Mathematical equations are expressed physically in our physical world. Plato's teleological worldview may not diverge as far from our scientific conception as might appear at first glance.

His notion of the Good might also be intelligible in modern terms. Plato sees the world as an organic whole, in which each part performs a vital function. We can see this biologically; every part of a biological organism has a function with respect to the whole. We can see this also with respect to any being of complexity, in inorganic nature as well as organic nature. It is the principle of unity that binds all things together, to make individual things into a unity and to bind the universe together as a whole. Plato thus may have identified the Good with the principle of unity. Things *are* insofar as they participate in unity, Goodness, intelligible order; things exist insofar as they are unified and coherent. The Good gives the Forms their coherent order; the Forms are forms of excellence, so what they share in common is participation in Goodness.

In the Hebrew Bible, we moved from universal goodness in chapter 1 to goodness in the human sphere in chapter 2. Likewise we moved in our discussion of Plato from the cosmic goodness described in the *Timaeus* to his discussions of human excellence in the *Meno, Protagoras, Gorgias*, and *Republic*. In the *Republic*, he presents the image of the tripartite soul: the goal of the soul is justice, the proper ordering of the soul so that each part performs its proper function, with reason ruling over appetite with the aid of the will. In the *Phaedrus*, too, Plato presents the soul as divided. In the earlier dialogues, however, Plato presents a different argument. Here he suggests that every soul wants what is genuinely good—to live a happy, balanced, fulfilling life. The reason we don't achieve what is good is that we are ignorant of what will make us genuinely happy. Thus the key to both excellence and happiness is knowledge of what is genuinely good for the *psyche*. The key to achieving excellence is the proper ordering of our soul. Just as the Demiurge crafted the world into an orderly whole, so our goal is to craft a soul in which each part sings its proper part in the choir. Goodness is order and balance, both in the cosmos and in our psyches.

Iris Murdoch is a modern Platonist who integrates the Platonic tradition in a modern light. In "On God and Good," she reinterprets the traditional concept of God in Platonic terms; the Good, she argues, is a single, perfect, transcendental non-representible real object of attention. Commitment to a moral ideal can be a powerful inspiration for our energy; we can contemplate the Good the way theists contemplate God. The Good is a magnetic force drawing and inspiring moral action. Virtue or excellence (*aretē*) is single, in that it unites and undergirds the many virtues. Likewise the Good is single, in that it is that which unifies and inspires diverse spheres of excellence: the courage of the mountain climber, the creativity of the artist, the sensitivity of the teacher who works with special needs children.

Murdoch argues that moral values are transcendent in that they are objective, rather than subjective and relative. Thus we sense in the power of an inspiring act of moral courage something that lives on behind the individual deed. There is a certainty that there exists an absolute standard of goodness, despite the relativity, ugliness, and flux we see in our world. Moreover, we are inspired by a transcendent ideal of perfection—an absolute standard that motivates us in a way no partial standard can. The moral ideal holds an objective authority for us; we strive to get ever closer to that ideal, even as we know that no finite being can ever fully achieve it. Murdoch argues further that this moral ideal possesses the necessity traditionally ascribed to God through the ontological proof. The idea of Good possesses an absolute certainty that is not merely psychological.

The Good possesses the necessity of reality. To see by the light of the Good is to see reality as it is, rather than through the partial vision clouded by our subjective needs and desires. The artist, scholar, and mathematician all aspire to this objectivity; we must do so when we are learning a language. These disciplines correspond to the traditional discipline of prayer: they demand our objective, focused attention, and bring us into the magnificent truth of what is. These are training for the ultimate discipline of the moral sphere; to see the complexity of a moral situation and the reality of what is good for all. The same honesty is demanded of the scholar, the artist, and the parent or child; and it is the Good that sheds light on how we are to balance these very different spheres of our life. For Murdoch, then, morality is the true mystical attunement; to seek unbiased guidance is the highest form of prayer. The radiance of the Good awakens our love and our desire to draw close to it. For Murdoch, Good is more absolute than God; we can do without God, but we cannot do without Good.

In chapter 3, we explored Chinese thought with its view that nature, as it is, is Good. The ancient Chinese belief system does not see a conflict between what ought to be and what is; for the *I Ching*, the *Tao Te Ching*, and some branches of Confucian thought, the way of nature is the way things ought to be. It is our goal to pattern ourselves according to the way of nature, the *Tao*. To follow our nature is to continue the *Tao*, which expresses itself in the rhythms of *yin* and *yang* and the principle of reversal—to restore equilibrium and homeostasis after disequilibrium. Human nature is naturally good; when humans attain harmony within themselves and extend these to the world of nature, the task of Heaven and Earth is completed.

In the *Tao Te Ching* we have an account of the coming to be of all things. It is not clear whether creation is a one-time event or a description of the mysterious process of formation by which things come to be determinate from the indeterminate. The text shows us the way of *wu-wei*, nonintrusive action, to stay attuned to the larger context from which things emerge. When we overvalue the formed, we lose the larger good of the whole—we forget that the beautiful flower depends also on the dirt, fertilizer, and entire ecosystem to emerge. We can act with assertiveness and creativity, as long as we remain attuned to the larger context of potential, and don't get attached to any one reified entity. We achieve greater effectiveness if we can be open to the many possibilities of the evolving situation, rather than remaining attached to any one purpose. Thus while Western ontology values Being, Taoism values non-being, emptiness, the vast, spacious openness of pure potential. Rather than superimposing our preconceived ideas upon a situation, we become aware of the interconnectedness of mutually defining opposites.

The Confucian *Tao* is prescriptive: it outlines defined courses of action: the way of the father, the way of the son, the way of the sage. The Taoist way in contrast is a non-course: to return to pure potentiality and follow the natural path that emerges. The Confucian sage rules by the power of ethical authority developed by living in cultured company; this authority is awe-inspiring and brings others to yield to it. Confucian moral virtue is the virtue of civilization; Taoist virtue is the subtle, lowly power of nature, in which the quiet and tranquil moves over the restless and agitated. Taoism and Confucianism, both built upon the goodness of nature, express the *yin* and *yang* of Chinese civilization itself. The Confucian sage inspires people to become responsible ethical agents through moral self-cultivation. The Taoist sage encourages people to cast off the masks of civilization and return to natural, spontaneous unself-conscious action, which in the eyes of Lao Tzu is a more authentic kind of virtue. The Absolute of Taoist tradition is the *Tao*, the unlimited Source of all. For Confucianism the Absolute may be Heaven or the harmony and equilibrium between Heaven, Earth, and Humanity. Good is an ongoing dance of finding balance amidst the uncertainties of life, and of finding harmony in the polarities of nature.

In a coda to chapter 3, we found in the philosophy of Alfred North Whitehead a modern parallel to the classical Chinese tradition. Whitehead's goal is to rethink the modern scientific ontology that denied the real existence of qualities in the world. He insists that the sights, sounds, and sensations of nature are real, and that values are as much a part of nature as facts. In fact, modern quantum physics shows relationship as an integral part of life even at the quantum level. Relationship is basic to our knowledge of the world; "if anything out of relationship, then complete ignorance to it." The entire fabric of nature is an interconnected web of experience; we only think that experience is anthropomorphic because we think all experience must be conscious. Even particles experience and respond to one another. The universe is a feeling universe; the selfish gene is only one side of the picture. There are also elements of cooperation and harmony throughout the ecosystem, as beings create an environment that supports their growth. The continuity between moments represents a primitive kind of memory; the universe is not a fabric of static things but an organism of interconnected events or occasions of experience, which continually choose to renew themselves and establish patterns of value in nature.

Like Murdoch, Whitehead is a Platonist; he recognizes an equivalent of Plato's Ideas or Forms, which he calls eternal objects. These are the constituent qualities without which the world would not be as it is. But unlike Plato and Murdoch, for Whitehead the real is more valuable than the ideal. Actuality is the ground of value; the greatest paper in the world is of little value until it is written. The first word of the paper makes it less than the potential masterwork—and yet more, because it is real.

Good for Whitehead is realized here on earth. God is that foundation of being that envisages all potentials and inspires us to crystalize new forms from the underlying pulse of creativity that flows throughout the universe. Whitehead insists that he includes God within his system for philosophical and not purely religious reasons. If there were just an underlying pulse of creativity and open potential, the world would have no direction. God is required to draw the choices of actual occasions into a harmonious whole. While every entity has free will to choose what it will be, God inspires choices that will blend with the creative order. For Plato, it is the One or the Good that guarantees unity, order, and intelligibility. For Whitehead, there is a personal willing God. And yet God needs other beings to realize values, to bring potentiality into actuality; the universe is the sum of our collective choices. There is an aesthetic beauty to the workings of nature that is akin to the Chinese vision of the web that has no weaver. And yet for Whitehead there is an artist; the universe is a collectively created symphony. God and humans together realize the Good.

The Biblical tradition tells us that God created the world and saw that all was good. How then does evil enter creation? In chapter 4, we saw that Augustine and Maimonides, separated by centuries and cultures, draw upon a common Biblical and Neoplatonic tradition to account for evil in creation. Both argue that every entity that exists inhabits a unique rung upon the great chain of being. Evil is lack of being or privation; judging things to be evil reflects a limited, subjective point of view. Things appear to be evil because they are in conflict with one another, or because they interfere with our limited desires. However, if we look at things in the context of the whole, we see that indeed, the whole of being is greater than the higher things alone. If we saw all events in context of the whole, we would achieve contentment and neither suffer nor harm others.

Both Augustine and Maimonides differentiate between moral evil and metaphysical, natural evil. Anything that has being is good; metaphysical evil is negation, the corruption or deprivation of being and thus goodness. Things begin intact; evil is that which deprives them of being or corrupts their goodness. Moral evil, too, is due to corruption or deprivation: it is the corruption of the original good will that we are given. Augustine is comforted by realizing that when he himself does evil, it is the result of his own free will, and does not have to be blamed upon God or a Manichean principle of evil.

Like Augustine, Maimonides affirms the Platonic assertion that all being is good, that God is the absolute good and God's bringing us into being is the greatest good. He affirms the notion of the great chain of being, in which God's intention is to bring about the greatest amount of being and thus good as possible. Maimonides' statement that God is the absolute good is problematic, as it conflicts with his strictures about the use of language with respect to God. All we can know about God is that God's existence is Necessary and all other beings are contingent, and thus there is an absolute disjunction between language about God and about all other beings. We cannot know anything positive about the essence of a being whose mode of existence is

Necessary; all we can know are the acts that emanate from God. Thus we can use language of action or of negation; we can deny anything of God that we can affirm of the contingent world. Negation also avoids introducing multiplicity in a God whose essence Maimonides insists is absolutely unified.

"Good" is thus for Maimonides an equivocal term; it means different things when applied to God and to creatures. In its absolute sense it simply points to God as the ultimate source of being and value. In 3.11 Maimonides asserts that if we realize this fact, we will neither hurt nor oppress ourselves or others; we will treat all beings as of intrinsic dignity and worth as expressions of the one God. Good also has different meanings when applied to humanity in its ideal state and in its actual state. In the ideal state of humanity, represented by Adam and Eve in the Garden of Eden, humans see only true and false, reality as it is. From an absolute standpoint, there is no evil; all being is good. Humans see evil when we look at reality from our individual, subjective point of view. From the perspective of an individual, death is an evil because it deprives us of our life. But from the perspective of the whole, death is necessary for it makes room for new life and the continuity of generations. Natural evils such as earthquakes and hurricanes simply happen; they are an unfortunate by-product of the fact of material existence. If the Infinite had not chosen to create a material universe, there would be no earthquakes and hurricanes—but we would also be deprived of the beauty of existence. Death and loss are the price we pay to enjoy the gift of our being as finite creatures. If we want to enjoy the splendors of existence, we must accept its consequences. Moral evil, he suggests, is also the result of a lack or deprivation. Whereas Augustine, developing the Christian notion of original sin, describes moral evil as due to the corruption of the will, Maimonides chooses the Socratic language of lack. Moral evil is due to ignorance, the lack of knowledge. If we had knowledge of God—which is equivalent to the Truth—we would harm neither ourselves nor others.

Maimonides thus suggests that while absolute Good is the equivalent of the Truth, that which is, in our actual state we use the terms "good" and "evil" to describe the world as distorted by our subjective, relative judgments. Thus eating from the tree of the knowledge of good and evil represents a deprivation of knowledge, which sees only true and false. In humanity's ideal state, the term "good" represents the absolute commandment of God: to know only the Truth, to know God. In our actual state, the terms "good" and "evil" represent the changing face of human morality, dictated by our subjective desires.

Augustine is a more conscious Platonist; his God is Goodness itself, a personal embodiment of the Form of the Good. Maimonides' God is at face value more austere: the Necessary Existent about whom no positive assertion can be made, the unknowable Neoplatonic One. Yet both assert that being itself is a good; God is the source of all being and goodness, and evil is simply lack, deprivation, or corruption. The Good for both thinkers is the Truth that is God, and for humans to know and contemplate Truth.

Thus human happiness for Augustine and Maimonides is found through contemplation of eternal truths—that is, through knowledge of God. In chapter 5, we saw that like Augustine and Maimonides, the Indian sacred texts known as the Upanishads suggest that peace and ultimate happiness are found through communion with the Divine, and that the *Bhagavad Gītā* offers four practical paths to achieve that communion: the paths of knowledge, action, devotion, and meditation. To Augustine and Maimonides, the Upanishads add that the Absolute has qualities not only of being and goodness, but awareness and joy. In fact, when we discover our true inner Self (*ātman*) we discover that it is one with the universal Spirit (*brahman*), which is existence, knowledge, and bliss. Like Plato, the Upanishads believe that knowledge has existential, transformative power. The Absolute for the Hindu tradition is *brahman*, originally the power of the sacrifice, but later conceived as an essential spirit, the fine essence undergirding all of reality. Ancient Indian thought saw the sacrifice as so essential to reality that the cosmos itself was said to be created and sustained by sacrifice. But by the end of the period of the Brāhmaṇas, the sacrifice had become internalized, so that it was not ritual knowledge but metaphysical knowledge that held the key to *brahman*. One who knew *brahman* became one with *brahman* and was liberated from *saṃsāra*, the cycle of birth and death. The absolute Good for this tradition was beyond moral good and evil; it was to transcend the world of distinction and find eternal freedom.

However, the *Bhagavad Gītā*, a popular devotional text, pointed out that to discover the Absolute by knowledge alone requires intense concentration. The *Gītā* thus sets forth two additional paths more accessible to the average person: continuing to act in the world, while letting go of attachment to the results of our actions (*karma yoga*); and a relationship of devotion to a loving personal God (*bhakti yoga*). For the *Gītā*, the personal God Krishna is more ultimate than the impersonal *brahman*, and the Good is to join Krishna in a relationship of loving devotion. The goal is not becoming one with *brahman*—a drop returning to the ocean—but eternal abiding with Krishna; the dualistic metaphysics of Sāṃkhya—in which many individual separate souls seek to get free of nature and return to the Lord—prevails over the nondualistic notion of union between the individual self (*ātman*) and *brahman*. And the path is one of non-attached action, devotional practice, and active meditation rather than pure contemplative knowledge.

Chapter 6 showed that like the ancient Chinese texts the *I Ching* and *Tao Te Ching*, Buddhism sees change as fundamental to reality. Like these ancient Chinese streams of thought, Buddhism suggests that by accepting change, we can let go of the grasping and frustration the Buddha saw as endemic to human life. The flame of our existence is fed by our desire, anger, and greed; when we abandon this, we "*nirvāṇa*," we cease to feed these flames and can exist in a way characterized by wisdom and compassion. Abandoning the limitations we have put upon ourselves by definitions of our identity, we experience freedom, flexibility, and vitality. Mahāyāna Buddhism in particular emphasizes that we can experience this new way of being and remain engaged in the world; moreover, this awareness can be a gift to others along the path. Buddhist meditation—in particular that of the Ch'an and Zen schools—emphasizes the mindfulness with which we approach every moment of our lives. Not only can we release ourselves from suffering, but we can appreciate the freshness of every moment. Zen teachings do this through humor, playfulness, and paradox, constantly undercutting the predilection of the human mind to attach itself to views and doctrines—including those of Buddhism and Zen.

Chapter 7 showed that Aristotle, like Buddhist meditation and the *Bhagavad Gītā*, offers an earthy, practical path to human flourishing. His ethical works reflect the tension we see in the Upanishads and the *Bhagavad Gītā* between the contemplative life of the philosopher and active, engaged life in society. He describes two forms of excellence or virtue: intellectual virtue, which is excellence of thinking; and practical virtue, which is excellence of moral qualities and actions. While Plato's Socrates teaches that virtue is a form of knowledge, that to know the good is to do it, Aristotle insists that moral excellence requires practice and habit. Discovering the principle of the mean and deliberating about practical action are important, but the key to developing a moral character is practice. Our actions create our character, and appropriate behavior requires the subtle art of sensitivity and attunement developed through active moral training.

Aristotle begins the *Nicomachean Ethics* by informing us that the good is that to which all things aim. The human good or *telos* is *eudaimonia*—the fulfillment and flourishing of the human being's potential. Human beings are fundamentally biological and have a function. The acorn's function is to become an oak tree; the human's function is active exercise of his or her ability to reason. When we actively exercise reason in matters of human action, we achieve moral excellence. When we exercise reason in theoretical matters—when we study mathematics, the unchanging principles of nature, and the metaphysical principles of being and divinity—we achieve intellectual excellence. In this we liken ourselves to the Unmoved Mover, who is the pure activity of thinking.

While much of the *Nicomachean Ethics* is concerned with the active moral life and the human virtues, chapters 7 and 8 of book 10 suggest that the ultimate fulfillment of our human *telos* lies in pure theoretical contemplation, like the life of the Unmoved Mover. As human beings, we find a secondary kind of flourishing in developing moral virtue. But we also have glimpses of a divine flourishing that will fulfill the divine part of our nature, and perhaps suggests our true divine potential. The question is whether Aristotle thought the ideal life consists of the pure activity of contemplation (the *dominant* view) or thought that the ideal is a balance of expressing all the diverse forms of excellence (the *inclusive* view).

The *Eudemian Ethics* offers an alternative vision of a mixed or integrated ideal of human flourishing in happiness as complete, inclusive virtue—not just excellence of one part of the soul, the part that studies, but the whole soul, including the part that engages in moral actions. Just as all the parts of one's body have to function well to be in physical health, it is likewise with the virtue of the soul insofar as it is a complete whole. Again, Aristotle suggests clearly that to express true excellence of soul, we must develop not only theoretical virtue but also moral virtue. At the end of the *Eudemian Ethics*, he suggests that our practical wisdom should aim for whatever balance makes contemplation and service of God possible. Service of God may simply mean the fulfillment of our natural *telos*, when we perfect our natural essence and purpose, imitating God and serving the divine order.

There is evidence even in the *Nicomachean Ethics* for an integrated ideal. Passages from the *Nicomachean Ethics* and throughout the Aristotelian corpus suggest that Aristotle uses the verb *theōria* ("to contemplate") for active engagement with many aspects of our world. Pericles studies political actions; friends learn from studying the virtuous actions of their friends. Thus Aristotle suggests a kind of contemplation in action, which bridges the gap between the exalted contemplation of *Nicomachean Ethics* 10 and the dynamic, active life in the *polis* Aristotle describes in the middle books of the treatise. While the focus of a political life may be directed toward political good and the ultimate focus of the philosophers' life the fruits of theoretical study, both will engage in learning about human beings and life in community.

In a coda to chapter 7, we saw that contemporary philosophers Alasdair Macintyre and Charles Taylor bring the Aristotelian tradition into the twenty-first century. Modern Kantians like John Rawls put justice and human rights at the center of moral argument. Macintyre, in contrast, argues that we need a conception of the purpose of our entire lives to see where justice fits into our overall scheme of value. Charles Taylor argues that we as human beings cannot exist without an orientation to the good. A self is not an objective, neutral entity that can be studied like other objects of empirical scientific research. Selves are inextricably oriented toward goals and the overall values around which we structure our lives.[1] Moreover, love for the good is itself among the most powerful motivators for moral action. Hence Socrates' notion that the unexamined life is not worth living; the articulation of our most deeply held moral values inspires not only love for philosophy but love for the good itself and for expressing the good in action.[2] Taylor thus offers a robust defense of Aristotle's ethical vision, expressed in the opening of the *Nicomachean Ethics*: every craft, activity, and action aims at some good.[3] In Aristotle's teleological universe, this includes the natural world, but all the more so the human. To be human is to have a function that sets us apart from nature: to use our reason to consciously direct us toward ends we choose. Alasdair Macintyre and Charles Taylor argue that this vision holds as true for moderns as for ancients. Moderns have gone astray in locating the sphere of morality narrowly in the question of rights and obligations, of what we ought to do. Macintyre and Taylor argue that ethics is most properly concerned with who we are, with how we orient our lives toward the good.

In chapter 8, we saw that the ninth-century Islamic philosopher Al-Fārābī took this integration one step further. Al-Fārābī suggests that the fruits of contemplation must express themselves in action; the philosopher who does not return to the cave to improve the social order has not fulfilled his or her role as philosopher. Al-Fārābī in fact suggests three models of happiness. The first is purely theoretical: to become a separated intellect, divorced from matter, contemplating eternal truths. This is beyond anything Aristotle might have envisioned. The second is an integrated ideal, which claims that *theoretical* perfection includes knowledge of ethics and politics as well as metaphysics. Theoretical knowledge begins with metaphysical knowledge of the beings that constitute the cosmos but continues on to humanity and to an understanding of how individuals and nations can achieve happiness. Al-Fārābī argues that false philosophers are those who gain theoretical knowledge but do not share it with others. Illusory philosophers learn theory, but do not perform acts of moral virtue. They thus fail to realize the reason for which philosophy is pursued: to practice virtuous actions, and to bring others as well as ourselves to happiness. In this remarkable statement, Al-Fārābī suggests that the purpose of philosophy is to achieve human flourishing and to teach others how to achieve human flourishing and fulfillment as well.

Al-Fārābī's altruism is in fact grounded in his metaphysics: the Neoplatonic notion of the great chain of being. Plotinus suggested that perfection naturally overflows, just as the seed ripens and produces fruit. When things come to maturity they ripen and overflow. Just as God's goodness brims over to create a world, so the wisdom of the philosopher overflows to help others reach fulfillment. When humans discover the key to flourishing, they cannot help but share it. God's goodness pours out and creates a world; prophets receive revelation and share it to create a religious community. The teacher receives the first teaching and then shares it with others. True knowledge must be expressed; contemplation cannot be separated from action.

As with Aristotle and Al-Fārābī, an important theme in Maimonides is the struggle to find the appropriate balance between contemplation and action. In chapter 9 we saw that Maimonides argues in *Guide of the Perplexed* 3.17 that moral perfection is only a stepping stone to intellectual perfection, that the ultimate perfection does not include moral qualities at all. However, he goes on to suggest at the end of 3.54 that beyond the perfecting of the rational soul itself lies the overflow from that perfection. Just as God's graciousness overflowed to create the earth, so knowledge of the attributes of God expressed in this world can flow into graceful human action. Plato asserts that those who spend their time contemplating the eternal Forms will take on these eternal qualities; he also asserts that humans should take as their goal the imitation of the divine. Maimonides asserts that while we cannot know God's essence, we can imitate God's attributes of action; when we understand God's kindness in creating a world, our own deeds will come to reflect that kindness. In *Guide* 3.11 he asserts that those who have true knowledge of the deity will neither hurt nor oppress themselves or others. Maimonides suggests that when human beings apprehend God and the Good, actions and desires fall into place; we express this understanding in our words, in our gestures of gratitude and thanksgiving, and in our lives. Contemplation is the gesture of continually returning to the Source to shed light on all reality, including human action.

In chapter 10, we saw that al-Ghazālī expresses this dialectic in his own life story. His autobiography describes several crises in which he is constrained to turn within and discover a truth by contemplative experience. He suggests that the truth known by revelation must be appropriated by each of us through direct experience. When we return to active life, the fruits of contemplation will express themselves in a renewed way of being in the world. The change is subtle but revolutionary. Outwardly we may engage in the same way of life, but our being is transformed by the reality we have touched. The qualities of God and the Good express themselves in our lives.

I indicated at the outset that my purpose in this study is not to discover a single, definitive model of God and the Good. Rather, my belief is that the search itself is intrinsically rewarding. In this spirit, Kenneth Seeskin has suggested a novel interpretation of Socrates' teaching that knowledge is virtue: the pursuit of knowledge itself entails acts of moral courage. Likewise, opening ourselves to a genuine search for the Absolute brings purpose, fulfillment, and challenge to our lives. Each approach we explore adds a color to the spectrum, a dimension without which the whole would be incomplete. To recognize the beauty and wisdom of each perspective expands our vision both as spiritual seekers and as moral agents.

Al-Ghazālī suggests that in the quest for God and the good, it is God and the good themselves that guide our human search. It is my hope that this small offering may aid others in their quest.

# Notes

## INTRODUCTION

1. See Victor Frankl, *Man's Search for Meaning*.
2. Pierre Hadot, "Spiritual Exercises,"107.
3. Dale S. Wright, *Philosophical Reflections on Zen Buddhism*, xii.
4. This is not to say that such contact is limited to this life; many traditions insist that it can indeed continue in an afterlife. What is fascinating is that modern accounts of near-death experiences focus on traditional virtues we find discussed in ancient philosophical thinkers that allow us to achieve fulfillment in this life as well. It seems that one feature of contemporary religious concern is a focus on experiencing the absolute in this life, accompanied by the promise that this experience will continue in the afterlife. See for example, Huston Smith, "Intimations of Mortality."

## 1. "GOD SAW THAT IT WAS GOOD": THE CREATION OF THE WORLD IN THE HEBREW BIBLE

1. I use the term "Hebrew Bible" to signify what Christians refer to as the Old Testament.
2. See G. W. Leibniz, "Principles of Nature and Grace Based on Reason," 209; cf. Martin Heidegger, *Introduction to Metaphysics*, 1–8; Jon Levenson, *Creation and the Persistence of Evil*, 5; Levenson, in *The Jewish Study Bible: Genesis*, 13. In the latter context, Levenson writes: "This clause [i.e., Gen. 1:2] describes things just before the process of

creation began. To modern people, the opposite of the created order is 'nothing,' that is, a vacuum. To the ancients, the opposite of the created order was something much worse than 'nothing.' It was an active, malevolent force we can best term 'chaos.' In this verse, chaos is envisioned as a dark, undifferentiated mass of water." Levenson notes that in the *midrash* Genesis Rabbah one rabbinic teacher, Bar Kappara, went so far as to uphold the notion that God created from primordial elements, but others rejected that notion, as comparing God to a king who had built his palace upon garbage. Levenson notes that "in the ancient Near East, however, to say that a deity had subdued chaos is to give him the highest praise." We should ponder this when we turn to Plato's account in the *Timaeus* as well. Cf. Israel Knohl, *Divine Symphony*, 12–14.

3. See Henri Bergson, *Creative Evolution*, 296–324. Compare the "anthropic principle," the notion that the universe has conspired to produce humanity as its crowning purpose. Our perception is that the universe appears fine-tuned to produce humanity—but this is no surprise, considering that we are the ones looking at the universe. See Paul Davies, *The Mind of God*, 175, 187, 200, 213, 215, 220.
4. JeeLoo Liu, *An Introduction to Chinese Philosophy*, 232, 266–67, 361 n. 31; Dan Lusthaus, *Buddhist Phenomenology*, 255; Junjiro Takakusu, "Buddhism as a Philosophy of 'Thusness,'" 98–104.
5. Others argue that the relationship may be the other way around: the goddess Tiamat may derive her name from the root *t-h-m*, deep, which also appears in Ugaritic, and may thus be a common Semitic noun. Nahum Sarna, *JPS Torah Commentary: Genesis*, 6, 353 n. 8.
6. Levenson, *Creation and the Persistence of Evil,* 5; Knohl, *Divine Symphony*, 12–14; Nahum Sarna, *Understanding Genesis*, 22.
7. Gen. 2:1.
8. *Mishnah Taʿanit* IV 2–3; *Tosefta Taʿanit* IV (III) 3–4. Moshe Weinfeld, "Sabbath, Temple, and the Enthronement of the Lord," 42–45. Weinfeld mentions that according to Persian Jewish custom, the liturgy of the evening Sabbath service contains the entire section of Gen. 1:1–2:3; Weinfeld, 51 n. 1.
9. Levenson, *Creation and the Persistence of Evil*, 11 and passim. Levenson traces a historical trajectory in which there gradually developed in ancient Israel the idea of creation without opposition. We see evidence of this in Psalm 104; Gen. 1:1–2:3 marks the full flowering of this view (Levenson, *Creation*, 53–77). A remnant of the older view may be seen in the special mention in Gen. 1:21 of God's creation of the sea monsters (*tanninim*), who were once the evil primordial foes that God had to conquer to make a habitable world. Now they are mere created beings, among God's other creatures. Israel Knohl makes another intriguing suggestion: that we can also see remnants of the combat myth in the duality between darkness upon the face of the deep and a spirit (or wind) of God sweeping over the face of the waters. Despite this duality, there is no evidence of struggle. God merely speaks and light appears; water separates so that dry land is revealed, with no evidence of struggle on the part of the water. See Umberto Cassuto, *A Commentary on the Book of*

*Genesis*, 50–51; Levenson, *Creation*, 54; Knohl, *Divine Symphony*, 14; Sarna, *JPS Torah Commentary: Genesis*, 10.

10. Saʿadya Gaon, *Book of Doctrines and Beliefs* I:2 (Qafih, trans., *Kitāb al-mukhtār fīʾl-ʿamānāt waʾl-iʿtiqādāt*, 42; Rosenblatt, trans., *Book of Beliefs and Opinions*, 48; Altmann, trans., *Book of Doctrines and Beliefs* in *Three Jewish Philosophers*, 61).
11. Gen. 8:22. Note that God's pronouncement takes place as a response to Noah's sacrifice. God's action of the deluge threatened to throw the world back into chaos; Noah's sacrifice of thanksgiving reestablishes a sense of order. God is pleased with this human gesture of establishing ritual; God's response is to assert that the rhythms of nature will be everlasting. As we have noted, the story of the world's creation is chanted in the Friday night Jewish Sabbath service. The service ritually affirms the successful establishment of the world order, crowned by the Sabbath. Scholars have also contextualized the Rosh Hashanah liturgy, which celebrates the birthday of the world, as marking the successful bringing-into-order of the world, which in the ancient Near East was seen as taking place every year.
12. This image of the jigsaw puzzle was suggested by Boston University student Jack Fischl, spring 2007, Boston University.
13. Edward Pechet, Boston University, February 2007.
14. E. W. Lane, *Arabic-English Lexicon*, s.v. *tayyib*; cited in Brown, Driver, and Briggs, *A Hebrew and English Lexicon of the Old Testament*, s.v. *tov*.
15. Brown, Driver, and Briggs, *Lexicon*, s.v. *tov*.
16. Psalm 34:8. Mitchell Dahood translates Psalm 34:8 not as "taste and see that the Lord is good," but as "taste and drink deeply" for the Lord "is sweet." As Wolfhart Heinrichs pointed out to me, this translation assumes that the verb *reʾu* derives from the root *r-w-h* "to be saturated, drink one's fill," rather than from *r-ʾ-h*, to see. R. J. McCarthy likewise translates the Arabic term *dhawq*, "taste," a metaphor for direct religious experience, as "fruitional experience." McCarthy writes: "The Hebrew verb is *taʿamu* (taste, relish, savor)—like the Arabic *taʿima*. I think, then, that *dhawq* is not simply a kind of cognition, but an immediate experience accompanied by savoring, or relishing, and enjoyment, i.e., what I like to call a fruitional (fruitive) experience" (Richard J. McCarthy, trans., Al-Ghazālī, *Freedom and Fulfillment*, 133 n. 162).
17. Plato, *Euthyphro* 10a. The *Euthyphro* is a philosophical dialogue written by Plato (427–347 BCE). Socrates (469–399 BCE) did not leave any writings; he was an oral teacher in Athens who questioned people in the public square, spurring them to examine and refine their beliefs. Plato was a student of Socrates. Plato wrote philosophy in the form of dialogues in which the character Socrates appears, often expressing Plato's own views.

    On the basis of testimony by Aristotle and other ancients, and modern word and conceptual studies, some scholars have classified certain Platonic dialogues as early, middle, or late, and suggested that the early dialogues present views of the historical Socrates, while in the middle and late dialogues Plato uses Socrates as a mouthpiece for his own evolving views. The *Euthyphro* is classified by these scholars as an early dialogue, one which expresses views that may be closer to those of the historical Socrates than views expressed in the later dialogues. Forms are not transcendent entities, but universal characteristics of things we see in our world. Piety is a quality that inheres in all pious actions. Socrates is interested in ethical questions rather than abstract metaphysics. See Terry Penner, "Socrates and the Early Dialogues," 125–131. This historical reasoning has recently been challenged by scholars such as Charles Kahn and Charles Griswold. See *New Perspectives on Plato, Modern and Ancient*, ed. Julia Annas, esp. Charles Kahn, "On Platonic Chronology," 93–128; Charles Griswold, "Comments on Kahn," 129–142; Julia Annas, "What Are Plato's 'Middle' Dialogues in the Middle Of?", 1–24; and Dorothe Frede, "Comments on Annas," 25–36.

18. In the Islamic world, this question was expressed in a debate between the Ashʿarites and the Muʿtazilites. The Ashʿarites insisted that God declares what is good; the Muʿtazilites, seen as radical rationalists, argue that God must respect that which is inherently good. For the Ashʿarites, humans cannot know good by unaided reason alone. Revelation is necessary to discern God's will. For the Muʿtazilites, humans can know the good by unaided reason, and God can only command that which is inherently good. See Daniel Gimaret, "*Muʿtazila*," 792–793; Merlin Swartz, *A Medieval Critique of Anthropomorphism*, 48–53.
19. Gen. 18:25.
20. In book 10 of Plato's *Republic*, Socrates argues that in fashioning blueprints for a world, a divine craftsman would create just one model of a bed or a chair (596b–d). The image comes close to the Aristotelian notion of four causes: an architect who wants to physically bring the work into being (the efficient cause) requires a blueprint by which to shape his work (the formal cause), physical material (the material cause), and a purpose for his or her creation (the final cause).
21. See for example Jon Levenson, in *Jewish Study Bible: Genesis*, 13; Marc Brettler, *How to Read the Bible*, 41; Knohl, *Divine Symphony*, 18–19. Knohl argues, for example, that the Yom Kippur rite of cleansing the Tabernacle is a way of symbolically reestablishing the original orderly nature of the world; *Divine Symphony*, 19.
22. See Mary Douglas, "The Abominations of Leviticus," in *Purity and Danger*, 69; Douglas, *Leviticus as Literature*, 152ff. For other interpretations of the foundations of the dietary system in Lev. 11, see Jacob Milgrom, *Leviticus 1-16*, 718–742. On the notion of a priestly theology, see Milgrom, *Leviticus: A Book of Ritual and Ethics*, 8–16; Milgrom, *JPS Torah Commentary: Numbers*, xxxvii–xlii, 444–447; Knohl, *Divine Symphony*, 9–35, 71–85; Jonathan Klawans, *Purity, Sacrifice, and the Temple*, 49–73; Klawans, *Impurity and Sin in Ancient Judaism*, 1–42.
23. Genesis Rabbah 9:5.
24. Genesis Rabbah 9:6–13.
25. Genesis Rabbah 9:7.
26. See Solomon Schechter, *Aspects of Rabbinic Theology*, 266–270.
27. Genesis Rabbah 3:7, 9:2. This interpretation is derived exegetically from several different verses, suggesting that the idea was in the air, and was attached to different

scriptural verses for support. James Kugel has likened this oral process to that of joke-telling, in which there may be many variations, as, for example, on a lightbulb joke; see Kugel, "Two Introductions to Midrash," 147.

28. See Levenson, *Jewish Study Bible: Genesis*, 15, comment to 1.4–25.
29. Whitehead points out that until the scientific revolution of the seventeenth century, aesthetic qualities were perceived to be real features of the world. The scientific revolution asserted that colors, sounds, scents were aspects of our mind that we project onto a sightless, scentless order. Whitehead's philosophy reasserted the objective facts of quality and beauty. Alfred North Whitehead, *Science and the Modern World*, 53–54. See below, chap. 3.
30. Ibid., 25.
31. Panpsychism has been defined as the belief that everything has a psychic aspect or dimension. See Charles Hartshorne, "Panpsychism," 442–453; Nagel, *Mortal Questions*, 181–195; T. L. S. Sprigge, *The God of Metaphysics*, 432–437, 483–486. On the continuum between other forms of feeling and consciousness, see Thomas Hosinski, *Stubborn Fact and Creative Advance*, 93–94. Hosinski points out that Whitehead gives the example of thirst, in which the body "feels" dry and "grasps the possibility" of something not present, water; humans become conscious of this more immediate physical sensation of the body. Whitehead thus suggests a continuum between mind and matter; there is a primitive element of "mentality" to even the smallest particles of matter, which sense and take into account their environment. Spinoza believes both (1) that God is identical with the scientific system of the universe and (2) that God/nature is at the same time both thought and extension, mind and matter. For an excellent, accessible introduction to Spinoza's metaphysics, see Steven Nadler, *Spinoza's Ethics*. On Spinoza's panpsychism, see Sprigge, *The God of Metaphysics*, 24–95; Margaret Wilson, "Spinoza's Theory of Knowledge," 101.
32. Rabbi Joseph Soloveitchik describes the two stories from the perspective of two different images of humanity, rather than two different images of God. The first story gives us "Adam I," the human being who scientifically investigates the cosmos. The second story depicts "Adam II," who is in relationship with a partner. He bases this portrait on the fact that man and woman are created together in Gen. 1, while in Gen. 2 the human being experiences existential loneliness before being given a partner. In contrast, feminist exegetes of the text tend to view more favorably the Gen. 1 account, in which man and woman are created together, equally in the image of God. Interestingly, in an early work of feminist exegesis, Phyllis Trible argues that the fact that woman is created last in the second story may be a hint that the female is the crown of creation. This range of exegetical possibilities shows that no text stands uninterpreted, and that what in the view of one reader is the plain sense of the text may be understood very differently by another reader. See Joseph B. Soloveitchik, *The Lonely Man of Faith*; Phyllis Trible, "Depatriarchalizing in Biblical Interpretation," 222.
33. See the interesting remarks by the science writer Natalie Angier in chap. 2, n. 6 below. Although in other contexts she has written in passionate defense of atheism, in

a recent *Boston Globe* interview she noted that we humans see meaning in our lives, and since we are part of the universe, the world must be a meaning-engendering universe.

34. See, e.g., Knohl, *Divine Symphony*, 37–40.
35. Brettler, *How to Read the Bible*, 46–47; cf. Susan Niditch, *Chaos to Cosmos*, 37.
36. Martin Buber, "The Tree of Knowledge," 20–21.
37. Sarna, *JPS Torah Commentary: Genesis*, 19, 25, 27.
38. See Ibn Ezra, *Commentary to Genesis* 2:9; Brettler, *How to Read the Bible*, 45–46. Buber and Sarna reject this view: Buber, "Tree of Knowledge," 16; Sarna, *JPS Torah Commentary: Genesis*, 19.
39. See Buber, "Tree of Knowledge," 16–17; Sarna, *JPS Torah Commentary: Genesis*, 19.
40. On Augustine and Maimonides, see chapter 4.
41. The eleventh-century Jewish philosopher Baḥya Ibn Paqūda devotes a chapter to such meditations on the various puzzling features of creation. See Baḥya Ibn Paqūda, *Book of Direction to the Duties of the Heart*, trans. Mansoor (Second Gate), 150–175; *Kitāb al-Hidāya ilā farāʾiḍ al-qulūb* (*Torat ḥovot ha-levavot*), trans. Qafih, 94–126.
42. On spiritual exercises in the ancient world, see Hadot, *Philosophy as a Way of Life*.

## 2. A DIVINE CRAFTSMAN SHAPES ALL FOR THE GOOD: PLATO'S REALM OF THE FORMS

1. While it is conventional to capitalize the *G* for the Biblical God, Plato's world includes a multiplicity of gods, so the convention is not as clear for Greek texts. We do not want to read the Biblical God into Plato. However, many Western readers find the small *g* distracting or confusing. Since Plato uses the definite article—he speaks of "the god"—and since he is clearly not talking about the gods of the Greek pantheon, we will here follow certain scholars who do use the capital *G* for God when speaking about Plato's idea of divinity.
2. Should the reader feel absolutely lost, however, there is no shame in skipping ahead to our summary below, "God and the Good in Genesis and the *Timaeus*."
3. See Eliot Deutsch, *Advaita Vedānta*, 27; T. M. P. Mahadevan, "Social, Ethical, and Spiritual Values in Indian Philosophy," 169.
4. Guthrie follows the many scholars who capitalize the G when referring to Plato's Forms and to the Good, which he sometimes speaks of as an abstract principle, and sometimes as a Form. Since the Good in Plato's dialogue the *Republic* seems to be a transcendent entity, I will follow this convention.
5. W. K. C. Guthrie, *A History of Greek Philosophy*, vol. IV, 506. He acknowledges his debt to Richard Lewis Nettleship, *Lectures on the Republic of Plato*, 218. Nettleship writes that the Good is the creative and sustaining cause of the world; Guthrie revises this formula, writing that the Good is the sustaining cause of the Forms, "which are in their turn the creative causes of natural objects and human actions" (Guthrie, 506). Elsewhere he explains that Plato uses the term "cause" (*aitia*) to describe the

formal and final cause, not simply efficient causation. It is what is responsible for the existence of a thing or the performance of an action; it is the "reason why" something exists" (ibid., 349–352).

6. The science writer Natalie Angier, who has elsewhere written in passionate defense of atheism, nevertheless asserted in an interview that we are significance creating beings: "I have this debate with my colleague Dennis Overbye, who argues that the universe is cold, the universe doesn't care. . . . I think he's setting himself apart from the universe. I say to Dennis, do you believe your life is meaningless? He says, no. Do you believe you're part of the universe? He says, yes. So how can you say the universe has no meaning? You are meaning, you are part of it. I think it's legitimate to see the universe as wanting to know itself." We look in the world and see significance; the universe has evolved meaning-bearing creatures. Plato would argue that this is because we are products of a universe in which significance is as fundamental as the fact of our existence. Interview with Natalie Angier by Harvey Blume, in *Boston Sunday Globe*, May 13, 2007, *Ideas*, E3.
7. See, e.g., Frances Cornford, *Plato's Cosmology*, 203.
8. Plato, *Timaeus* 28b–c. Donald Zeyl points out that there are three primary terms that Plato uses to refer to the universe. In the *Timaeus*, *ouranos* ("heaven," "the heavens") properly designates the realm of the fixed stars; he also uses it to refer to the universe as a whole. Plato uses the term *kosmos* ("order," world," "world order") to refer to the world as an orderly system. Finally, he uses *to pan* (lit. "the whole" or "the all") to consider the universe in its totality. I use the English form cosmos when referring to our common conception of the universe as a whole. See Zeyl, trans., *Plato's Timaeus*, 14 n. 16.
9. *Timaeus* 28a.
10. The sixteenth-century philosopher Spinoza, for example, will argue that all of existence—which he terms "God" or "nature"—is eternal and self-caused.
11. *Timaeus* 28c.
12. *Timaeus* 29a, 30c–d.
13. *Timaeus* 30a. If we examine this argument carefully, we see that Plato has articulated two distinct meanings of "becoming." The first one is expressed in 27d: "What is that which is *always real* and *has no becoming*, and what is that which is *always becoming* and is *never real*? That which is apprehensible by thought with a rational account is the thing that is always unchangeably real; whereas that which is the object of belief together with unreasoning sensation is the thing that becomes and passes away, but never has real being." In this passage Plato speaks of that which is always becoming, that which is perpetually in the process of change. As we have seen, here in 27d Plato is describing two orders of reality: the realm of Being, that which eternally *is* the same and never *becomes* or changes in any way, and the realm of Becoming, that which changes, comes to be, and passes away. Being is static; becoming is a process. He then goes on to ask of the world as a whole: "So, concerning the whole Heaven or World—let us call it by whatsoever name may be most acceptable to it—we must ask the question which, it is agreed, must be asked at the outset of

inquiry concerning anything: Has it always been, without any source of becoming; or has it come to be, *starting from some beginning*? It has come to be; for it can be seen and touched and it has body, and all such things are sensible; and as we saw, sensible things, that are to be apprehended by belief together with sensation, are things that become and can be generated" (28b–c). Plato's translator Francis Cornford points out that the meaning of the term "becoming" has shifted radically here. Earlier, Plato distinguished between the world of Being, which is eternal and fully real, and the realm of Becoming, which is always in flux and thus does not possess the same degree of reality. In the new passage (28b–c), Timaeus asks about becoming in terms of *having a specific beginning*, coming into existence. Timaeus here asks whether the world has always existed and is without a beginning, or whether it came to be at a certain point. He does not ask whether the world is in a continuous process of becoming and change, in which new elements are continually arising and old elements passing away. Kenneth Seeskin refers to this as the "instability of the sensible world." Rather, he asks whether the world has *come to be, starting from some beginning*, that is, whether it has *come into existence* after not existing. He goes on to argue that something that has come into existence requires a cause to bring it into existence; he compares the cause of the world to a father, maker, or craftsman. This is an agent who begets or fashions that which comes into existence.

What is important about this distinction is that the argument Timaeus makes for the existence of God works only on the assumption of his second meaning of becoming, "to come into existence at a certain point." The first dichotomy—between that which always *is* and never becomes, and that which *is always becoming*, and never *is*—does not prove that the world as a whole has a specific moment of origin, and thus does not prove the existence of a God who brought it to its present state. The world as a whole could be an eternal process of becoming and change, a process that has no origin and thus needs no originator. The process of things coming to be and passing away could be continuous and without a beginning. It might need a cause or ground for its being, but one that continually sustains the process, not a cause that brings it into existence at a certain point. For such a sustaining cause or ground of existence, the terms "father," "maker," and" craftsman" are not necessarily appropriate, and Plato's proof would not work (Cornford, *Plato's Cosmology*, 25; Seeskin, *Maimonides on the Origin of the World*, 42) The search would not be for a "parent" or "artist," an originator or shaper of the cosmic order; it would be inappropriate to speak of a god who brought order out of chaos if the state of change had no precise beginning.

However, if Plato believes that the process of becoming or change is perpetual and beginningless, then why does the *Timaeus* feature what looks like an account of creation or shaping? Interpreters from ancient times through the present day have suggested that the creation story may be metaphorical. See Cornford, *Plato's Cosmology*, 24–25; Seeskin, *Maimonides on the Origin of the World*, 42–43; Richard Sorabji, *On Time, Creation, and the Continuum*, 275.

14. On the ancient Greek interpreters, see John Dillon, *The Middle Platonists*, 7. Cornford upholds the metaphorical view, along with Taylor, Cherniss, and Taran. The literal reading of the story as a real creation (or rather, shaping) in time is upheld by Vlastos, Hackforth, Sorabji, and Robinson. Cornford, *Plato's Cosmology*, 25–27; cf. Seeskin, *Maimonides on the Origin of the World*, 18–19, Sorabji, *On Time, Creation, and the Continuum*, 275, Donald Zeyl, trans., *Plato's Timaeus*, xx–xxv, esp. xxi and citations in xxi nn. 28 and 29.
15. *Republic* 500b–d. Plato thus suggests that philosophers are infused with the desire to imitate the Forms—much like Socrates' injunction in the *Theaetetus* that we must strive as much as possible to imitate God. On the imitation of God, see below, chapter 9.
16. Plato, *Republic* 508d–509b.
17. Zeyl, trans., *Plato's Timaeus*, lxv–lxvi.
18. A likeness, an image, is of course not identical to the model, but a reflection or approximation of the original, as a son resembles a father.
19. We do not perceive space with our senses, nor do we know space the way we know the Forms. Nevertheless, since space provides a permanent matrix for all becoming, it must be everlasting and indestructible like the Forms. What Plato might mean by "bastard reasoning" is that we cannot perceive it directly, but if we subtract all the other elements of our world, we can deduce that space is necessary as their matrix.
20. Aristotle, *Metaphysics* 1029a12–27. It is not clear whether Aristotle himself holds that prime matter actually exists, but the later Aristotelian tradition developed this assertion and attributed it to Aristotle.
21. *Timaeus* 50a–b.
22. Seeskin, *Maimonides on the Origin of the World*, 50–51.
23. Ibid., 51.
24. Here Plato seems to mix metaphors. On the one hand, this characterless nature sounds like Aristotelian prime matter. On the other, when he adds that the part of it that has been made fiery appears at any time as fire, it sounds like we have the image of a mirror or screen, although we could also have the image of space appearing fiery or watery (51a–b).
25. This works well to describe the container in motion that contains moving particles in the pre-creation chaotic state (52d–53c).
26. Seeskin, *Maimonides on the Origin of the World*, 53.
27. Plotinus, *Enneads* 3.6.14: "But would this mean that if there were no Matter nothing would exist? Precisely as in the absence of a mirror, or something of similar power, there would be no reflection. A thing whose very nature is to be lodged in something else cannot exist where the base is lacking—and it is the character of a reflection to appear in something not itself." See Seeskin, *Maimonides on the Origin of the World*, 51.
28. See Zeyl, trans., *Plato's Timaeus*, lxv–lxvi; Cornford, *Plato's Cosmology*, 194.

29. See Walter Burkert, *Structure and History in Greek Mythology and Ritual*, 28; quoted in Brettler, *How to Read the Bible,* 39.
30. *Timaeus* 47d–48a.
31. Seeskin, *Maimonides on the Origin of the World*, 54.
32. See *Timaeus* 29b–c.
33. As Seeskin notes, this world of sensation stands between pure order and pure chaos. Seeskin, *Maimonides on the Origin of the World*, 45.
34. *Republic* 500b–501c.
35. Exodus 15:11.
36. See Jeffrey Tigay, "Moses and Monotheism," in *JPS Torah Commentary: Deuteronomy*, 433–435; Jon Levenson, *Sinai and Zion*, 56–70.
37. Knohl, *The Divine Symphony,* 12–13. This is indeed one of the possibilities that the fourth-century Church father Augustine rejects in his search for the source of evil. If everything that God created is good, how did evil creep in? Was it somehow contained in primordial matter? See Augustine, *Confessions* 7:13.
38. Genesis Rabbah 1:5.
39. Genesis Rabbah 3:7, 9:2.
40. Isaiah 45:5.
41. Isaiah 45:7. See also Deut. 4:35: "The Lord alone is God; there is none beside him." And Deut. 4:39: "The Lord alone is God in heaven above and on earth below; there is no other."
42. Isaiah would thus emphatically reject the notion that the world was created from a preexistent unformed chaos, which would be responsible for the evil element in the world. For Isaiah, God creates all—including the possibility of evil.
43. Cornford, *Plato's Cosmology*, 165–177.
44. *Republic* 501a–c.
45. Vlastos, "Creation," 411–412; Seeskin, *Maimonides on the Origin of the World*, 47; Cornford, *Plato's Cosmology*, 27, 176.
46. Seeskin, *Maimonides on the Origin of the World*, 41; Dillon, *The Middle Platonists*, 7.
47. See Stephen Hawking, *A Brief History of Time*, 56–63; Michio Kaku, *Hyperspace*, 114–117; Norbert Samuelson, *Judaism and the Doctrine of Creation*, 222–226.
48. Dillon, *The Middle Platonists*, 3.
49. Ibid., 5.
50. See Henry Allison, *Benedict de Spinoza*, 50, who explains that this metaphor depicts the relationship between the one substance (God-nature) and its attributes (thought and extension). He in turn traces the metaphor to Léon Brunschvicg, *Spinoza et ses contemporains*, 67–68; it is also cited by E. M. Curley, *Spinoza's Metaphysics*, 144. Curley translates: "A thought, in itself one and indivisible, may be expressed with complete exactness in an infinity of languages. . . . No one of the translations contains the thought and they all manifest it in its entirety. Just as there is a perfect parallelism between the different texts which express one and the same thought, so also there is an intimate and perpetual correspondence between the different attributes which proceed from one unique activity. Ultimately, from the point of

view of absolute reality, all these attributes are only one and the same thing." Thus thought and extension are two expressions of one substance, God-nature.

51. *Timaeus* 52d–53c.
52. Michael Frede, introduction to Plato, *Protagoras*, xxv–xxvi.
53. See Julia Annas, *An Introduction to Plato's Republic*, 246.
54. See R. M. Hare, *Plato*, 44–45.
55. David Ross, *Plato's Theory of Ideas*, 43.
56. See Gerasimos Santas, "The Form of the Good in Plato's *Republic*," 232–263, especially 240–252; cf. Santas, "Aristotle's Criticism of Plato's Form of the Good: Ethics Without Metaphysics?," 142–145.
57. Plato, *Republic* 353a–e; see Dorothea Frede, "Plato's Ethical Theory."
58. Nettleship, *Lectures on the Republic of Plato*, 222–225; see Monte Ransome Johnson, *Aristotle on Teleology*, 278–279.
59. Nettleship, *Lectures on the Republic of Plato*, 224–225, n. 1 (by the editor). For contemporary reflections on teleology in nature, see Johnson, *Aristotle on Teleology*, 287–294.
60. At *Phaedo* 75b, Plato even uses the language of striving; things are striving to reach their ideal form but, in the sensible world, always fall short of the absolute ideal.
61. See for example Konrad Gaiser, "Plato's Enigmatic Lecture 'On the Good.'"
62. Hans-George Gadamer argues that Plato's "one" is not that of Plotinus, "the sole existent and 'trans-existent' entity. Rather, it is that which on any given occasion provides what is multiple with the unity of whatever consists in itself. As the unity of what is unitary, the idea of the good would seem to be presupposed by anything ordered, enduring, and consistent. That means, however, that it is presupposed as the unity of many" (Gadamer, *The Idea of the Good in Platonic-Aristotelian Philosophy*, 31).
63. Cf. Frede, "Plato's Ethical Theory."
64. Plato, *Phaedo* 99c. Translation my own, with the aid of Tyler Travillian. See also trans. C. J. Rowe, *Phaedo*, 238: "and that what is good and binding really (*hōs alēthōs*) binds and holds together, that they don't believe at all"; compare G. M. E. Grube in *Five Dialogues*, 138. As Dorothea Frede writes, "the Good is the intelligible inner principle that determines the nature of every object capable of goodness in the sense that it is able to fulfill its function in the appropriate way" (Frede, "Plato's Ethical Theory"). Rowe translates the first part of the passage: "But their capacity to be now located in the way in which it is possible for them [*auta*, loosely generalising from the case of the earth] 'to be placed best,' i.e., their capacity to be situated in the best way possible" (Rowe, 238).
65. C. J. Rowe notes, "Atlas, in myth, is a Titan (and so a god) who holds up the sky; the real Atlas, Socrates suggests, is the *dynamis* just mentioned, which holds everything together—but the people in question go searching (hopelessly) for a stronger one" (Rowe, 238).
66. Cf. Rowe, 238. As Frede points out, in *Republic* 10 Plato explains further that in each case it is the use or function that determines a thing's goodness. "Aren't the

virtue or excellence, the beauty and correctness of each manufactured item, living creature, and action related to nothing but the use [*chreia*] for which each is made or naturally adapted?" Similarly, in *Republic* 1 (353a–e) Socrates explains that the excellence or virtue of every object is its ability to fulfill its own task, work, or function (*ergon*). For a human being, as mentioned earlier this is living and doing well, which is also living happily (Frede, "Plato's Ethical Theory"). We will see almost the identical line of explanation in Aristotle's *Eudemian Ethics*. Goodness is what allows a human being to live well, do well, and be happy.

67. Plato, *Republic* 6 (509b). While Plato suggests that the Good is beyond essence (*ousia*), this does not necessarily mean that the Good is beyond being (*on*). At 518d, Socrates says that the soul becomes able to endure "contemplation of what is [*to on*] and the brightest of what is [*tou ontos to phanotaton*] and this, we say, is the Good." We can make sense of this distinction linguistically. *Ousia* is the quality of having or participating in being, which Plato ascribes to the Forms, the objects of knowledge; it is the being-what-it-is of each of the Forms. Since the presence of the Good gives the Forms their being, the Good may be identified with *on*, being—or more precisely, the brightest of what is (*tou ontos to phanotaton*)—although it is itself beyond *ousia*, the quality of having being, possessed by the Forms. Robert Wood suggests that in 518d, *on* is used as a generic term for both the brightest of what is (the Good) and *ousia*, possessed by the forms. That is, the soul becomes able to contemplate the entire realm of being, including both the Forms and the Good. The Good is in some sense one, while those things that possess being are many. For this lucid interpretation of *Republic* 509b, I am indebted to Tyler Travillian, Department of Classics, Boston University, who guided me to the work of Robert E. Wood; see, e.g., Wood, "Plato's Divided Line," 537 and n. 31; Wood, "Phenomenology and the Perennial Task of Philosophy" 255. See also Stanley Rosen, *Plato's Sophist*, 212–213, who argues that *ousia* is the whole, a differentiated unity, rather than a pure monad; Martin Kavka, *Jewish Messianism and the History of Philosophy*, 43–44; Santas, "Aristotle's Criticism of Plato's Form of the Good," 137–160; Joe Sachs, trans., *Plato's Republic*, 206. On Plato's notion of the Good as the One, see Kenneth Sayre, *Plato's Late Ontology*, 171–174; Gaiser, "Plato's Enigmatic Lecture 'On the Good,'" 5–37; Dillon, *The Middle Platonists*, 1–9.

68. Ben-Ami Scharfstein explains: "If you try to think of a world in which the quality of oneness or unity is absent, you see that it is the one—the nature of which is to be fundamentally and indivisibly single—that clarifies the world by making it possible to distinguish between one thing and another. Every distinguishable thing is a one for itself, its oneness being (or accounting for) its unity and identity. This is because nothing can exist unless it is, so to speak, held together by being one rather than many. And so, if unity or oneness did not exist and was not basic, nothing would exist, not even manyness, plurality, or multiplicity, which is made up of ones, unities" (Scharfstein, *Ineffability*, 150).

69. See also the interesting interpretation of Kenneth Sayre, *Plato's Literary Garden*, 185–188. Sayre interprets the Good as establishing a "field of being" in which there

are standards by which to judge objective values, and in which "there are objective distinctions between things shaped accurately and only approximately, between things done well and things done poorly, between things seen correctly and things seen otherwise" (186). Sayre argues further that the unhypothetical first principle of all is not the Good but the entire field of being of the Forms. Finally, Sayre argues that while goodness and beauty are closely connected, we cannot simply identify the Good of the Republic with the Form of Beauty in the *Symposium*. He notes that in the *Philebus* Plato identifies the Good as a unified trio of beauty, proportion, and truth, which are responsible for what is good in any mixture, and concludes that there are three dialogues that feature the Good, and each emphasizes one of these aspects. The *Republic*'s discussion of the Divided Line emphasizes the aspect of Truth, the *Symposium* that of Beauty, and the *Philebus* that of Proportion (192–195). See also Sayre, *Plato's Late Ontology*, 171–174.

70. Cf. Guthrie, *History of Greek Philosophy*, vol. 5, 434. David Roochnik pointed out to me a further angle to be noted. Jacob Klein has emphasized that in Greek mathematics, one is not considered a number. One is the *archē*, the root principle of all numbers, but since it cannot be counted, it is not itself a number. Still, it is the root of limit and thus the root of intelligibility. Unity defines things and makes them what they are. Perhaps then just as one is not a number, so Good is not strictly speaking a Form and is not itself intelligible. It is beyond being; it is that which makes all being intelligible. It is that beyond form which gives form to all things. See Jacob Klein, *Greek Mathematical Thought and the Origin of Algebra*; see also Gadamer, *The Idea of the Good*, 31–32.
71. See Santas, "The Form of the Good in Plato's *Republic*," esp. 232–241, 247–252; Santas, "Aristotle's Criticism of Plato's Form of the Good," 137–145.
72. I wrote this sentence before I saw the interpretation of Robert E. Wood, with which it is in substantial agreement; see Wood, "Plato's Divided Line," 537.
73. Plato, *Meno* 87e–89a; *Republic* 505a, 505e.
74. However, the *Republic* certainly challenges the view espoused by Socrates in Plato's early dialogues that the soul is unified and characterized by intellect, such that intellectual understanding translates seamlessly into moral virtue. In the *Republic*, the psyche is presented as divided, with the desiring part warring with the rational part of the soul. Virtues seem likewise to be divided among groups of people: the military class excels in courage, while the artisans are ruled by appetite. It is only the philosophers who excel in wisdom.
75. Plato, *Republic* 439–441.
76. Ibid, 441e. The just person "puts himself in order, is his own friend, and harmonizes the three parts of himself like three limiting notes in a musical scale—high, low, and middle. . . . Only then does he act . . . he believes that the action is just and fine that preserves this inner harmony and helps achieve it" (*Republic* 443d–e).
77. For contrasting views of the so-called Socratic paradoxes, see Gerasimos Santas, "The Socratic Paradoxes," 642–643; Roslyn Weiss, *The Socratic Paradox and Its Enemies*.

78. Plato, *Gorgias* 467c–468e, 499d–501c; Aristotle, *Nicomachean Ethics* 1094a.
79. Jonathan Lear uses the metaphor of the "organization of desire" to describe Aristotle's ethics. Lear, *Aristotle*, 152–208.
80. *Gorgias* 507a–b.
81. *Gorgias* 507c.
82. *Gorgias* 507e–508a. On this theme, see also *Timaeus* 90a–d.
83. *Republic* 443d–e, 432a.
84. *Republic* 433a–434a, 443c–e. Plato suggests that the cause of injustice is *pleonexia*, always wanting to outdo others, seeking what belongs to others (359c, 343e). Its opposite is doing or having one's own, the definition of justice (434a, 441d–e). See Plato, *Republic*, trans. G. M. A. Grube, 20 n. 18. In the *Bhagavad Gītā* we will find a similar theme—that each person should do his or her own duty and not the duty of others. See below, chapter 5.
85. Compare Aristotle on the difference between selfishness—which stems from gratifying the lower parts of our soul—and genuine self-love, in which we award the highest part of our soul the greatest share of our attention. No one will blame us for putting our efforts into the generous, caring, compassionate, and wise parts of our selves. Putting these parts of our selves first makes us the opposite of selfish people. See Aristotle, *Nicomachean Ethics*, 1168b16–1169a18, and below, chapter 7.
86. *Timaeus* 90c5.
87. *Timaeus* 90c5–6.
88. *Timaeus* 90d2; see 43a–44a.
89. *Timaeus* 90b–d.
90. *Crito* 48b4–11. He continues: "From what has been agreed let us consider this: would it be just or unjust to leave this place without the consent of the Athenians? If it is just we shall. If it is not, we shall not."
91. *Apology* 28b.
92. *Apology* 30a.
93. *Republic* 443d–e.
94. *Republic* 618d.
95. Alasdair Macintyre writes: "Remarkable . . . Iris Murdoch has once again put us all in her debt."
96. Iris Murdoch, "On 'God' and 'Good,'" in *The Sovereignty of Good*, 55–56.
97. Ibid., 56. Cf. Murdoch, *Metaphysics as a Guide to Morals*, 468.
98. See "Iris Murdoch and Jiddu Krishnamurti Talk."
99. Murdoch, "On 'God' and 'Good,'" 58.
100. Ibid., 58–59. I am reminded of the original Yiddish title of Abraham Joshua Heschel's biography of the Hasidic rabbi of Kotzk, whom Heschel compared with the nineteenth-century existentialist Soren Kierkegaard. The English translation renders the title *A Passion for Truth*; the original Yiddish title spoke of the *Passion for Integrity*.
101. Peter Berger, *The Sacred Canopy*.

102. Cf. *Phaedo, Republic.*
103. Murdoch, "On 'God' and 'Good,'" 63.
104. Cf. Rabbi Tarfon in the rabbinic ethical treatise known as *Chapters of the Fathers* (*Pirke Avot*): "The task is not yours to complete, but neither are you free to desist from it."
105. Ibid., 62–63.
106. See below.
107. Murdoch, "On 'God' and 'Good,'" 63; Confucius, *Analects* 7:30, trans. Slingerland, 74; see Herbert Fingarette, *Confucius: The Secular as Sacred*, 38ff.
108. Is this certainty purely psychological? As Murdoch notes, cult leaders also possess complete confidence that their religious visions are real. Murdoch does argue for a positive psychological payoff: the conviction of an objective goodness can inspire someone in a concentration camp to selfless acts of moral greatness. Nevertheless, she argues that what motivates and inspires him or her is more than an "as if" or "it works." It is a real moral ideal. She cautions that "we must avoid here, as in the case of God, any heavy material connotation of the misleading word 'exist.'" On the other hand, the purely psychological conviction of certainty does not seem strong enough to do justice to the reality of goodness.
109. Murdoch, 65.
110. Ibid.
111. Ibid., 66.
112. Ibid., 66.
113. Ibid., 69.
114. David Tracy, "Iris Murdoch and the Many Faces of Platonism," in *Iris Murdoch and the Search for Human Goodness*, ed. Maria Antonaccio and William Schweiker (Chicago: University of Chicago Press, 1996), 75.
115. Murdoch, "The Sovereignty of Good Over Other Concepts," in *The Sovereignty of Good*, 89; *Metaphysics as a Guide to Morals*, 478–479.
116. "Sovereignty," 92.
117. "Sovereignty," 96, 91.
118. "Sovereignty," 96–97.
119. "Sovereignty," 97.
120. "Sovereignty," 100.
121. Cf. Murdoch, *The Fire and the Sun*, 43.
122. "Sovereignty," 100–101.
123. "Sovereignty," 101–102.
124. Stephen Menn's analysis of the role of Good in Plato and Aristotle suggests the following. For Plato *nous* searches for and loves the good. For Aristotle, *nous*—the quest and love for the Good—is in some sense the Good itself.
125. "Sovereignty," 103.
126. He illustrates the metaphor with mathematical examples, such as the triangle a mathematician draws, or equal figures we perceive with our senses.

127. "Sovereignty," 103.
128. Taylor, *Sources of the Self*, 95–96, citing Murdoch, 74, and 99: "If there were angels they might be able to define good but we would not understand the definition." He adds: "Anyone who has read Murdoch's book will see the extent of my debt to her in what I have written here" (Taylor, 534 n. 4).
129. Murdoch, *Metaphysics as a Guide to Morals*, 473.

## 3. CHANGE AND THE GOOD: CHINESE PERSPECTIVES

1. *Yin* originally represented the dark (north), shady side of the mountain: it is the principle of darkness, earth, cold, femininity, rest, receptivity, night, below, still, silence. *Yang* was the sunny, south side of the mountain: it is the principle of light, heat, masculinity, activity, expansion, day, above, speech, Heaven. See John B. Henderson, "Cosmology," in *Encyclopedia of Chinese Philosophy*, 191.
2. See Laurence Thompson, *Chinese Religion*, 3; Karyn L. Lai, *An Introduction to Chinese Philosophy*, 207, 216.
3. See JeeLoo Liu, *An Introduction to Chinese Philosophy*, 34.
4. Ibid., 35; Tu Wei-Ming, "The Continuity of Being: Chinese Visions of Nature," 46; Tu, *Centrality and Commonality*, 10.
5. While the *Tao* is never conceived of as a personal Being, "Heaven" (*Tian*) sometimes does have the characteristic of a personal will. Heaven is a complex concept in Chinese thought. *Tian* is a kind of higher power, conceived by some as an anthropomorphic being, and by others (such as Chuang Tzu and Hsun Tzu) as the impersonal workings of nature. Heaven was sometimes conflated with the Lord on High or Supreme Ancestor, who issued a mandate to the emperor (the "Son of Heaven") to rule the world with ritual correctness. In Confucian times, writes Edward Slingerland, " 'Heaven' refers to an anthropomorphic figure—someone who can be communicated with, angered, or pleased—rather than a physical place. From Zhou times on, Heaven is viewed as the source of normativity in the universe, the all powerful Being who, when pleased with proper ritual conduct, charges its representative on earth with the Mandate to rule, as well as the power of virtue that made realizing the Mandate possible. Heaven is also viewed as responsible for everything beyond the control of human beings (things relegated to 'fate') and—in Confucius' view—for revealing to human beings the set of cultural practices and texts collectively known as 'the Way' " (*Confucius: Analects*, trans. Edward Slingerland, 239, 240). Confucius says the following about Heaven: (a) "at fifty I understood the Mandate of Heaven" (*Analects* 2.11); (b) "Heaven has bestowed virtue on me. What can Huan Tui do to me?" (7.23); (c) "Since the death of King Wen, is not the course of culture (*wen*) in my keeping? If it had been the will of Heaven to destroy this culture, it would not have been given to a mortal (like me.) But if it is the will of Heaven that this culture should not perish, what can the people of Kuang do to me?" (9.5); (d) "Alas there is no one that knows me! . . . but there is Heaven that

knows me" (14:37). For Confucius, Heaven is probably not a full-fledged anthropomorphic God, but a vaguely conceived moral force, a source of moral norms, a moral order (as Herbert Creel expresses it, in the sense that we say "Heaven helps those who help themselves" or "Heaven only knows"; see Creel, "Confucius and the Struggle for Human Happiness," 171). While Heaven embodies a kind of morality and perhaps even has the anthropomorphic nature of intention and will, the *Tao* does not. None of these ancient Chinese thinkers conceive of the *Tao* as a personal being. See *Readings in Classical Chinese Philosophy*, ed. P. J. Ivanhoe and Bryan Van Norden, 357, 360.

6. 1.11. Quoted by Liu, *An Introduction to Chinese Philosophy*, 35. *The I Ching: Book of Changes*, trans. R. Wilhelm and C. F. Baynes, 320. This is also known as *The Great Commentary* (*Dazhuan*) or the *Commentary on the Appended Phrases* (*Zixi zhuan*).
7. *Commentary on the Appended Phrases* I.5; trans. Richard John Linn in T. De Bary and Irene Bloom, *Sources of Chinese Tradition*, 321. Wing-Tsit Chan translates: "The successive movement of yin and yang constitutes the Way (*Tao*). What issues from the Way is good, and that which realizes it is the individual nature. The man of human-heartedness (*ren*) sees it and calls it human-heartedness. The man of wisdom sees it and calls it wisdom. And the common people act according to it daily without knowing it. In this way the Way of the superior man is fully realized" (Wing-Tsit Chan, *A Source Book in Chinese Philosophy*, 266). Liu translates: "One cycle of yin; one cycle of yang, this is called *Tao*. What continues it is Good. What completes it is nature" (*An Introduction to Chinese Philosophy*, 36).
8. Liu, *An Introduction to Chinese Philosophy*, 37; see Lik Kuen Tong, "The Appropriation of Significance," 373–393.
9. Liu, *An Introduction to Chinese Philosophy*, 24–29; Chan, *A Source Book in Chinese Philosophy*, 262.
10. Liu, *An Introduction to Chinese Philosophy*, 37–38; Lai, *Introduction to Chinese Philosophy*, 216. Fung Yu-Lan describes the concept of *chung/zhong*, the mean, as similar to the Aristotelian mean: one is to have emotions that are appropriate and in due proportion to the situation. The mean is "neither too much nor too little," and is just right in relation to time; Confucians often use the word *shih* (time or timely) together with *chung* to refer to the "timely mean." Fung Yu-Lan, *A Short History of Chinese Philosophy*, 172–173.
11. Chan, *A Source Book in Chinese Philosophy*, 98. De Bary translates: "What Heaven has ordained is called [human] 'nature'; to follow that nature is called the Way. To cultivate that Way is called 'instruction.' The Way cannot be departed from for even an instant. If it could, it would not be the Way. . . . Before the feelings of pleasure, anger, sorrow, and joy are aroused, is called [the state of] centrality. After these are aroused, if they preserve equilibrium [centrality] it is called [the state of] harmony. Harmony is the universal path" (De Bary and Bloom, *Sources of Chinese Tradition*, 735–736).
12. Liu, *An Introduction to Chinese Philosophy*, 38; see Tu, "The Continuity of Being," 45–47; Tu, *Centrality and Commonality*, 10; "Maintaining Perfect Balance ('The Doctrine

of the Mean')," in *The Four Books: The Basic Teachings of the Later Confucian Tradition*, trans. Daniel K. Gardner, 111.

13. Note that while we are used to the spelling *Tao Te Ching*, the pronunciation is closer to "Daodejing." The text is traditionally attributed to Lao Tzu, an honorific name that means "Old Master." He is identified either as (1) Lao Tzu, who is recorded as having conversations with the time of Confucius (around 500 BCE) or (2) a figure named Lao Tan (around 375 BCE), which would put him after Confucius but before the philosopher Chuang Tzu, who lived ca. 365–285 BCE. Modern scholars generally agree that the book we have today is a compilation, drawn together from the sayings of a certain tradition, perhaps with internal commentary even within chapters. Many scholars believe the text reached something like its present form in the third century BCE (about 225 BCE); this is known as the "received," or Wang Bi, version of the text. This text has been called *Tao Te Ching*—the *Classic of the Way* (*Tao*) *and Its Power/Virtue* (*Te*). Two versions of the text recently found in a tomb at Mawangdui are firmly dated to the second half of the second century BCE. In these manuscripts, the order of the two parts of the text is reversed; the section on *Te* precedes that on *Tao*, so it would properly be called the *Te Tao Ching* (Henricks, trans., *Te-Tao Ching*, xvi–xviii). Because many scholars do see in the *Tao Te Ching* a firm editorial hand with a coherent philosophical perspective, it is regarded as acceptable to refer to both the text and its author as Lao Tzu, or the Lao Tzu tradition. For an earlier dating of the received text, see however, William H. Baxter, who focuses on the rhetorical patterns and pronunciations of the work itself. He concludes that the text was probably composed around 400 BCE, after Confucius but before Chuang Tzu; William H. Baxter, "Situating the Language of the *Lao-tzu*," 231–233. Philip Ivanhoe, *The Daodejing of Laozi*, xv–xvii; Ivanhoe, "The Concept of *de* ('Virtue') in the Laozi," 253 n. 1; Brook Ziporyn, "Ironies of Coherence and the Discovery of the Yin," chap. 4 of *Ironies of One and Many*; A. C. Graham, *Disputers of the Tao*, 215–217.
14. See, e.g., Benjamin Schwartz, "The Thought of the *Tao-te-ching*," 192; Liu, *An Introduction to Chinese Philosophy*, 133–136; Isadore Robinet, "The Diverse Interpretations of the Laozi," 132–134. On the question of whether Chinese thought teaches creation *ex nihilo*, see Robert Neville, "From Nothing to Being."
15. Note the paradox that the *Tao* is here described as unchanging, while in many passages its essential nature is described as the changing flow of nature's opposites. Like chapter 40, this passage may reflect a Taoist creation myth. Ellen Marie Chen has argued that there is a Taoist creation myth according to which being emerges from nothing, flowers into the ten thousand things, reaches its limit, and returns to an original nothing. See Neville, "From Nothing to Being," 25, 33 n.12, for the series of Chen articles. As Neville suggests, this view of the *Tao* may be reading a temporal view of creation *ex nihilo* into an atemporal context. That is, the movement from *Tao* to one to two to ten thousand things may be an ongoing spontaneous process of change, rather than a temporal sequence from nothing to being. In any event, this does not remove the enigma of the *Tao*: while *Tao* expresses

itself through change, there is an aspect of *Tao* that is described as solitary and unchanging. Perhaps there is a dimension of Taoist thought that describes *Tao* as an unmoved mover, the unmoved principle of all change. But perhaps it is more accurate to say that the *Tao* is simply constant in its nature; it is unchanging in its changingness. It is that fountain from which the entire universe—changing and unchanging—constantly emerges.

16. Lao Tzu, *Tao Te Ching*, trans. Stephen Addiss and Stanley Lombardo. All translations are taken from this edition. There are no page numbers in this translation, only chapter numbers.
17. For a full picture of the *Tao Te Ching* in the context of early Taoist accounts of the origin of the world, see now Thomas Michael, *The Pristine Dao*, 7–31.
18. We find similar notions in Aristotle and Plotinus. Neither thinker describes a real creation. In Plotinus, the language of emanation or radiation is used to describe the relationship of ontological priority, the dependence of all things on a principle that is prior logically, not temporally. That is, all things depend on the One, while the One does not depend on anything. Likewise here, all things depend on the *Tao*, while the *Tao* stands solitary and alone, unchanging (chapter 25). One "engenders" two in the sense that the two, three, and ten thousand things are all dependent on the One. On the relationship of the One to the many in Lao Tzu, see A. C. Graham, *Disputers of the Tao*, 221–222; Robinet, "Diverse Interpretations," 130; Liu, *An Introduction to Chinese Philosophy*, 136; Schwartz, "The Thought of the *Tao-te-ching*," 192.
19. Wing-Tsit Chan, trans., *The Way of Lao Tzu*, 176; Chan, *A Source Book in Chinese Philosophy*, 161. See also Max Kaltenmark and Roger Greaves, *Lao Tzu and Taoism*, 39–40.
20. Schwartz, "The Thought of the *Tao-te-ching*," 193–194.
21. *Tao Te Ching* 28, 32; see Graham, *Disputers of the Tao*, 221, describing the *Tao* as "the undivided."
22. Ziporyn thus focuses on the *Tao* as a way of transition between non-being and being, a way that things come into being. In order to sustain itself, *yang* activity—outward, outgoing, and bright—must contain and make preeminent its "opposite," receptive, inward, dark passivity (*yin*). Coherence, intelligibility, a hewed-out form emerge from incoherence, the unhewn block of wood. A bas-relief emerges from an unhewn block; content emerges from a context. Ziporyn, *Ironies of One and Many*, chapter 4; see also Graham, *Disputers of the Tao*, 220–226.
23. The uncarved block is pre-value. There is not yet any distinguishing between the bas-relief that has been sculpted out—the desired, artistic, valued product—and the leftover material. Thus the uncarved block represents that which has not yet been valued. However, it also represents the whole block, including the pre-valued and what has been carved out; this is because in the original, before anything has been valued or separated, there is no distinction between carved and uncarved. Once something has been valued, things fall on one side of the divide: valued or unvalued. Thus Ziporyn writes: "The unhewn itself is in this sense technically pre-value, the whole from which both value and anti-value emerge" (Ziporyn, *Ironies of One and Many*, chapter 4); see also Graham, *Disputers of the Tao*, 223–225. Consider

also Neville, who describes spontaneous change as that which harmoniously embraces the past—the *yin* elements, or context—while transforming them in unexpected ways. Natural, effortless action creates novelty by attentiveness to context. See Neville, "From Nothing to Being," 26–27.

24. On the theme of the mother, see Schwartz, "The Thought of the *Tao-te-ching*," 194; Kaltenmark and Greaves, *Lao Tzu and Taoism*, 37–41; Liu, *An Introduction to Chinese Philosophy*, 138–139.
25. *Te* is a term commonly glossed in early Chinese texts as deriving from the Chinese for "get"; it is the virtue or power that one "gets" from the *Tao* (Burton Watson, "Introduction" in *Tao Te Ching*, trans. Addiss and Lombardo, xiii). As David Nivison expresses this idea, "*De* thus is what the thing 'gets' from the *dao* to be itself. Here is a curious bit of philosophical philology of very early date. The words '*de*,' 'virtue,' and '*de*,' 'get' are (and were) exact homophones; so 'virtue' must be a metaphysical 'getting' " ("The Paradox of 'Virtue,' " in *The Ways of Confucianism*, 33 and n. 10). The relationship between *Tao* and *Te* is sometimes expressed in the following way: the *Tao* is universal and not determined; the *Te* is the virtue or power that gives a person efficacy, enabling him or her to accomplish particular actions. The universal *Tao* expresses itself in the individual's *Te*. See Kaltenmark and Greaves, *Lao Tzu and Taoism*, 27–28; Chan, trans., *The Way of Lao Tzu*, 11; Nivison, *The Ways of Confucianism*, 33. The royal *Te* was originally the magical effect a sage cultivated through rites of sacrifice. It came to mean the natural effect a person had on others. The Confucian sage was said to have such a *Te*, a kind of moral charisma, that had a powerful effect on the people he ruled; Confucius also suggested that any person could cultivate this kind of moral power. Taoists had a related sense of *Te*, as the natural effect the Taoist sage had upon both people and natural beings around them. Ivanhoe and Van Norden, *Readings in Classical Chinese Philosophy*, 357–358; Ivanhoe, "The Concept of Virtue (*de*) in the *Laozi*," 242–250.
26. We read a similar sentiment about giving orders in chapter 34: "It clothes and nourishes all beings / But does not become their master / Enduring without desire / It may be called slight / All beings return to it, / But it does not become their master / It may be called immense. / By not making itself great, / It can do great things." The fact that the *Tao* does not give orders can be looked at from two points of view. On the one hand, one might see that which does not give orders as small, lowly, insignificant. But in Lao Tzu's reversal of values, the fact that the *Tao* does not become master of things is its greatness. By not making itself lord over things, the *Tao* presents a different model of greatness and true mastery. See Ziporyn, *Pattern and the Pendulum*, 208.
27. Graham, *Disputers of the Tao*, 223–226.
28. Is *Tao* transcendent as well as immanent? Is the *Tao* simply the totality of the infinite possibilities, or a force that pervades these possibilities? Or is *Tao* the transcendent realm from which the possibilities emerge? For various interpretations, see Liu, *An Introduction to Chinese Philosophy*, 134–138; Robinet, "The Diverse Interpretations of the *Laozi*," 132–140.

29. Homer H. Dubs, "Taoism," 272, quoted by Chan, *The Way of Lao Tzu*, 8. Dubs notes that Lao Tzu did not perceive a contradiction in asserting the existence of non-existence; in fact, he recognized the need to assert the reality of non-existence. On various meanings of the *Tao* in the *Tao Te Ching*, see Robert G. Henricks, "Re-exploring the Analogy of the *Dao* and the Field," 171–173. On *Tao* as the substance of all things, see Robinet, "The Diverse Interpretations of the *Laozi*," 134–140; Ziporyn, *Pattern and the Pendulum*, 204–206.
30. Plato, *Republic* 508e–509c.
31. One modern scholar points out that this is a radical solution to the problem of creation. In Western thought, the pre-Socratic thinker Parmenides declared that what is not cannot be. Thus Western thought developed the problem of creation *ex nihilo*: if non-being is really nothing, how can something arise out of nothing? See "Taoism," 272, quoted by Chan, *The Way of Lao Tzu*, 8. From the pre-Socratic thinker Parmenides, all we have are fragments; see Proclus, *Commentary on Plato's Timaeus* 1.345.18, lines 3–8; Simplicius, *Commentary on Aristotle's Physics* 116.28–28B.2; Plato, *Sophist* 242a; Sextus Empiricus, *Against the Mathematicians* 7.114 = 18B7. Trans. R. D. McKirahan Jr. and rev. Patricia Curd in *Readings in Ancient Greek Philosophy from Thales to Aristotle*, 2nd ed., ed. S. Marc Cohen, Patricia Curd, and C. D. C. Reeve (Indianapolis: Hackett, 2000), 27–28.
32. *Tao Te Ching*, chapter 4.
33. See below.
34. *Tao Te* Ching, chapters 4, 8, 34.
35. *Chuang Tzu: Basic Writings*, trans. Burton Watson, chapter 6, 86–87.
36. Fung Yu-Lan, *A Short History of Chinese Philosophy*, 116–117.
37. See Ziporyn, *Pattern and the Pendulum*.
38. "Discerning the rhythms of the situation" is a formulation suggested to me by a lecture of Robert Neville to Core Humanities, CC 102, spring 2002.
39. *Tao Te Ching*, chapter 3. Graham prefers to translate *wu-wei* as "doing nothing," to emphasize that it is a way of doing, not pure passivity; Graham, *Disputers of the Tao*, 232–234. On *wu-wei* and its relationship to *de*, see Liu, *An Introduction to Chinese Philosophy*, 142–144; Ivanhoe, "The Concept of *de* ('Virtue') in the Laozi," 242–250.
40. *Tao Te Ching*, chapter 20; Ivanhoe, "The Concept of *de* ('Virtue') in the Laozi," 242–250.
41. H. G. Creel, "On the Opening Words of the 'Lao-Tzu,'" 302; Creel, *Shen Pu-hai*, 167–169; Chan, *Way of Lao Tzu*, 6–7; Ivanhoe, *Classics of Chinese Philosophy*, 357.
42. See Brook Ziporyn, trans., *Zhuangzi*, appendix 2; Ziporyn, *Pattern and the Pendulum*, 193ff; Chad Hansen, *A Daoist Theory of Chinese Thought*, 83–85; Schwartz, "The Thought of the *Tao-te-ching*," 190; Creel, "On the Opening Words of the 'Lao-Tzu,'" 299–330; Liu, *An Introduction to Chinese Philosophy*, 132–133.
43. See Ziporyn, trans., *Zhuangzi*, appendix 2; Ziporyn, *Pattern and the Pendulum*, 193ff; Graham, *Disputers of the Tao*, 220. On contrasts between the *Tao* of Confucius and Lao Tzu, see now Thomas Michael, "Confucius and Laozi." In conversation, Michael suggested to me a different way of interpreting the opening lines of the *Tao Te Ching*.

He argues that the *Tao* that can be spoken of is not a fixed, stamped *Tao,* or way of doing things. Rather, it should open up into an expansive understanding. One can understand the *Tao* of being a father, but in order to fully fulfill the role of father, one must go beyond the fixed, stamped *Tao* to a more expansive notion. I interpret this as what Western traditions call "going beyond the letter of the law."

44. Sidney Rosenfeld, a longtime professor of German at Oberlin College, comes to my mind.
45. Ivanhoe, "The Concept of *de* ('Virtue') in the Laozi," 240–242. Sidney Rosenfeld again comes to mind.
46. Ivanhoe, "The Concept of *de* ('Virtue') in the Laozi," 242–243.
47. On *ziran* (*tsu-jen*), see Robinet, "The Diverse Interpretations of the *Laozi,*" 143–144; Liu Xioagan, "Naturalness (*Tzu-jan*), the Core Value in Taoism," 211–227; Liu, "An Inquiry Into the Core Value of Laozi's Philosophy," 211–237.
48. Ivanhoe, "The Concept of *de* ('Virtue') in the Laozi," 245–246. Compare Charles Griswold, "Happiness, Tranquility, and Philosophy."
49. Ivanhoe, "The Concept of *de* ('Virtue') in the Laozi," 245–246.
50. *Tao Te Ching*, chapter 38; Ivanhoe, "The Concept of *de* ('Virtue') in the Laozi," 247–248. Ivanhoe suggests a parallel difference in Confucian and Taoist conceptions of government by *wu-wei*. The Confucian leader rules by the power of moral authority, like the teacher who commands respect, who engenders responsibly acting students. The Daoist who rules by *wu-wei* invites a different response; when the people abandon their artificial desires, they will naturally be satisfied with the simple life of their agricultural village, abandoning "competition, contention, and strife" (Ivanhoe, 250).
51. Liu, *An Introduction to Chinese Philosophy*, 39.
52. For the relationship between Whitehead and Chinese thought, see, for example, Robert Neville, "Whitehead on the One and the Many," 387–393; John Berthrong, *Concerning Creativity: A Comparison of Chu Hsi, Whitehead, and Neville.*
53. Even what we call an individual is itself a community of cells, which cooperate to make organs, which cooperate to make larger systems of the organism.
54. Whitehead, *Science and the Modern World*, 103.
55. This point is articulated by the rationalist Bertrand Russell as well.
56. Whitehead, *Science and the Modern World*, 103–104.
57. Ibid., 105.
58. The example of a paper conceived in one's head and the commitment of the first word was given by the late Clyde Holbrook, who first introduced me to the wonders of Whitehead, in the course Modern Religious Thought at Oberlin College, 1976–77.
59. Whitehead, *Science and the Modern World*, 105.
60. "Ground of being" is a term popularized by the twentieth-century theologian Paul Tillich to suggest an impersonal or pre-personal depth/dimension of God. The term has entered the common theological vocabulary; I do not mean to suggest that Whitehead himself uses the term or is influenced by Tillich. I use the phrase because it captures the way Whitehead blurs the personal and impersonal

dimensions of divinity, and it works better to describe Whitehead's God than "being" alone.

61. Ibid. Thus, despite his strong Platonic leanings, on this issue Whitehead comes closer to Aristotle, for whom forms exist only in their instantiation in real objects. While Whitehead does argue for a realm of eternal objects that are required for nature rather than emergent from it, he sees value in the real integration and syntheses of these objects in the histories we create in our world.
62. Whitehead, *Religion in the Making*, 115.

## 4. THE HARMONY OF REASON: AUGUSTINE AND MAIMONIDES ON GOOD AND EVIL

1. For Whitehead on the problem of evil, see Whitehead, *Religion in the Making*, 91–96. In brief, Whitehead sees evil as inconsistency and instability; the universe exhibits a drive toward stability and consistency. See also below, n. 7.
2. See Harry A. Wolfson, "What Is New in Philo?," 439–460; Herbert Davidson, "The Study of Philosophy as a Religious Obligation."
3. We have seen that the relationship between the Good and being in the work of Plato himself is a complex one. In *Republic* 509b Plato writes that the objects of knowledge derive their existence, or being (*einai*), and essence (*ousia*) from the Good, while the Good itself is beyond essence (*ousia*) in dignity and power. We noted above that while he suggests that the Good is beyond essence (*ousia*), this does not necessarily mean that the Good is beyond being (*on*). See above, chap. 2, n. 67.
4. See above, chap. 2, n. 67.
5. *Enneads* 5.4.1. See Seeskin, *Maimonides on the Origin of the World*, 96–99; Dominic J. O'Meara, *Plotinus; An Introduction to the Enneads*, 44–49.
6. See Arthur O. Lovejoy, *The Great Chain of Being*, 61ff. He offers a definition of the principle of plenitude, or the great chain of being, on p. 52. Maimonides expresses this principle in *Guide* 3.25: "The entire purpose consists in bringing into existence the way you see it everything whose existence is possible" (*Dalālat al-hāʾirīn*, ed. Joel, 366 line 20; Pines, trans., 504). "What is primarily intended—namely, the bringing into being of everything whose existence is possible, existence being indubitably a good" (*Dalālat al-hāʾirīn*, ed. Joel, 368 line 1; Pines, trans., 506).
7. Augustine, *Confessions* 7.13. As Whitehead expresses the idea, evil is when things are at cross-purposes; *Religion in the Making*, 94 .
8. Augustine, *Confessions* 7.12–13.
9. Augustine, *Confessions* 7.12.
10. Augustine, *Confessions* 7.3; *On the Free Choice of the Will* 1.4.7–8; 2.16.27.
11. Augustine, *Confessions* 7.3; *On the Free Choice of the Will* 1.4.7–8; 2.16.27.
12. The Stoics taught that we can always choose happiness, which lies in *apatheia*, the lack of suffering (*pathos*). We always have the choice of our own attitude. See, e.g.,

Epictetus, *The Handbook (The Encheiridion)*. Spinoza was also much influenced by the Stoics.

13. Augustine, *On the Free Choice of the Will* 3.18–20: 106–111.
14. Augustine, *Confessions* 7.3.
15. Augustine, *Confessions* 7.3.
16. Augustine, *Confessions* 7.12.
17. Augustine, *Confessions* 7.5.
18. Augustine, *Confessions* 7.15.
19. Augustine, *Confessions* 7.15.
20. Augustine, *Confessions* 7.10.
21. Augustine, *Confessions* 7.15.
22. Beings exist in God; all beings are held in God's truth just as Forms exist in the Mind of God. God exists in an eternity outside time; God is the eternal source of our temporal world. Philosophical language expresses this by saying that God is the ontological and epistemological ground of existence. What this means is that God is the condition for the possibility of both anything *existing* and of anything's *being known.*

    We have seen that for Plato to be is to be intelligible. Plato conceives of the Good as a source of both being and knowledge, which he compares to light. Light is that which illumines and shows that the order of being is an intelligible order. Thus for the Platonic and Neoplatonic traditions upon which Augustine is drawing, one cannot really separate being from intelligibility. To be is to be capable of being known. God is both Being and Truth; God's light gives both being and intelligibility. Dark chaotic matter has no distinctions, and thus cannot be known. To understand is to make distinctions between things. In the One, argues Plotinus, there are no distinctions and thus there is no intelligibility. The One is not conscious and does not think. When the One becomes conscious, intellect is its first emanation. The term "emanation" draws on the metaphor of light. From the undifferentiated one, the light of intelligibility radiates.
23. *Confessions* 7.16.
24. Plato, *Republic* 571a–579d; Aristotle, *Nicomachean Ethics* 1166b; Augustine, *On the Free Choice of the Will* 1.4; 1.11; 1.13; 1.16; 2.19; 3.1.
25. Augustine thus maintains the profound conviction that contemplating eternal verities is the source of happiness. Plato, too, describes contemplating the eternal Forms in quasi-mystical language: one *sees* the Forms, a gestalt vision of the interconnected nature of all eternal verities. The philosopher who contemplates the Forms would not desire to leave that vision; he or she would have to be persuaded to return to the cave and instruct humankind to see the Truth (*Republic* 520a–d). In contrast, the Bible begins with humanity living in a paradise in which all is good, but human beings choose to leave that perfect reality. For Maimonides, it is the imagination that tempts humanity. Living in a world of pure Truth, human beings are tempted by imagining that the world might be other than it is, and better. For Augustine, it is through corruption of the will that humanity is tempted to leave

the world of pure Truth and turn aside to corrupt things. Both thinkers see the goal as a return to pure contemplation, an eternal being with God.

26. Maimonides, *Guide* 1.2.
27. See Lawrence B. Berman, "The Ethical Teachings of Maimonides Within the Context of Islamicate Civilization," 19–20, 24–27.
28. Ibid. While Sara Klein-Braslavy and Warren Zev Harvey argue that it is the imagination that clouds our perceptions, Howard Kreisel and Lawrence Kaplan argue that relative, generally accepted opinions are not cognized directly by the imagination, but rather by the practical intellect—the rational faculty—as a result of the power of the imagination. In either case, the judgment of the rational faculty becomes dominated by the desires of the imagination. Klein-Braslavy and Harvey also argue that there is in fact an absolute "good" that is incumbent upon the original, ideal human being guided only by intellect. However, this *good* is not different from the *true*, since its dictum is to pursue humanity's true, natural end, which is intellectual perfection, and to cognize only intelligibles. They argue that there is thus indeed a universal morality of true and false, and not only a conventional, shifting morality of relative "good" and "evil." See Sara Klein-Braslavy, *Maimonides' Interpretation of the Adam Stories in Genesis*, 133–136, 148–149; Warren Zev Harvey, "Maimonides and Spinoza on Knowledge of Good and Evil," 177–183 (Hebrew),140–145 (English); Howard Kreisel, *Maimonides' Political Thought*, 73–74, 102; Lawrence Kaplan, "I Sleep, but My Heart Waketh," 150–154, n. 19; Berman, "Ethical Views of Maimonides," 29; Berman, "Maimonides on the Fall of Man," 11.
29. Maimonides, *Guide* 3.11.
30. Cf. Kenneth Seeskin, "The Positive Contribution of Negative Theology," 49.
31. Sara Klein-Braslavy and Warren Zev Harvey have focused on the well-known Aristotelian strand; Shlomo Pines and Howard Kreisel have focused on the strand I am going to trace here. See notes below, esp. 61, 63, and 65. Shlomo Pines suggested that there are four "discourses" in the *Guide*: (1) a traditional religious one, including anthropomorphic expressions in the Bible; (2) an "Aristotelian" strand; (3) a critical strand, showing the impossibility of metaphysics; (4) and a Sufi discourse in *Guide* 3.51. For more on Pines' view, see below, n. 63. Alexander Altmann calls attention to the Neoplatonic strand in Maimonides' approach to speaking about God, also noted by Julius Guttmann. In recent years, Alfred Ivry has been pointing out diverse Neoplatonic elements in Maimonides' thought. See Pines, "Maimonides' Halachic Works and the *Guide of the Perplexed*," 10–11; Alexander Altmann, "Maimonides on Intellect and the Scope of Metaphysics," 121–122; Julius Guttmann, "*Torat ha-Elohim shel ha-Rambam*," 59; Guttman, *Ha-filosofya shel ha-yahadut*, 151; Alfred Ivry, "Neoplatonic Currents in Maimonides' Thought," 15–40; Ivry, "Islamic and Greek Influences on Maimonides' Philosophy," 139–132; Ivry, "Maimonides and Neoplatonism," in *Neoplatonism and Jewish Thought*, 137–156; Ivry, "Providence, Divine Omniscience, and Possibility," 143–159; Sara Klein-Braslavy, *Maimonides' Intepretation of the Story of Creation*, 104–113, 168–174; Klein-Braslavy, *Adam Stories*, 137–149; Howard Kreisel, *Maimonides' Poliical Thought: Studies in Ethics, Law, and the*

*Human Ideal*, 93–124, 63–92; Warren Zev Harvey, "Ethics and Meta-ethics, Aesthetics and Meta-Aesthetics in Maimonides," 131–138; Shlomo Pines, "Truth and Falsehood Versus Good and Evil: A Study in Jewish and General Philosophy in Connection with *Guide of the Perplexed* I:2," 95–157.

32. *Guide* 3.13 (Pines translation: 453). Parenthetical numbers give references to Pines' English translation of Maimonides' *Guide*.
33. *Guide* 3.25 (503).
34. Klein-Braslavy, *Adam Stories*, 143. Human beings also have an absolute good, which is God's intention in creating them: to achieve intellectual perfection; ibid., 145.
35. Aristotle, *Nichomachean Ethics* 1094a.
36. Maimonides, *Guide* 3.12. *Dalālat al-hāʾirīn*, ed. Joel, 318 line 20; *Guide of the Perplexed*, trans. Pines, 442.
37. Maimonides, *Guide* 3.12. *Dalālat al-hāʾirīn*, ed. Joel, 323 line 18; *Guide of the Perplexed*, trans. Pines, 448.
38. Maimonides, *Guide* 3.10. *Dalālat al-hāʾirīn*, ed. Joel, 317 lines 5–6; *Guide of the Perplexed*, trans. Pines, 440.
39. Maimonides, *Guide* 3.10. *Dalālat al-hāʾirīn*, ed. Joel, 317 line 10; *Guide of the Perplexed*, trans. Pines, 440.
40. I do not mean to suggest that the notion that being itself is good or beautiful is only Neoplatonic. In a study in progress, I discuss the Aristotelian roots of this idea, for example in Aristotle's assertion at *Metaphysics* 12.7, 1072b that the Unmoved Mover exists in a way that is good or beautiful (*kalōs*). For an argument that Aristotle conceives of God as not only Mind (*Nous*) but the Good, see Stephen Menn, "Plato and Aristotle on God as *Nous* and the Good." In 3.25, Maimonides explains that the fundamental principle of the nature of coming to be and passing away is that "the entire purpose consists in bringing into existence the way you see it everything whose existence is possible" (*Dalālat al-hāʾirīn*, ed. Joel, 366 line 20; trans. Pines, 504). Later in the same chapter, he speaks of "what is primarily intended—namely, the bringing into being of everything whose existence is possible, existence being indubitably a good" (*Dalālat al-hāʾirīn*, ed. Joel, 368 line 1; trans. Pines, 506). It is interesting that Maimonides speaks of "the intention" rather than "God's intention," as if this is simply an impersonal cosmic process. He expresses here the principle of plenitude. See Lovejoy, *Great Chain of Being*, which offers a definition of the principle of plenitude on p. 52. See below on Pines' remarks, n. 63.
41. Maimonides, *Dalālat al-hāʾirīn* 1.59, ed. Joel, 95; trans. Pines, 139. On parallel statements in Islamic mystical authors and Baḥya Ibn Paqūda, see Diana Lobel, *A Sufi-Jewish Dialogue*, 38–39.
42. However, note the very different way this metaphor is used by Hua Yen Buddhists, who assert that in fact the ocean cannot be conceived of independently of the waves: "The waves are waves which are none other than water—the waves themselves show the water. The water is water, which is no different from waves—the water makes the waves. Waves and water are one, yet that does not hinder their difference. Water and waves are different, yet that does not hinder their unity." See

Liu, *An Introduction to Chinese Philosophy*, 263, quoting Thomas Cleary, trans., "Cessation and Contemplation in the Five Teachings," 58.

43. Compare this with Baḥya Ibn Paqūda's distinction between essential and active attributes. Essential attributes belong to God as God, independent of creation. Maimonides rejects the notion of essential attributes, as they introduce multiplicity into God. But Baḥya's essential attributes, which he insists are distinct in name alone, describe three aspects of divinity that are conceptually quite similar to the conception of a Necessary Existent in Avicenna and Maimonides: God is one, existent, and eternal. On the Necessary Existent in Avicenna, see the following note. See Baḥya, *Duties of the Heart*, trans. Mansoor, 132–134; trans. Qafih, 73–77.
44. *Mishneh Torah*, *Book of Knowledge* (Sefer ha-madda') 1:2–3, in *A Maimonides Reader*, 43–44; trans. Bernard Septimus in *A Jewish Philosophy Reader*, ed. Frank, Leaman, and Manekin, 223. On Avicenna's theory of Necessary Existence, see Fazlur Rahman, "Ibn Sīnā's Theory of the God–World Relationship," 38–52.
45. For if the universe were eternal, then every possibility would at some time be realized—one of which would be for all existents to cease to be. If there were not some being that eternally is, there would be nothing to bring the world back into existence. Given that we are here, there must be an eternal being who is the ground of this world's existence. If, on the other hand, the universe is created in time, then there must be a Creator. In either case, we are assured that there is some principle of Being that grounds our being. Necessary Existence simply means that existence will never totally disappear. As Warren Zev Harvey notes, Maimonides bases this proof on the Aristotelian notion that the world is in fact eternal. See Warren Zev Harvey, "Maimonides' First Commandment, Physics, and Doubt," 149–162.
46. *Guide* 1.50–60. See Seeskin, "The Positive Contribution of Negative Theology," 36–38.
47. *Guide* 1.58; Altmann, "Maimonides on the Intellect and the Scope of Metaphysics," 123; Wolfson, *Maimonides on Negative Attributes*, 428–429; Diana Lobel, " 'Silence Is Praise to You,' " 33.
48. *Guide* 1.58 (136). We see here the imagery of emanation Maimonides drew from Plotinus. For metaphors of emanation in Plotinus, see *Enneads* 5.2.1 for overflow; 3.8.10 for a flowing river, 5.3.12 for light, 5.1.6 for perfume. I am grateful to Kenneth Seeskin for the Plotinus passages, which I was having trouble locating. See also 5.8.12 for the notion that as long as there is a One—that is eternally—there will always be a radiation from the source. It is not that God decided at a certain moment to create a world; flowers naturally emit a beautiful fragrance, and light radiates outward.
49. *Guide* 1.54, 3.53. See Seeskin, "The Positive Contribution of Negative Theology," 42; Seeskin, "Sanctity and Silence"; Altmann, "Maimonides on the Intellect," 119–120; Hyman, "Maimonides on Religious Language," 185–186.
50. *Guide* 1.54.
51. On the complex dialectic between positive and negative discourse in Maimonides, see Elliot Wolfson, "Via Negativa in Maimonides and Its Impact on

Thirteenth-Century Kabbalah"; Seeskin, "Sanctity and Silence"; Lobel, "Silence Is Praise to You."

52. See Josef Stern, "Maimonides on Language and the Science of Language," 206–212; Stern, "Logical Syntax as a Key to a Secret of the *Guide of the Perplexed*," 155–166.
53. *Guide* 3.12. Recall our discussion in chapter 2 of the Hindu Brahman and Plato's Good as sources of Being, truth, and value.
54. In the "language of human beings," the fact that the world exists shows that it conformed to God's "intention" in overflowing God's being to others.
55. *Guide* 3.10 (440). We have seen that Whitehead, too, suggests that values are woven into the fabric of nature. His reasoning is similar to that of Maimonides and other heirs of the Neoplatonic tradition. The realization of existence is an embodiment of value. Every being strives to be; every moment beings achieve realization of their natures. Whitehead, *Science and the Modern World*, 105.
56. Of course, strictly speaking, from the point of view of Maimonides' negative theology, we can no more say that God is "good" than we can say that God is "one" or "existent." But neither can God be "that which conforms to purpose," because God has no purpose other than God's existence. See *Guide* 3.13. On equivocal terms, see Maimonides, *Treatise on Logic*, 59; Aristotle, *Categories*, 1.1a.1–6; Hyman, "Maimonides on Religious Language," 177–179.
57. *Guide* 3.10 (440); 3.12 (443).
58. *Guide* 1.72; 2.1. Cf. the felicitous translation of Chaim Rabin of *Guide* 2.1: "It has been definitely proved by demonstration that the whole universe of existing things is like one organism in which everything hangs together" (*Maimonides: Guide of the Perplexed*, 93).
59. *Guide* 3.10–12.
60. *Guide* 3.10 (440); 3.12. See Kenneth Seeskin, *Maimonides: A Guide for Today's Perplexed*, 59. As Sara Klein-Braslavy points out, this is Maimonides' interpretation of the *midrash* in Genesis Rabbah found written in the Torah of Rabbi Meir, which we discussed in chap. 1. In a play on words between two like-sounding Hebrew terms, "death" (*mavvet*) and "very" (*me'od*), the rabbinic Sage interpreted Gen. 1:31, "God saw all that he had made, and behold, it was very good" as "death (*mavvet*) is good." Maimonides adds that even the existence of matter is good—despite the fact that matter brings with it lack, decay, and death—in that matter brings existence into actuality, in however imperfect a form. *Story of Creation*, 109–110.
61. *Guide* 3.12. Warren Zev Harvey, Sara Klein-Braslavy, and Howard Kreisel have each undertaken substantive studies of the question of good and evil in Maimonides. Harvey and Klein-Braslavy have focused attention on Maimonides' statement in *Guide* 3.13 that the good is "that which conforms to our purpose," and have deduced from it what they see as several derivative meanings of good, including the one discussed here, that good is Truth, Existence, or God. Kreisel believes that the more foundational statement of Maimonides is his assertion in 3.25 that good is the "realization of a noble end," and that existence has intrinsic worth, and is thus good. I have benefited greatly from the substantial textual investigations that

each of these studies has contributed, both of key passages in Maimonides and of thinkers such as al-Fārābī, Avicenna, al-Ghazālī, and Spinoza. I believe my position, simplified for the purpose of this study, is in harmony with elements of each of these approaches. My own approach suggests that God is the absolute Truth and Existent; another way of saying this is that God is the absolute "Good," and thus that what God confers—existence—is an overflow of that "good." God is the absolute Being, and God confers the absolute good of existence on other beings. This says nothing about the relative "goods" we choose when we have lost sight of our absolute, objective purpose, which is knowledge of God. Harvey argues: "The term 'good,' like 'perfect', may denote the ontic truth: existent reality or God. This use, however, is not—as in Plato—the primary and literal use of the term, but is merely a figurative use 'in accordance with the language of man' " (Harvey, "Maimonides and Spinoza," 140 English; 177 Hebrew). He thus argues that good is a univocal, rather than an equivocal term. It has one primary sense for Maimonides: that which conforms to our purpose.

If we grant this point—that existence is good because it conforms to God's purpose—this is simply to say that it is the product of God's will and wisdom, which Maimonides takes to be one. Along these lines, Klein-Braslavy sums up her detailed argument by interpreting Gen. 1:31 as follows: " 'God said,' signifies that God willed the world into existence. God 'saw' intends that the world conformed to God's 'wisdom.' And that the world was 'good' signifies that existence itself is the purpose of our existence" (*Story of Creation*, 113). That is to say, existence is an intrinsic "good" because it flows from an absolute, objective existent—i.e., the Necessary Existent—who has no purpose outside of its Existence. There is no value outside its existence to which it could conform as "good." Its purpose is simply to be. We could therefore say that God is not "Good" any more than God is "One" or "Existent." But as the Necessary Existent, God is the absolute source of value from which all value flows. See below, n. 63, for Pines' articulation of this position. On the primary and metaphorical uses of "good," see below, n. 65.

See Harvey, "Maimonides and Spinoza" (Hebrew), 165–185 (English trans., 131–146); Klein-Braslavy, *Story of Creation*, 104–113, 168–174; Klein-Braslavy, *Adam Stories*, 137–149; Kreisel, *Maimonides' Political Thought*, 93–124, 63–92; Harvey, "Ethics and Meta-ethics," 131–138; Ehud Benor, *Worship of the Heart*, 193 n. 87; Stephen Menn, "Aristotle and Plato on God as *Nous* and as the Good," esp. 547–551, and his excellent summary at 570–573.

62. *Guide* 3.11.
63. In an article published posthumously on "Truth and Falsehood Versus Good and Evil," Shlomo Pines explains this as follows: "When certain philosophers refer to knowledge of good and evil or (as we did above) to moral judgments, the assumption is that there exists a class of cognition and a class of propositions and judgments whose validity is a function of the opposition between good and evil, the existence of each of these contraries presupposing the existence of the other. Now Maimonides rejects the intellectual validity of this conception of the good and

relegates it to the sphere of universally held opinions. Opinions of this kind relating to good and its antithesis evil may be useful, indeed necessary, for the preservation of the human race, as they help to curb destructive appetites but do not correspond to what really exists, which is apprehended by the intellect. However, 'the good' is an equivocal term. As Maimonides states in *Guide* 3.19, 'the good is being,' which means that judgments concerning 'the good' (when it is given the above sense) are (to use the terminology of *Guide* I, 2) concerned with what is true (and false)" (Pines, "Truth and Falsehood," 141). Pines adds in a note: "And not with good and evil. This inference is not spelled out in *Guide* III:10, a chapter in which Maimonides is concerned with establishing the proposition that 'evil' is relative and has no independent existence" (Pines, "Truth and Falsehood," 141 n. 131).

Thus in *Guide* 1.2, Maimonides describes the arising of relative good and evil, which have no objective, independent, or strictly logical status; these concepts arise when we look at the universe from our limited, subjective point of view, based on our own desires and imaginings. And then there is absolute good (which is being, and so beyond relative good and evil), which is simply Necessary Existence. It is the condition of all existence and value, and as the absolute standard of truth and value it transcends "good" and "evil." It is beyond "existence," "oneness," and "goodness" because it is the condition for all three. This is God. Necessary Existence is the absolute good, and God's overflow of existence is a sharing of that good to create a universe. Cf. Kreisel, *Maimonides' Political Thought*, 121.

See also Pines' remarks to his introduction to the *Guide*, p. cxxxii: "In III:25 Maimonides, speaking of the final end of the universe and rebutting the anthropomorphic illusions to which men are prone, states that the primary purpose is to bring into existence everything that is capable of existence. For being is a good. This is a formulation of the 'principle of plenitude,' whose history is traced in A. O. Lovejoy's Great Chain of Being." On the principle of plenitude, see above, including nn. 6 and 40. See Pines, "Truth and Falsehood Versus Good and Evil," 95–157.

64. *Guide* 1.73 (209, Premise 10: A Call to the Reader's Attention); Warren Zev Harvey, "Maimonides and Spinoza on Good and Evil," 168 (Hebrew), 132 (English). Recall Augustine's succinct statement in *Confessions* 7.15: "Falsehood is nothing but the supposed existence of that which is not."
65. Klein-Braslavy, *Adam Stories*, 133–136, 145–149; cf. al-Fārābī, *The Political Regime*, 72–74 (Hyderabad ms. 42–44); trans. F. Najjar, in *Medieval Political Philosophy*, ed. Lerner and Mahdi, 34–35. The final question we must ask: Is this Platonic or Neoplatonic strand in Maimonides his true voice? Does he believe that this ontological use of the term "good" is its primary sense, or a derived, metaphorical usage? There are two questions here. One is a question about the way we use language. The second is a deeper question about good. Does Maimonides believe that God is intrinsically good and identical with being, as Plato and Plotinus believe? On one level, the Necessary Existent simply is. When we reach the level of God, we are beyond the language of good and evil—indeed, we are beyond language. Nevertheless, it seems clear to me that for Maimonides, it is the Necessary Existent that is

the absolute good. What we call good and evil in the "language of human beings," which is relative, is that which conforms to our purposes, or that which achieves a noble aim. But the Absolute for Maimonides is God, who grants being, and our purpose or noble aim is to know God and to further being, while God's "purpose" or "noble aim" is to confer being.

Maimonides, as a medieval Neoplatonic Aristotelian, believes that this world receives an overflow from the divine Being, which he terms "good." In *Guide* 3.13 Maimonides explains that there is a constant overflow of good from one thing to another, as he has explained in 2.11. To deprive a being of existence—i.e., that overflow—is "evil." But evil has no real existence; it is simply the deprivation of existence, which is divine overflow. Creation is "good" in that it is an overflow from God, who is Reality and Truth. In the "language of man" we speak of good as that which conforms to God's purpose. But this kind of "good" is different from the sense in which God and existence are good; just as God's "purpose" and "providence" are different from the way those words are used with respect to the human sphere. As Harvey points out, God's intention or purpose is simply God's action. We only infer that this reality is God's "purpose" because it is here. The language of overflow lends itself to some of his rapturous expressions of divine presence and immanence, which have given rise to interpreting Maimonides as a "mystical" thinker, or at least one expressing a kind of intellectualist mysticism. On Maimonides' rapturous Neoplatonic expressions, see Altmann, "Maimonides on the Intellect," 121–122.

66. See above at n. 49 and below, chap. 9.
67. Pers. comm. Also noted in Rémi Brague, *The Law of God*, 203. Professor Brague comments: "To be sure, equating 'covenant' and 'the nature of being' in this context is not totally arbitrary: God's covenant with Noah (Gen. 9:9–17) concerns the whole of what we would call nature." This would tie in with Maimonides' interpretation of "all my goodness," which God shows Moses in Exodus 33:19 as all of created reality.
68. On "suchness" or "thusness" in Buddhism, see above, chap. 1, n. 4.
69. See below, chap. 9.
70. See introduction to *Perek ḥeleq in Mishnah ʿim perush rabbenu Moshe ben Maimon*, trans. Qafih, 199; trans. Sheilat, Maimonides, *Haqdamot ha-Rambam la-Mishnah*, 132 (Hebrew), 362 (Arabic); English translation in *A Maimonides Reader*, ed. Twersky, 405.

## 5. YOU ARE THE ABSOLUTE: PHILOSOPHIES OF INDIA

1. See Gavin Flood, *An Introduction to Hinduism*, 23–35; Klaus Klostermaier, *A Short Introduction to Hinduism*, 5–8; David Kinsley, *Hinduism: A Cultural Perspective*, 10–11.
2. Flood, *Introduction to Hinduism*, 33–34.
3. Thomas Hopkins, *The Hindu Religious Tradition*, 11.
4. Alf Hiltebeitel, "Hinduism," 337; Klaus Klostermaier, *A Survey of Hinduism*, 62–63.

5. Flood, *Introduction to Hinduism*, 35; Klostermaier, *Short Introduction*, 16; Kinsley, *Hinduism*, 11.
6. *Hymns from the Ṛig Veda*, trans. Wendy Doniger in *The Ways of Religion: An Introduction to the Major Traditions*, ed. Roger Eastman: "The Hymn of Creation," "The Hymn of the Person," "The Golden Embryo," 22–27; Jeanine Miller, "The Hymn of Creation: A Philosophical Interpretation," 64–85; "*Ṛig Veda*" in Kessler, *Eastern Ways of Being Religious*, 52–54; for other commentary, see Zaehner, *Hinduism*, 41–46; *Bhagavad Gītā*, trans. Edgerton, 113–118.
7. While in the *Ṛig Veda* the purpose of the sacrifice is to connect with and appease the gods, in the Brāhmaṇas the ritual becomes an end in itself; the gods themselves are believed to have gained their place in the cosmos through the sacrifice. At the end of the Brāhmaṇa period, in texts known as the Āraṇyakas, the sacrificial ritual is internalized; for example, sacrifice is compared to the alternation of breathing and speaking. The priests who practice the sacrifice internally thus come to have cosmic importance. For the Brāhmaṇas, the ritual is all of reality; for the Āraṇyakas, the priest becomes one with the ritual. Thus it is a short step to the Upanishads, in which the individual becomes one with all of reality.

   The distinction between Brāhmaṇas and Āraṇyakas is not absolute. Some of the esoteric sections teaching the mystical significance of ritual actions and words came to be known as Āraṇyakas—texts to be recited in the forest wilderness, outside the village—while others came to be known as Upanishads. The *Bṛihadāraṇyaka*—which opens with a meditation on the horse sacrifice—is considered both an Āraṇyaka and an Upanishad. Many of the texts of the Brāhmaṇas set forth the mystical significance of details of the rituals. See Hopkins, *Hindu Religious Tradition*, 20, 30, 31–35, 38; Flood, *Introduction to Hinduism*, 36, 40, 75; *Upanishads*, trans. Patrick Olivelle, xxxii.
8. Hopkins, *Hindu Religious Tradition*, 28; Kinsley, *Hinduism*, 11.
9. This account of the evolution of the term *brahman* follows the somewhat simplified presentations of Franklin Edgerton, Gavin Flood, Thomas Hopkins, and R. C. Zaehner. For example Hopkins, who presents the original meaning of *brahman* as the power of the sacred utterance and the sacrifice, uses the term "*brahman* power" to explicate a statement from the *Atharva Veda*: "Who knows the thread of the thread, he would know the great *brahman* [power]" (10.8.37). In this account, the meaning of *brahman* evolved from the power of the sacrifice and the sacred word to that passively dynamic principle that sustains the universe. See similar descriptions by Edgerton, trans., *The Bhagavad Gītā*, 116–117; Flood, *Introduction to Hinduism*, 84; Zaehner, 36–56, esp. 37, 47. Patrick Olivelle notes that among its many meanings, *brahman* may mean a "formulation of truth," "the Veda," or "the ultimate essence of the cosmos," but "always retains its verbal character as 'the sound expression' of all reality" (Olivelle, trans., *Upanishads*, lvi). For scholarly studies of the many meanings of *brahman*, see Jan Gonda, *Notes on Brahman*; Louis Renou and Liliane Silburn, "Sur la notion de 'Brahman'"; Paul Thieme, "Brahman"; Hermann Oldenberg, *Die Religion des Veda*. Jan Gonda traces the original meaning of the term to

the root *bṛh* "to be great," and hence "power." Hermann Oldenberg summarizes the basic meaning of *brahman* as the sacred formula and the power in it. Thieme traces the root meaning to "forming" or "formulation"—poetic formulation and then formulation of truth. Renou notes the context of the life-or-death riddle, a theme developed by J. C. Heesterman, who writes: "*brahman* is distinguished by its enigmatic or paradoxical nature. The *brahman*, then, is the formulation of the cosmic riddle, a riddle that cannot be solved by a direct answer but only formulated in paradoxical terms that leave the answer—the (hidden) connection (*bandhu, nidāna*) between the terms of the paradox—unexpressed" (Heesterman, "Brahman," 295). In Renou's phrase, *brahman* is the "connective energy compressed in riddles" ("*Sur la notion de 'Brahman,'*" 43; Heesterman, "Brahman," 295). Heesterman emphasizes the context of the *brahmodya*, the verbal contest, which formed part of the Vedic ritual: "It consists of a series of rounds of verbal challenges and responses. In each round two contestants put riddle questions to each other. The point of the riddle contest is to show that one has 'seen' or understood the hidden 'connection' by responding with a similar, if possible even more artfully contrived, riddle. The one who holds out longest and finally reduces his opponent to silence is the winner, the true *brahman*, holder of the hidden connection . . . the live 'connection' that holds together the cosmos" (Heesterman, "Brahman," 295). As the concept of *brahman* evolved, "identification made it possible to concentrate the whole of the spoken and acted proceedings of the ritual in the person of the single sacrificer, who in this way internalizes the whole of the ritual, that is, the transcendent cosmic order, and so becomes identical with *brahman*. . . . Here the development leads over to the Upanisadic doctrine of the unity of *ātman*, the principle of individuation or the individual 'soul,' and *brahman*, which gave rise to the monistic philosophy of the Vedānta" (Heesterman, "Brahman," 296).The complex, multilayered account of Heesterman thus affirms the evolution of the concept of *brahman* from the power of the word or verbal formulation—through the dimension of the cosmic enigma, enacted through the verbal contest and the sacrifice—to the ultimate essence underlying the cosmos. J. C. Heesterman, "Brahman," in *Encyclopedia of Religion*. See also Heesterman, *The Inner Conflict of Tradition*, 71–74. For Jan Gonda's response to Renou on the notion of the enigma, see his *Notes on Brahman*, 57–61.

10. Hopkins, *Hindu Religious Tradition*, 19–20, Olivelle, trans., *Upanishads*, lvi; Edgerton, trans., *The Bhagavad Gītā*, 116.
11. Kimberley Patton has undertaken a comparative study of the phenomenon of ritual beginning in the sphere of the gods, in Vedic religion and five other religious traditions: ancient Greek, Zoroastrian, Old Norse, Jewish, Christian, and Islamic. Kimberley Patton, *Religion of the Gods: Ritual, Paradox, and Reflexivity*.
12. *Śatapatha Brāhmaṇa* 10.2.5.11. Cited Flood, *Introduction to Hinduism*, 84, from Julius Eggeling, trans., *The Śatapatha Brāhmaṇa*.
13. Hopkins, *Hindu Religious Tradition*, 32–34, 37–38, Zaehner, *Hinduism*, 37, 47; Edgerton, trans., *The Bhagavad Gītā*, 116–117. Brereton explicates the mysterious concept of *brahman* by pointing out that while for the later Vedānta tradition, *brahman* has

a specific meaning and designation, for the Upanishads, "the *brahman* remains an open concept. It is simply the designation given to whatever principle or power a sage believes to lie behind the world and to make the world explicable. It is the reality sought by the householder who asks a sage: 'Through knowing what, sir, does this whole world become known?' " (*Muṇḍaka Upaniṣad* 1.13). Joel Brereton, "Upanishads," 118.

14. Hopkins, *Hindu Religious Tradition*, 31; Olivelle, trans., *Upanishads*, xxxii; Zaehner, *Hinduism*, 37.
15. Flood, *Introduction to Hinduism*, 84.
16. See "The Hymn of the Person," in *Hymns from the Ṛig Veda*, trans. Doniger, in *Ways of Religion*, 24–25.
17. The Upanishads, originally part of the Brāhmaṇas, are also known as the Vedānta, "the end of the Vedas"; since the Upanishads come to focus upon metaphysical concerns, the term "Vedānta" has come to signify the mystical philosophy based on these Upanishadic teachings. The term "Upanishad" itself suggested a body of secret teachings; in its conventional etymology, the term was said to mean "to sit near," and referred to the practice of students sitting near their teachers and learning the sacred scriptures. Recently scholars have argued that the term *upaniṣad* actually signifies "connection" or "equivalence." The Upanishads reveal the secret teachings of the interconnections of beings in the universe, and ultimately the reality that lies at the heart or summit of this chain of connections. The *upaniṣad* is the subordination of one thing to another; one would arrange things in a progression in order to identify the dominant reality behind an object. Brereton, "*Upanishads*," 124–125; Olivelle, trans., *Upanishads*, xxxii, lii–liii; Hiltebeitel, "Hinduism," 341; Hopkins, *Hindu Religious Tradition*, 36–37. On the meaning of *upaniṣad* as equivalence, see Louis Renou, " *'Connection' en védique; 'cause' en buddhique*"; H. Falk "*Vedisch upaniṣad*."
18. Olivelle points to this as the final *upaniṣad*, or equation: that between the individual Ātman, the essential I, and the ultimately real; Olivelle, trans., *Upanishads*, lvi.
19. Cf. these passages from the *Bṛihadāraṇyaka Upanishad*: "As a spider might come out with his thread, as small sparks come forth from the fire, even so from this Self come forth all vital energies [*prāṇa*], all worlds, all gods, all beings. The mystic meaning [*upaniṣad*] thereof is 'the Real of the real.' Vital energies, verily are the real. He is their Real" (*Bṛihadāraṇyaka Upanishad* 2.1.20). "Hence, now, there is the teaching 'Not thus! Not so!' [*neti, neti*], for there is nothing higher than this, that he is thus. Now the designation for him is the Real of the real. Verily, breathing creatures are the real. He is their Real" (*Bṛihadāraṇyaka Upanishad* 2.3.6). Trans. Robert Ernest Hume, *Thirteen Principal Upanishads*, 95, 97. I thank Joel Brereton for tracking down these passages.
20. *Chāndogya Upanishad* 6.1–16; Hopkins, *Hindu Religious Tradition*, 43; Brereton, "Upanishads," 122–124.
21. *Chāndogya Upanishad* 6.8.
22. *Chāndogya Upanishad* 6.9–16. Compare Olivelle, trans., *Upanishads*, 153–156: "The finest essence here—that constitutes the self of this whole world; that is the truth;

that is the self [*ātman*]. And that's how you are [*tat tvam asi*], Śvetaketu!" Olivelle suggests that this is the final *upaniṣad*, the final equation or connection; *brahman* is the summit of the hierarchical scheme of the cosmos, and the final equation to be made is between the individual *ātman* and *brahman*; Olivelle, trans., *Upanishads*, lvi. Olivelle's translation appears to follow the persuasive argument of Joel Brereton, "*Tat Tvam Asi* in Context." Brereton argues that the refrain "*tat tvam asi*" traveled to the later parables from its original formulation in the case of the tree: "'This finest essence which you do not see, my dear, from this finest essence stands this so great *nyagrodha* tree' . . . As the *nyagrodha* tree exists because of an invisible essence so also both the world and Śvetaketu himself have such an essence as their true nature and true self." Thus he argues that each parable shows that "there is an invisible essence from which all things evolve, to which all things devolve and which is thus the inner reality of all things" (105). Just as the tree and the world are pervaded by the finest essence, which is the truth and the self for them, so also is Śvetaketu in the same condition, a being pervaded by a finest essence, which is his truth and self. He would thus translate the refrain as follows: "That which is this finest essence, that the whole world has as its self. That is the truth. That is the self. In that way are you, Śvetaketu" (109). Or: "That which is this finest essence—this whole world has that as its self. That is the real. That is the self. Thus are you, Śvetaketu!" (Brereton, "*Upanishads*," 124). In classical Vedāntic exegesis, such as that of Śaṅkara, "That" is taken to refer to Being and "You" to *ātman* (102–103). Brereton's point is rather that "that" is a description of the condition of Śvetaketu. Although I certainly cannot say that I remember Sanskrit grammar well enough to make a learned evaluation of the issue, the linguistic argument he brings from other passages seems convincing. See also the response of Julius Lipner, "The Self of Being and the Being of Self: Śaṃkara on 'That You are' (*tat tvam asi*)," 55 n. 9; see also Daniel Raveh, "*Ayam aham asmīti:* Self-consciousness and Identity in the Eighth Chapter of the *Chāndogya Upaniṣad* vs. Śaṅkara's *Bhaṣya*."

23. *Chāndogya Upanishad* 8.1–3.
24. Brereton and Hopkins point out, for example, that while the teacher Uddālaka suggests that the world evolved progressively out of Being and so must evolve progressively back, Yājñavalkya suggests that once we awaken to the knowledge that Being alone is real we become one with Being itself; the self that is the subject of the individual is also the self of the world. Even a cursory reading of the fourth chapter of the *Bṛihadāraṇyaka Upanishad* reveals a great diversity of creation myths and models of the relationship between the One and the many. *Chāndogya Upanishad* 6:9–6:16; *Bṛihadāraṇyaka Upanishad* 4.3.44, 4.4.8; S. Radhakrishnan, *The Principal Upanishads*, 78–90; Hopkins, *Hindu Religious Tradition*, 43–47; Brereton, "*Upanishads*," 129–130.
25. *Bṛihadāraṇyaka Upanishad* 4.2–4.5; see Brereton, "Upanishads," 126–130; Hopkins, *Hindu Religious Tradition*, 40–43, 45–47.
26. See *Māṇḍūkya Upanishad* and the teaching of Prajāpati in *Chāndogya Upanishad* 8.7–12; see also Brereton, "Upanishads," 127–128; Hopkins, *Hindu Religious Tradition*,

39–40. See also the interesting study of Daniel Raveh, who highlights the surprisingly worldly description of the fourth state (*turiya*) in *Chāndogya* 8.12.3; Raveh, "*Ayam ahama asmīti*," 329.

27. S. Radhakrishnan and Charles Moore, *A Source Book in Indian Philosophy*, 507; Eliot Deutsch and J. A. B. van Buitenen, *A Source Book of Advaita Vedānta*; Deutsch, *Advaita Vedānta: A Philosophical Reconstruction*; Richard King, *Indian Philosophy: An Introduction to Hindu and Buddhist Thought*, 185, 217. However, scholars of Indian philosophy remind us that the Advaita Vedānta is only one tradition of the six schools of classical Indian philosophy. There are even other nondualistic positions that are equally authoritative in Indian philosophy. On the qualified nondualism of Rāmānuja, see John Carman, *The Theology of Rāmānuja: An Essay in Interreligious Understanding*, esp. 114–133, 158–166; Carman, "Rāmānuja," in *The Encyclopedia of Religion*, 211–213; on the view that outside the Advaita Vedānta, there may be a plurality of individuals, see Kalidas Bhattacharyya, "The Status of the Individual in Indian Metaphysics," 299–319; for the variety of approaches in Indian philosophy, see also other essays in that volume, as well as King, *Indian Philosophy*.
28. Deutsch, *Advaita Vedānta* 47–65; R. N. Danbekar, "*Vedānta*," *Encyclopedia of Religion*; Zaehner, *Hinduism*, 83.
29. Śaṅkarācārya, *Shankara's Crest-Jewel of Discrimination*, trans. Swami Prabhavananda and Christopher Isherwood, 103–104. Scholars dispute whether the great scholar of nondualist Vedānta Śaṅkara is the author of this text, but it is clearly from the Advaita (nondualist) school. See David Lorenzen, "Śaṅkara," in *Encyclopedia of Religion*, 64.
30. *Bṛihadāraṇyaka Upanishad* 3.2.13, 4.4.3–4; see Brereton, "Upanishads," 132–133; Flood, *Introduction to Hinduism*, 86; William K. Mahoney, "*Karman:* Hindu and Jain Concepts," 263.
31. See Wendy Doniger O'Flaherty, "Karma and Rebirth in the Vedas and Purāṇas," 3–37.
32. Flood, *Introduction to Hinduism*, 86; Hopkins, *Hindu Religious Tradition*, 50–51; Brereton, "Upanishads," 131–133; Brian K. Smith, "*Saṃsāra*," 56–57; and the articles collected by O'Flaherty in *Karma and Rebirth in Classical Indian Traditions*.
33. The term is derived from the Sanskrit root *dhṛ*, "to sustain, support, uphold." William Mahoney succinctly describes the multifaceted notion of *dharma* as follows. It is the essential foundation of something and thus truth; that which is established, customary, or proper and thus traditional or ceremonial; it is one's duty, responsibility, or imperative and thus one's moral obligation; it is that which is right, virtuous, meritorious and thus ethical; and it is that which is required and thus legal. The underlying connotation is therefore that of correctness—the way things are and should be. In the Vedic period it is closely connected with *ṛita*, the universal cosmic order in which all things have a place and function. However, whereas *ṛita* is an impersonal order, *dharma* refers to personal actions required to maintain cosmic order. In the *Ṛig Veda*, these actions are incumbent upon the gods, especially

Varuṇa. Later, the actions become prescribed for each class and station of human being. See William Mahoney, "*Dharma*: Hindu *Dharma*," 329.

34. The term *mokṣa* and its feminine synonym *mukti* are derived from the root *muc*, meaning "release." The notions of *saṃsāra* and release from *saṃsāra* are not in evidence in Vedic texts; the earliest evidence we have for these concepts is from texts of the sixth century BCE. The concept of *mokṣa* is developed in both the *Mahabharata* and the *Laws of Manu*; it appears infrequently in the Upanishads and the *Bhagavad Gītā* (see below, n. 57). In a late 1950s issue of *Philosophy East and West*, Professors J. A. B. van Buitenen and Daniel H. H. Ingalls present contrasting accounts of these ideals of *dharma* and *mokṣa*. Van Buitenen maintains there was an inevitable tension between the world-affirming ideal of *dharma* and the world-renouncing ideal of liberation from *saṃsāra*. Ingalls maintains that the two ideals were for the most part integrated within Hindu culture and were only put in tension by sporadic challenges. In a final footnote, Ingalls minimizes the differences between the two papers. He argues that van Buitenan was speaking of the psychological tension felt by those religious "professionals" or innovators—presumably those who sought total release from the world—whereas he was speaking of the social reality for the majority of Hindu believers. See van Buitenen, "*Dharma* and *Moksha*," 33–40; Ingalls, "*Dharma* and *Mokṣa*," 41–48. Wendy Doniger O'Flaherty notes that the tension between *dharma* and *mokṣa* is often described as a tension between Vedic and Upanishadic/Vedāntic worldviews; "Karma and Rebirth," 4.
35. King, *Indian Philosophy*, 182–183; Radhakrishnan and Moore, 424–425; Edeltraud Harzer, "*Sāṃkhya*," 47–51.
36. Radhakrishnan and Moore, *Source Book in Indian Philosophy*, 424–425, 453–454; King, *Indian Philosophy*, 166–196. The term "yoga" derives from the root *yuj*, "to bind together, hold fast, control, unite, or yoke." See Mircea Eliade, "Yoga," 519; Flood, *Introduction to Hinduism*, 94. See also Franklin Edgerton, "The Meaning of *Sāṃkhya* and *Yoga*," 1–45; Edgerton, *Bhagavad Gītā*, 166.
37. King, 211–212; Eliade, "Yoga," 522.
38. Of course the great nondualist Vedānta philosopher Śaṅkara will interpret even the most blatantly dualistic passages to suggest complete nondualism. See the *Bhagavad Gītā: with the commentary of Sri Śaṅkarāchārya*, trans. A. Mahadeva Sastry.
39. See Hopkins, *Hindu Religious Tradition*, 40–43.
40. The term is based on the Sanskrit root *kṛ*, meaning "to act, do, or bring about." The concept is that action creates; by doing something one creates something. Action has real and tangible effects. There is linguistic speculation that the root *kṛ* may be related to the Indo-European term "ceremony," which has both a sacred dimension—ritual acts prescribed according to norms—and a social dimension, acts that keep the world running smoothly. These two dimensions are present in the Hindu concept as well, and are related to the Hindu concept of *dharma*, the action that keeps the world functioning (see above, n. 33). In the Vedic context, *karma* was sacrificial action. It was originally believed that the gods were free to accept or

reject sacrificial gifts and respond as they pleased. Over time the ritual came to be seen as autonomous; if the priest performed the ritual correctly, the gods were forced to respond. Thus the concept of *karma* gradually became detached from the ritual context and came to be seen as an impersonal and autonomous system of cause and effect. The Upanishads envision two paths to afterlife reward: the way of the fathers, for those who performed rituals with hopes of material rewards, leads to rebirth on earth; the way of the gods, for those who renounce worldly rewards and practice ascetically, does not lead to earthly rebirth. In the *Bṛihadāraṇyaka Upanishad,* the source of reward is extended from the realm of ritual, sacrificial action to all action: "Truly one becomes good through good action, bad by bad" (*Bṛihadāraṇyaka Upanishad* 3.2.13). See Mahoney, "*Karman,*" 261–266.

41. Klostermaier, *Short Introduction*, 40–42.
42. In some ways we can see the Upanishads as akin to Plato and the *Bhagavad Gītā* as akin to Aristotle. Plato presents a realm of unchanging eternal Being and Truth; the way to happiness is knowledge of that Truth, the interconnected web of Forms. The Upanishads similarly picture an eternal unchanging Reality; supreme fulfillment arises through transformative knowledge of that Reality. Aristotle's thought, we shall see, is more like the *Bhagavad Gītā* in emphasizing a practical path to happiness.
43. *Bhagavad Gītā* 2.11–30.
44. *Bhagavad Gītā* 3.6.
45. 3.20–24. Krishna offers a subtle teaching on action. When we take delight in the Self alone, there is no reason to act, but there is also no reason not to act. We thus act purely for the sake of the maintenance of the world order. Two Judeo-Arabic thinkers, Baḥya Ibn Paqūda in the eleventh century and Maimonides in the twelfth, offer a similar teaching on action for its own sake. The highest way of action is to act with no motive of reward. The eleventh-century Islamic thinker al-Ghazālī, however, argues that only God can act with no motive; we human beings all have a motive for action. Thus our highest motive should be to act purely for God's sake. Ghazālī, *Ihyā ʿulūm al-dīn* (Egypt, 1352/1934–44) 4:474, "Clarifying Statements of Masters on *Ikhlāṣ* (Devotion)," translated in Lobel, *A Sufi-Jewish Dialogue*, 172. Compare Baḥya's view in Lobel, *A Sufi-Jewish Dialogue* 152ff, 240–241; Baḥya Ibn Paqūda, *Kitāb al-Hidāya ilā farāʾiḍ al-qulūb* (*Torat ḥovot ha-levavot*) 5.1: Qafih, 243, Mansoor, 274; 8.13: Qafih, 340, Mansoor 362. Maimonides, *Mishneh Torah, Hilkhot teshuvah*, 10.2, *A Maimonides Reader*, 83–84; introduction to *Pereq ḥeleq in Mishnah ʿim perush rabbenu Moshe ben Maimon*, trans. Josef Qafih, 199–200; trans. Yitzhaq Shilat in idem, *Haqdamot ha-Rambam la-Mishnah*, 132–133 (Hebrew), 362–363 (Arabic); English translation in *A Maimonides Reader*, 405–406.
46. This is in fact a teaching of the Sāṃkhya school.
47. *Bhagavad Gītā* 3.27–29.
48. *Bhagavad Gītā* 4.15–23. Edgerton, *The Bhagavad Gītā*, 126. The point was formulated this way by David Eckel in his lecture and handout on the *Bhagavad Gītā* in Boston's Core Curriculum, CC 102, spring 2002.
49. *Bhagavad Gītā* 4.18–20, 5.2.

50. See *Bhagavad Gītā* 9.26–34. Any person, no matter how low ranking, can achieve salvation through devotion to Krishna. See Hopkins, *Hindu Religious Tradition*, 93–94.
51. *Bhagavad Gītā* 9.26.
52. *Bhagavad Gītā* 9.22; 4.14. In 4.14, Krishna asserts that knowledge of Krishna as one who is above *karma* frees one from *karma*.
53. *Bhagavad Gītā* 9.27.
54. *Bhagavad Gītā* 4.9–14.
55. *Bhagavad Gītā* 12.1–7; cf. 9.22.
56. *Bhagavad Gītā* 12.7.
57. Zaehner, *Hinduism*, 57–79, esp. 78–79. As noted above (n. 34) the term "liberation" (*mokṣa*) itself is relatively rare in both the Upanishads and the *Bhagavad Gītā*. The term appears in the relatively late Upanishads: "He who is the maker of all. . . . The Cause of *saṃsāra* and *mokṣa*, of continuance and of bondage" (*Śvetāśvatara Upanishad* 6.16); "One should stand free from determination, free from conception, free from self-conceit. This is the mark of liberation [*mokṣa*]" (*Maitri Upanishad* 6.30); "The mind, in truth, is for mankind the means of bondage and release [*mokṣa*]; for bondage, if to objects bound; from objects free—that's called release [*mokṣa*]!" (*Maitri Upanishad* 6.34). The *Bhagavad Gītā* employs the word *mokṣa* in at least three passages: "Those who strive toward release [*mokṣāya*] from old age and death, taking refuge in Me, they know that *brahman* completely, as it relates to the self and all action" (7.29); "They who know, through the eye of knowledge, the distinction between the field and the knower of the field, as well as liberation [*mokṣam*] of beings from material nature [*prakṛiti*], they go to the Supreme" (13.34); "The understanding [*buddhi*] which understands action and nonaction, what is to be done and what is not to be done, danger and freedom from danger, bondage and liberation [*mokṣam*], that is the understanding [*buddhi*] of *sattva*" (18.30). The root *muc* also provide terms to specify those who seek release: "Knowing this, the ancients who sought liberation [*mumukṣubhis*] also performed action" (4:15); and one who is released is referred to with the adjective form *mukta*: "The sage whose highest aim is release [*munir mokṣaparāyanas*] from whom desire, fear, and anger have departed, is forever liberated [*mukta*]" (5.28). The substantive form appears as *vimokṣa*—"the divine destiny [leads] to liberation [*vimokṣāya*]" (16.5)— or *nirvimokṣa* with the same meaning. See A. M. Esnoul, "*Mokṣa*," in *Encyclopedia of Religion*. I thank Joel Brereton for providing passages from G. A. Jacobs, *A Concordance to the Principal Upaniṣads and the Bhagavadgītā*. Translations here from Hume, trans., *Thirteen Principal Upanishads*; Winthrop Sargeant, trans., *The Bhagavad Gītā*; David White, trans., *The Bhagavad Gītā: A New Translation with Commentary*.
58. In this spirit, Ralph Waldo Emerson, influenced by the *Gītā*, writes: "It is easy in the world to live after the world's opinion; it is easy in solitude to live after our own; but the great man is he who in the midst of the crowd keeps with perfect sweetness the independence of solitude" (*Self-Reliance*, in *The Essential Writings of Ralph Waldo Emerson*, 136).

59. In the Sāṃkhya metaphysic that predominates in the *Gītā*, the spirit (*purusha*) is seen as passive, while nature is seen as active. Likewise, in the older Upanishadic model, in which *ātman* is identified with *brahman*, *ātman-brahman* is pictured as an eternal Witness comprising three qualities or aspects: existence (*sat*), consciousness (*cit*), and joy (*ānanda*).
60. Eknath Easwaran, *The End of Sorrow: The Bhagavad Gītā for Daily Living*, 247–248.
61. *Bhagavad Gītā* 3.31. See also 3.9: "Action imprisons the world unless done as sacrifice. Freed from attachment, perform action as sacrifice!"
62. Cited by Easwaran, *The End of Sorrow*, 253.
63. *Bhagavad Gītā* 4.13–14; Easwaran, *The End of Sorrow*, 63–64, 253–254.
64. *Bhagavad Gītā* 2.48, 50.
65. *Bhagavad Gītā* 2.48.
66. See above, chap. 4. On the possibility that the notion of *karma yoga* had an actual historical influence on that of *wu-wei*, see Victor Mair, *The Tao Te Ching: The Classic Book of Integrity and the Way*, 140–153.

## 6. COMPASSION, WISDOM, AWAKENING: THE WAY OF BUDDHISM

1. Rupert Gethin, *The Foundations of Buddhism*, 9–11; Luis O. Gomez, "Buddhism in India," 351–354; Hopkins, *The Hindu Religious Tradition*, 53–55; Gary Kessler, "Buddhist Ways of Being Religious," in *Eastern Ways of Being Religious*, 100. On the doctrine of *karma*, see Padmanabh S. Jaini, "Karma and the Problem of Rebirth in Jainism"; James P. McDermott, "Karma and Rebirth in Early Buddhism," in *Karma and Rebirth in Classical Indian Traditions*, ed. Wendy Doniger O'Flaherty.
2. Kessler, "Buddhist Ways of Being Religious," 99–100; Gomez, "Buddhism," 354.
3. Gethin, *Foundations*, 17–27, 34, 164–168; Gomez, "Buddhism," 384.
4. Donald Lopez, "Introduction" to *Buddhism in Practice*, 17–18; reprinted in Kessler, 102. For a discussion of the complexity of discerning the core teachings that can be traced back to the Buddha *Śākyamuni*, see Gomez, "Buddhism," 353. Gomez suggests that it is difficult to determine whether early Buddhism actually had a metaphysics; some early strata of Buddhist literature suggest a radical rejection of knowledge and ritual, focusing instead on the joy of renunciation and abstention from conflict. Metaphysical formulations of the doctrine of liberation may have developed at a later stage.
5. Walpola Rahula, *What the Buddha Taught*, 45–46; Gomez, "Buddhism," 355. The four truths are summarized succinctly as sorrow, its cause, its cessation, and the path leading to cessation. See Gomez, "Buddhism," 357.
6. See *Wisdom of Buddhism*, ed. Christmas Humphreys, 57–70; Gethin, *Foundations*, 59–83, 133–162; Gomez, "Buddhism," 355; Lopez, *Buddhism in Practice*, 18–19; reprinted in Kessler, 102.
7. *Bṛihadāraṇyaka Upanishad* 2.1.20, 3.1.6. See above, chap. 5, n. 19.
8. See above, chap. 5.

9. *Saṃyutta nikāya* 1.135, *Milindapanha* 25–28, cited by Gethin, *Foundations*, 139; Humphreys, *Wisdom of Buddhism*, no. 35, 79–80; Edward Conze, *Buddhist Scriptures*, 148; *Milandapanho*, 34–38; reprinted in Carl Olson, *Original Buddhist Sources*, 57–58.
10. A very insightful explication of the five *skandhas* can be found in Rahula, *What the Buddha Taught*, 20–26, and in Gethin, *Foundations*, 135–136.
11. *Kena Upanishad* 1.2.
12. Rahula, *What the Buddha Taught*, 24–25; Gethin, *Foundations*, 136.
13. Rahula, *What the Buddha Taught*, 53–54; Gethin, *Foundations*, 141–142. Buddhist metaphysical speculation is soteriological in intent. Since the goal is the cessation of suffering, one needs to understand how suffering arises; thus causation is a central topic of philosophical speculation in Buddhism. See Gomez, "Buddhism," 357. On the concept of *karma* in early Buddhism, see above, n. 1; see also Muzuno Kogen, "Karman, Buddhist Concepts," 266–268.
14. Gethin, *Foundations*, 140–144; Joseph Goldstein, "Ego and Self," in *Insight Meditation: The Practice of Freedom*, 93–94.
15. Pema Chödrön, *When Things Fall Apart: Heart Advice for Difficult Times*, 9–10.
16. Chödrön, "The Facts of Life," 17–19.
17. Ibid., 19.
18. Ibid., 20.
19. Ibid.; cf. Thich Nhat Hanh, *Zen Keys: A Guide to Zen Practice*, 53–54.
20. Chödrön, "The Facts of Life," 21.
21. Ibid., 22.
22. Ibid.
23. See above, chap. 3.
24. *Saṃyutta nikāya* 3.66–67; Gethin, *Foundations*, 136; Humphreys, *Wisdom of Buddhism*, no. 33, 77.
25. Gethin, *Foundations*, 136–137.
26. Humphreys, *Wisdom of Buddhism*, no. 34, 78–79.
27. Van Buitenen ties together the root meaning of *dharma* that we have seen in Hinduism with the ontological meaning assumed in early Buddhism: "*dharmas*, as the forces that are active in maintaining the world, efficacious potencies set loose for constructive purposes are known in early Buddhism. . . ." See Van Buitenen, "*Dharma* and *Moksha*," 35–36.
28. Humphreys, *Wisdom of Buddhism*, no. 36, 80–81; Coomaraswamy and Horner, *The Living Thoughts of Gotama the Buddha*.
29. *Saṃyutta nikāya* 35.28 (Pali Texts Society), cited in Rahula, *What the Buddha Taught*, 95–97.
30. King, *Indian Philosophy*, 80; see *Bṛihadāraṇyaka Upanishad* 1.5.3.f.
31. King, *Indian Philosophy*, 80; Gethin, *Foundations*, 137, citing *Majjhima nikāya* 1, trans. Bikkhu Nanamoli and Bhikkhu Boodhi, *The Middle Length Discourses of the Buddha: A New Translation of the Maddhima nikāya*, 138–139, 232–233; *Saṃyutta nikāya* 2.125, 249; 3.67–68, 88–89, 104, 105, 187–188.

32. *Majjhima nikāya* 1 (Pali Texts Society), 486; Rahula, *What the Buddha Taught*, 41; Humphreys, *Wisdom of Buddhism*, no. 36, 80–81.
33. *Majjhima nikāya* 1 (Pali Texts Society), 487; 3, p. 245; *Suttanipāta* (Pali Texts Society) 5.232, 41; Rahula, *What the Buddha Taught*, 41; Gethin, *Foundations*, 75.
34. Humphreys, *Wisdom of Buddhism*, 81.
35. *Udāna* (Columbo, 1929), 129; cited in Rahula, *What the Buddha Taught*, 37.
36. *Udāna*, trans. Masefield, 80; cited in Gethin, *Foundations*, 76–77.
37. Gethin, *Foundations*, 77. See also Thomas Kasulis, "*Nirvāṇa*," 448–450, 453–454.
38. Gethin, *Foundations*, 75.
39. Gethin, *Foundations*, 75–76; Kasulis, "*Nirvāṇa*," 448.
40. Gethin, *Foundations*, 77.
41. *Saṃyutta nikāya* 4 (Pali Texts Society), 100–101; Rahula, *What the Buddha Taught*, 62–63; Humphreys, *Wisdom of Buddhism*, no. 37, 54–55. Rahula suggests the Buddha was aware how challenging psychologically was his teaching of no-self; he sees the Hindu teaching of *ātman* as a psychological crutch. Cf. the anecdote cited by Rahula, *What the Buddha Taught*, 63.
42. Humphreys, *Wisdom of Buddhism*, no. 16, 53–54.
43. Rahula, *What the Buddha Taught*, 40.
44. Ibid., 38.
45. Gethin, *Foundations*, 147; Steven Collins, *Selfless Persons: Imagery and Thought in Theravada Buddhism*.
46. *Saṃyutta nikāya* 1 (Pali Text Society), 5; cited by Rahula, *What the Buddha Taught*, 72.
47. It is true that for Maimonides, the seeker never becomes the Necessary Existent, but neither does the Buddhist seeker become *nirvāṇa*; the person *nirvāṇa*-s or ceases to interact with existence in a way characterized by anger, desire, and greed.
48. On the modern phenomenon of engaged Buddhism, see also Christopher Queen and Sallie King, *Engaged Buddhism: Buddhist Liberation Movements in Asia*.
49. A third phenomenon we will not explore here is the rise of devotional Buddhism.
50. *Majjhima nikāya* 3, p. 63; *Saṃyutta nikāya* 2, pp. 28, 95; Rahula, *What the Buddha Taught*, 53–54.
51. *Saṃyutta nikāya* 22.95, quoted in Nyanatiloka, trans., *Word of the Buddha*, 12; Philip Novak, *The World's Wisdom*, 68–69.
52. Whitehead, *Science and the Modern World*.
53. See "The Heart Sutra" in Conze, *Buddhist Wisdom Books*; Novak, *World's Wisdom*, 79–80.
54. Śāntideva's *Śikṣāsamuccaya* 257; quoted in William Theodore de Bary, *Buddhist Tradition in India, China, and Japan*, 100–101; Novak, *World's Wisdom*, 78. See further on this below.
55. Gethin, *Foundations*, 235–237; on the Perfection of Wisdom literature, see Conze, *Buddhist Wisdom Books*.
56. Nāgārjuna, *Mūlamadhyamakakārikā* (Root Verses on the Middle) 24.18, 15.3; Candrakīrti, *Prasannapadī* 247–248, cited by King, *Indian Philosophy*, 120–121; Gethin, *Foundations*, 238–242.

57. Gethin, *Foundations*, 238.
58. Nāgārjuna, *Mūlamadhyamakakārikā* 24.14, trans. M. David Eckel, in *A Question of Nihilism*, 275 (includes translation of chapters 18, 24, 25 of Bhāvaviveka's *Prajñāpradīpa*, commentary to Nāgārjuna's *Mūlamadhyamakakārikā*). See also Frederick Streng, *Emptiness*, 213.
59. Nāgārjuna, *Mūlamadhyamakakārikā*, 25.19; trans. Eckel, 314; Streng, *Emptiness*, 217.
60. Śāntideva, *Śikṣāsamuccaya* 257; quoted in de Bary, *Buddhist Tradition*, 100–101; Novak, *World's Wisdom*, 78.
61. Cf. *The Fundamental Wisdom of the Middle Way: Nāgārjuna's Mūlamadhyamakakārikā*, trans. Garfield, 332–333.
62. Cf. Gethin, *Foundations*, 226–228; David Snellgrove, "Celestial Buddhas and Bodhisattvas," 134.
63. Śāntideva, *Śikṣāsamuccaya* 280–281; quoted in Conze, *Buddhist Texts Through the Ages*, 131–132; Novak, *World's Wisdom*, 81.
64. Conze, *Buddhist Scriptures*, 164–167.
65. Śāntideva, *Śikṣāsamuccaya* 257; quoted in de Bary, *Buddhist Tradition*, 100–101; Novak, *World's Wisdom*, 78.
66. Heinrich Dumoulin, "Ch'an," 185. This stanza is actually late in origin, from a period in which Ch'an was already firmly established in China. Although Ch'an tradition maintains that it is a teaching transmitted from mind to mind outside the textual tradition, Ch'an's relationship to sacred texts is in fact more complex. Ch'an accepts the Buddhist canon, puts great emphasis on beloved Mahāyāna sutras, and continues devotional practices such as the chanting of scripture. Note that even its anti-textual stories are delivered through texts! Dale Wright thus suggests that masters such as Huang Po are not rejecting textual study per se. Rather, they warn against clinging to the text as one would to a devotional object, forgetting that its real purpose is to open one to experience. Texts have a way of obscuring the very reality to which they point. Huang Po thus rejects a kind of gluttony in reading texts—devouring knowledge about enlightenment, rather than reading through the text to the reality at its heart. Knowledge about enlightenment is not awakening; sometimes one needs to ritually shred the text in order to arrive at its true meaning. Wright thus suggests that Huang Po is proposing a new way of reading for genuine insight. See Wright, *Philosophical Meditations on Zen Buddhism*, 29–34. See also the studies collected by Steven Heine in *The Zen Canon*.
67. De Bary and Bloom, *Sources of Chinese Tradition*, 492–493; de Bary, *Buddhist Tradition*, 209–211. For an alternative perspective on the Bodhidharma story, see John McRae, *Seeing Through Zen*, 22–28.
68. Dumoulin, "Ch'an," 186.
69. Ibid., 187.
70. I follow the translation and textual explication of McRae, *Seeing Through Zen*, 61–62.
71. See Liu, *Introduction to Chinese Philosophy*, 308; Lai, *Introduction to Chinese Philosophy*, 263–264. John McRae urges that we look at the verses attributed to these two teachers as a conceptual pair, since Hui-neng's verses are clearly formulated in

response to those attributed to Shen-hsiu. He finds the key to Shen-hsiu's verse in a passage from a treatise attributed to Shen-hsiu that likens the enlightened mind to votive lamps ("lamps of eternal brightness"). It then appears that the act of rubbing the mirror clear of dust is being compared to maintaining Buddhist monastic regulations. The body is being likened to the *bodhi* tree, where Buddha attained enlightenment, the mind is the place enlightenment takes place, and the enlightened mind is the bright surface of the mirror. McRae suggests that the verse is not meant to depict gradual enlightenment but the continual practice of perfections that is the *bodhisattva* ideal. McRae, *Seeing Through Zen*, 65.

72. Thich Nhat Hanh, *Zen Keys*, 34. Dale Wright points out that Chinese Buddhism was indeed text-centered. The transmission of Buddhism from India to China required a massive project of translation and interpretation of texts. Scholars specialized in philology, history, or classification of texts; monks memorized and ritually recited sutras. New texts arose, along with new translations of old texts, variant editions, copious commentaries, and, amid all these texts, the discovery of printing. The critique of text arose in the midst of a culture that produced the largest and most influential canon of texts in East Asian Buddhism. Wright, *Philosophical Meditations*, 28; for his nuanced presentation of the Ch'an attitude toward texts, see above, n. 66.
73. Thich Nhat Hanh, *Zen Keys*, 38.
74. Rahula, *What the Buddha Taught*, 68.
75. Ibid., 93.
76. See for example Paul Reps, *Zen Flesh, Zen Bones*, stories 75, 82.
77. Ibid., 94. For an account of enlightenment (*satori*) as a series of deepening experiences, see that of Hakuin, from Orategama, in *Semmon hōgoshū* 2.81–85; in de Bary, *Buddhist Tradition*, 381–388; see also excerpt in Novak, *World's Wisdom*, 101–102. On the need for ongoing practice, see especially the teachings of Dōgen. Dōgen was critical of the use of the *kōan*, with its emphasis on the instantaneous experience of enlightenment; he emphasized instead sitting meditation (*zazen*), ongoing practice, and the integration of meditation practice with everyday life; see de Bary, *Buddhist Tradition*, 357–376. We have seen the debate from the inception of the Ch'an school between those who advocate a process of gradual enlightenment and thus who argue that enlightenment can only be a sudden, instantaneous transformation. This is often discussed as a distinction between the Northern and Southern schools of Zen, although the reality is more nuanced. See Chan, "The Zen (Ch'an) School of Sudden Enlightenment," in *A Source Book in Chinese Philosophy*, 427–428; Liu, *Introduction to Chinese Philosophy*, 304–309, 314–316; Fung Yu-Lan, *A Short History of Chinese Philosophy*, 258–265; Heinrich Dumoulin, *Zen Buddhism: A History*, 1:107–154. For primary texts see "The Platform Scripture of the Sixth Patriarch" and "The Recorded Conversations of Shen-Hui," in Chan, *Source Book*, 430–444; Philip Yampolsky, trans., *The Platform Sutra of the Sixth Patriarch*; Yampolsky, "The Platform Sutra of the Sixth Patriarch," in de Bary and Bloom, *Approaches to the Asian*

*Classics*, 241–250; and the perspective of John McRae, above, nn. 70–71. On Dōgen, see also Dumoulin, *Zen Buddhism*, 2:51–119.

78. *Zen Keys*, 94. Attributed to Chinese Ch'an master Ch'ing-yüan Wei-hsin (Japanese: *Seigen Ishin*) of the T'ang dynasty by Masao Abe, *Zen and Western Thought*, 4: "Thirty years ago, before I began the study of Zen, I said, 'Mountains are mountains, waters are waters.' After I got insight into the truth of Zen through the instructions of a good master, I said, 'Mountains are not mountains, waters are not waters.' But now, having attained the abode of final rest [that is, Awakening], I say, 'Mountains are really mountains, waters are really waters.' And then he asks, 'Do you think these three understandings are the same or different?'" Abe gives the story in English; his footnote cites the Chinese (Song dynasty) canonical source *Wu-têng Hui-yüan* in a Japanese edition: *Gotōegen* (English title: A Summary of Five Buddhist Books), ed. Imaeda Aishin (Tokyo: Rinrōkaku Shoten, 1971), 335. This story can also be found in the *Hsu Chuan Teng Lu*, a biographical collection. See *Taishō shinshū daizōkyō*, ed. Takakusu Junjirō and Watanabe Kaigyoku et al., 85 vols. (Tokyo: Taishō Issaikyō kankōkai, 1924–1935). The latter source can be found online at the Chinese Buddhist Electronic Text Association (CBETA) Web site: http://cbeta.org/result/normal/T51/2077_022.htm; it is unfortunately not translated into English. I thank my colleague Gina Cogan for her meticulous tracking down of this source.

    As my colleague Tom Michael pointed out, the method of double negation is found in both the Diamond Sutra and Nāgārjuna. For the Diamond Sutra, see Conze, *Buddhist Wisdom Books*; for Nāgārjuna, see above.

79. *Zen Keys*, 55. The source is Mumon, *The Gateless Gate*, 7; see *Zen Flesh, Zen Bones*, 96.
80. See Chan, *Source Book*, 429. The literal meaning of *kōan* is "an official document," which points to an important decision and the final determination of truth and falsehood. Steven Heine has enriched Western understanding of *kōans* by adding to the irreverent aspect, the mythological, ritual, legal, and political dimensions of *kōan* discourse; see Heine, *Opening a Mountain: Kōans of the Zen Masters*. For early accounts of the use of the *kōan*, see "The Recorded Conversations of Zen Master I-Hsuan," in Chan, *Source Book*, 444–449. For the history of the *kōan*, see Isshū Miura and Ruth Fuller Sasaki, *Zen Dust, the History of the Koan and Koan Study in Rinzai (Lin-Chi) Zen*. For the importance of the master-disciple relationship in the practice of the *kōan*, see Dumoulin, "Ch'an," 100.
81. See Chan, *Source Book*, 429.
82. *Zen Keys*, 54. See *Zen Flesh, Zen Bones*, stories 36, 76, 82.
83. *Zen Keys*, 87–89. On Dōgen's (n. 77 above) approach to the integration of practice and life, see de Bary, *Buddhist Tradition*, 361.
84. Huang Po, quoted in *Zen Keys*, 80. See *The Zen Teachings of Huang Po on the Transmission of Mind*, trans. John Blofeld. For contemporary meditations on themes in Huang Po's Buddhism, see Wright, *Philosophical Meditations on Zen Buddhism*. On the doctrine of Buddha nature, see Sallie B. King, *Buddha Nature*. For the Ch'an school's

views on Mind in the context of other schools of Chinese Buddhism, see Liu, *Introduction to Chinese Philosophy*, 309–312, 319–323. For the idealistic schools of Hua-Yen and Tien-T'ai Buddhism see ibid., 248–303; Chan, *Source Book*, chap. 25: "The One and All Philosophy: Fa-Tsang of the Hua Yen School"; Robert M. Gimello, "Apophatic and Kataphatic Discourse in Mahāyāna: A Chinese View"; Brook Ziporyn, *Evil and/or/as the Good*; Ziporyn, *Being and Ambiguity*.

85. *Zen Keys*, 82. Sallie B. King, through analysis of key texts in the development of the theory, likewise argues that the doctrine of Buddha nature is not *ātman*-like monism, but thoroughly Buddhist; see *Buddha Nature*.
86. *Zen Keys*, 82. On Ch'an views on Mind and nature, see Liu, *Introduction to Chinese Philosophy*, 319–323. Sallie King points out that the *Awakening of Faith in the Mahāyāna* shows the beauty of the language of "thusness." Thusness or suchness (tathātā) has an adjectival quality. It points out simply that things are as they are. It doesn't have the negative connotation of emptiness; the word thusness suggests there really is something real. On the other hand, the term reminds us not to reify what is as a substantive entity. King, *Buddha Nature*, 102; King cites *Da Sheng Qi Xin Lun, Taishō* 32, no. 1666; 576a; Yoshito S. Hakeda, *The Awakening of Faith*.

## 7. THE GOOD IS THAT TO WHICH ALL THINGS AIM: ARISTOTLE ON GOD AND THE GOOD

1. Stephen Menn argues that this is not so in the *Metaphysics*. Aristotle does seem to identify the Unmoved Mover as both *Nous* and as Good-in-itself, although he does not accept Plato's Form of the Good. Stephen Menn, "Aristotle and Plato on God as *Nous* and as the Good," 543–573.
2. *Nicomachean Ethics* (*NE*) 1096a30.
3. *NE* 1098a.
4. *NE* 1139b; see also *Posterior Analytics*, *De Anima*.
5. *NE* 1098a, 1102b–1103a.
6. *NE* 1098a, 1102a–b.
7. *NE* 1103a; Allen Speight, handout for Boston University Core Humanities CC 102.
8. Plato, *Protagoras* 360d. Cf. *Meno* 88b.
9. *NE* 1103b.
10. *NE* 1105b.
11. *NE* 1106b.
12. And one can only expect the degree of precision proper to the investigation of human beings; we cannot be as exact in moral philosophy as in mathematics. *NE* 1098a.
13. See for example, C. D. C. Reeve, trans., Aristotle, *Politics*, xxvi.
14. This point was suggested to me by David Roochnik.
15. Alfred North Whitehead termed this teleological urge of entities to realize themselves "satisfaction."

16. *NE* 1097b29–1098a20. Note that for Aristotle, form is the organizing principle of a thing; for the human being, it is the structural principle that allows the body to be alive and to function properly. Our soul is the form of our body; it is not something independent, but is that which enables our body to live and perform its function.
17. *NE* 1101a.
18. *NE* 1100a–b.
19. This may point to a subtle difference between the ideals of Plato and Aristotle. Plato's philosopher would naturally prefer to remain contemplating the Good—a fixed, static ideal. But see now Andrea Wilson Nightingale and Charles Griswold for a re-evaluation of Plato's ideal and relationship to the real. See below, nn. 81–82.

    If Hindu liberation is a static ideal of becoming one with the All, and Ch'an or Zen Buddhist *satori* is a moving goal of responding anew to each moment, Aristotle's *eudaimonia* is more like Zen enlightenment. Awakening takes place every moment; it is not a fixed and static ideal. Aristotle's *eudaimonia* is a way of living and not a state one attains.
20. *NE* 1141b. The image of Thales goes back to Plato's *Theaetetus*, where Socrates reports a story that Thales fell into a well while gazing at the stars because he did not see what was at his feet (174a–b). Andrea Wilson Nightingale suggests that Plato, Aristotle, and other fourth-century thinkers portrayed earlier thinkers as impractical contemplatives who were detached from and ignorant of human affairs. Andrea Wilson Nightingale, *Spectacles of Truth in Classical Greek Philosophy*, 22–24, 204.
21. *NE* 1100b.
22. In *Metaphysics* Δ.13, Aristotle distinguishes three senses of the word *teleios*: (1) having all of its parts (cf. "the complete time of a thing); (2) being best of its kind (cf. "perfect); (3) having reached its end ("fully realized," "fully developed," as of an adult in comparison to a child). David Keyt argues that in book 10 (1177a), Aristotle has the second or third sense in mind: *perfect* or *fully realized* happiness is found in contemplation. David Keyt, "Intellectualism in Aristotle," 149–150.
23. For a solution to the problem that distinguishes between happiness and complete happiness, see John Cooper, "Contemplation and Happiness: A Reconsideration," and below, n. 68.
24. The problem was first posed this way by W. F. R. Hardie, "The Final Good in Aristotle's Ethics." It was further developed in the central article by J. L. Ackrill, "Aristotle on Eudaimonia"; the terms have been adopted and the conceptions debated in much of contemporary Aristotelian scholarship. Thomas Nagel uses the terms "dominant" and "comprehensive"; Nagel, "Aristotle on Eudaimonia," 7–14. Keyt uses "inclusivist" and "exclusionary"; Keyt, "Intellectualism in Aristotle," 139. See also Gabriel Richardson Lear, *Happy Lives and the Highest Good*, 47–70. Roger Crisp argues for a position he calls "aretic inclusivism"; Crisp, "Aristotle's Inclusivism."
25. John Cooper, *Reason and the Human Good in Aristotle*, 175–177.
26. *NE* 1177b–1178a. David Roochnik has recently put this question in a different light, seeing a continuum between the *theōria* described in *NE* 10.7 and other aspects of the activity of understanding our world. I will return to this point later, as it seems

to me a key to developing a unified interpretation of Aristotle's ethics. Roochnik, "What Is *Theōria? Nicomachean Ethics* 10.7–8."

27. For a strong articulation of the dominant or intellectualist view, see Richard Kraut, *Reason and the Human Good in Aristotle*. Richardson Lear describes the inclusive or comprehensive view as suggesting that the middle-order goods (the ones that are desired both for their own sake and for the sake of the final good) are *included* in the final good, as parts of a whole. She resolves the tension by suggesting a form of the dominant view: that one value is the organizing principle or dominant value shaping the life. This value is more important than any other value, and is the principle around which the middle order goods are organized. Richardson Lear, *Happy Lives and the Highest Good*, 25–28, 37–46, 67–70. Richardson Lear further argues that the relationship between middle-order goods and the final end will be the key to understanding in what way we choose morally virtuous action for the sake of contemplation. Ibid., 46. The final good is self-sufficient in that it is sufficient in itself as a goal worthy of choice, an ultimate goal of all our actions, projects, and decisions. This one purpose is thus enough to make us feel satisfied with our lives. A self-sufficient final end makes all the actions leading up to it worthy, and we don't need any other goal or instrumental good to make our life desirable. Would choosing everything for the final end of contemplation make a life worth choosing? Ibid., 48, 52–53. Finally, she argues that one could add goods to *eudaimonia* and improve the quality of one's life; nevertheless it is most choiceworthy as a *telos*. There are things one could add to improve one's contemplation, for it is not just the highest good in rank; it is highest as an overall *purpose* or organizing principle. Self-sufficiency gives us the confidence that no matter what life may bring us, we will be able to make of it a life worth choosing. Ibid., 66–68, 70–71.
28. It has been debated whether the term "life" (*bios*) refers to a biographical life of one individual, or a way of engagement that can represent one aspect of a person's total life. For example, Simone de Beauvoir engaged in the literary life and the philosophical life; Henry Kissinger participated in the academic life and the life of politics. John Cooper claims that the term *bios* can only refer to one way or mode of life lived by one person, to the exclusion of other ways of life. David Keyt, in contrast, brings passages from Plato and Aristotle in which a *bios* refers to one phase or aspect of a person's life, as in the examples of Simone de Beauvoir and Kissinger. However, Gabriel Richardson Lear has responded by reminding us that Aristotle speaks in book 1 of the *NE* of three distinct ways of life. She argues that he is not pointing to three *activities* that are mutually exclusive, but to three ways of life, each of which has a distinct orienting principle. The question is whether we make our ultimate end contemplation or political activity, even if our lives include both pursuits. What we are really asking is, what is the ultimate aim of our life? Cooper, *Reason and the Human Good in Aristotle*, 159–160; David Keyt, "Intellectualism in Aristotle," 145–146; Richardson Lear, *Happy Lives and the Highest Good*, 66–71; Sarah

Broadie, *Ethics with Aristotle*, 26–27. Broadie distinguishes between the happiness of the happy person; a happy life (as when we wish happiness to a newly wedded pair); and the abstract quality of happiness which all particular happy lives have in common. Broadie, 27; see also p. 55 n. 22.

29. Gabriel Richardson Lear defines "dominant end" as the target, the one goal that predominates, and makes the whole choiceworthy. Her suggestion creates a bridge between the language of "dominant" and "inclusivist" interpretations; it provides an interpretation of the "dominant" view that brings it into harmony with the "inclusivist" or "comprehensive" view. See her articulate formulation, *Happy Lives and the Highest Good*, 66–71.
30. Aristotle, *Metaphysics* 12.7 (1072b).
31. Ibid.
32. See Richard Norman, "Aristotle's Philosopher-God"; Menn, "Aristotle and Plato on God as *Nous* and as the Good," 543–573.
33. *NE* 1178b5.
34. *NE* 1178b.
35. But is this who we really are even according to Aristotle? In book 10 Aristotle defines the human being as *nous*, which in this context he identifies with the activity of *theōria*, pure theoretical understanding, separate from the body-mind compound (1178a). In book 9, he argues similarly, but with an important difference. He states that the intellectual part of oneself appears to be a person's real self (1166a18); and again in 1166a22 that a person's real self would seem to be his thinking part. But most tellingly he says at 1169a that someone is called "continent" or "incontinent" because his intellect is or is not his master, on the assumption that this is what each person is. In the last passage especially, it is clear that he is talking about practical reason, or at least reason as integrated; the example of continence must include practical reason, and cannot be pure *theōria*.

David Keyt points out that at closer inspection, even the statements in 10.7 that seem uncompromisingly intellectualist turn out to be somewhat qualified. Mind (*nous*) "most of all" is a human being; *nous* "would seem to be a human being most of all." We find the same qualifications in his statements about who we are in book 9. Keyt argues that this means that *nous* is not all of what we are; we also have other parts of ourselves. However, Dominic Scott looks at the phrase "most of all" (*malista*) in a different way. He brings evidence that to say something is most of all x is to say that it is unqualifiedly x, the paradigm or standard by which other things are judged. Thus he argues that for Aristotle theoretical *nous* is what we truly are, while practical intellect is defined by this intellectual standard, and is thus a kind of approximation of our true essence. Theoretical *nous* is the paradigm of the way we are intellect, but we are practical *nous* in a secondary, looser sense. See *NE* 10.7 (1178a2, a6–7); 9.4 (1166a 22–23); 9.8 (1169a2); Keyt, "Intellectualism in Aristotle," 150; Dominic Scott, "Primary and Secondary *eudaimoniâ*," 228, 230–33; cited by Richardson Lear, *Happy Lives and the Highest Good*, 90.

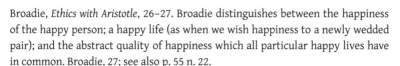

36. Here Aristotle is speaking in his precise, technical sense about pure theoretical wisdom (*sophia*). This narrow, restricted sense of *sophia* accords with his definition of knowledge of things that are eternal, necessary, and unchanging in other works. He has defined wisdom here in contradistinction to practical reasoning (*phronēsis*), which decides about moral action. Theoretical wisdom studies things that cannot be other than they are; practical wisdom decides about things that we can change, and results in choice and action. Here in book 6, the term *nous* (elsewhere, more broadly "mind") is defined technically as knowledge of first principles, and *epistēmē* as demonstrative science; wisdom is thus knowledge of the first principles of demonstrative science. When we actualize our knowledge, we experience the flourishing of our human capabilities.
37. Anthony Kenny, *Aristotle on the Perfect Life*, 94. I am not sure the passage goes so far as to claim that virtue is incomplete without a moral dimension, but it does suggest that all aspects of developing our human virtues are part of human flourishing. Moreover, this holistic model is certainly implied in Aristotle's initial formulation in book 1: "*Eudaimonia* is activity of the soul in accordance with virtue" (1098a). The problem is still the meaning of the addendum: "and if there is more than one virtue, with the best and most complete."
38. *EE* 1219a35–39.
39. The passage goes on: "Virtue is of two forms, virtue of character and intellectual virtue; for we praise not only the just, but also the intelligent and wise" (*EE* 1220a4–6).
40. Kenny himself argues that while Aristotle presents a clear inclusivist position in the *Eudemian Ethics*, in *Nicomachean Ethics* book 10 he presents a dominant, intellectualist view of *eudemonia* as consisting in theoretical contemplation. However, he also argues that in book 1, Aristotle leaves room for rather than argues for the identification of contemplation with perfect or complete happiness—an identification he does not make until book 10. Kenny, *Aristotle on the Perfect Life*, 17–19.
41. Aristotle draws here on a tradition we find in Plato's *Theaetetus* 174a–b, that Thales had his head up, contemplating the stars, and so fell into a well. Nightingale, *Spectacles of Truth*, 22–23, discusses the way the early Greek thinkers were depicted as "theorizers."
42. The word translated "complete" is sometimes translated "perfect." *Teleion* means "end-y," "relating to ends." He argues that something is more end-y if it is pursued for its own sake rather than if it is pursued for the sake of something else. Happiness is most end-y, because it is pursued always for its own sake, and never for the sake of anything else. However, he also uses the term in another context. This is his argument from the function of a human being. The good for a human being is activity of the soul in accordance with virtue, and if there is more than one virtue, then in accordance with the best and most complete or perfect. Now, Kenny asks, does he mean here the most complete, that is "inclusive," or the most supreme? In the very next line, Aristotle speaks of a complete life, as opposed to a partial or interrupted one. He says that one swallow does not make spring, nor does one day;

nor does one day or a short time make us blessed and happy. However, should we argue that he has changed the meaning of "complete" from the technical definition he gave just before the function argument, that completeness refers to what is desired for its own sake and not for the sake of something else? So we have two alternatives. Either he means that the best and most complete is the one supreme virtue always desired for its own sake, never for the sake of anything else, or he means that it is the most inclusive, as he goes on to say in the next sentence—that a life must be complete, i.e., not incomplete.

In the *Eudemian Ethics*, this statement is less ambiguous. There, he argues that life may be complete or incomplete, and the activity of what is incomplete is itself incomplete. Thus happiness must be the activity of a complete life in accordance with complete virtue. This would seem to argue that complete virtue means an inclusive whole, of which all the various virtues—virtues of character as well as virtues of thought—are a part. Nightingale points out that Aristotle tends to slide from an "is" to an "ought," from the value-neutral language of physics—of *kinēsis* (movement) and actualization (*energeia*)—to the notion that something that is an end is more choiceworthy. Nightingale, *Spectacles of Truth*, 216 and n. 59; Kenny, *Aristotle on the Perfect Life*, 19ff.

43. I thank Tyler Travillian for unraveling the complexities of this passage. See translations of Michael Woods, trans., *Aristotle: Eudemian Ethics, Books I, II, and VIII*, 42; Kenny, *Aristotle on the Perfect Life*, 95, 98–99; *Eudemian Ethics*, trans. H. Rackham, 475–476.
44. See Kenny, *Aristotle on the Perfect Life*, 96–97.
45. Likewise, in *NE* 6.13 (1145a10), Aristotle argues that practical wisdom is not really a governor over wisdom or the better part of the intellect, any more than medical science is an authority over health. Medicine doesn't make use of health, but rather sees how to produce health. Just so, practical wisdom does not use wisdom, but tells us how to achieve it. Thus it issues orders and arranges for the sake of health or wisdom, but not by means of wisdom. Similarly, political science does not govern the gods, but arranges things in the state that enable their service.
46. I am greatly indebted to Tyler Travillian and Tom Marre for their aid in the translation and interpretation of this entire passage.
47. *Euthyphro* 13e. See Kenny, *Aristotle on the Perfect Life*, 102; Gregory Vlastos, "Socratic Piety," in *Socrates: Ironist and Moral Philosopher*, 162–164, 173–177. We know from many passages in the *Apology* and elsewhere that Socrates considered the cultivation of justice to be the purpose of life. We should always ask ourselves in every situation whether what we are doing is just: if it is, we should do it, if not not: "You are wrong, sir, if you think that a man who is any good at all should take into account the risk of life or death; he should look to this only in his actions, whether what he does is right or wrong, whether he is acting like a good or bad man" (*Apology* 28b). "I went to each of you privately and conferred upon him what I say is the greatest benefit, by trying to persuade him not to care for any of is belongings before caring that he himself should be as good and as wise as possible" (*Apology* 36c).

"The most important thing is not life, but the good life . . . and [it still holds] that the good life, the beautiful life, and the just life are the same . . . we must examine next whether it is just for me to attempt to escape from here without the permission of the Athenians, or whether it is not just. If it appears to be just, let us try it; and if not, let us give it up" (Crito 48b–c). Socrates says explicitly that his supreme service of God is to spur everyone in Athens to care for the excellence of his or her soul, for excellence (virtue, *aretē*) is more important than anything. Thus Aristotle too could include moral action as a form of service of God—the many noble things by which we fulfill our *telos*. Another way of putting together the middle and the last book of the *NE* is to note that the subject of the middle books is practice and habituation—making virtue continuous and active. The contemplative life contains these features as well: there is a practice required for intellectual virtue. We need moral virtue to practice intellectual virtue; thus the contemplation of 10.7 may represent the apex of the life of virtue we have been developing. Contemplation must then involve more than pure rumination about truths already known; it must involve active appreciation of one's understanding. I thank two of my Boston University students, Inelis Garcia-Pena and Yankel Polak, for these insights.

48. *Apology* 30a–b.
49. The notion of noble moral action as an approximation of contemplation is the insight of Richardson Lear, *Happy Lives and the Highest Good*, 78–92, 189–196. See below, n. 76.
50. Note that Aristotle's Unmoved Mover, which he identifies in the *Metaphysics* as the good and a principle of teleological order, may have an aspect of both separateness and immanence; he likens the good in the universe to both the order of an army and its leader. See quote from *Metaphysics* below, and the discussions of Menn, "Aristotle and Plato on God as *Nous* and as the Good," 549–551, 556; and Monte Ransome Johnson, *Aristotle on Teleology*, 273–276, 276–286. We are accustomed to thinking that while for Plato, there is an absolute good, Aristotle denies such a good. Stephen Menn, however, argues that Aristotle does not deny an absolute, immaterial Good-in-Itself existing separately from the many good things. Aristotle says explicitly: "It is clear then from what has been said that there is a substance which is eternal and unmovable and separate from sensible things," which he identifies as the good or end of the universe: "We must consider also in which of two ways the nature of the universe contains the good and the highest good, whether as something separate and by itself, or as the order of the parts. Probably in both ways, as an army does; for its good is found both in its order and in its leader, and more in the latter; for he does not depend on the order but it depends on him." Aristotle, *Metaphysics* XII:10, 1075a 12-5; 1076a 5, quoting Homer, *Iliad* 2.204. He identifies the good as *nous*, the virtue of thinking, both as striving and as end: "Anaxagoras makes the good a motive principle; for his 'reason' moves things. But it moves them for an end, which must be something other than it, except according to our way of stating the case; for, on our view, the medical art is in a sense health." We participate in *nous* insofar as we think. *Nous* is that which inspires the heavens to revolve, and

that is the absolute good. (*Metaphysics* 1073a3–5; 1075a12–15). Thus, Menn argues that though Aristotle rejects a Form or Idea of the Good, he accepts in principle an absolute good in itself (Menn, "Aristotle and Plato on God as *Nous* and as the Good," 549–551, 563).

Monte Ransome Johnson takes issue with Menn. Johnson denies that Aristotle is committed to the position that the first principle is a separate Good-itself, although he does go on to add: "If Aristotle does endorse the existence of a highest good in nature, or even a 'separate good,' then it must be something attainable by humans." Thus he comes close, in fact, to Menn's position: "The most obvious candidate for a 'highest good in nature,' that is also attainable by humans, is intelligence (nous), and the activity of theoretical science and wisdom. Aristotle says that nous 'either is itself also something divine, or is the most divine part in us.' . . . This is 'the intelligence, i.e. the god' of *Eudemian Ethics* (*ho nous kai ho theos*, 1217b30–31), and 'the god, i.e. the intelligence' of *Nicomachean Ethics* (*ho theos kai ho nous*, 1096a24–25). It may be that this intelligence is in ontological terms a separately existing good. Aristotle in fact says that 'the [happiness] of the nous is separate' (*NE* X:8, 1178a22)." So he, too, holds plausible the notion that *nous* is in ontological terms a separately existing good, one in which humans can participate. What he wants to deny is that there is one universal good, which would make it like a Platonic Form. Menn is mindful of this problem as well. The debate between them seems to be on the definition of "separate." Johnson makes a forceful argument that Aristotle's teleology is thoroughly immanent throughout nature. The highest good for a human being is *nous*, but other organisms achieve their distinct good in other ways, by fulfilling their immanent nature and function. See Johnson, *Aristotle on Teleology*, 273–276, 276–286.

51. Cf. C. D. C. Reeve, trans., *Aristotle, Politics*, xlv.
52. Gabriel Richardson Lear points out that inclusivists tend toward saying that *eudaimonia* is the happy life itself, or that package of goods that constitutes a happy life. But that doesn't tell us the principle or goal around which such a life is organized. Richardson Lear, *Happy Lives and the Highest Good*, 51. On this question, see the useful discussion of completeness and self-sufficiency in C. D. C. Reeve, *Practices of Reason: Aristotle's Nicomachean Ethics*, 114–122.
53. Richardson Lear, *Happy Lives and the Highest Good*, 4.
54. *De Anima* 417a32, 417a25. Roochnik, "What Is *Theōria*?," 71. This example is reminiscent of Avicenna's distinction between a scribe who knows how to write and a scribe who is actually engaged in writing. He uses this distinction to contrast the active intellect with the acquired intellect. The image is echoed in Maimonides, *Guide* 3.51.
55. Roochnik thus disagrees with Richard Kraut, who argues that *theōria* thinks about knowledge already acquired. Roochnik, "What Is *Theōria*?," 72, quoting Kraut, *Aristotle on the Human Good*, 73.
56. On prodigies such as autistic savants who can see complex algorithms, see for example the popular work of Oliver Sachs, *The Man Who Mistook His Wife for a Hat.* Huston Smith links such savants with the phenomenon of what he terms "religious

savants," such as Emmanual Swedenborg. See his provocative talk "Intimations of Immortality: Three Case Studies."

57. Amelie Oksenberg Rorty, for example, draws a bridge between books 9 and 10 of the *Nicomachean Ethics* by arguing that in observing (*theōrein*) our friends, we can contemplate the species "humanity." She need not go so far, argues Roochnik; in his mundane use of *theōria*, Aristotle does offer examples of theorizing the contingent. What distinguishes the different forms of knowledge—theoretical, practical, and productive—is that practical and productive knowledge modify the object of study (ethics modifies the human being, art or craft modifies/creates a product), while theoretical knowledge changes only the knower, not the object of knowledge. Such knowledge is loved because of itself, rather than for an external benefit. *NE* 1177b1; Amelie Oksenberg Rorty, "The Place of Contemplation in Aristotle's *Nicomachean Ethics*," 379; Roochnik, "What Is *Theōria*?," 74.

    Richard Kraut, like Nightingale and Roochnik, admits that Aristotle includes both more broad and more restrictive uses of *theōria*. He acknowledges that whenever a person closely observes or studies something, he or she is engaged in *theōria*. However, he would restrict the kind of *theōria* Aristotle describes in 10.7–8 to "the activation of theoretical wisdom," an activity that "does not take human happiness as an object of study (*NE* VI:12, 1143b18–20) and is contrasted to practical wisdom." Nevertheless, no matter which form of *theōria* one is engaged in, Kraut acknowledges that it is an active engagement of one's attention, and not a mere capacity or disposition. Kraut, *Cambridge Companion to Plato*, 15–16 n. 2.

58. Roochnik sees the close connection between the exalted and the mundane forms of *theōria* even in the paradigmatic expression of the Unmoved Mover's exalted *theōria* in *Metaphysics* 12.7: "Since [the Unmoved Mover's] actualization is pleasure, its mode of being—which it engages in forever—is like that which is best for us during a short time" (1072b 14–18). What does it mean, Roochnik asks, to say that the Unmoved Mover is pleasure? Pleasure, for Aristotle—like seeing and understanding—is an activity that is perfectly complete and whole in every moment. Pleasure takes us out of time. Seeing, understanding, and pleasure are not "processes whose end-point is distinct from the activity leading to that end-point" (Roochnik, "What Is *Theōria*?," 79). When we are actively engaged in knowing, we are absorbed in a timeless activity like that of the Unmoved Mover, who is always "thinking about thinking."

    Alfred North Whitehead, whose thought we have discussed in earlier chapters, is called a panpsychist for making a similar point but broadening it beyond the human species to all beings in the universe. All beings "take into account" (prehend) their environment and other beings. The universe is alive and aware, and our human consciousness is simply the most exalted form of the awareness that takes place throughout all of nature. Even inanimate particles "take into account" one another and "respond" to their environment.

59. Plato, *Apology* 38a.

60. David Roochnik pointed me to this felicitous phrase in Nussbaum, *The Fragility of Goodness: Luck and Ethics in Greek Tragedy and Philosophy*, 261.
61. Aristotle, *Metaphysics* 1.1 (980a).
62. See Roochnik, "What Is *Theōria?*," 80–81.
63. On the aristocratic nature of Aristotle's vision of activity for its own sake, not for the sake of a practical end, see Nightingale, *Spectacles of Truth*, 250–255; and Ericksen, 99, 108–118.
64. On the role of music in the education of the free person, see *Politics* 8.3 and Nightingale, *Spectacles of Truth*, 242–245. Nightingale argues that Aristotle's view of music is that it trains youth to be spectators of the good and the beautiful, an activity akin to *theōria*. Nightingale, *Spectacles of Truth*, 250–252. See Menn, "Plato and Aristotle on God as *Nous* and as the Good." Nightingale has suggested that we look at the category of the sublime, of Aristotle's expression that philosophy begins in wonder. She points out, however, that while philosophy for Aristotle *begins* in wonder, wonder ceases for Aristotle when we have completed our investigation and come to know. On the other hand, the notion of wonder in study does reappear in Aristotle's work on the investigation of animals. We derive an aesthetic wonder from the beauty of the natural world.
65. Nightingale describes the highest level of *theōria* this way: "When the human theorizer contemplates the 'first principles and causes,' he thereby contemplates god. The most advanced human theorist, then, theorizes divine thinking. By engaging in this highest form of *theōria*, the human mind assimilates itself to god: since the possession of the faculty of *nous* makes humans (potentially) akin to god, the actualization of this faculty marks the fullest flourishing of human nature" (Nightingale, *Spectacles of Truth*, 240).
66. *Politics* 7.2 (1324a14–15).
67. *Politics* 7.2 (1324a14–15).
68. See Cooper, "Contemplation and Happiness," 204–212.
69. Maimonides seems to suggest just this view. See *Guide* 3.51 (621).
70. *NE* 6.5 (1140b9–10).
71. *NE* 9.9 (1169b34). See Rorty, "The Place of Contemplation in Aristotle's *Nicomachean Ethics*," 377–394.
72. On this mode of thinking as free, unwearied, and aristocratic, see Nightingale, Ericksen, 99, 108–118.
73. *Politics* 1324a35.
74. *Politics* 1325b15–23.
75. Nightingale discusses this passage in terms of Aristotle's aristocratic values; he valorizes actions that are "free." Political actions are less free because they are active in relation to others, whereas contemplation is active only in relation to oneself. Nightingale, *Spectacles of Truth*, 235.
76. Richardson Lear, *Happy Lives and the Highest Good*, 4, 85, 121, 193–196.
77. Ibid., 90–91.

78. Ibid., 201.
79. Ibid., 206.
80. On the "blind spot," see now Nightingale, *Spectacles of Truth*, 102–105. I arrived at the image before reading her perceptive discussion. She uses the image in a different way: when the philosopher sees the Forms, he or she cannot see this world clearly, and when engaged in practical and political work in the world, one cannot see the Forms as clearly. She comes to the surprising conclusion that the philosopher's vision is actually broader when in this world, because one can look to the Forms and to this reality, whereas when engaged in theoretical contemplation one can only see the Forms and is blind to the imitations. Nightingale, *Spectacles of Truth*, 130.
81. Julia Annas, *An Introduction to Plato's Republic*, 247. On the devaluation of the imperfect world, see Charles Griswold, "Longing for the Best: Plato on Reconciliation with Imperfection," 101–136.
82. Nightingale, *Spectacles of Truth*, 98–100. She also argues that the philosopher is not reluctant to take part in ordinary practical life, but only to take political office. She argues that Plato in the *Republic* is defending a philosophical life that combines contemplation and action, not a contemplative life separated from ordinary human affairs. She supports this with Socrates' claim that the philosophers "must not be allowed to do what is permitted at present . . . namely to remain there and to refuse to go down among those prisoners and to have a share in their labors and honors" (*Republic* 519c–d). Since "at present" philosophers do not engage in pure contemplation of the Forms, she deduces that Plato must be referring to the practice of allowing philosophers to avoid political office, although they are perforce engaged in practical activities in the world. Nightingale, *Spectacles of Truth*, 132–134. She points out that Aristotle, too, acknowledges that one can exercise moral virtue in private life as well as in politics (*NE* 1179a2–6); Nightingale, *Spectacles of Truth*, 213, 215.
83. David Hume, *A Treatise of Human Understanding* 1.4.7. "I dine, I play backgammon, I converse and am merry with my friends; and when after three or four hours amusement, I return to these speculations, they appear so cold and strained and ridiculous that I cannot find in my heart to enter them any further."
84. Plotinus, *Enneads* 4.8.1, trans. A. H. Armstrong, 397.
85. Judah Halevi, in his twelfth-century philosophical dialogue known as the *Kuzari*, echoes the Talmudic story of the four who went into a garden (*pardes*), taken by the tradition as a symbol of mystical knowledge. Only Rabbi Akiva enters in peace and leaves in peace. Halevi comments that Rabbi Akiva was able to conduct himself freely in both worlds, i.e., the physical world and the spiritual world. See *Jerusalem Talmud, Hagigah* 77b; Judah Halevi, *Kuzari* III:65; Lobel, *Between Mysticism and Philosophy: Sufi Terms for Religious Experience in Judah Halevi's Kuzari*, 117. Halevi, *Kitāb al-radd waʾl-dalīl fīʾl-dīn al-dhalīl* (*al-Kitāb al-Khazari*), ed. David Baneth and Haggai Ben-Shammai, 140; English trans. Hartwig Hirschfeld, 190.

86. Nightingale points out that this journey follows the model of civic *theōria* in ancient Athens—the journey to a foreign sanctuary to bring back a report of one's viewing of sacred objects.
87. See *Nicomachean Ethics* 1178b5. See Lobel, *Between Mysticism and Philosophy*, 158 and 246–247 n. 62, for the way Judah Halevi expresses this tension between his own impulse to solitary contemplation and absorption in the divine, and his sense that one needs to actively engage in the life of community.
88. The *Nicomachean Ethics* presents a teleological model, moving toward the ideal of pure understanding. In the *Eudemian Ethics*, Aristotle emphasizes that the moral steps must be included in the final perfection. In the *NE*, this seems like a concession; insofar as we are human, we must engage in moral action (1178b5). In the *Eudemian Ethics* it is clearer that being noble individuals is a constitutive part of the ideal human life and not a mere instrumental means. However even in the *Eudemian Ethics*, he emphasizes that we should devote as little attention as possible to the nonrational parts of our soul. *EE* 8.3 (1249b).
89. Nightingale argues that in divorcing *theōria* from an effect on *praxis*, and suggesting that as a private person, Aristotle's philosopher is not obliged to return from the theoretical journey to report on his or her findings, Aristotle in effect rendered theoretical contemplation essentially amoral. Nightingale, *Spectacles of Truth*, 222.
90. Plato, *Republic* 501a–b.
91. *Republic* 500b–d.
92. Immanuel Kant, *Foundations of the Metaphysics of Morals*, trans. Lewis White Beck, ak 434; *Grounding for the Metaphysics of Morals*, trans. James W. Ellington, 40.
93. Immanuel Kant, *Critique of Practical Reason*, trans. Lewis White Beck, 169 (ak 161).
94. Kant, *The Conflict of the Faculties* (*Streit der Facultaten*), trans. Mary J. Gregor, 115.
95. See Kant, *Grounding for the Metaphysics of Morals*.
96. See John Rawls, *A Theory of Justice*.
97. See Michael Sandel, *Liberalism and the Limits of Justice*.
98. Alasdair Macintyre, *After Virtue: A Study in Moral Theory*, 202–203.
99. Charles Taylor, *Sources of the Self: The Making of the Modern Identity*, 8.
100. Ibid.
101. Ibid.
102. Ibid., 9.
103. John Rawls, *A Theory of Justice*, 587.
104. Taylor, *Sources of the Self*, 15.
105. Ibid., 15–16.
106. Taylor, *Sources of the Self*, 18. Taylor thus implicitly rejects Peter Berger's analysis of the sociology of knowledge in *A Sacred Canopy*: that in all societies, we project our values outward and then are confronted with them as if they are objective values that exist apart from our projection. Berger of course is aware that in modern pluralistic societies they are no longer as absolute and unquestioned as they once were.

107. Taylor, *Sources of the Self*, 33–34, 63–65.
108. Ibid., 122.
109. Aristotle, *NE* 1094a.

## 8. THE PHILOSOPHER AS TEACHER: AL-FĀRĀBĪ ON CONTEMPLATION AND ACTION

1. See *Politics* 7.2 (1324a13–29), 7.3 (1325a16–1326b20); *Aristotle's Politics*, trans. C. D. C. Reeves, xlii–xliii.
2. *saʾādah*: "felicity, flourishing."
3. Al-Fārābī, *Kitāb al-jadal* (Book of Dialectic), in *al-Manṭiq ʿinda al-Fārābī*, 69:10–18; Miriam Galston, "The Theoretical and Practical Dimensions of Happiness as Portrayed in the Political Treatises of al-Fārābī," 95–96.
4. Ibn Bājjah and Jamāl al-Dīn ʿAlawī, *Rasāʾil falsafiyyah li-Abī Bakr Ibn Bajjah: Nuṣūs falsafiyyah ghayr manshūrah*, 197; Shlomo Pines, "The Limitations of Human Knowledge According to al-Farabi, Ibn Bajja, and Maimonides," 82; cited by Galston, "Theoretical and Practical Dimensions," 100; Ibn Tufayl, *Ḥayy Ibn Yaq Yaqẓān*, ed. Gauthier, 13–14; trans. Lenn Goodman, 100.
5. The separate intellect humans can become is, however, lower than what Fārābī terms the "Active Intellect." The concept of the Active Intellect is a complex one. Its function is to bring the pure potential of our minds into activity; it is mentioned first by Aristotle. (See below, nn. 9, 10, 19, and at n. 24). It is the tenth intellectual emanation from the Divine, and the one with which human intellects can unite, in what is sometimes referred to as a kind of intellectualist mysticism. On the notion of intellectualist mysticism, see Lobel, *A Sufi-Jewish Dialogue*, 21–26 and 249 nn. 1–4; al-Fārābī, *Mabādiʾ ārāʾ ahl al-madīnah al-fāḍilah* (Principles of the Opinions of the Inhabitants of the Virtuous City), trans. Richard Walzer, 205–206; Galston, "Theoretical and Practical Dimensions," 101–102.
6. al-Fārābī, *Madīnah*, trans. Walzer, 206.
7. "The rational faculty is partly practical reason and partly theoretical reason; practical reason is made to serve theoretical reason. Theoretical reason, however, is not made to serve anything else, but has as its purpose to bring humans to happiness" (al-Fārābī, *Madīnah*, trans. Walzer, 208). He goes on to explain that "when this happiness becomes known through theoretical reason and is set up as an aim and desired by the appetitive faculty, and when the deliberative faculty discovers what ought to be done in order to attain that with the assistance of the faculty of representation and the senses, and when those actions are performed by the instruments of the appetitive faculty, the actions of man will all be good and noble." Virtue flows from knowledge; virtue and noble actions lead to happiness. Nevertheless, happiness proper is said here to consist in becoming an intelligible being alone.

8. al-Fārābī, *Madīnah*, trans. Walzer, 201:15–16; Galston, "Theoretical and Practical Dimensions," 101–102.
9. The notion that the active intellect—that which brings the human mind from potentiality to actuality—is a transcendent being is not explicit in Aristotle. It is first clearly articulated by Aristotle's Greek commentator, Alexander of Aphrodisias. Alexander, *De anima*, 89, in *Scripta minora* 2.1 ed. I Bruns, containing Alexander's *De anima* (1–00) and *De intellectu* (106–113); cf. *De intellectu*, 110, lines 1–3. Cited by Herbert Davidson, "Alfarabi and Avicenna on Active Intellect," 112; Davidson, *Alfarabi, Avicenna, and Averroes, on Intellect*, 13–14. This account appears also in al-Fārābī's *Treatise on the Intellect*, where he comments on Aristotle's use of the term "intellect" in *De anima*. Al-Fārābī, *Risālah fīʾl-ʾaql fīʾl-ʾaql* (Treatise on the Intellect), ed. M. Bouyges, S.J, 26:9–27:7, 3':3–5; Galston, "Theoretical and Practical Dimensions," 102.
10. The text says that the function of what al-Fārābī calls the Active Intellect—the tenth divine emanation—is to enable people to become a separate substance like it. *Kitāb al-siyāsah al-madaniyyah* (The Political Regime), ed. Fauzi Najjar, 32:6–9, 35:10–11, 55:9–10, 72:15–18; Galston, "Theoretical and Practical Dimensions," 102.
11. *Fuṣūl muntazaʾah* (Selected Aphorisms), ed. Fauzi Najjar, nos. 28, 45:6–46:16; *Fuṣūl al-madanī: The Aphorisms of the Statesman*, ed. D. M. Dunlop, no. 25, 39–40 (English), 120–121 (Arabic); Galston, 103.
12. *Taḥṣīl al-saʾādah*, 16:15–17; 15:16–16:15; *The Attainment of Happiness*, in *al-Fārābī's Philosophy of Plato and Aristotle*, trans. Muhsin Mahdi, 24–25; Galston, "Theoretical and Practical Dimensions," 104. The marginal numbers of the Hyderabad manuscript also appear in the margins of Mahdi's English translation.
13. *Taḥṣīl al-saʾādah*, 39:10–40:3, 45:12–47:3; *Attainment of Happiness*, trans. Mahdi, 43–44, 48–49.
14. *Taḥṣīl al-saʾādah*, 45–46; *Attainment of Happiness*, trans. Mahdi, 48–49. Al-Fārābī in this work also formulates a celebrated statement: that the philosopher, supreme ruler, king, lawgiver, and imam are different expressions of one idea. He adds that although the term "philosopher" stands primarily for theoretical excellence, in order for a philosopher to reach the ultimate in theoretical virtue, the practical virtues must be included as well. 42:12–44:2; trans. Mahdi, 46–47. On this passage, see Muhsin Mahdi, *Alfarabi and the Foundation of Islamic Political Philosophy*, 183–192. For another interpretation, see Joshua Parens, *An Islamic Philosophy of Virtuous Religions: Introducing Alfarabi*, 103–108.
15. Al-Fārābī expresses such a comprehensive portrait of happiness in several other contexts as well. In the *Selected Aphorisms* (*Fuṣūl muntazaʾah*), al-Fārābī suggests that theoretical philosophy is useful because it makes true virtue possible. To act morally, we need to achieve a state of genuine virtue; to attain true virtue, we have to know what virtue is. Like Aristotle, al-Fārābī holds that a philosopher must behave morally not merely from habit or having obeyed the authority of another, but out of genuine knowledge of what is right. But al-Fārābī goes further; he asserts that

to attain true virtue, we must also know what happiness is. "A deed is only right and a virtue when a person rightly knows the virtues which are thought to be virtues, but are not so, and has accustomed himself to the actions of the real virtues. . . . This is a condition which does not come and is not perfected except after experience, perfect knowledge of demonstration and perfection in the natural sciences . . . until he attains lastly to the knowledge of happiness which is in truth happiness. It is that which is sought for itself and not for anything else, at any time whatever." *Fuṣūl* nos. 94, 95:14–96:8; *Aphorisms of the Statesman*, trans. Dunlop, 89:72; Galston, "Theoretical and Practical Dimensions," 108.

16. Al-Fārābī reiterates this point later in the same aphorism. In this passage, he writes about a person who has almost reached the ultimate goal, the state of speculative knowledge that brings happiness. At this level, we have achieved knowledge of existents and their ultimate causes; we see existence in the light of the divine. At the same time, we continue to inquire into the goal for which human beings are brought into existence—the perfection we are here to attain—and to investigate all the things by which humans reach this perfection. Then (and only then, al-Fārābī implies), we are able to pass to the practical part of philosophy; it now becomes possible to attain the ultimate goal and do what we must do. *Fuṣūl* no. 94, 96:15–97:8; *Aphorisms of the Statesman,* trans. Dunlop, 89:74; Galston, "Theoretical and Practical Dimensions," 108–110.
17. *Fuṣūl* no. 98, 101:1–7; *Aphorisms of the Statesman*, trans. Dunlop, 93:76–77. Galston points out that al-Fārābī here, as elsewhere, shows respect for conventional morality, which he argues prepares one for true virtue based on reason. Galston, "Theoretical and Practical Dimensions," 111.
18. *Madīnah*, trans. Walzer, 244:7–16, 204:15–206:10; Galston, "Theoretical and Practical Dimensions," 111–112.
19. The text speaks of union with the Active Intellect, the tenth intellectual emanation discussed above, nn. 5, 9, 10 and below at n. 24. *Siyāsah*, 79:15–17.
20. *Siyāsah*, 80:3–5; Galston, "Theoretical and Practical Dimensions," 113.
21. We have seen above that the *Political Regime* described happiness in purely intellectual terms as becoming a separate intellect. Galston thus surmises that it is possible that this text conceives of happiness in purely private intellectual terms, while revelation allows one to govern others well and bring them to happiness, without necessarily enhancing one's own fulfillment. Galston, "Theoretical and Practical Dimensions," 112–113.
22. *Taḥṣīl al-saʿādah*, 42:12–44:2; *Attainment of Happiness*, trans. Mahdi, 46–47.
23. As we will see in our discussion of Maimonides, we can harmonize these views by seeing governance as the natural overflow from a self-sufficient intellect.
24. See above, nn. 5, 9, 10, 19. See Galston, "Theoretical and Practical Dimensions," 133–135 and references there.
25. He adds that something is in vain when it exists, but is not accompanied by the end for which it exists.

26. *Jadal* 70:7–14; trans. Galston, "Theoretical and Practical Dimensions," 144.
27. *Jadal* 69:10–18; *Siyāsah* 73:11–12; *Fuṣūl* nos. 53, 62:2–5; *Aphorisms* 49:48 (English), 133–134 (Arabic); *Madīnah*, trans. Walzer, 208:10, Galston, "Theoretical and Practical Dimensions," 114–115.
28. *Fuṣūl* no. 53, 62:2–5; *Aphorisms* 49:48 (English), 133–134 (Arabic).

## 9. THE IMITATION OF GOD: MAIMONIDES ON THE ACTIVE AND THE CONTEMPLATIVE LIFE

1. *Guide of the Perplexed* 3.54 (635).
2. Maimonides seems to define "mind" and "soul" interchangeably; by "soul," he means rational soul.
3. Lawrence Kaplan, "'I Sleep, but My Heart Waketh': Maimonides' Conception of Human Perfection," 154–155.
4. *Guide* 3.27, 3.54.
5. We can see here the influence of Platonic political philosophy. In the *Republic*, Plato argues that philosophers have a duty to return to the cave to teach the masses; philosophers are in debt to the *polis*, because they were nourished by the *polis* and allowed to study. Socrates expresses this view before dying as well; he has an obligation to obey the laws of the city, for he is grateful that the city enabled him to study and practice philosophy. Aristotle takes a similar approach in the *Politics*; the city's laws must enable the elite to pursue the philosophical way of life and achieve the supreme philosophical achievement. Plato, *Republic* 520a–c; *Crito* 48b–53a; Aristotle, *Politics* 1333a–b; C. D. C. Reeves, trans., *Politics*, xlvii.
6. In *Guide* 3.27 (511–512); 3.54 (635–636).
7. Maimonides insists in 1.54 that morality is not an end in itself; moral qualities are only a disposition to respond to others, he asserts, and have no use if we are alone (*Guide* 3.54 [635]; 3.27 [510–511]). However, Maimonides' testimony is divided on this issue. Maimonides' claim that morality has no place when we are alone contradicts his statement in *Guide* 3.12 that most evils are self-inflicted; we harm ourselves through greed for luxuries our souls don't truly need (*Guide* 3.12 [445–446]). Morality does, then, have a place when we are alone. Similarly, in *Guide* 3.53 he asserts that walking in the way of moral virtues is *tsedaqah*, doing justice to our rational soul (*Guide* 3.53 [631]). Thus Maimonides does seem to find some intrinsic merit to development of the moral virtues. In fact, in *Guide* 3.54, Maimonides defines moral perfection as the *wisdom* of possessing moral virtues (*Guide* 3.54 [635]). His terminology reflects Aristotle's concept of moral wisdom (*phronēsis*) as a genuine rational virtue and the Greek notion of the sage or wise person who is wise in human affairs. We find both notions likewise embedded in Maimonides' *Laws of Moral Dispositions* in the model of the wise person (*ḥakham*) whose moral practice follows the golden mean (*Mishneh Torah, Laws of Moral Dispositions* [*Hilkhot De'ot*] 1:5; *A Maimonides Reader*, 52).

8. This level of achievement belongs to human beings alone. Maimonides draws from Aristotle the notion that intellect is what differentiates us from all other species, what makes human beings distinctly human. However, in *Nicomachean Ethics* 10.7, Aristotle goes on to argue that the conception of purely theoretical matters is in fact a divine capacity; it makes us like gods. Thinking is thus clearly an activity that could go on in a disembodied afterlife. However, it is not clear that Aristotle himself would uphold the conception of an afterlife, since he insists that form must be embodied in matter. For Aristotle the soul is simply the form of the human body, that which enables it to perform its function. For Maimonides it is otherwise. Maimonides, like al-Fārābī, envisions an afterlife without the body. For Maimonides, being embodied is an unfortunate temporary condition. The state we seek is a purely intellectual contemplation of the divine after death. It is medieval Aristotelians who developed Aristotle's notion of the active intellect, that part which comes from without, to allow it to become acquired intellect and achieve immortality. This is a development of the medieval notion of developing an acquired intellect, which can achieve conjunction with the divine active intellect and achieve immortality. See Davidson, *Alfarabi, Avicenna, and Averroes on Intellect*, 201–202.
9. See the passionate textual investigation of Menachem Kellner, "Is Maimonides' Ideal Person Austerely Rationalist?"
10. Alexander Altmann has shown that this philosophical schema of four perfections was in fact taught by the Arabic philosopher Ibn Bājjah. Altmann, "Maimonides' Four Perfections."
11. *Guide* 3.54 (636).
12. Even if Maimonides, like Aquinas, leaves open the possibility of eternal creation—that the universe proceeds eternally from God—he nevertheless also believes that God's laws do in some sense govern this universe. *Guide* 3.54 (637–638). On Maimonides' views on creation, see Norbert Samuelson, "Maimonides' Doctrine of Creation"; Warren Zev Harvey, "A Third Approach to Maimonides' Cosmogony-Prophetology Puzzle"; Sara Klein-Braslavy, "The Creation of the World and Maimonides' Interpretation of Gen. I–V"; Lawrence Kaplan, "Maimonides on the Miraculous Element in Prophecy"; Herbert Davidson, "Maimonides' Secret Position on Creation." On Maimonides' doctrine of providence, see Charles Raffel, "Providence as Consequent Upon the Intellect: Maimonides' Theory on Providence"; Zvi Diesendruck, "Samuel and Moses Ibn Tibbon on Maimonides' Theory of Providence"; Aviezer Ravitzky, "Samuel Ibn Tibbon and the Esoteric Character of the Guide of the Perplexed"; Ehud Benor, "Models for Understanding Evil in *The Guide of the Perplexed*."
13. *Guide* 1.54 (125).
14. *Guide* 3.53 (631–632).
15. *Guide* 3.53 (632); 3.12 (444).
16. The taking on of God's attributes is a Sufi motif; the servant of God annihilates his or her qualities of ego, and comes to reflect God's attributes. This motif is reflected in the philosopher's speech in Judah Halevi's *Kuzari*, where the person becomes the

limbs of the Active Intellect. Halevi, *Kitāb al-radd wa'l-dalīl fī'l-dīn al-dhalīl (al-Kitāb al-Khazari)*, ed. Baneth and Ben-Shammai, 4; English trans. Hirschfeld, 33. For the idea that the highest human ideal is the overflow or expression of rational perfection, see *Guide* 2.11; Warren Zev Harvey, "Maimonides on Human Perfection, Awe, and Politics," 9–10; see also "Political Philosophy and *Halakhah* in Maimonides," 198–212; English translation, 58–59; Howard Kreisel, *Maimonides' Political Thought*, 125–158; David Shatz, "Worship, Corporeality, and Human Perfection," 100; Shatz, "Maimonides' Moral Theory," 186.

17. The conclusion of the *Guide* is thus very different from Aristotle's conclusion of the *Nicomachean Ethics*. There Aristotle pokes fun at the idea that the gods would engage in human affairs such as making contracts. Aristotle's God does not exercise providence over individuals. God is "thinking about thinking," at best aware of the general principles of nature; if the gods are not involved in human affairs, it is unlikely Aristotle believes the Unmoved Mover is. Aristotle's God did not create the world, does not sustain it actively through loving-kindness. While Plato's God in the *Timaeus* is said to create or shape the world out of goodness, so that all could share in the goodness and orderliness of the divine, Aristotle's God is simply present as an underlying sustaining cause of the universe.
18. Hermann Cohen, *Religion of Reason out of the Sources of Judaism*, trans. Simon Kaplan, 95–96; Cohen, *Ethics of Maimonides*, trans. Almut Bruckstein, 103–105; Cohen, *Characteristik der Ethic Maimunis*; Steven Schwarzschild, "Moral Radicalism and 'Middlingness' in the Ethics of Maimonides"; Julius Guttmann, *Philosophies of Judaism*, 200–203.
19. See Lawrence V. Berman, "The Political Interpretation of the Maxim: The Purpose of Philosophy Is the Imitation of God"; Menachem Kellner, *Maimonides on Human Perfection*; David Hartman, *Maimonides: Torah and Philosophic Quest*.
20. See Maimonides, *Book of Commandments* (*Sefer ha-mitsvot*), commandment 3, ed. Josef Qafih, 59; trans. in Twersky, *A Maimonides Reader*, 432. Ehud Benor suggests that it is not clear whether Maimonides believes we can contemplate God through the study of the commandments; he omits the commandments in his statement in *Guide* 3.28. But see Hannah Kasher, who points out that *Guide* 3.26 suggests an analogy between contemplation of the wisdom expressed in the commandments and expressed in nature. Ehud Benor, *Worship of the Heart: A Study in Maimonides' Philosophy of Religion*, 35 and 179–180 n. 48; Hannah Kasher, "Talmud Torah as a Means of Apprehending God in Maimonides' Teachings," 75; cf. Hartman, *Maimonides*, 204. Divine legislation is also part of the natural world; see *Guide* 2.40 (382): "the Law, although it is not natural, enters into what is natural," and David Shatz, "Worship, Corporeality, and Human Perfection," 86 and n. 21; Josef Stern, "The Idea of a *ḥoq* in Maimonides' Explanation of the Law," 99–109; Warren Zev Harvey, "Political Philosophy and *Halakhah* in Maimonides,"; English translation by Sam Friedman in *Jewish Intellectual History in the Middle Ages*, ed. Westport, 47–64.
21. Kellner, *Maimonides on Human Perfection*, 43–45.

22. See chapter 5 of the ethical treatise known as Eight Chapters (*Shemonah peraqim*): *Haqdamah le-massekhet Avot* in *Ethical Writings of Maimonides*, trans. Charles Butterworth, 75–78; Yizhaq Sheilat, *Haqdamot ha-Rambam la-mishnah*, 241–244 (Hebrew), 385–388 (Arabic); and the *Laws of Ethical Characteristics* in the *Code of Jewish Law* (*Mishneh Torah: Hilkhot de*ʿ*ot*): *Mishneh* ʿ*im perush rabbenu Moshe ben Maimon*, trans. Josef Qafih, 387–391. Mishneh *Torah*, "Laws of Ethical Characteristics" (*Hilkhot De*ʾ*ot*) in Twersky, ed., *A Maimonides Reader*, 3:3, p. 57.
23. See the remarks of Howard Kreisel, *Maimonides' Political Thought*, 307 n. 35, with which I substantially agree.
24. Kenneth Seeskin noted that in *Guide* 3.11 Maimonides accepts the classic formulation of the Socratic paradox. Seeskin, "The Positive Contribution of Negative Theology," 49.
25. *Republic* 500b–d.
26. Plato, *Theaetetus* 176e.
27. See Menachem Kellner, *Maimonides on Human Perfection*, 42. For studies of *imitatito Dei* in Judaism and in Maimonides, see David S. Shapiro, "The Doctrine of the Image of God and *Imitatio Dei*"; Martin Buber, "*Imitatio Dei*"; Berman, "Political Interpretation of the Maxim"; Warren Zev Harvey, "Holiness: A Command to *Imitatio Dei*"; Kenneth Seeskin, *Searching for a Distant God*, 91–106; Howard Kreisel, *Maimonides' Political Thought*, 125–158; Steven Harvey, "Maimonides in the Sultan's Palace," 47–75; Berman, "The Ethical Views of Maimonides Within the Context of Islamicate Civilization," 17–19, 23–24; Steven Harvey, "Avicenna and Maimonides on Prayer and Intellectual Worship"; Kaplan, "'I Sleep But My Heart Waketh.'" On Maimonides' conception of holiness, see Menachem Kellner, "Spiritual Life."
28. Ehud Benor argues that from the standpoint of Aristotelian virtue ethics, the matter is not quite so simple. Maimonides acknowledges that habituation to ethical virtues takes time and practice. Why should contemplation of God's attributes follow necessarily in assimilation of those attributes and expressing them in action? He responds that to achieve intellectual perfection, we must develop practical virtues. When we have sensitized ourselves ethically, we will develop a concept of God that sees God's creation of the world as an ethical outpouring of loving kindness. Our ethical sensitivity—temporarily put on hold due to the intensity of our contemplation—will be re-activated and energized by our love of God. Aristotle argued that "pleasure completes the action" like a bloom upon youth; Benor argues that for Maimonides, passionate love for God is the crowning pleasure that flows from intellectual contemplation. Our passionate love will awaken a desire to arouse ourselves from contemplation and return to the world of action, in imitation of God's overflow in creating the world. He suggests that statutory prayer—in which we are obliged to petition for things that will aid the world—may reflect a transitional state in which we are roused to turn from pure contemplation to action on behalf of others. Benor's resolution of the Socratic paradox—that virtue is a form of knowledge—is parallel to that of Kenneth Seeskin: virtue is a form of knowledge, because we must develop ourselves morally to achieve knowledge. See

Benor, *Worship of the Heart*, 54–61; Seeskin, *Dialogue and Discovery: A Study in Socratic Method*, 144–145.

29. Warren Zev Harvey, "Maimonides on Human Perfection, Awe, and Politics," 9–10; see also "Political Philosophy and *Halakhah* in Maimonides."
30. Compare this with Baḥya Ibn Paqūda's distinction between essential and active attributes. Essential attributes belong to God as God, independent of creation. Maimonides rejects the notion of essential attributes as introducing multiplicity into God. But Baḥya's essential attributes, which he insists are distinct in name alone, describe three aspects of divinity that are conceptually quite similar to the conception of a Necessary Existent in Avicenna and Maimonides: God is one, existent, and eternal. On the Necessary Existent in Avicenna, see following note. See Baḥya, *Duties of the Heart*, trans. Mansoor: 132–134; trans. Qafih, 73–77.
31. *Mishneh Torah*, Book of Knowledge (*Sefer ha-madda*ʿ 1:2–3), *A Maimonides Reader*, 43–44. Translated by Bernard Septimus in *A Jewish Philosophy Reader*, ed. Daniel J. Frank, Oliver Leaman, Charles Manekin, 223. On Avicenna's theory of Necessary Existence, see Fazlur Rahman, "Ibn Sīnā's Theory of the God-World Relationship," 38–52.
32. *Guide* 2.37, 373–374; cf. *Mishneh Torah*, Laws of Foundations of the Torah (*Yesode ha-Torah*) 7:7.
33. See Berman, "Political Interpretation of the Maxim," 53–61; Shlomo Pines, "The Limitations of Human Knowledge According to Al-Farabi, ibn Bajja, and Maimonides."
34. Harvey, "Awe, Perfection, and Human Politics," 11. Altmann notes similarly that Maimonides makes a strong statement that the ordinary practice of worship and morality is not to be compared to the ultimate purpose, which is apprehension of God. Thus, Maimonides distinguishes between ordinary practices of worship and morality and the imitation of divine attributes, which does not flow from practical reasoning but from "theoretical, metaphysical considerations," from the apprehension of God. The imitation of God (*imitatio Dei*) is, therefore, "but the practical consequence of the intellectual love of God and is part and parcel of the ultimate perfection." Altmann, "Maimonides' Four Perfections," 24.
35. See above, chap. 3.
36. See *Ḥayy Ibn Yaqdhān: Roman philosophique d'Ibn Thofail*, 116–117; Ibn Ṭufayl's *Ḥayy Ibn Yaqẓān*, trans. Lenn Evan Goodman, 146–147.
37. Avicenna writes that reason is the tongue of angels; they have no words, only reason. We should strive to imitate the heavenly bodies, who engage in wordless praise of the Divine. Avicenna, *Risālah fī mahiyyat al-salāh* (*Treatise on Prayer*) in *Traités mystiques d-Ibn Sina*, 33; trans. A. J. Arberry, *Avicenna on Theology*, 53. Maimonides expresses the same idea, quoting Psalm 19:2–4: "The heavens declare the glory of God [and the firmament speaks of his handiwork;] there is no speech, there are no words, neither is their voice heard." The heavens thus declare the praise of God and make known his wonders without speech or words. The beauty of the heavens is itself a praise of the divine. *Guide* 2.4 (159–160). The Jewish daily prayer known as the *Qedushah*, or holiness prayer, likewise bids the earthly Jewish congregation to join the angels in their worship of the divine. See *Ha-siddur ha-shalem* (*Daily Prayer*

*Book*), trans. Philip Birnbaum, 71–74. Avicenna suggests that intellectual worship of the divine is a contemplative person's acknowledgment of our ontological position in the universe as beings dependent on the Necessary Existent. For a somewhat different interpretation of Avicenna's view of worship and prayer, see Steven Harvey, "Avicenna and Maimonides on Prayer and Intellectual Worship."

38. See Hartman, *Maimonides*, 192–195. On the knowledge and love for God in Maimonides, see most recently the illuminating essay of Daniel Lasker, "Love of God and Knowledge of God in Maimonides' Philosophy," 329–345.
39. See Shatz, "Maimonides' Moral Theory," 186–187.
40. *Bhagavad Gītā* 3.22–26.
41. *Misneh Torah*, Laws of Repentance (*Hilkhot teshuvah*), 10:2. See also *Commentary to the Mishneh,* introduction to *Pereq ḥeleq*; Qafih, 199; Shilat, 132 (Hebrew), 362 (Arabic); *A Maimonides Reader*, 405–412.

## 10. THE DANCE OF HUMAN EXPRESSION: AL-GHAZĀLĪ AND MAIMONIDES

1. It is true that recent studies of Ghazālī's autobiography suggest that his account is highly stylized and shaped by his theological system. Regardless of the chronological sequence of events, his narrative nevertheless probably reflects a process of genuine realization. See Eric Ormsby, "The Taste of Truth: The Structure of Experience in al-Ghazālī's *al-Munqidh min al-dalāl,*" 133–135, 147–152; Montgomery Watt, *Muslim Intellectual: A Life of al-Ghazālī*, 47–57, 133–151. For analyses of the levels of ascent and the ways of knowing God, see, e.g., Binyamin Abrahamov, "Al-Ghazālī's Supreme Way to Know God," 141–168; Scott Girdner, *Reasoning with Revelation: The Significance of the Qurʾānic Contextualization of Philosophy in al-Ghazālī's* The Niche of Lights (*Mishkāt al-anwār*), 77–84, 663–672; Fadlou Shehadi, *Ghazālī's Unique Unknowable God*, 43–47.
2. Ghazālī, *Al-Munqidh min al-dalāl*, 69–70; trans. Watt, *The Faith and Practice of al-Ghazālī,* 19; trans. McCarthy, *Freedom and Fulfillment*, 63.
3. Ghazālī, 76–77; trans. Watt, 24; trans. McCarthy, 66
4. Ghazālī, 122–126; trans. Watt, 56–58; trans. McCarthy, 89–90.
5. Ghazālī, 128–129; trans. Watt, 60–61; trans. McCarthy, 92–93.
6. Ghazālī, 132; trans. Watt, 63; trans. McCarthy, 94.
7. For the view that the supreme way to know God for Ghazālī is itself rational, see Abrahamov, "Al-Ghazālī's Supreme Way to Know God." One way to understand this might be to say that the rational intellect is active and creative, while the intuitive mind is receptive to illumination from the divine. This distinction was suggested to me by Binyamin Abrahamov in private communication.
8. Ghazālī, 134; trans. Watt, 64; trans. McCarthy, 95.
9. Ghazālī, 132–134; trans. Watt, 64; trans. McCarthy, 94–95.
10. Ormsby, "The Taste of Truth," 134, 148. Ormsby notes that it is shaped not only by his actual journey but by the theological structure he sets forth, and by his desire to portray even his crises as part of a meaningful structure of experience. He notes

that it is also shaped by contrasting pairs of events, states, or faculties: the senses as unreliable vs. the highest sense of *dhawq*; leaving of teaching and returning to teaching; dreams as erring and as revealing prophetic truth; the intellect as erring, and finding its true role as guide toward prophecy; the tongue as knotted, and discovering the directness of taste, 149–152. Finally, Ormsby notes two themes that shape the work: the quest for certitude, and the quest for integrity between realization and practice, 139–140.

11. Ghazālī, 133–134; trans. Watt, 64; trans. McCarthy, 95.
12. Ghazālī, 137–140; trans. Watt, 64; trans. McCarthy, 95.
13. See Hava Lazarus-Yafe, "Symbolism of Light in the Writings of Al-Ghazālī," in *Studies in Al-Ghazālī*, 304–306.
14. See Girdner, *Reasoning with Revelation*, 77–84, 663–672; Shehadi, *Ghazālī's Unique Unknowable God*, 43–47.
15. Ghazālī, 134; trans. Watt, 67–71; trans. McCarthy, 96–99.
16. See David Shatz, "Worship, Corporeality, and Human Perfection: A Reading of *Guide of the Perplexed*, III:51–54," 97–108, 111–119.
17. The Bible tells us that Moses and Aaron died "by the mouth of the Lord" (Deut. 34:5, Num. 33:38). The Talmudic tradition extrapolates from this that they died "by a kiss." It was said that Miriam also died by the mouth (i.e., the word) of the Lord, but that the text did not express it as a kiss, as such would be unbecoming to say of a woman (Bava Batra 17a). Maimonides relates the image of a kiss to Song of Songs 1:2: "Let him kiss me with the kisses of his mouth, for your love is better than wine." He learns from this that these three died in the pleasure of divine contemplation; he understands the metaphor of the kiss to suggest the joy one derives from the perception of God, and the intense love it awakens. *Guide* 3.51 (628).
18. Benor, *Worship of the Heart*, 51–53. See above, chap. 7, n. 65, for Nightingale's argument that for Aristotle, both god and the human contemplator theorize the abstract principles of nature. Nightingale describes the highest level of *theōria* this way: "when the human theorizer contemplates the 'first principles and causes,' he thereby contemplates god. The most advanced human theorist, then, theorizes divine thinking. By engaging in this highest form of *theōria*, the human mind assimilates itself to god: since the possession of the faculty of *nous* makes humans (potentially) akin to god, the actualization of this faculty marks the fullest flourishing of human nature" (Nightingale, *Spectacles of Truth*, 240).
19. Introduction to *Pereq ḥeleq, Maimonides Reader*, 405; trans. Qafih, 199; Shilat, 132 (Hebrew), 362 (Arabic).

## CONCLUSION

1. Taylor, *Sources of the Self*, 33–34, 63–65.
2. Ibid., 122.
3. Aristotle, *Nicomachean Ethics* 1094a.

# Bibliography

## PRIMARY SOURCES


Aristotle. *Athenian Constitution; Eudemian Ethics; Virtues and Vices*. Greek and English. Trans. H. Rackham. Loeb Classical Library. Cambridge, Mass.: Harvard University Press, 1992.

——. *The Basic Works of Aristotle*. Ed. Richard McKeon. New York: Random House, 1941.

——. *The Categories; On Interpretation*. Greek and English. Trans. Harold P. Cooke and Hugh Tredennick. Loeb Classical Library. Cambridge, Mass.: Harvard University Press, 1983.

——. *Eudemian Ethics: Books I, II, and VIII*. Translated with a commentary by Michael Woods. 2nd ed. New York: Oxford University Press, 1992.

——. *Aristotle's Metaphysics*. Trans. Joe Sachs. Santa Fe, N. M.: Green Lion Press, 2002.

——. *A New Aristotle Reader*. Ed. J. L. Ackrill. Princeton: Princeton University Press, 1987.

——. *Aristotle's Nicomachean Ethics*. Trans. Joe Sachs. Newbury, Mass.: Focus Publishing, 2002.

——. *Nicomachean Ethics*. Trans. Terence Irwin. Indianapolis: Hackett, 1985.

——. *Nicomachean Ethics*. Trans. Martin Ostwald. New York: Prentice Hall, 1962.

——. *Politics*. Trans. C. D. C. Reeve. Indianapolis: Hackett, 1998.

Augustine. *Confessions*. Trans. R. S. Pine-Coffin. New York: Penguin, 1961.

——. *On Free Choice of the Will*. Trans. Thomas Williams. Indianapolis: Hackett, 1993.

Avicenna, and A. J. Arberry. *Avicenna on Theology*. Westport, Conn.: Hyperion Press, 1979.

Baḥya Ibn Paqūda. *The Book of Direction to the Duties of the Heart*. Ed. and trans. Menahem Mansoor. Littman Library of Jewish Civilization. London: Routledge and Kegan Paul, 1973.

——. *Kitāb al-Hidāya ilā farāʾiḍ al-qulūb*. Ed. and trans. A. S. Yahuda. Leiden: Brill, 1912.

——. *Kitāb al-Hidāya ilā farāʾiḍ al-qulūb* (*Torat ḥovot ha-levavot*). Ed. and trans. Josef Qafih. Jerusalem, 1973.

*Bhagavad Gītā*. Trans. Barbara Stoler Miller. New York: Penguin, 1995.

*The Bhagavad Gītā: A New Translation with Commentary*. Trans. David White. New York: Lang, 1993.

*The Bhagavad Gītā*. Trans. Winthrop Sargeant. Albany: State University of New York Press, 1984.

*The Bhagavad Gītā: with the commentary of Sri Śaṅkarāchārya*. Trans. A. Mahadeva Sastry. Madras: Samata Books, 1977.

*The Bhagavad Gītā*. Trans. Franklin Edgerton. Cambridge, Mass.: Harvard University Press, 1972.

Chuang Tzu. *Zhuangzi: The Essential Writings, with selections from traditional commentaries.* Trans. with introduction and notes by Brook Ziporyn. Indianapolis: Hackett, 2009.

—. *Chuang Tzu: Basic Writings*. Ed. and trans. Burton Watson. New York: Columbia University Press, 1964.

Cohen, Hermann. *Charakteristik der ethik Maimunis*. Leipzig: Gustav Fock, 1908.

—. *Ethics of Maimonides*. Trans. with commentary by Almut Sh. Bruckstein. Madison: University of Wisconsin Press, 2004.

—. *Religion of Reason out of the Sources of Judaism*. Trans. Simon Kaplan. Atlanta: Scholars Press, 1995.

Confucius. *Confucius: Analects*. Ed. and trans. Edward G. Slingerland. Indianapolis: Hackett, 2003.

Coomaraswamy, Ananda Kentish, and I. B. Horner. *The Living Thoughts of Gotama the Buddha*. Ann Arbor, Mich.: University Microfilms International, 1978.

Doniger, Wendy. *Hymns from the Ṛig Veda*. New York: Penguin. "The Hymn of Creation," "The Hymn of the Person," "The Golden Embryo" reprinted in *The Ways of Religion: An Introduction to the Major Traditions*, ed. Roger Eastman. New York: Oxford University Press, 1999.

Epictetus. *Handbook of Epictetus*. Trans. Nicholas P. White. Indianapolis: Hackett, 1983.

Al-Fārābī. *Al-Fārābī on the Perfect State: Abu Nasr al-Fārābī's Mabādiʾ ārāʾ ahl al-madīnah al-fāḍilah: A Revised Text with Introduction, Translation, and Commentary*. Ed. and trans. Richard Walzer. New York: Clarendon Press, 1985.

—. *Al-Fārābī's Philosophy of Plato and Aristotle*. Ed. and trans. Muhsin Mahdi. Ithaca: Cornell University Press, 1969.

—. *Al-Fārābī's The Political Regime (Kitāb al-siyāsah al-madaniyyah, also known as the Treatise on the Principles of Beings)*. Ed. Fauzi M. Najjar. Beirut: Imprimerie Catholique, 1964.

—. *Al-Fārābī: Risālah fīʾl-'aql*. Ed. Maurice Bouyges. Beirut: Imprimerie Catholique, 1938.

—. *Fuṣūl al-madanī: Aphorisms of the Statesman*. Ed. and trans. D. M. Dunlop. Cambridge: Cambridge University Press, 1961.

—. *Fuṣūl muntazaʾah (Selected Aphorisms)*. Ed. and trans. Fauzi Najjar. Beirut: Dar aal-Mashreq, 1971.

—. *Kitāb al-Jadal*. In *al-Manṭiq ʿinda al-Fārābī*, vol. 3. Ed. Rafiq Ajam. Beirut: Dar al-Mashreq, 1986.

—. *Taḥṣīl al-sa'ādah* (*The Attainment of Happiness*). Ed. Ja'far al-Yasin. Beirut: Al-Andalus, 1981.

Gardner, Daniel K., trans. *The Four Books: The Basic Teachings of the Later Confucian Tradition.* Indianapolis: Hackett, 2007.

Al-Ghazālī. *The Faith and Practice of al-Ghazālī.* Ed. and trans. W. Montgomery Watt. Oxford: Oneworld, 1995.

—. *Freedom and Fulfillment: An Annotated Translation of al-Ghazālī's al-Muniqidh min al-dalāl and Other Relevant Works of al-Ghazālī.* Ed. and trans. Richard Joseph McCarthy. Boston: Twayne, 1980.

—. *Al-munqidh min al-dalāl.* Damascus, 1939.

Hakeda, Yoshito S. *The Awakening of Faith.* New York: Columbia University Press, 1967.

Huang Po. *The Zen Teachings of Huang Po on the Transmission of Mind.* Trans. John Blofeld. New York: Grove Press, 1959.

Hume, David. *A Treatise of Human Nature.* Buffalo: Prometheus Books, 1992.

*The I Ching; or, Book of Changes.* Bollingen Series 19. Trans. Richard Wilhelm and Cary F. Baynes. New York: Pantheon, 1950.

Ibn Bājjah. *Rasāʾil falsafiyyah li-Abī Bakr Ibn Bājjah: Nuṣūs falsafiyyah ghayr manshūrah*, ed. Jamāl al-Dīn ʻAlawī. Bayrut: Dār Al-Thaqāfah, 1983.

Ibn Ezra, Abraham. *Ibn Ezra's Commentary on the Pentateuch*, trans. H. Norman Strickman and Arthur M. Silver. New York: Menorah Publishing, 1988.

Ibn al-Ṭufail. *Ḥayy Ben Yaqdhān; Roman philosophique d'ibn Thofail.* Ed. and trans. Leon Gauthier. Beirut: Imprimerie Catholique, 1936.

—. *Ibn Ṭufayl's Ḥayy Ibn Yaqzān.* Ed. and trans. Lenn Evan Goodman. Los Angeles: Gee Tee Bee, 1983.

*The Jewish Study Bible.* Ed. Adele Berlin, Marc Zvi Brettler, Michael A. Fishbane. New York: Oxford University Press, 2004.

Judah Halevi. *Kitāb al-radd waʾl-dalīl fīʾl-dīn al-dhalīl (al-Kitāb al-Khazari).* Ed. D. H. Baneth and Haggai Ben-Shammai. Jerusalem: Magnes Press, 1977.

—. *Kuzari.* Trans. Hartwig Hirschfeld. New York: Schocken, 1964.

—. *Sefer ha-Kuzari: maqor ve-targum.* Trans. Yosef Qafih. Kiryat Ono: Mekhon Mishnat ha-Rambam, 1996.

Kant, Immanuel. *The Conflict of the Faculties = Der Streit der Fakultaten.* Trans. Mary J. Gregor. New York: Abaris Books, 1979.

—. *Critique of Practical Reason and Other Writings in Moral Philosophy.* Chicago: University of Chicago Press, 1949.

—. *Foundations of the Metaphysics of Morals.* Trans. Lewis White Beck. Indianapolis: Bobbs-Merrill, 1969.

—. *Grounding for the Metaphysics of Morals; with On a Supposed Right to Lie Because of Philanthropic Concerns.* Trans. James W. Ellington. Indianapolis: Hackett, 1993.

Lao Zu. *The Daodejing of Laozi.* Trans. Philip J. Ivanhoe. New York: Seven Bridges Press, 2001.

—. *Tao Te Ching.* Trans. Stephen Addiss and Stanley Lombardo. Indianapolis: Hackett, 1993.

—. *The Tao Te Ching: The Classic Book of Integrity and the Way.* Trans. Victor Mair. New York: Bantam, 1990.

—. *Te-Tao Ching. A New Translation Based on the Recently Discovered Ma-Wang-Tui Texts.* Trans. Robert G. Henricks. New York: Ballantine Books, 1989.

—. *Tao Te Ching.* Trans. D. C. Lau. New York: Penguin, 1963.

—. *The Way of Lao Tzu (Tao-Te Ching).* Trans. Wing-Tsit Chan. Indianapolis: Bobbs-Merrill, 1963.

Leibniz, Gottfried Wilhelm. *Principles of Nature and Grace Based on Reason.* In *Philosophical Essays*, ed. Roger Ariew and Daniel Garber. Indianapolis: Hackett, 1989.

Maimonides, Moses. *Dalālat al-hāʾirīn.* Trans. Solomon Munk. Rev. I. Joel. Jerusalem, 1929.

—. *Ethical Writings of Maimonides.* Trans. Charles Butterworth with Raymond Weiss. New York: New York University Press, 1975.

—. *Guide of the Perplexed.* Trans. Shlomo Pines. Chicago: Chicago University Press, 1963.

—. *The Guide of the Perplexed.* Trans. Chaim Rabin. Indianapolis: Hackett, 1995.

—. *Haqdamot ha-Rambam la-Mishnah.* Trans. Yitzhaq Sheilat. Jerusalem: Maʾaliyot, 1992.

—. *A Maimonides Reader.* Ed. Isadore Twersky. New York: Behrman House, 1972.

—. *Maimonides' Treatise on Logic: Maqāla fī ṣināʾat al-manṭiq (Millot ha-higgayon).* Arabic and Hebrew edition and English translation by Israel Efros. New York: American Academy for Jewish Research, 1938.

—. *Mishnah ʿim perush rabbenu Moshe ben Maimon.* Jerusalem: Mossad Harav Kook, 1964–1968.

—. *Mishneh Torah: Ha-yad ha-ḥazakah.* Ed. Nachum L. Rabinovitch. Yerushalayim: Hotsaʾat Maʿaliyot, 1984.

—. *Sefer ha-mitsvot: makor ve-targum.* Trans. Yosef Qafih. Yerushalayim: Mosad Ha-Rav Kuk, 1971.

*The Majjhima nikāya.* Ed. J. Kashyap and Rahula Sankrityayana. London: Pali Texts Society, 1888.

—. *The Middle Length Discourses of the Buddha: A New Translation of the Majjhima nikāya.* Trans. Bikkhu Namoli and Bikkhu Bodhi. Boston: Wisdom Publications in association with the Barre Center for Buddhist Studies, 1995.

*The Milindapanho; Being Dialogues Between King Milinda and the Buddhist Sage Nāgasena.* Ed. V. Trenckner. London: Williams and Norgate, 1880.

Nāgārjuna. *The Fundamental Wisdom of the Middle Way: Nāgārjuna's Mūlamadhyamakakārikā.* Ed. and trans. Jay L. Garfield. New York: Oxford University Press, 1995.

—. *Mūlamadhyamakakarikā: The Philosophy of the Middle Way.* Trans. David J. Kalupahana. Albany: State University of New York Press, 1986.

Plato. *Five Dialogues: Euthyphro, Apology, Crito, Meno, Phaedo.* Ed. and trans. G. M. A. Grube. Indianapolis: Hackett, 1981.

—. *Gorgias.* Trans. Donald Zeyl. Indianapolis: Hackett, 1987.

—. *Phaedo.* Ed. C. J. Rowe. Cambridge Greek and Latin Classics. Cambridge: Cambridge University Press, 1993.

—. *Protagoras.* Trans. Stanley Lombardo and Karen Bell. Indianapolis: Hackett, 1992.

—. *Protagoras and Meno.* Trans. W. K. C. Guthrie. New York: Penguin Books, 1956.

——. *Republic*. Trans. Allen Bloom. New York: Basic Books, 1991.

——. *Republic*. Trans. G. M. A. Grube and C. D. C. Reeve. Indianapolis: Hackett, 1992.

——. *Plato's Republic*. Trans. Joe Sachs. Newburyport, Mass.: Focus Publishing, 2007.

——. *Timaeus*. Trans. Frances Cornford. New York: Prentice Hall, 1981.

——. *Timaeus*. Trans. Donald Zeyl. Indianapolis: Hackett, 2000.

Plotinus. *Enneads*. Ed. and trans. A. H. Armstrong. 7 vols. Cambridge, Mass.: Harvard University Press, 1984.

Proclus. *Commentary on Plato's Timaeus*. Trans. Harold Tarrant. Cambridge: Cambridge University Press, 2007.

Radhakrishnan, S. *The Principal Upaniṣads*. Atlantic Highlands, N.J.: Humanities Press, 1992.

Saʿadya Gaon. *The Book of Beliefs and Opinions*. Trans. Samuel Rosenblatt. New Haven: Yale University Press, 1976.

——. *The Book of Doctrines and Beliefs*. Trans. Alexander Altmann. Oxford: East and West Library, 1946. In *Three Jewish Philosophers: Philo, Saadya Gaon, Judah Halevi*. New York: Athenium, 1982.

——. *Kitāb al-mukhtār fīʾl-ʿamānāt waʾl-iʿtiqādāt*. Trans. Josef Qafih. Jerusalem: Sura Institute, 1972–1973.

*The Samyutta-nikāya of the sutta-pitaka*. Ed. L. N. Feer, Caroline A. F. Rhys Davids, and Pali Text Society. London: Pub. for the Pali Text Society by H. Frowde, 1884; Oxford: Pali Text Society, 1975–1998.

Śaṅkarācārya. *Shankara's Crest-Jewel of Discrimination (Viveka-Chudamani), with A Garland of Questions and Answers (Prasnottara Malika)*. Trans. Swami Prabhavananda and Christopher Isherwood. Hollywood, Calif.: Vedanta Press, 1971.

Śāntideva. *Śikṣāsamuccaya: A Compendium of Buddhist Doctrine*. Trans. Cecil Bendall and W. H. D. Rouse. Delhi: Motilal Banarsidass, 1981.

*Satapatha-Brāhmaṇa*. Trans. Julius Eggeling. 5 vols. Oxford: Clarendon Press, 1882–1900.

Simplicius. *On Aristotle's Physics 5*. Ancient Commentators on Aristotle. Trans. J. O. Urmson and Peter Lautner. Ithaca: Cornell University Press, 1997.

*The Sutta-nipata, Being a Collection of Some of Gotama Buddha's Dialogues and Discourses*. London: Pub. Ed. V. Fausboll for the Pali Text Society, by H. Frowde, 1885.

*Udāna*. Columbo, 1929.

*The Udāna*. Trans. Peter Masefield. Oxford: Pali Text Society, 1994.

*The Upanishads*. Trans. Eknath Easwaran. Tomalas, Calif.: Nilgiri Press, 1987.

*Upanishads: A New Translation*. Trans. Patrick Olivelle. Oxford: Oxford University Press, 1996.

*Thirteen Principal Upanishads*. Trans. Robert Ernest Hume. 1885. New York: Oxford University Press, 1885.

*The Word of the Buddha: An Outline of the Teaching of the Buddha in the Words of the Pali Canon*. Trans. Theo Nyanatiloka. Kandy: Buddhist Publication Society, 1968.

Zhuangzi. *Zhuangzi: The Essential Writings*. Ed. and trans. Brook Ziporyn. Cambridge, Mass.: Hackett, 2009.

## SECONDARY SOURCES


Abe, Masao. *Zen and Western Thought*. Honolulu: University of Hawaii Press, 1989.

Abrahamov, Binyamin. "Al-Ghazālī's Supreme Way to Know God." *Studia Islamica* 77 (1993): 141–168.

Ackrill, J. L. "Aristotle on Eudaimonia." In *Essays on Aristotle's Ethics*, ed. A. O. Rorty, 15–34. Berkeley: University of California Press, 1980.

Allison, Henry E. *Benedict de Spinoza: An Introduction*. New Haven: Yale University Press, 1987.

Altmann, Alexander. "Maimonides' Four Perfections." In *Essays in Jewish Intellectual History*, ed. Alexander Altmann, 65–76. Hanover, N.H.: Brandeis University Press, 1981.

—. "Maimonides on the Intellect and the Scope of Metaphysics." In *Von der Mittelalterlichen zur Modernen Aufklarung: Studien zur jüdischen Geistesgeschichte*, 60–129. Tubingen: Mohr, 1987.

Annas, Julia. *An Introduction to Plato's Republic*. New York: Oxford University Press, 1981.

Annas, Julia, and C. J. Rowe. *New Perspectives on Plato, Modern and Ancient*. Washington, D.C.: Center for Hellenic Studies, 2002.

Antonaccio, Maria, and William Schweiker. *Iris Murdoch and the Search for Human Goodness*. Chicago: University of Chicago Press, 1996.

Baxter, William H. "Situating the Language of the *Lao-Tzu:* The Probable Date of the *Tao-Te-Ching*." In *Lao-Tzu and the Tao-Te-Ching*, ed. Livia Kohn and Michael Lafargue, 231–253. Albany: State University of New York Press, 1998.

Benor, Ehud. "Models for Understanding Evil in *The Guide of the Perplexed*" [Hebrew]. *Iyyun* 34 (1985).

—. *Worship of the Heart: A Study of Maimonides' Philosophy of Religion*. SUNY Series in Jewish Philosophy. Albany: State University of New York Press, 1995.

Berger, Peter L. *The Sacred Canopy: Elements of a Sociological Theory of Religion*. Garden City: Doubleday, 1967.

Bergson, Henri, and Arthur Mitchell. *Creative Evolution*. New York: Modern Library, 1944.

Berman, Lawrence V. "The Ethical Views of Maimonides Within the Context of Islamicate Civilization." In *Perspectives on Maimonides*, ed. Joel L. Kraemer and Lawrence V. Berman, 13–32. London: Littman Library of Jewish Civilization, 1996.

—. "Maimonides on the Fall of Man." *AJS Review* 5 (1980): 1–15.

—. "The Political Interpretation of the Maxim: The Purpose of Philosophy is the Imitation of God." *Studia Islamica* 15 (1961): 53–61.

Berthrong, John H. *Concerning Creativity: A Comparison of Chu Hsi, Whitehead, and Neville*. SUNY Series in Religious Studies. Albany: State University of New York Press, 1998.

Bhattacharyya, Kalidas. "The Status of the Individual in Indian Metaphysics." In *The Indian Mind: Essentials of Indian Philosophy and Culture*, ed. Charles Alexander Moore, 299–319. Honolulu: East–West Center Press, 1967.

Birnbaum, Philip. *Daily Prayer Book: Ha-siddur ha-shalem*. New York: Hebrew Pub. Co., 1977.

Bond, George Doherty. *The Word of the Buddha: The Tipiṭaka and Its Interpretation in Theravada Buddhism*. Ceylon: Gunasena, 1982.

Brague, Rémi. *The Law of God: The Philosophical History of an Idea*. Chicago: University of Chicago Press, 2007.

Brereton, Joel. "*Tat Tvam Asi* in Context." *Zeitschrift der Deutschen Morgenländischen Gesellschaft* 136 (1986): 98–109.

——. "The Upanishads." In *Eastern Canons: Approaches to the Asian Classics*, ed. Wm. de Bary and I. Bloom, 115–135. New York: Columbia University Press, 1990.

Brettler, Marc Zvi. *How to Read the Bible*. Philadelphia: Jewish Publication Society, 2005.

Broadie, Sarah. *Ethics with Aristotle*. New York: Oxford University Press, 1991.

Brown, Francis, S. R. Driver, and Charles A. Briggs. *A Hebrew and English Lexicon of the Old Testament*. Oxford: Clarendon Press, 1966.

Brunschvicg, L. N. *Spinoza et ses contemporains*. Bibliothèque de philosophie contemporaine. Paris: F. Alcan, 1923.

Buber, Martin. "*Imitatio Dei*." In *Contemporary Jewish Ethics*, ed. Menachem Marc Kellner, 152–161. New York: Sanhedrin Press, 1978.

——. "The Tree of Knowledge (Genesis 3)." In *On the Bible*, ed. Martin Buber and Nahum Norbert Glatzer, 14–21. New York: Schocken, 1968.

Burkert, Walter. *Structure and History in Greek Mythology and Ritual*. Sather Classical Lectures 47. Berkeley: University of California Press, 1979.

Carman, John. "Rāmānuja." In *Encyclopedia of Religion*, 12:211–213.

——. *The Theology of Rāmānuja: An Essay in Interreligious Understanding*. New Haven: Yale University Press, 1974.

Cassuto, Umberto. *A Commentary on the Book of Genesis*. Jerusalem: Magnes Press, Hebrew University, 1961.

Chan, Wing-Tsit. *A Source Book in Chinese Philosophy*. Princeton: Princeton University Press, 1963.

Charles, David. "Aristotle on Well-Being and Contemplation." *Proceedings of the Aristotelian Society*, suppl. 73 (1999): 205–223.

Chödrön, Pema. "The Facts of Life." In *The Places That Scare You: A Guide to Fearlessness in Difficult Times*, 17–22. Boston: Shambhala, 2002.

——. *When Things Fall Apart: Heart Advice for Difficult Times*. Boston: Shambhala/Random House, 1997.

Cleary, Thomas F. *Entry Into the Inconceivable: An Introduction to Hua-Yen Buddhism*. Honolulu: University of Hawaii Press, 1983.

Cohen, S. Marc, Patricia Curd, and C. D. C. Reeve, eds. *Readings in Ancient Greek Philosophy: From Thales to Aristotle*. 2nd ed. Indianapolis: Hackett, 2000.

Collins, Steven. *Selfless Persons: Imagery and Thought in Theravada Buddhism*. Cambridge: Cambridge University Press, 1982.

Conze, Edward. *Buddhist Scriptures*. New York: Penguin, 1959.

——. *Buddhist Wisdom Books, containing the Diamond Sutra and the Heart Sutra*. New York: Harper and Row, 1972.

Cooper, John M. "Contemplation and Happiness: A Reconsideration." *Synthese* 72 (1987): 187–216.

——. *Reason and the Human Good in Aristotle*. Indianapolis: Hackett, 1986.

Cornford, Frances. *Plato's Cosmology: The Timaeus of Plato.* New York: Humanities Press, 1952.

Creel, H. G. "Confucius and the Struggle for Human Happiness." In *Chinese Thought: From Confucius to Mao Tse-tung*. Chicago: University of Chicago Press, 1953. Reprinted in *The Ways of Religion: An Introduction to the Major Traditions*, ed. Roger Eastman, 166–176. New York: Oxford University Press, 2000.

—. "On the Opening Words of the 'Lao-Tzu.'" *Journal of Chinese Philosophy* 10.4 (1983): 299–329.

Creel, H. G. and Pu-Hai Shen. *Shen Pu-Hai: A Chinese Political Philosopher of the Fourth Century b.c.* Chicago: University of Chicago Press, 1974.

Crisp, Roger. "Aristotle's Inclusivism." *Oxford Studies in Ancient Philosophy* 12 (1994): 111–136.

Curley, E. M. *Spinoza's Metaphysics: An Essay in Interpretation.* Cambridge, Mass.: Harvard University Press, 1969.

Danbekar, R. N. "*Vedānta.*" In *Encyclopedia of Religion*, 15:207–214.

Davidson, Herbert. "Alfarabi and Avicenna on Active Intellect." *Viator* 3 (1972): 109–178.

—. *Alfarabi, Avicenna, and Averroes on Intellect: Their Cosmologies, Theories of the Active Intellect, and Theories of Human Intellect.* New York: Oxford University Press, 1992.

—. "Maimonides' Secret Position on Creation." In *Studies in Medieval Jewish History and Literature*, ed. Isadore Twersky, 16–40. Cambridge, Mass.: Harvard University Press, 1979.

—. "The Study of Philosophy as a Religious Obligation." In *Religion in a Religious Age*, ed. S. D. Goitein, 53–68. Cambridge, Mass.: Association for Jewish Studies, 1974.

Davies, Paul. *The Mind of God: The Scientific Basis for a Rational World.* New York: Simon and Schuster, 1992.

De Bary, Wm. Theodore. *The Buddhist Tradition in India, China, and Japan.* New York: Vintage Books, 1972.

De Bary, Wm. Theodore, and Irene Bloom. *Approaches to the Asian Classics.* New York: Columbia University Press, 1990.

—. *Sources of Chinese Tradition.* New York: Columbia University Press, 1999.

Deutsch, Eliot. *Advaita Vedānta: A Philosophical Reconstruction.* Honolulu: East–West Center Press, 1969.

Deutsch, Eliot, and J. A. B. Van Buitenen. *A Source Book of Advaita Vedānta.* Honolulu: University Press of Hawaii, 1971.

Diesendruck, Zvi. "Samuel and Moses Ibn Tibbon on Maimonides' Theory of Providence." *Hebrew Union College Annual* 11 (1936): 341–356.

Dillon, John Myles. *The Middle Platonists: 80 b.c. to a.d. 220.* Ithaca: Cornell University Press, 1996.

Douglas, Mary. "The Abominations *of* Leviticus." In *Purity and Danger: An Analysis of Concepts of Pollution and Taboo*, 41–57. London: Routledge, 1984.

—. *Leviticus as Literature.* Oxford: Oxford University Press, 1999.

Dubs, Homer H. "Taoism." In *China*, ed. Harley Farnsworth Macnair, 266–289. Berkeley: University of California Press, 1946.

Dumoulin, Heinrich. "Ch'an." In *Encyclopedia of Religion*, 3:184–192.
—. *Zen Buddhism: A History*. 2 vols. New York: Macmillan, 1988.
Eastman, Roger, ed. *The Ways of Religion: An Introduction to the Major Traditions*. New York: Oxford University Press, 1999.
Easwaran, Eknath. *The End of Sorrow: The Bhagavad Gītā for Daily Living.* Tomales, Calif.: Nilgiri Press, 1993.
Eckel, M. David. *A Question of Nihilism: Bhāvaviveka's Response to the Fundamental Problems of Mādhyamika Philosophy*. Diss., Harvard University, 1980.
Edgerton, Franklin. *The Bhagavad Gītā*. Cambridge, Mass.: Harvard University Press, 1972.
—. "The Meaning of *Sankhya* and *Yoga*." *American Journal of Philology* 45 (1924): 1–45.
Eliade, Mircea. "Yoga." In *Encyclopedia of Religion*, 15:519–523.
Emerson, Ralph Waldo. *The Essential Writings of Ralph Waldo Emerson*. Ed. Brooks Atkinson. Modern Library Classics. New York: Modern Library, 2000.
*Encyclopedia of Chinese Philosophy*. New York: Routledge, 2003.
*Encyclopedia of Islam*. Leiden: Brill, 2007.
*Encyclopedia of Religion*. New York: Macmillan, 1987.
Ericksen, Trond Berg. *Bios Theoretikos: Notes on Aristotle's Nicomachean Ethics* X.6–8. Oslo: Universitetsforl, 1976.
Esnoul, A. M. "*Mokṣa*." In *Encyclopedia of Religion*, 10:28–29.
Falk, H. 1986. "Vedisch *Upaniṣad*." *ZDMG* 136 (1986): 80–97.
Fingarette, Herbert. *Confucius: The Secular as Sacred*. New York: Harper and Row, 1972.
Flood, Gavin D. *An Introduction to Hinduism*. New York: Cambridge University Press, 1996.
Frank, Daniel H., Oliver Leaman, and Charles Harry Manekin. *The Jewish Philosophy Reader*. London: Routledge, 2000.
Frankl, Viktor Emil. *Man's Search for Meaning: An Introduction to Logotherapy*. Boston: Beacon, 2006.
Frede, Dorothea. "Plato's Ethical Theory." *Stanford Encyclopedia of Philosophy*, 1997. Updated May 2009.
Fung Yu-Lan. *A Short History of Chinese Philosophy*. Trans. Derk Bodde. New York: Free Press, 1948.
Gadamer, Hans-Georg. *The Idea of the Good in Platonic-Aristotelian Philosophy*. Trans. P. Christopher Smith. New Haven: Yale University Press, 1986.
Gaiser, Konrad. "Plato's Enigmatic Lecture 'On the Good.'" *Phronesis* 25.1 (1980): 5–37.
Galston, Miriam. "The Theoretical and Practical Dimensions of Happiness as Portrayed in the Political Treatises of al-Fārābī." In *The Political Aspects of Islamic Philosophy: Essays in Honor of Muhsin S. Mahdi*, ed. Charles E. Butterworth, 95–151. Cambridge, Mass.: Center for Middle Eastern Studies, Harvard University, 1992.
Garrett, Don. *The Cambridge Companion to Spinoza*. New York: Cambridge University Press, 1996.
Gethin, Rupert. *The Foundations of Buddhism*. New York: Oxford University Press, 1998.
Gimaret, Daniel. "*Muʿtazila*." In *Encyclopedia of Islam*, 792–793.
Gimello, Robert. "Apophatic and Kataphatic Discourse in Mahayana: A Chinese View." In *Philosophy East and West* 26 (1976): 117–136.

Girdner, Scott. *Reasoning with Revelation: The Significance of the Qur'ānic Contextualization of Philosophy in al-Ghazālī's The Niche of Lights (Mishkāt al-anwār)*. Diss., Boston University, 2010.

Goldstein, Joseph. *Insight Meditation: The Practice of Freedom*. Boston: Shambhala, 1993.

Gomez, Luis O. "Buddhism: Buddhism in India." In *Encyclopedia of Religion*, 2:351–385.

Gonda, Jan. *Notes on Brahman*. Utrecht: Beyers, 1950.

Graham, A. C. *Disputers of the Tao: Philosophical Argument in Ancient China*. La Salle, Ill.: Open Court, 1989.

Griswold, Charles L. "Happiness, Tranquility, and Philosophy." In *In Pursuit of Happiness*, ed. Leroy Rouner, 13–32. Notre Dame: University of Notre Dame Press, 1995.

—. "Longing for the Best: Plato on Reconciliation with Imperfection." *Arion* 11.2 (2003): 101–136.

Guthrie, W. K. C. *A History of Greek Philosophy*. 6 vols. Cambridge: Cambridge University Press, 1962–1981.

Guttmann, Julius. *Ha-filosofya shel ha-yahadut*. Jerusalem: Mossad Bialik, 1953.

—. *Philosophies of Judaism: The History of Jewish Philosophy from Biblical Times to Franz Rosenzweig*. New York: Holt, 1964.

—. "Torat ha-Elohim shel ha-Rambam." In *Essays in Honour of the Very Rev. Dr. J. H. Hertz, Chief Rabbi of the United Hebrew Congregations of the British Empire, on the Occasion of His Seventieth Birthday*, ed. Isidore Epstein, Joseph H. Hertz, Ephraim Levine, and Cecil Roth, 53–69. London: E. Goldston, 1942.

Hadot, Pierre. *Philosophy as a Way of Life: Spiritual Exercises from Socrates to Foucault*. Trans. Arnold Ira Davidson. Malden, Mass.: Blackwell, 1995.

Hanh, Thich Nhat. *Zen Keys: A Guide to Zen Practice*. New York: Doubleday, 1995.

Hansen, Chad. *A Daoist Theory of Chinese Thought: A Philosophical Interpretation*. New York: Oxford University Press, 1992.

Hardie, W. F. R. "The Final Good in Aristotle's Ethics." *Philosophy* 40, no. 154 (1965): 277–295.

Hare, R. M. *Plato*. New York: Oxford University Press, 1982.

Hartman, David. *Maimonides: Torah and Philosophic Quest*. Philadelphia: Jewish Publication Society of America, 1976.

Hartshorne, Charles. "Panpsychism." In *A History of Philosophical Systems*, ed. Vergilius Ture Anselm Ferm, 442–453. New York: Philosophical Library, 1950.

Hartshorne, Charles, and Creighton Peden. *Whitehead's View of Reality*. New York: Pilgrim, 1981.

Harvey, Steven. "Avicenna and Maimonides on Prayer and Intellectual Worship." Forthcoming in *Proceedings* of the Workshop "Exchange and Transmission Across Cultural Boundaries: Philosophy, Mysticism and Science Across the Mediterranean World" at the Institute for Advanced Studies at the Hebrew University of Jerusalem, 2005.

—. "Maimonides in the Sultan's Palace." In *Perspectives on Maimonides: Philosophical and Historical Studies*, ed. Joel L. Kraemer and Lawrence V. Berman, 47–75. London: Littman Library of Jewish Civilization, , 1996.

Harvey, Warren Zev. "Ethics and Meta-Ethics, Aesthetics and Meta-Aesthetiics in Maimonides." In *Maimonides and Philosophy: Papers Presented at the Sixth Jerusalem Philosophical Encounter, May*, ed. Shlomo Pines and Yirmiyahu Yovel, 131–138. Dordrecht: Nijhoff, 1985.

—. "Holiness: A Command to *Imitatio Dei*." *Tradition* 16 (1977): 7–28.

—. "Maimonides' First Commandment, Physics, and Doubt." In *Hazon Nahum: Studies in Jewish Law, Thought, and History Presented to Dr. Norman Lamm on the Occasion of His Seventieth Birthday*, ed. Norman Lamm, Yaakov Elman, and Jeffrey S. Gurock, 149–162. New York: Yeshiva University Press, 1997.

—. "Maimonides on Human Perfection, Awe, and Politics." In *the Thought of Moses Maimonides: Philosophical and Legal Studies*, ed. Ira Robinson, Lawrence Kaplan, and Julien Bauer, 1–15. Lewiston, N.Y: Edwin Mellen Press, 1990.

—. "Maimonides and Spinoza on Knowledge of Good and Evil" [Hebrew]. *Iyyun* 28 (1978): 165–185.

—. "Maimonides and Spinoza on Knowledge of Good and Evil." Trans. Yoel Lerner. In *Jewish Intellectual History in the Middle Ages*, ed. Joseph Dan, 131–146. Westport, Conn.: Praeger, 1994.

—. "Political Philosophy and *Halakhah* in Maimonides" [Hebrew]. *Iyyun* 29 (1980): 198–212.

—. "Political Philosophy and *Halakhah* in Maimonides." Trans. Sam Friedman. In *Jewish Intellectual History In the Middle Ages*, ed. Joseph Dan, 47–64. Westport, Conn.: Praeger, 1994.

—. "A Third Approach to Maimonides' Cosmogony-Prophetology Puzzle." *Harvard Theological Review* 74.3 (1981): 287–301.

Harzer, Edeltraud. "*Sāṃkhya*." In *Encyclopedia of Religion*, 13:47–51.

Hava Lazarus-Yafe, "Symbolism of Light in the Writings of Al-Ghazālī," in *Studies in Al-Ghazzālī*, 264–348. Jerusalem: Magnes Press, Hebrew University, 1975.

Hawking, Stephen. *A Brief History of Time: From the Big Bang to Black Holes*. Toronto: Bantam Books, 1996.

Heesterman, Jan. "Brāhmaṇas and Āraṇyakas." In *Encyclopedia of Religion*, 2:296–298.

—. "Brahman." In *Encyclopedia of Religion*, 2:294–296.

—. *The Inner Conflict of Tradition*. Chicago: University of Chicago Press, 1985.

Heidegger, Martin. *An Introduction to Metaphysics*. New Haven: Yale University Press. 1959.

Heine, Steven. *Opening a Mountain: Kōans of the Zen Masters*. New York: Oxford University Press, 2001.

—. *The Zen Canon*. New York: Oxford University Press, 2004.

Henricks, Robert G. "Re-exploring the Analogy of the *Dao* and the Field." In *Religious and Philosophical Aspects of the Laozi*, ed. Mark Csikszentmihalyi and P. J. Ivanhoe, 161–174. Albany: State University of New York Press, 1999.

Hiltebeitel, Alf. "Hinduism." In *Encyclopedia of Religion*, 6:336–360.

Hopkins, Thomas J. *The Hindu Religious Tradition*. Belmont, Calif.: Wadsworth, 1971.

Hosinski, Thomas E. *Stubborn Fact and Creative Advance: An Introduction to the Metaphysics of Alfred North Whitehead*. Lanham, Md.: Rowman and Littlefield, 1993.

Humphreys, Christmas. *The Wisdom of Buddhism*. New York: Random House, 1961.

Hyman, Arthur. "Maimonides on Religious Language." In *Perspectives on Maimonides: Philosophical and Historical Studies*, ed. Joel L. Kraemer and Lawrence V. Berman, 175–191. London: Littman Library of Jewish Civilization, 1996.

Ingalls, Daniel H. H. "Dharma and Mokṣa." *Philosophy East and West* 7 (1957): 41–48.

Ivanhoe, Philip. "The Concept of *de* ('Virtue') in the Laozi." In *Religious and Philosophical Aspects of the Laozi*, ed. Mark Csikszentmihalyi and P. J. Ivanhoe, 239–257. Albany: State University of New York Press, 1999.

Ivanhoe, P. J., and Bryan W. Van Norden. *Readings in Classical Chinese Philosophy*. New York: Seven Bridges Press, 2001.

Ivry, Alfred. "Islamic and Greek Influences on Maimonides' Philosophy." In *Maimonides and Philosophy: Papers Presented at the Sixth Jerusalem Philosophical Encounter*, ed. Shlomo Pines and Yirmiyahu Yovel, 139–156. Dordrecht: Nijhoff, 1985.

——. "Maimonides and Neoplatonism: Challenge and Response." In *Neoplatonism and Jewish Thought*, ed. Lenn Evan Goodman, 137–156. Albany: State University of New York Press, 1992.

——. "Neoplatonic Currents in Maimonides' Thought." In *Perspectives on Maimonides*, ed. Joel Kraemer, 115–140. London: Littauer, 1996.

——. "Providence, Divine Omniscience, and Possibility: The Case of Maimonides." In *Divine Omniscience and Omnipotence in Medieval Philosophy*, ed. Tamar Rudavsky, 143–159. Dordrecht, Holland; Boston; Hingham, Ma: D. Reidel Pub. Co, 1985.

Jacob, G. A. *A Concordance to the Principal Upaniṣads and the Bhagavadgītā*. Delhi: Motilal Banarsidass, 1971.

Jaini, Padmanabh S. "Karma and the Problem of Rebirth in Jainism." In *Karma and Rebirth in Classical Indian Traditions*, ed. O'Flaherty, 217–240. Berkeley: University of California Press, 1980.

Johnson, Monte Ransome. *Aristotle on Teleology*. Oxford: Oxford University Press, 2005.

Kaku, Michio. *Hyperspace: A Scientific Odyssey Through Parallel Universes, Time Warps, and the Tenth Dimension*. New York: Oxford University Press, 1994.

Kaltenmark, Max, *Lao Tzu and Taoism*. Trans. Roger Greaves. Stanford: Stanford University Press, 1969.

Kaplan, Lawrence. "I Sleep, but My Heart Waketh: Maimonides' Conception of Human Perfection." In *The Thought of Moses Maimonides: Philosophical and Legal Studies*, ed. Ira Robinson, Lawrence Kaplan, and Julien Bauer, 130–166. Lewiston, N.Y.: Edwin Mellen Press, 1990.

——. "Maimonides on the Miraculous Element in Prophecy." *Harvard Theological Review* 70.4 (1977): 233–256.

Kasher, Hannah. "*Talmud Torah* as Means of Apprehending God in Maimonides' Teachings" [Hebrew]. *Jerusalem Studies in Jewish Thought* 5 (1986): 72–83.

Kasulis, Thomas. "*Nirvāṇa*." In *Encyclopedia of Religion*, 10:448–456.

Kavka, Martin. *Jewish Messianism and the History of Philosophy*. New York: Cambridge University Press, 2004.

Kellner, Menachem. "Is Maimonides' Ideal Person Austerely Rationalist?" *American Catholic Philosophical Quarterly: Journal of the American Catholic Philosophical Association* 76.1 (2002): 125.

——. *Maimonides on Human Perfection*. Brown Judaic Studies 202. Atlanta: Scholars Press, 1990.

——."Spiritual Life." In *The Cambridge Companion to Maimonides*, ed. Kenneth Seeskin, 273–299. New York: Cambridge University Press, 2005.

Kenny, Anthony John Patrick. *Aristotle on the Perfect Life*. Oxford: Oxford University Press, 1992.

Kessler, Gary E. *Eastern Ways of Being Religious: An Anthology*. Mountain View, Calif.: Mayfield, 2000.

Keyt, David. "Intellectualism in Aristotle." In *Essays in Ancient Greek Philosophy*, vol. 2, ed. John Peter Anton, Anthony Preus, and Philosophy Society for Ancient Greek, 364–387. Albany: State University of New York Press, 1978.

King, Richard. *Indian Philosophy: An Introduction to Hindu and Buddhist Thought*. Washington, D.C.: Georgetown University Press, 2007.

King, Sallie B. *Buddha Nature*. Albany: State University of New York Press, 1991.

Kinsley, David. *Hinduism: A Cultural Perspective*. 2nd ed. Englewood Cliffs, N.J.: Prentice Hall, 1993.

Klawans, Jonathan. *Impurity and Sin in Ancient Judaism*. New York: Oxford University Press, 2000.

——. *Purity, Sacrifice, and the Temple: Symbolism and Supersessionism in the Study of Ancient Judaism*. Oxford: Oxford University Press, 2006.

Klein, Jacob. *Greek Mathematical Thought and the Origin of Algebra*. Trans. Eva Brann. Cambridge, Mass.: MIT Press, 1968.

Klein-Braslavy, Sara. "The Creation of the World and Maimonides' Interpretation of Gen. I–V." In *Maimonides and Philosophy: Papers Presented at the Sixth Jerusalem Philosophical Encounter, May*, ed. Shlomo Pines and Yirmiyahu Yovel, 65–71. Dordrecht: Nijhoff, 1985.

——. *Maimonides' Interpretation of the Adam Stories in Genesis* (Hebrew). Jerusalem: Reuben Mass, 1986.

——. *Maimonides' Interpretation of the Story of Creation* (Hebrew). Jerusalem: Reuben Mass, 1978.

Klostermaier, Klaus K. *A Short Introduction to Hinduism*. New York: Oxford University Press, 1998.

——. *A Survey of Hinduism*. Albany: State University of New York Press, 1989.

Knohl, Israel. *The Divine Symphony: The Bible's Many Voices*. Philadelphia: Jewish Publication Society, 2003.

Kogan, Barry. "What Can We Know and When Can We Know It? Maimonides on the Active Intelligence and Human Cognition." In *Moses Maimonides and His Time*, ed. Eric Ormsby, 121–137. Washington, D.C.: Catholic University of America, 1989.

Kogen, Muzuno. "*Karman*, Buddhist Concepts." In *Encyclopedia of Religion*, 8:266–268.

Kraut, Richard. *The Cambridge Companion to Plato*. Cambridge: Cambridge University Press, 1992.

Kreisel, Howard. *Maimonides' Political Thought: Studies in Ethics, Law, and the Human Ideal*. Albany: State University of New York Press, 1999.

Kugel, James. "Two Introductions to Midrash." *Prooftexts: A Journal of Jewish Literary History* 3.2 (1983): 131–157.

Lai, Karyn L. *An Introduction to Chinese Philosophy*. New York: Cambridge University Press, 2008.

Lane, Edward William. *Arabic-English Lexicon*. Cambridge: Islamic Texts Society, 1863; repr. 1984.

Lasker, Daniel. "Love of God and Knowledge of God in Maimonides' Philosophy." In *Écriture et réécriture des textes philosophiques médiévaux: Volume d'hommage offert à Colette Sirat*, ed. Jacqueline Hamesse and Olga Weijers, 329–346. Turnhout: Brepols, 2006.

Lear, Jonathan. *Aristotle: The Desire to Understand*. Cambridge: Cambridge University Press, 1988.

Leibniz, Gottfried Wilhelm. "Principles of Nature and Grace Based on Reason." In *Philosophical Essays*, ed. Roger Ariew and Daniel Garber, 206–212. Indianapolis: Hackett, 1989.

Lerner, Ralph, and Muhsin Mahdi. *Medieval Political Philosophy: A Sourcebook*. New York: Free Press of Glencoe, 1963.

Levenson, Jon D. *Creation and the Persistence of Evil: The Jewish Drama of Divine Omnipotence*. San Francisco: Harper and Row, 1988.

—. *Sinai and Zion: An Entry Into the Jewish Bible*. Minneapolis: Winston Press, 1985.

Lipner, Julius. "The Self of Being and the Being of Self: Śaṃkara on 'That You Are' (*tat tvam asi*)." In *New Perspectives on Advaita Vedanta: Essays in Commemoration of Professor Richard de Smet, SJ*, ed. Bradley Malkovsky, 51–69. Leiden: Brill, 2000.

Liu, JeeLoo. *An Introduction to Chinese Philosophy: From Ancient Philosophy to Chinese Buddhism*. Malden, Mass.: Blackwell, 2006.

Liu Xioagan. "An Inquiry Into the Core Value of Laozi's Philosophy." In *Religious and Philosophical Aspects of the Laozi*, ed. Mark Csikszentmihalyi and Philip J. Ivanhoe, 211–237. Albany: State University of New York Press, 1999.

—. "Naturalness (*tzu-jan*), the Core Value in Taoism: Its Ancient Meaning and Its Significance Today." In *Lao-Tzu and the Tao-Te-Ching*, ed. Livia Kohn and Michael Lafargue, 211–228. Albany: State University of New York Press, 1998.

Lobel, Diana. *Between Mysticism and Philosophy: Sufi Language of Religious Experience in Judah Ha-Levi's Kuzari*. Albany: State University of New York Press, 2000.

—. "'Silence Is Praise to You': Maimonides on Negative Theology, Looseness of Expression, and Religious Experience." *American Catholic Philosophical Quarterly: Journal of the American Catholic Philosophical Association* 76.1 (2002): 25–49.

—. *A Sufi-Jewish Dialogue: Philosophy and Mysticism in Baḥya Ibn Paqūda's* Duties of the Heart. Philadelphia: University of Pennsylvania Press, 2007.

Lopez, Donald S. *Buddhism in Practice*. Princeton: Princeton University Press, 1995.

Lorenzen, "Śaṅkara." In *Encyclopedia of Religion*, 13:64–65.

Lovejoy, Arthur O. *The Great Chain of Being: A Study of the History of an Idea*. The William James Lectures Delivered at Harvard University, 1933. Cambridge, Mass.: Harvard University Press, 1964.

Lusthaus, Dan. *Buddhist Phenomenology: A Philosophical Investigation of Yogācāra Buddhism and the Ch'eng Wei-Shih Lun*. London: Routledge Curzon, 2002.

Macintyre, Alasdair C. *After Virtue: A Study in Moral Theory*. Notre Dame: University of Notre Dame Press, 1984.

Mahadevan, T. M. P. "Social, Ethical, and Spiritual Values In Indian Philosophy." In *The Indian Mind: Essentials of Indian Philosophy and Culture*, ed. Conference East–West Philosophers and Charles Alexander Moore, 152–171. Honolulu: East–West Center Press, 1967.

Mahoney, William. "*Dharma:* Hindu *Dharma*." In *Encyclopedia of Religion*, 4:329–332.

—. "Enlightenment." In *Encyclopedia of Religion*, 5:107–109.

—. "*Karman:* Hindu and Jain Concepts." In *Encyclopedia of Religion,* 8:261–266.

McDermott, James P. "Karma and Rebirth in Early Buddhism." In *Karma and Rebirth in Classical Indian Traditions*, ed. O'Flaherty, 165–192.

McRae, John. *Seeing Through Zen*. Berkeley: University of California Press, 2003.

Menn, Stephen. "Aristotle and Plato on God as *Nous* and as the Good." *Review of Metaphysics* 45.3 (1992): 543–573.

—. *Plato on God as* Nous. Carbondale: Southern Illinois University Press, 1995.

Michael, Thomas. "Confucius and Laozi: Two Visions of the Dao of Antiquity." In *Metaphilosophy and Chinese Thought: Interpreting David Hall*, ed. Ewing Chinn and Henry Rosemont, 169–178. New York: Global Scholarly Publications, 2005.

—. *The Pristine Dao: Metaphysics in Early Daoist Discourse*. Albany: State University of New York Press, 2005.

Milgrom, Jacob. *The JPS Torah Commentary: Leviticus*. Philadelphia: Jewish Publication Society, 1989.

—. *The JPS Torah Commentary: Numbers.* Philadelphia: Jewish Publication Society, 1989.

—. *Leviticus: A Book of Ritual and Ethics*. Continental Commentaries. Minneapolis: Fortress Press, 2004.

—. *Leviticus 1-16: A New Translation with Introduction and Commentary*. New York: Doubleday, 1991.

Miller, Jeanine. "The Hymn of Creation: A Philosophical Interpretation." In *The Essence of Yoga: Essays on the Development of Yogic Philosophy from the Vedas to Modern Times*, ed. Georg Feuerstein and Jeanine Miller, 64–85. Rochester, Vt.: Inner Traditions, 1998.

Miura, Isshū, and Ruth Fuller Sasaki. *Zen Dust: The History of the Koan and Koan Study in Rinzai (Lin-Chi) Zen*. Kyoto: First Zen Institute of America in Japan, 1966. Excerpt in *The Ways of Religion*, ed. Roger Eastman, 139–144.

Murdoch, Iris. *The Fire and the Sun: Why Plato Banished the Artists*. Oxford: Clarendon Press, 1977.

—. *Metaphysics as a Guide to Morals*. New York: Penguin, 1993.

—. *The Sovereignty of God*. London: Routledge and Kegan Paul, 1974.

Murdoch, Iris, and Jiddu Krishnamurti. "Talk." HYPERLINK "http://www.youtube.com/watch?v=_-9fsZW_OZI" http://www.youtube.com/watch?v=_-9fsZW_OZI. Accessed Oct. 17, 2010.

Nadler, Steven. *Spinoza's Ethics: An Introduction*. Cambridge: Cambridge University Press, 2006.

Nagel, Thomas. "Aristotle on *Eudaimonia*." In *Essays in Aristotle's Ethics*, ed. Amelie O. Rorty, 7–14. Berkeley: University of California Press, 1980.

—. *Mortal Questions*. Cambridge: Cambridge University Press, 1979.

Nettleship, Richard Lewis. *Lectures on the Republic of Plato*. Ed. Godfrey Rathbone Benson Charnwood. London: Macmillan and Co., 1929.

Neville, Robert. "From Nothing to Being: The Notion of Creation in Chinese and Western Thought." *Philosophy East and West* 30.1 (1980): 21–34.

—. "Whitehead on the One and the Many." *Southern Journal of Philosophy* 7 (1969–1970): 387–393.

Niditch, Susan. *Chaos to Cosmos: Studies in Biblical Patterns of Creation*. Chico, Calif.: Scholars Press, 1985.

Nightingale, Andrea Wilson. *Spectacles of Truth in Classical Greek Philosophy: Theōria in Its Cultural Context*. New York: Cambridge University Press, 2004.

Nivison, David. *The Ways of Confucianism: Investigations in Chinese Philosophy*. Ed, with an introduction by Bryan Van Norden. Chicago: Open Court, 1996.

Norman, Richard. "Aristotle's Philosopher-God." *Phronesis* 14.1 (1969): 63–74.

Novak, Philip. *The World's Wisdom: Sacred Texts of the World's Religions*. San Francisco: HarperSanFrancisco, 1994.

Nussbaum, Martha Craven. *The Fragility of Goodness: Luck and Ethics in Greek Tragedy and Philosophy*. New York: Cambridge University Press, 1986.

O'Flaherty, Wendy Doniger, ed. *Karma and Rebirth in Classical Indian Traditions*. Berkeley: University of California Press, 1980.

—. "Karma and Rebirth in the Vedas and Purāṇas." In *Karma and Rebirth in Classical Indian Traditions*, ed. O'Flaherty, 3–37. Berkeley: University of California Press, 1980.

Oldenberg, Hermann. *Kleine Schriften*. Wiesbaden: Steiner, 1967.

—. *Die Religion des Veda*. Stuttgart, 1917.

Olson, Carl. *Original Buddhist Sources: A Reader*. New Brunswick, N.J.: Rutgers University Press, 2005.

O'Meara, Dominic J. *Plotinus: An Introduction to the* Enneads. Oxford: Oxford University Press, 1995.

Ormsby, Eric. "The Taste of Truth: The Structure of Experience in al-Ghazālī's *al-Munqidh min al-dalāl*." In *Islamic Studies Presented to Charles J. Adams*, ed. Wael B. Hallaq and Donald P. Little, 133–152. Leiden: Brill, 1991.

Patton, Kimberley C. *Religion of the Gods: Ritual, Paradox, and Reflexivity*. New York: Oxford University Press, 2009.

Penner, Terry. "Socrates and the Early Dialogues." In *The Cambridge Companion to Plato*, ed. Richard Kraut, 121–169. Cambridge: Cambridge University Press, 1992.

Pines, Shlomo. "The Limitations of Human Knowledge According to Al-Farabi, ibn Bajja, and Maimonides." In *Studies in Medieval Jewish History and Literature,* ed. Isadore Twersky and Jay Michael Harris, 82–109. Cambridge, Mass.: Harvard University Press, 1979.

—. "Maimonides' Halachic Works and the *Guide of the Perplexed.*" In *Maimonides and Philosophy: Papers Presented at the Sixth Jerusalem Philosophical Encounter, May,* ed. Shlomo Pines and Yirmiyahu Yovel, 1–14. Dordrecht: Nijhoff, 1985.

—. "Truth and Falsehood Versus Good and Evil: A Study in Jewish and General Philosophy in Connection with *Guide of the Perplexed* I:2." In *Studies in Maimonides,* ed. Isadore Twersky, 195–157. Cambridge: Harvard University Press, 199.

Queen, Christopher S., and Sallie B. King. *Engaged Buddhism: Buddhist Liberation Movements in Asia.* Albany: State University of New York Press, 1996.

Radhakrishnan, S., and Charles Alexander Moore. *A Source Book in Indian Philosophy.* Princeton: Princeton University Press, 1957.

Raffel, Charles. "Providence as Consequent Upon the Intellect: Maimonides' Theory on Providence." *Association for Jewish Studies Review* 12 (1987): 25–71.

Rahman, Fazlur. "Ibn Sīnā's Theory of the God-World Relationship." In *God and Creation: An Ecumenical Symposium,* ed. David B. Burrell and Bernard McGinn, 38–56. Notre Dame: University of Notre Dame Press, 1987.

Rahula, Walpola. *What the Buddha Taught.* New York: Grove Press, 1974.

Raveh, Daniel. "*Ayam aham asmīti:* Self-Consciousness and Identity in the Eighth Chapter of the *Chāndogya Upaniṣad* vs. Śaṅkara's *Bhaṣya.*" *Journal of Indian Philosophy* (April 2008) 36:319–333. Published online Dec. 7, 2007.

Ravitzky, Aviezer. "Samuel Ibn Tibbon and the Esoteric Character of the Guide of the Perplexed." *Association for Jewish Studies Review* 6 (1981): 87–123.

Rawls, John. *A Theory of Justice.* Cambridge, Mass.: Belknap Press of Harvard University Press, 1971.

Reeve, C. D. C. *Practices of Reason: Aristotle's Nicomachean Ethics.* New York: Oxford University Press, 1992.

Renou, Louis. "'Connection' en védique; 'cause' en buddhique." In *Dr. C. Kunhan Presentation Volume,* 55–60. Madras: Adyar Library, 1946.

Renou, Louis, and Liliane Silburn. "Sur la notion de 'Brahman.'" Journal Asiatique 237 (1949): 7–46. Reprinted in *L'Inde fondamentale: Études d'indianisme réunies et présentées par Charles Malamoud,* 83–116. Paris: Hermann, 1978.

Reps, Paul. *Zen Flesh, Zen Bones: A Collection of Zen and pre-Zen Writings.* Garden City, N.Y.: Anchor/Doubleday, 1961.

Richardson Lear, Gabriel. *Happy Lives and the Highest Good: An Essay on Aristotle's Nicomachean Ethics.* Princeton: Princeton University Press, 2004.

Robinet, Isadore. "The Diverse Interpretations of the *Laozi.*" In *Religious and Philosophical Aspects of the Laozi,* ed. Mark Csikszentmihalyi and P. J. Ivanhoe, 127–259. Albany: State University of New York Press, 1999.

Roochnik, David. "What Is *Theōria? Nicomachean Ethics* Book 10.7–8." *Classical Philology* 104 (2009): 69–81.

Rosen, Stanley. *Plato's Sophist: The Drama of Original and Image*. New Haven: Yale University Press, 1983.

Ross, W. D. *Plato's Theory of Ideas*. Oxford: Clarendon Press, 1953.

Rorty, Amelie Oksenberg. "The Place of Contemplation in Aristotle's *Nicomachean Ethics*." In *Essays on Aristotle's Ethics*, ed. Amelie Rorty, 377–394. Berkeley: University of California Press, 1980.

Rouner, Leroy S. *In Pursuit of Happiness*. Notre Dame: University of Notre Dame Press, 1995.

Sacks, Oliver W. *The Man Who Mistook His Wife for a Hat and Other Clinical Tales*. New York: Summit Books, 1985.

Samuelson, Norbert. *Judaism and the Doctrine of Creation*. New York: Cambridge University Press, 1994.

—. "Maimonides' Doctrine of Creation." *Harvard Theological Review* 84.3 (1991): 249–271.

Sandel, Michael J. *Liberalism and the Limits of Justice*. New York: Cambridge University Press, 1982.

Santas, Gerasimos. "Aristotle's Criticism of Plato's Form of the Good: Ethics Without Metaphysics?" *Philosophical Papers* 18.2 (1989): 137–160.

—. "The Form of the Good in Plato's *Republic*." In *Essays in Ancient Philosophy*, vol. 2, ed. John Peter Anton, Anthony Preus, and Philosophy Society for Ancient Greek, 232–263. Albany: State University of New York Press, 1983.

—. "The Socratic Paradoxes." *Journal of Philosophy*, Oct. 10 (1963).

Sarna, Nahum M. *The JPS Torah Commentary: Genesis*. Philadelphia: Jewish Publication Society, 1989.

—. *Understanding Genesis*. Heritage of Biblical Israel, vol. 1. New York: Jewish Theological Seminary of America, 1966.

Sayre, Kenneth. *Plato's Late Ontology: A Riddle Resolved*. Princeton: Princeton University Press, 1983.

—. *Plato's Literary Garden: How to Read a Platonic Dialogue*. Notre Dame: University of Notre Dame Press, 1995.

Scharfstein, Ben-Ami. *Ineffability: The Failure of Words in Philosophy and Religion*. Albany: State University of New York Press, 1993.

Schechter, Solomon. *Aspects of Rabbinic Theology*. Major Concepts of the Talmud. New York: Schocken, 1961.

Schwartz, Benjamin. "The Thought of the *Tao-te-ching*." In *Religious and Philosophical Aspects of the Laozi*, ed. Mark Csikszentmihalyi and P. J. Ivanhoe, 189–209. Albany: State University of New York Press, 1998.

Schwarzschild, Steven. "Moral Radicalism and 'Middlingness' in the Ethics of Maimonides." In *The Pursuit of the Ideal: Jewish Writings of Steven Schwartschild*, ed. Menachem Kellner. Albany: State University of New York Press, 1990.

Schwarzschild, Steven, and Menachem Marc Kellner. *The Pursuit of the Ideal: Jewish Writings of Steven Schwarzschild*. SUNY Series in Jewish Philosophy. Albany: State University of New York Press, 1990.

Scott, Dominic. "Aristotle on Well-Being and Intellectual Contemplation: Dominic Scott." *Supplement to the Proceedings of the Aristotelian Society* 73.1 (1999): 225–242.

Seeskin, Kenneth. *Dialogue and Discovery: A Study in Socratic Method*. Albany: State University of New York Press, 1987.

—. *Maimonides: A Guide for Today's Perplexed*. West Orange, N.J.: Behrman House, 1991.

—. *Maimonides on the Origin of the World*. New York: Cambridge University Press, 2005.

—. "The Positive Contribution of Negative Theology." In *Jewish Philosophy in a Secular Age*, 31–69. Albany: State University of New York Press, 1990.

—. "Sanctity and Silence: The Religious Significance of Maimonides' Negative Theology." *American Catholic Philosophical Quarterly* 76 (2002): 7–24.

—. *Searching for a Distant God: The Legacy of Maimonides*. New York: Oxford University Press, 2000.

Shapiro, David S. "The Doctrine of the Image of God and *Imitatio Dei*." In *Contemporary Jewish Ethics*, ed. Menachem Marc Kellner, 127–151. New York: Sanhedrin Press, 1978.

Shatz, David. "Maimonides' Moral Theory." In *The Cambridge Companion to Maimonides*, ed. Kenneth Seeskin, 167–192. New York: Cambridge University Press, 2005.

—. "Worship, Corporeality, and Human Perfection: A Reading of *Guide* III:51–54." In *The Thought of Moses Maimonides*, ed. Ira Rosenbloom, Lawrence Kaplan, and Julien Bauer, 77–129. Lewiston, N.Y.: Edwin Mellen Press, 1990.

Shehadi, Fadlou. *Ghazālī's Unique Unknowable God: A Philosophical Critical Analysis of Some of the Problems Raised by Ghazālī's View of God as Utterly Unique and Unknowable*. Leiden: Brill, 1964.

Smith, Huston. "Intimations of Immortality: Three Case Studies." Ingersoll Lectures on Immortality. *Harvard Divinity Bulletin* (winter 2001–2002): 12–15.

Snellgrove, David. "Celestial Buddhas and Bodhisattvas." In *Encyclopedia of Religion*, 3:134–143.

Soloveitchik, Joseph Dov. *The Lonely Man of Faith*. New York: Doubleday, 1992.

Sorabji, Richard. *Time, Creation, and the Continuum: Theories in Antiquity and the Early Middle Ages*. Ithaca: Cornell University Press, 1983.

Sprigge, Timothy L. S. *The God of Metaphysics*. Oxford: Clarendon Press, 2006.

Stern, Josef. "Logical Syntax as a Key to a Secret of the *Guide of the Perplexed*." *Iyyun* 38.5 (1989).

—. "Maimonides on Language and the Science of Language." In *Maimonides and the Sciences*, ed. R. S. Cohen and Hillel Levine, 173–226. Dordrecht: Kluwer, 2000.

—. "The Idea of a *Hoq* in Maimonides' Explanation of the Law." In *Maimonides and Philosophy: Papers Presented at the Sixth Jerusalem Philosophical Encounter, May*, ed. Shlomo Pines and Yirmiyahu Yovel. Dordrecht: Nijhoff, 1985.

Streng, Frederick. *Emptiness: A Study in Religious Meaning*. Nashville: Abingdon, 1967.

Suzuki, D. T., and William Barrett. *Zen Buddhism: Selected Writings of D. T. Suzuki*. Garden City, N.Y.: Doubleday, 1956.

Swartz, Merlin L. *A Medieval Critique of Anthropomorphism: Ibn Al-Jawzī's Kitāb Akhbār aṣ-ṣifāt*. Islamic Philosophy, Theology, and Science 46. Leiden: Brill, 2002.

Takakusu, Junjiro. "Buddhism as a Philosophy of 'Thusness.'" In *The Indian Mind: Essentials of Indian Philosophy and Culture*, ed. Charles Alexander Moore,86–117. Honolulu: East–West Center Press, 1967.

Taylor, Charles. *Sources of the Self: The Making of the Modern Identity*. Cambridge, Mass.: Harvard University Press, 1989.

Thompson, Laurence G. *Chinese Religion: An Introduction*. Belmont, Calif.: Dickenson, 1969.

Thieme, Paul. "Brahman." In *Zeitschrift der Deutschen Morgenländischen Gesellschaft* 102 (1952): 91–129. Reproduced in Paul Thieme, *Kleiner Schriften*, 11:100–138.

Tigay, Jeffrey H. "Moses and Monotheism." In *The JPS Torah Commentary: Deuteronomy*, ed. Jeffrey H. Tigay, 433–435. Philadelphia: Jewish Publication Society, 1996.

Tong, Lik Kuen. "The Appropriation of Significance: The Concept *of Kangu-Tung* in the *I Ching*." *Journal of Chinese Philosophy* 17.3 (2008): 315–344.

Trible, Phyllis. "Depatriarchalizing in Biblical Interpretation." In *The Jewish Woman: New Perspectives*, ed. Elizabeth Koltun, 217–240. New York: Schocken, 1976.

Tu Wei-Ming. *Centrality and Commonality: An Essay on Confucian Religiousness*. Albany: State University of New York Press, 1989.

——. "The Continuity of Being: Chinese Visions of Nature." In *Confucian Thought: Selfhood as Creative Transformation*, 35–50. Albany: State University of New York Press, 1985.

Van Buitenen, J. A. B. "*Dharma* and *Moksha*." *Philosophy East and West* 7 (1957): 33–40.

Vlastos, Gregory. "Creation in the *Timaeus*: Is It a Fiction?" In *Studies in Plato's Metaphysics*, ed. R. E. Allen, 401–419. New York: Humanities Press, 1965.

——. "Socratic Piety." In *Socrates: Ironist and Moral Philosopher*, 157–178. Ithaca: Cornell University Press, 1991.

Watt, W. Montgomery. *Muslim Intellectual: A Study of al-Ghazali*. Edinburgh: University Press, 1963.

Weinfeld, Moshe. "Sabbath, Temple, and the Enthronement of the Lord." In *Alter Orient und Altes Testament: Veröffentlichungen zur Kultur und Geschichte des Alten Orients und des Alte Testaments*, ed. Kurt Bergerhof, Manfried Dietrich, and Oswald Loretz, 501–512. Neukirchen-Vluyn, 1971.

Weiss, Roslyn. *The Socratic Paradox and Its Enemies*. Chicago: University of Chicago Press, 2006.

Whitehead, Alfred North. *Religion in the Making*. New York: Macmillan, 1926.

——. *Science and the Modern World*. New York: Macmillan, 1946.

Wilson, Margaret. "Spinoza's Theory of Knowledge." In *The Cambridge Companion to Spinoza*, ed. Don Garrett, 89–141. Cambridge: Cambridge University Press, 1996.

Wolfson, Elliot. "Via Negativa in Maimonides and Its Impact on Thirteenth-Century Kabbalah." In *Maimonides Studies* V, ed. Arthur Hyman and Alfred Ivry, 393–442. New York: Yeshiva University, 2008.

Wolfson, Harry Austryn. *Maimonides on Negative Attributes*. New York, 1945.

——. "What Is New in Philo?." In *Philo: Foundations of Religious Philosophy in Judaism, Christianity, and Islam*, 4th rev., II:439–460. Cambridge, Mass.: Harvard University Press, 1968.

Wood, Robert E. "Phenomenology and the Perennial Task of Philosophy: A Study of Plato and Aristotle." *Existentia* 12.3–4 (2002): 253–263.

——. "Plato's Divided Line: The Pedagogy of Complete Reflection." *Review of Metaphysics* 44.3 (1991): 525–547.

Wright, Dale. *Philosophical Meditations on Zen Buddhism.* New York: Cambridge University Press, 1998.

Yampolsky, Philip B. "The Platform Sutra of the Sixth Patriarch." In *Approaches to the Asian Classics*, ed. William Theodore De Bary and Irene Bloom. Companions to Asian Studies, 241–250. New York: Columbia University Press, 1990.

——. *The Platform Sutra of the Sixth Patriarch; The Text of the Tun-Huang Manuscript with Translation, Introduction, and Notes.* Records of Civilization: Sources and Studies 76. New York: Columbia University Press, 1967.

Zaehner, R. C. *Hinduism.* New York: Oxford University Press.

Ziporyn, Brook. *Being and Ambiguity: Philosophical Experiments with Tiantai Buddhism.* Illinois: Open Court Press, 2004.

——. *Evil and/or/as the Good: Intersubjectivity and Value Paradox in Tiantai Buddhist Thought.* Cambridge, Mass.: Harvard University Press, 2000.

——. *Ironies of One and Many: Coherence in Early Chinese Thought* (Albany: State University of New York Press, forthcoming).

# Index